D0849743

Romantic Origins

Also by Leslie Brisman:

Milton's Poetry of Choice and Its Romantic Heirs

Romantic Origins

LESLIE BRISMAN

Cornell University Press

ITHACA AND LONDON

Cornell University Press gratefully acknowledges a grant from the Andrew W. Mellon Foundation that aided in bringing this book to publication.

First published 1978 by Cornell University Press.
Published in the United Kingdom by Cornell University Press Ltd.,
2–4 Brook Street, London W1Y 1AA.

International Standard Book Number 0-8014-1024-X
Library of Congress Catalog Card Number 77-90898
Printed in the United States of America by York Composition Co.
Librarians: Library of Congress cataloging information appears on the last page of the book.

For Susan

Authority and Reason on her wait,
As one intended first.

Milton, *Paradise Lost*

Contents

We plant a new way of life, a new instinct, a second nature, that withers the first. It is an attempt to gain a past *a posteriori* from which we might spring, as against that from which we do spring.

Nietzsche, *The Use and Abuse of History*

Do not all spiritual creations contain in themselves the insoluble riddle of their origins?

Hermann Cohen, *Religion of Reason*

Romantic Origins

Introduction

> Why does this thought come into my mind again and again,
> always in more and more vivid colors?—that in former times,
> investigators, in the course of their search for the origin of things,
> always thought that they found something which would be of the
> highest importance for all kinds of action and judgment: yea,
> that they even invariably postulated that the salvation of mankind
> depended upon insight into the origin of things. . . . In former
> ages thinkers used to move furiously about, like wild animals in
> cages, steadily glaring at the bars which hemmed them in, and at
> times springing up against them in a vain endeavor to break
> through them: and happy indeed was he who could look through
> a gap to the outer world and could fancy that he saw something
> of what lay beyond and afar off.
>
> Nietzsche, *The Dawn of Day*

In the Preface to his Second Discourse, Rousseau offers a word
of caution to those who would read him on the state of nature
and those who would develop their own fictions about man's
beginnings: "It is no light undertaking to separate what is
original from what is artificial in the present nature of man, and
to know correctly a state which no longer exists, which perhaps
never existed, which probably never will exist, and about which
it is nevertheless necessary to have precise notions in order to
judge our present state correctly."

Coupled here are two great motivating powers behind Rousseau's work and that of the Romantic movement he is often
credited with fathering: the desire to know correctly a state
which no longer exists, and the desire to express one's awareness
of the fictionality of such a state. Variously applied to reflections
on society, language, sexuality, and the growth of the soul, both

these desires can be said to impel Rousseau's *Social Contract, On the Origin of Languages, On the Origin and Foundations of Inequality, Julie,* and the *Confessions.* For the English Romantic poets, the "state which no longer exists" has manifestations in medievalism, primitivism, revisions of myths about cosmic creation, and—most centrally—accounts of the development of the poet's own creativity. In the Preface to *The Errors of Ecstasie* (1822) George Darley wrote, "Since the time of Rousseau, it has been the tendency of imaginative writers to embody their own history in their works." Darley's poem is an example of how much more interested the Romantics were in mythic than in factual autobiography, states which perhaps never existed rather than states which, from the ordinary march of time, no longer exist.

The concomitant desire, to acknowledge one's awareness of the fictionality of poetic reconstructions of the past, is variously expressed or repressed. Generations of readers—including Blake—seem to have repressed their awareness of Rousseau's qualifications about *his* myths of the past. About their own myths of origins, the Romantic poets could be—as the chapters on Shelley and Keats here attempt to demonstrate—richly ironic. Keats toys playfully at the opening of *Lamia* with a vision of primeval fancy, yet characteristically he persists in the query, What happens if we take more seriously than nature herself the faith in a reinvigoration that comes from the earth? (Wallace Stevens called this Keatsian myth he inherited "a cure of the ground," and enjoyed the fruit of the ambiguity about whether the ground or we are being cured.) Shelley's extraordinary visions of dream origins, from *Alastor* through *The Triumph of Life,* are balanced by cool awareness of the way these visions originate in deceptions of language or the mythmaking imagination. Blake seems to require that the poet willfully renounce or postpone his self-consciousness about metaphor for the sake of exploration of the mythic past, and the chapter on Blake explores his obsessive return to a story of first motions. The chapter on Coleridge synthesizes a myth of original interruption less persistent than Blake's but no less seminally recurred to at moments of crisis within and outside his poems. Coleridge the man at times may well have repressed awareness of his myth as fiction and genuinely conceived himself to be the interrupted philosopher. George Darley, if one understands him as repressing awareness of the relation between biographical and created versions of his poetic origin, looks rather small beside the major Romantic poets; if one understands his achievements as imaginative representations of a complex about being inferior and belated—and understands him to be challenging the priority of an extrapoetic "complex"—he grows in stature, and I include him to test generalizations about romantic origins against what the eighteenth century would have called a less original genius.

In imagining Rousseau to be the begetter of the double desire concerning exploration of the past, I borrow his own insistence that one speculate, whatever the fictions, about origins. One could say about the notion that the interest in romantic origins dates from Rousseau what Michel Foucault says of a whole age of speculation like Rousseau's: "It was of little importance whether this origin was considered fictitious or real, whether it possessed the value of an explanatory hypothesis or a historical event." The interest in origins is as old as literature itself, and the nation that prided itself on Arthurian romance—let alone a renaissance tradition rich in its returns to classical fonts—was never without its special fascination with idealized beginnings. Perhaps Rousseau came to be mythologized as a seminal figure in the history of myths of origins because coupled with his extraordinary rhetorical achievement was the bald fact of his being literally and symbolically outside an ongoing English tradition, and thus in a position to be recognized as uttering the prophetic cry for a new beginning.

What threatened to be an English mode of repetition could be distinguished from what the Romantics took to be a new, French beginning as arguments about imaginative originality may be distinguished from those about imagined origins. William Duff, in his *Essay on Original Genius* (1767), defined the quality named in his title as "that native and radical power which the mind possesses, of discovering something new and uncommon." Sir Joshua Reynolds, in the *Discourses on Art*, summed up the established view that "by imitation only, variety, and even originality of invention is produced." Originality meant newness in the sense of modest individuality, and was perceived as an achievement to be gained by following—or, for some, swerving from—a model predecessor. The concern with romantic or idealized origins, on the other hand, frees the writer from "following" anyone and impels him to leap over the grounds of individuality in search of an ultimate antecedence. This Emersonian "newness," in the words of Thomas Weiskel, "seems to offer to the poet the truly primary power of the god, the original or external power reigning before his own first poetic spirit got its start at birth." In place of wit, the poetry of judgment, and descriptive nature poetry, there emerges a new willingness to vaunt beyond irony and to explore, through the negative sublime, the landscape of the mind. Myth, narrative romance, and the reworkings of personal memory play increasingly important roles; they signal a new interest in fictional antecedence as a repetition of nothing less than God's original *I am*.

The myths about origins studied in this book are all forms of exuberance, either (like Darley's) energetic accommodations with the past, or (like Byron's) reworkings of stories of fall and loss into abundant recompense. The concern for origins has its melancholy side too, and there is poetic justice—if not an extraordinary feat of the continuity of literary history—in the fact that contemporary French criticism, parallel to the French reading of Freud, barely covers with shimmering leaves of rhetoric the dark and rocky paths that lead back to primal scenes of language. In *De la grammatologie*, Jacques Derrida looks forward to a new science of language which would "restore the absolute youth, the purity of its origin, before a history and a fall which has perverted the relationships between inside [speech] and outside [writing]." But this strange zeal for a new mode of discourse forms its own commentary on the history of sign-making as it is recapitulated in individual poems. It helps explain why Wordsworth's boy of Winander must die, why Blake's Tharmas struggles in watery pools, why Shelley's Shape-all-light dissolves the scene which brings her into being. Derrida evokes the more somber aspect of the myth of Narcissus in ruminating on the fictionality of wellsprings or sources: "There are no simple origins, for what is reflected is split *in itself* and not only as an addition to itself of its image; the reflection, the image, the double, splits what it doubles." The whole process of image-making as it is understood from Rousseau to Saussure is founded on a conscious or unconscious "forgetting of a simple origin."

Valéry thought the interest in origins and originality a shady business: "We say that an author is original if we cannot trace the hidden transformations that others underwent in his mind; we mean to say that the dependence of what he does on what others have done is excessively complex and irregular." What is a matter of misstatement on the part of the critic is a misery for the poet. Writing about Maurice Blanchot, Paul de Man expresses the romantic melancholy attendant on poetic interest in origins: "The poet can only start his work because he is willing to forget that this presumed beginning is, in fact, the repetition of a previous failure, resulting precisely from an inability to begin anew. When we think that we are perceiving the assertion of a new origin, we are in fact witnessing the reassertion of a failure to originate."

Whether as a defense mechanism against such despair or, less obliquely, a literary mechanism for channeling the otherwise requisite unconsciousness into formal expression, Romantic poets developed a safeguard to their myths of origin: there are two births, and while one is subject to repetition and the "failure to originate," the other remains pure. In Genesis, man is given a double birth from the earth and from God; Christian tradition expands the temporal distinction by picturing a first birth from nature and a second birth through faith in Christ. To the Romantic poets Rousseau bequeathed the habit of regarding adolescence or the growth of consciousness as a second birth, with faith in the mind's own powers replacing faith in external deity. Though subject to attendant anxieties, the second birth is ultimately more sure, more one's *own*, than one's first, natural origin. Sometimes, as in the account Shelley's Rousseau gives in *The Triumph of Life*, the second birth is represented as temporally and spatially localizable. Sometimes the sublimity of the metaphoric birth is veiled by a radiant mist that leaves uncertain whether it may be supposed antecedent or subsequent to the birth from nature. Natural birth comes to mean not simply literal emergence into life but emergence into a bondage to nature like that Blake images in caterpillar babies, mandrakes, and chained figures of youthful energy. If the whole cycle of repetition, so shockingly re-created in "The Mental Traveller," is associated with the first birth, then the second birth, whether pictured as a winged child breaking out of the mundane shell or Albion reemerging after having cast himself into the Furnaces of affliction, is at a moment whose time is always, potentially, now.

With startling simplicity, John Clare conceived the re-presentations of both births to be poetic achievements. When he wrote, "I found the poems in the fields / And only wrote them down," he summed up the romantic happiness of a myth of natural origins without anxiety. In "A Vision," the darkness is held off by the idea of a second origin, and a rejection of earth substitutes for the fear of being rejected by earth: "I gave my name immortal birth / And kept my spirit with the free." It is possible to find parallel alternates in Wordsworth's desire to write lyrical ballads in the language of common men and his difficult achievements of poetic voice in near-apocalyptic encounters. More often, however, the Romantic poets associate ordinary language and ordinary experience with the first birth and reserve the development of symbolic language and poetic experience for the second. Finding the origin of the imagination in the use of signs, Condillac summarized the root linguistic process that would be expanded and illustrated by Wordsworth and his heirs: "As soon as the memory is formed, and the habit of the imagination is in our power, the signs recollected by the former, and the ideas revived by the latter, begin to free the soul from her dependence in regard to the objects by which she was surrounded." For the poets, anxiety associated with a failure to originate could thus be diffused by supposing the soul not yet freed from her earlier dependence. Blake's mythmaking and Wordsworth's memory come to be less threatened themselves and more like guarantees of the separateness and viability of the second birth.

If the Romantics' myths of origins were less successful or less overt, poems would be more like dreams, and the origins of the imagination more like the origins of the unconscious. Without collapsing suggestive analogy into identity, one can compare what is with what is not on the far side of consciousness. Beside Condillac's understanding of the development of the imagination in a symbolic universe, consider this translation into psychoanalytic terms:

The *origin* of the unconscious must be sought in the process that introduces the subject into a symbolic universe. One could describe, abstractly, two stages in this process. At a first level of symbolization, the network or web of significant oppositions is cast onto the subjective universe; but no particular signified is caught in any *single* mesh. What is simply introduced, along with this system coextensive to experience, is pure difference, scansion, the bar: in the "fort-da" gesture, the edge of the bed. This is, need we repeat it, a purely mythical stage, but the prenomena of psychotic language show that it can reappear "secondarily," in "regression," in the form of the uncontrollable oscillation of a pair of differential elements.

The second level of symbolization is that which, following Freud, we called primal repression, and following Lacan, metaphor. [Jean Laplanche and Serge Leclaire, "The Unconscious: A Psychoanalytic Study"]

A psychoanalytic reading of the poets' myths of origin might consider them, as second births, symptoms of what Freud calls "primal repression" or enlargements of what Lacan denominates "metaphor." But psychosis differs radically from poetry in the mode of reappearance of what Laplanche and Leclaire call the "purely mythical stage." In psychotic language, the "pure difference" of an earlier stage is returned to regressively. In poetic language, the "pure difference" of the mythic state is creatively reimagined. Not regressing, the poet rather creates the second birth as a form of anteriority. Hence the myth of a fall from celestial state, discussed in the Byron chapter below, but perceivable, in other ways, in the work of Shelley, Wordsworth, Blake, and a whole mode of starry descendentalism that takes the fall of Lucifer as a paradigm. When Coleridge longs to revive within him the symphony and song of a visionary maid, he expresses the desire to return not to the pre-interruption state of nature but to an antecedent realm where the poet glows with supernatural power. And when Keats's Saturn and Thea fade into nature, the belatedness of Apollo, second-generation celestial, is transformed into primariness, while predestined godhood dies into life. Returning to a second birth given both primary importance and something like temporal priority, the poets step outside the circle of imitation, repetition, and belatedness; they return to the sources of their power.

I have placed Wordsworth last in this book, and concluded Chapter 7 with a look at the Snowdon passage, itself granted climactic position in *The Prelude*. For all the antagonism of a concern for origins to the idea of circles of repetition, the reader may feel that in the end is my beginning. I imagine that Wordsworth would have agreed, both in his general desire to stand at the head of a new movement in literary history, and in the specific return, in the Snowdon episode, to a more original—in the sense of older—source of grandeur. We speak of the domestication of the sublime among the Romantics, and imply by the process a movement away from an earlier, undomesticated, *unheimlich* art to a later cultivated simplicity whose significance may depend on our awareness that more majestic forms have been borrowed for incidents from common life. The paradox revolves around the ambiguity of natural origins and their first or revised temporality. On the one hand the eighteenth-century idea of the sublime is the original one, and the attempt to generate emotion like it out of incidents less remote or incidents of a new, fancied remoteness is a derivative. On the other hand, Wordsworth and his heirs believed that both everyday incidents and the new forms of romance they explored could compete with the old high art for an original—an earlier—place in consciousness. Hence the rich ambiguity available to the poet (discussed here in the chapters on Keats and Darley) when he attempts to adhere to a notion of the small and the natural as the beginnings of the awesome.

As a setting for the sublime, before the vision is interpreted as a paradigm of the mind, Snowdon looks as though it could more readily make Edmund Burke smile with approbation from somewhere high in heaven than could "Strange Fits of Passion" arouse tears such as angels weep. Why does the greatest Romantic long poem end with a traditional setting for grandeur, instead of concluding more polemically with, for example, the no less extraordinary boy of Winander episode? Burke's seminal work, whose title is perhaps too often remembered in abbreviated form, is *A Philosophical Enquiry into the Origins of Our Ideas of the Sublime and Beautiful.* One cannot approach the sublime without enquiry into, or shocked recognition of, origins. And if the origin of the sublime, as Burke shows, is in the instinct of self-preservation, then all confrontations with death, from the startlingly simple Lucy poems to the momentous mountain vision, are equally available as metaphors for beginnings. So strong is the originating power, the achieved sense of standing at a beginning in episodes of confronted self-consciousness, that only an episode mellowed by its more original—in the sense of older—setting could help the poet wind to a close. In *The Triumph of Life* and

The Fall of Hyperion, Shelley and Keats found emblems of beginnings resistant to temporal naturalization, and it is part of the glory of these poems that in breaking off they remain at origins, heavy with a sense of something evermore about to be.

The late Thomas Weiskel warned that "the equation 'meaning equals origin'—as if we could, even in principle, specify origins! —charms interpretation like a false Duessa, but it is not a necessary error." This is the error that so pained Coleridge, the error of reducing poetic ends to natural origins by confusing sources and analogues with those romantic quests for rebeginning which remain so centrally involved in what poems mean. Each of the Romantic poets differs from the others in the nature and mode of representing the return to beginnings. If they discovered individual resolutions to the problems of belatedness, resolutions available only in *fictions* of origin, they discovered as well sources of originality that "mean intensely and mean good."

In taking my epigraphs from Nietzsche throughout this book I accord that great demystifier of origins the first word, hoping that he will not have the last. Even the equivalent of the one line from Hermann Cohen could be quoted from *Beyond Good and Evil:* "The things of highest value must have some other indigenous origin; they cannot have been derived from this ephemeral, seductive, deceptive, inferior world, this labyrinth of delusion and greed." But what Cohen asserts with conviction Nietzsche derides as "the typical prejudice by which the metaphysicians of all time can be recognized." The exploration of romantic origins necessarily follows what Nietzsche dismisses as the faith of metaphysicians, "faith in the antithetical nature of values." Perhaps in the end it will prove appropriate to borrow Nietzsche's term "antithetical" to designate the mode of literary criticism that specially valorizes the pursuit of poets' reimagined origins.

CHAPTER 1

Coleridge and the
Ancestral Voices[1]

They place that which comes at the end (unfortunately, for it ought not to come at all!)—namely, the "highest concepts," which means the most general, the emptiest concepts, the last smoke of evaporating reality—in the beginning, *as* the beginning. This again is nothing but their way of showing reverence: the higher *may* not grow out of the lower, may not have grown at all. Moral: whatever is of the first rank must be *causa sui*.

Nietzsche, *Twilight of the Gods*

Through the large and complex web of Coleridge's writing about the imagination we can pick out two threads: the imagination is a "reconciling and mediatory power"[2] in search of the middle ground between polar terms; and it is a power of origination, in search of the origin of things. Quantitatively, it may be the first activity or meaning of imagination that applies most often in Coleridge's prose. He labors to polarize, whether by borrowing another thinker's set of terms or elaborating a philosophic duality; sometimes he draws up lists or, in the notebooks, connects words by his own shorthand symbol for "is polarly related to." Here I am concerned with the imagination polarizing and mediating between polarities insofar as these efforts bear on the second concern of imagination, the nature of origination. The imagination is both in search of the origin of things, where natural and literary things come from, and in search of the nature of originality, what it means to take the self as source.

Coleridge's familiar definitions ask to be taken as a starting place. In the *Biographia Literaria* he distinguishes imagination from fancy, and primary from secondary imagination. (These distinctions themselves exemplify the imagination's effort to polarize and mediate.) "The primary imagination I hold to be the living Power and prime Agent of all human Perception, and as a repetition in the finite mind of the eternal act of creation in the infinite *I am*." Just as the envisioned relation of one's own *I am* to the infinite *I am* telescopes the whole quest for origination, lesser paths backward are discovered in the notion that perception is a *repetition* of an original act or assertion. The secondary imagination, which "dissolves, diffuses, dissipates, in order to recreate," has more to do with imagination as a mediatory power, though *recreate* emphasizes the relation to a presumably more original creation. Coleridge considers the secondary imagination an echo of the primary, "coexisting with the conscious will, yet still as identical with the primary in the kind of its agency." The term *echo* directs the secondary imagination back to an original voice, and the notion of an individual "conscious will" implies a past relation to a divine or primal will.

Exercising secondary imagination, a poet may be said to make a beginning not by insisting on a point of absolute origin but by willfully reoriginating thought and approaching his primary aesthetic act like a moral act for which he assumes responsibility. "A finite will," Coleridge writes in *Aids to Reflection*, "*constitutes* a true Beginning; but with regard to the series of motions and changes by which the free act is manifested and made *effectual,* the *finite* Will *gives* a beginning only by coincidence with that *absolute* Will, which is at the same time *Infinite* Power."[3] Since he takes upon himself the beginnings of things, the poet stakes out a point in time he declares to be free of prior causality, thus exercising the equivalent of free will—that which, "by whatever means, has its principle in itself, so far as to *originate* its actions."[4]

i

If the imagination is concerned with the nature of origin, nothing is less imaginative, Coleridge insists, than trying to trace one poet's words to another. The labor of relationship—the poet's task of coming into relationship with more original poetic voices, the critic's task of deciphering such relationships—must be distinguished from the mere laboriousness of collecting verbal echoes. Coming across a moment in Petrarch that reminds him of Milton, Coleridge notes,

What noble Petrarch abstracted from his own Heart, why should not nobler Milton, in nobler Times, have received from the same Oracle—nothing can be baser than Parallelisms, when brought to invalidate the originality of a certainly original mind—nothing more pleasing than when they are merely to shew how the hearts of great men have sympathized in all ages.[5]

In such statements about poetic influence we can hear both bitterness at parallelism-hunters and yearning after the springs of such secret sympathy. The poet or critic who finds that sympathy is engaged in the imaginative labor of uncovering or creating relationship—imaginative because relationship reconciles and mediates like imagination itself. On the other hand, commentators who "only hunt out verbal parallelism"[6] have no relationship with Coleridge. Theirs is a perverse kind of secondary imagination, for where Coleridge hunted in foreign and obscure sources, they would only "echo" his original researches, dissolving, diffusing, dissipating, in order to uncreate. Not so the hearts of great men; the idea of literary likeness as community, the idea that coincidence of thought establishes, beyond all barriers of time, a sense of feeling, points to the fundamental human needs and poetic aspirations of Coleridge.

The desire to use verbal parallelisms as evidence of origins comes from an inability, in Coleridge's phrase, "to imagine the origination of a fine thought."[7] The critic's problem, like that of the poet who borrows, is a failure of imagination. If poets have difficulty being original, it is no wonder critics have difficulty imagining poets' originality:

The first rule I have observed in notes on Milton and others, is to take for granted that no man had ever a thought originate in his own mind; in consequence of which, if there is anything in a book like it before, it was certainly taken from that. And you may go on, particularly by their likenesses, to the time of the Deluge, and at last it amounts to this: that no man had a thought but some one found it, and it has gone down as an heirloom which one man is lucky enough to get and then another.[8]

It makes a certain sense, Coleridge concedes, "with regard to certain wit and to certain stories"; only in relation "to the production of genius" is source-hunting baleful. The impulse to read back is the impulse to naturalize, to resist the power of genius and see a given work as an outgrowth rather than a new dispensation. But if source-hunting is a kind of naturalization, its special danger is that it masquerades as itself a form of creative activity. "Those who have more faith in parallelism than myself . . . "[9] Coleridge begins, and then records his own discovery of a Miltonic borrowing. Even in the complaint about those who take source-hunting back to the Deluge, imagination is at work, however facilely, envisioning a humanistic line from us back to our antediluvian ancestors. The sublimated search for origins is clearer in this passage from the letters:

If they find a fine passage in Thomson, they refer it to Milton; if in Milton to Euripides or Homer; and if in Homer they take for granted its pre-existence in the lost works of Linus or Musaeus. It would seem as if it was part of their Creed, that all Thoughts are traditional, and that not only the Alphabet was revealed to Adam but all that was ever written in it that was worth writing.[10]

One stretches the notion of continuity too far in thinking of such a passage as a minor literary achievement, part of the Coleridgean corpus if not part of the body of literature all given with the alphabet to Adam. Yet what is expressed here as critical ire is essentially poetic zeal, and the path back to Adam is legitimately taken in the boldest and most "original" of Coleridge's lyrics.

ii

"Kubla Khan," which in the end apotheosizes poetic zeal, is both about a search for origins and itself a prime object for source-hunting critics. Coleridge pointed to *Purchas his Pilgrimage* as the "source" of the poem, or at least as the source of the reverie that started this dreamy journey back. A little glance at a more "original" state of the poem in manuscript copy reveals Coleridge to be in closer relation to the great men who have sympathized in all ages than he appears to be in the published text. In the manuscript, the lady sings of Mount Amara, a Miltonic place, in place of the final version's Mount Abora.

Before considering the reason for the change we need to consider why Coleridge should have thought of Milton at all. For the Romantic poet the attempt to recapture paradise is felt primarily as the attempt to recapture *Paradise Lost.* Milton's poem is itself symbolic of paradise renewed through song, of poetry getting us back to origins. No less than the work of source-hunting scholars, poetry is false surmise, and the difference between paradise and poem finds its fit emblem in the difference between a false paradise and the true one. That of Eden is not that of Ethiopia, or other myths:

> Nor where Abassin Kings their issue guard,
> Mount Amara, though this by some supposed
> True Paradise under the Ethiop line.
> [*Paradise Lost,* IV. 280–82]

The false paradise is where Ethiopian emperors guarded their younger sons to prevent revolt against the royal line, passed from father to oldest son. The post-Miltonic poet is preeminently a younger son, one who feels the special privilege of paradisal place but one who feels no less that he is cut off from the real line and the reality about him.

To cite Milton is to assert one's relation to the imperial line; to alter Milton would then be to revolt against one's status as younger son imprisoned in a false paradise of poetic belatedness. Like a Bolingbroke authenticating his coup by appealing to genealogy, the poet wishing the crown to pass to him claims a prior line. Coleridge does not swerve from Milton; he takes the line of origination further back. As a source-hunter, Coleridge simply reaches beyond Milton to Purchas—whom Milton also read, and who has, in fact, a whole chapter on Amara. As a poet Coleridge does something more original: he changes Amara to Abora.

John Beer suggests that the name is related to a myth of origins, the sun as "Abora, parent of light," and that the name may also be related to the place of Christ's baptism, Beth Abara.[11] Whatever the associations with other place names, we must read the change not simply as a change in place; the quarrel, after all, is not about geography, about the relative ages of civilizations, but about priority of the inspired word. "Abora" could thus stand not simply for the *place* Christ was baptized, but for the most original speech, the Father's infinite *I Am* repeated in a finite mode at the time of Christ's baptism: "Thou art my beloved son." Even in its purely linguistic associations, "Abora" points to first things. Coleridge, who was fascinated by the way the Hebrew *ab-ba* seems to father language (the sounds bring forth the alphabet) as well as signify "father," delighted generally in the potential insights of word-sources. "In disciplining the mind," he advised, "one of the first rules should be, to lose no opportunity of tracing words to their origin."[12] Whatever he intended as discipline, Coleridge himself practiced imaginative, rather than historical, etymology. If "Abora" is the *aboriginal* word, then we are back to Adam and his alphabet, the aleph-bet of language, origin of words.

In the beginning was the Word: Kubla Khan does not "build," as he does in Purchas, but simply "decrees" a pleasure dome. As Coleridge says about Milton's God, this is the power of the

Word over chaos. Other readings of "Kubla Khan" provide other ways of approaching the problem of origins. But whether one interprets imagery in terms of sexual, literary, or more generally mythic quest, the direction is back to a source, back to some sense in which this is a poem about sources. Milton's description of Eden shows the prelapsarian unity of origins and ends when waters from the fresh fountain, divided into four rivers, "unite their streams." With the fall, things will fall apart, the center will not hold; finding the stream divided and then, at the end of this long and very beautiful sentence of description of paradise, reunited, we realize that this is the paradisal place, the original place from which there has been as yet no falling away. Coleridge's paradise is more tenuous; he claimed not to have been able to hold on to an original vision, and some critics have furthered the division in not finding the place in the first stanza related to that in the second. He expresses the fragile but still paradisal unity in the image of the stream "where was heard the mingled measure / From the fountain and the caves." A characteristic Romantic trope, this ambiguous "where" stands for the very difficulty of locating the wellspring or paradisal place of original Voice. Susan H. Brisman points out that since the mingled measure is heard midstream, the stream itself serves, as in Milton, to express not diffusion from a source but the coming together that keeps the essential, the "original," unity of place.

In purely natural terms, there can be nothing original; every natural phenomenon is traceable to natural causes, every body of water derivable from other waters. Nature is imaged in her streams, which change, but are the same: "Nature is a line in constant and continuous evolution. Its *beginning* is lost in the super-natural: and for our *understanding,* therefore, it must appear as a continuous line without beginning or end. But where there is no discontinuity there can be no origination, and every appearance of origination in *nature* is but a shadow of our own casting."[13] Perhaps this is the shadow of the dome of pleasure that is projected on the waves, for what Kubla Khan creates is, precisely, an original place. (We might, incidentally, interpret the shadow of the ship in *The Rime of the Ancient Mariner* like-wise: both shadows are signs of the projected will, the self originating an act and impressing itself on a scene.) If the will is "a power of *originating* an act or state," Kubla Khan's pleasure dome is the supreme act of will, echoing or standing for divine decree.

In contrast to nature's streams, whose beginnings are "lost in the super-natural," this sacred river is discovered in the super-natural place of beginnings. The Alph is the Aleph, stream of origination, and suggests besides—though more by contrast than by similarity—the river Alpheus. In classical mythology, Alpheus is the river that defies metamorphosis as stasis; the thwarted stream goes underground, still pursuing, still flowing, so that sexual conflict ends not in degenerated immobility but in the regenerated stream. Unthwarted by Coleridgean caverns meas-ureless to man, Alpheus just goes on, imaging the kinds of reconciliation that compose the redeemed natural life of genera-tion. When Milton refers to Alpheus in *Lycidas,* the tradition of the ongoingness of the stream directs attention to the blockage that has taken place: "Return Alpheus, the dread voice is past / That shrunk thy stream." [14] The shrinking has been; it is now in the past, and in relation to an original or authoritative voice of the past. The renewed continuity of the stream can represent, for Milton, poetic continuity.

We can first observe the rather different relation of "dread voice" to continuity for Coleridge in a curious piece of prose about the nature of imitation: "In all well laid out grounds what delight do we feel from that balance and antithesis of feelings and thoughts! How natural! we say;—but the very won-der that caused the exclamation, implies that we perceived art at the same moment." As Coleridge proceeds, the art-nature synthesis draws him up to contemplation of the place of all synthesis, the "original" place:

There alone are all things at once different and the same; there alone, as the principle of all things, does distinction exist unaided by division: there are will and reason, succession of time and unmoving eternity, infinite change and ineffable rest!

> Return Alpheus! the dread voice is past
> Which shrunk thy streams!
>   —Thou honour'd flood,
> Smooth-*flowing* Avon, crown'd with vocal reeds,
> That strain I heard, was of a higher mood!
> But now my *voice* proceeds.[15]

Perhaps invoking Alpheus here is only formulaic, cited the way one might cite, say, Eliot's typist—"Well now that's done: and I'm glad it's over"—relying on allusion to let down the level of talk from some awkwardly false height. Yet regardless of the value of Coleridge's rapture here, the passage establishes the symbolic distinction between "dread voice" and "my [more trivial] voice," between a higher strain and a more natural tone.

What shrinks the streams of Alpheus? In *Lycidas* the distinction is between an orthodox or authoritative voice and a milder one associated with pastoral, with poetry. The *Lycidas* distinction may be said to stand for that encountered throughout Milton's poetry. Verse is responsive to a higher voice that, by itself, shatters the leaves with which poetic art would cover the rock of nature. Readers of *Paradise Lost* learn to accept the voice of God the Father as authoritative voice, and to be grateful to the poet for recognizing that its strain does shrink the streams. There are, to be sure, a few moments in *Paradise Lost* and *Paradise Regained* where a Biblical text, directly cited, represents the higher voice to which the poet's words act as meliorating commentary; but more generally, within Milton's own lines there are moments that represent a higher voice, and moments that seem more a human response to such a voice.

For Coleridge the myth can be said to be reversed. Discussing Wordsworth, one could read the distinction between voices as analogous to Milton's: there is a higher voice especially in *The Prelude* associated with Miltonic voice, and there is Wordsworth's own, more "natural" voice. Coleridge, on the other hand, may be said to pre-empt authoritative voice, and make the myth of discontinuity the interruption of his own poetic voice by the prosaic accents of the natural man. The story of the composition of "Kubla Khan," part of the "story" of the poem, is that the poet was, in the middle, "unfortunately called out by a person on business from Porlock."

This splendid fiction, prefixed to the poem from the 1816 edition on, might be called a primal scene of interruption. A fabricated story of interruption has this advantage over inherited accounts of man's ejection from an inspired or paradisal state: it allows its creator to externalize interruption while retaining a deeper awareness (and perhaps ultimately a happy rather than merely a repressed awareness) that the writer is his own interrupter. If we think of the original, pre-interruption writer as inspired, and the interrupter as the natural man, we can say that Coleridge the person is his own person from Porlock.

Like *Lycidas,* "Kubla Khan" figures within it the interruption of poetic voice. But for Coleridge the break from vision does not come, as it does for Milton, from the rumbling of a more thunderous voice:

> O fountain Arethuse, and thou honoured flood
> Smooth-sliding Mincius, crowned with vocal reeds,
> That strain I heard was of a higher mood:
> But now my oat proceeds. . . .

For Coleridge the oat cannot proceed, and we are left only with the preceding vision. When the vision breaks, there is a resetting of what has been spoken and a self-consciousness about what has been lost, what is to be, now, only in the statement of the loss: "could I revive within me / Her symphony and song. . . . "

What does it mean to displace discontinuity from Phoebus to Porlock? Milton is, on many levels, the uncouth swain surprised at the voices he hears, and our final surprise at the separation of poet and swain attests to the strength of their identification throughout *Lycidas*. Coleridge describes his delight in *Lycidas*, finding *"the Poet* appearing & wishing to appear *as the Poet*—a man likewise? For is not the Poet a man?"[16] Elsewhere he comments that Shakespeare's poetry "does not reflect the individual Shakespeare; but John Milton himself is in every line of the Paradise Lost."[17] This ease in the relation of poet to man permits the struggle over discontinuity to take place between poet-man and higher voice. But for Coleridge, literary stance parallels biographical fact: the natural man keeps getting in the way of the poet, and the poet reacts by reflecting or reconstructing the conflict in verse. Coleridge is haunted not by the ghosts of the past but by the specter of himself as natural man. There are, to be sure, various forms: sometimes the specter appears as a Giant Worrier; sometimes a figure menacing for his overt geniality; sometimes a more reductive, practical-willed Spectre of Urthona. In fortification against this giant of selfhood, whatever his forms, Coleridge's prose plagiarisms are hasty efforts to assimilate precursors to the poet's—one can as well say The Poets'—side. Coleridge's battle is thus not with his ancestors, though his efforts to assimilate them may shadow forth the conflict with the natural man: "And 'mid this tumult Kubla heard from far / Ancestral voices prophesying war." What happens to the commanding geniuses, decreers of the pleasure domes of the imagination? "In times of tumult," Coleridge says in the *Biographia,* certain men are "destined to come forth as the shaping spirit of Ruin, to destroy the wisdom of ages in order to substitute the fancies of a day, and to change kings and kingdoms, as the wind shifts and shapes the clouds."[18] "Kubla Khan" may be said to separate genius into the creative figure of Kubla and the ruinous figure of the man from Porlock who, interrupting the ancestral line, the line of vision, comes in with his fancies of the day.

The Porlock in Coleridge is the serpent in this garden, the interrupter of this bliss. We do not actually hear his voice in the poem, which remains paradisal, though we hear of it in the note and we sense its force in the structure of the poem. In one context Coleridge does give voice to his "Porlock," as I would like to call the specter for short. But before turning there to wonder, as Eve does at the serpent, "how cams't thou speakable of mute?" let us pause to picture this sly tempter. I personify this aspect of Coleridge for convenience, but nothing is more essential to Porlock than that he be conceived as a person. He is *the person,* as opposed to *the poet* in the poet. At best, he is what makes the conversational Coleridge so personable; at worst, he is what keeps the poet from producing works like *Lycidas*—a poem, as John Crowe Ransom has said, "nearly anonymous." Like Milton's serpent, Porlock stands before one "uncalled," with "gentle dumb expression" that turns one, invariably, to regard him. To the extent that he is no poet this Porlock is always dumb, though in fact he can be, as Coleridge the man was, unquenchably garrulous. More than dumb, Porlock's expression is gentle. He is all smiles, all sweet, adoring, reasonable talk, genuinely delighted, like Milton's Satan—one "long in populous city pent"—to behold "this flowery plat."

As Coleridge interprets the Eden story, Eve is "tempted by the same serpentine and perverted understanding, which [was] framed originally to be the interpreter of the reason and the ministering angel of the spirit." [19] Porlock is such a "perverted understanding," unwilling to recognize his subordinate status of interpreter to a more original text. Why should there be any priority of one "Reason" over another? Why should not knowledge of evil solve the whole problem? What kind of language is prohibition? How can an original word decree? "The gods are first, and that advantage use / On our belief, that all from them proceeds" (*Paradise Lost,* IX. 718–19). The serpent and Porlock understand no such "proceeding." "I question it," says Milton's serpent, and Porlock is the constant questioner of the notion that some other voice is more original.

I compare Porlock to the serpent not to establish a literary parallelism between Milton and Coleridge but to suggest how

Porlock avails himself of the strength of his precursors. By himself, Porlock could not gain access to a Coleridge lyric, anymore than undisguised daytime anxieties, according to Freud, could break into the dreamwork. If "Kubla Khan" internalizes the fact of interruption and becomes, more than an interrupted poem, a poem about interruption, it does so in a manner like that by which dreams absorb the Porlocks of conscious waking life. Here is Freud: "The daytime thought, which was not in itself a wish but on the contrary a worry, was obliged to find a connection in some way or other with an infantile wish which was now unconscious and suppressed, and which would enable it—suitably decocted, it is true—to 'originate' in consciousness." [20] Coleridge's Porlock, less a wish fulfillment of genial personality than a personification of Freud's Daytime Worry, makes allies within the more primary dreamwork. One can see the poet returning to Kubla's or Milton's paradise the way dreams return to the scenes of infantile desire; but the more important connection is that between the Freudian alliance with infantile wish and Coleridge's turn, after a stanza break, to the lost Abyssinian maid. Freud tells us that the materials of conscious life are "relegated to a secondary position in respect to the formation of dreams." [21] Porlock knows and wrestles with his secondariness, making strange alliances through which he can "reoriginate" in a poem (as Milton's serpent does entering Eden) and thus penetrate the wish-fulfillment character of lyric vision.

iii

To find Porlock speaking *in propria persona* we must step outside the poetry proper, for in prose—as in Freud's perception-consciousness system generally—such spirits may find voice without disguise. Porlock speaks in the climactic thirteenth chapter of the *Biographia Literaria*—the volume, like Eden, is about to be broken off—when the disquisition on the imagination is interrupted by a "letter from a friend whose practical judgement I have had ample reason to estimate and revere." We can think of Blake's dictum that corporeal friends are spiritual enemies, for however we may value the human relief that this interruption brings, it reduces or at least deflects argument the way a worrying friend does who interrupts us while we are hardest at work. The restated conflict becomes the one with our friend Porlock, not with some philosophic ancestor. This, to be sure, has a great advantage, for philosophically Coleridge is belated, while in conflict with Porlock he has the primariness of his German sources imputed to him. If I am my reading, my natural self cannot claim to antedate but only to interrupt me; a child entering the library while his father is attempting to assimilate his ancestors less threatens than lightens the mode of generational conflict. These analogues are intended to suggest that if the disquisition before the break in the *Biographia* chapter is to a dangerous extent paraphrased Schelling, then it is only in the "friend's" letter that Coleridge seems to speak in his own (more childlike and friendly) voice. But let us retain our construct and continue to designate his own, easy, personal, and belated voice, *Porlock*. This is, as Coleridge himself later confessed, his natural self:

Such is my *nature* . . . that I can do nothing well by *effort*. Hence it is, that I often converse better than I compose, and hence too it is that a collection of my letters written before my mind was so much oppressed would, in the opinion of all who have ever seen any of them, be thrice the value of my set publications. Take as a specimen [Satyrane's] letters, which never received a single correction, or that letter addressed to myself as from a friend, at the close of the first volume of the Literary Life, which was written without taking my pen off the paper except to dip it in the inkstand. You will *feel* how much more ease and felicity there are in these, compared with the more elaborate pages of the Sermon, etc.[22]

Such, to be sure, is his "nature," and if we love him we love him for the Porlock in him, for the "ease and felicity" of the natural man. If I still call this Porlock a serpent in the garden, it is because the relaxation of the will that lets the "natural man" take over is to some extent a fall. The voice of practical judgment is a lesser voice, a sensible Understanding in distinction from a higher Reason.

Taking the structure of the *Biographia* chapter as a kind of narrative, we can allegorize the intervention in a manner analogous to Coleridge's own allegorization of the story of the fall:

In the temple language of Egypt the serpent was the symbol of the understanding in its twofold function, namely, as the faculty of means to proximate or medial ends, analogous to the instinct of the more intelligent animals . . . and again as the discursive and logical faculty possessed individually by each individual . . . in distinction from the *nous,* that is, intuitive reason, the source of ideas and absolute truths, and the principle of the necessary and the universal in our affirmations and conclusions. Without or in contravention to the reason . . . this understanding . . . becomes the sophistic principle, the wily tempter to evil by counterfeit good; the pander and advocate of the passions and appetites: ever in league with, and always first applying to, the desire, as the inferior nature in man, the woman in our humanity; and through the desire prevailing on the will (the manhood, *virtus*) against the command of the universal reason, and against the light of reason in the will itself.[23]

If these terms seem terribly weighty to apply to the ultimately good-humored stratagem of having Porlock interrupt Reasoning Coleridge, we need to add that lightness is, after all, part of Porlock's temptation. He appeals to "the woman in our humanity," the gentler sex's love for gentler prose. He is the great enlightener, who would question the burden of the mystery and substitute science and love, his own more earthy sweetness and his own kind of light.

What is the "light of Reason" he interrupts? Chapter XIII of the *Biographia* begins with the citation of Raphael's speech in *Paradise Lost,* Book V, about the "one life": "O Adam, One Almighty is from whom / All things proceed, and up to him return." If the speech outlines the great, Miltonic, imaginative vision, we can say that these first two lines sum up the nature of imagination as the power to make manifest the glory of beginnings. To see the world in this view of cosmic unity is to see, *pace* Satan, *pace* Porlock, all things from Him proceeding. The lines that follow give us imagination in its mediating power, its power of standing between and holding polarities together. Permanence and flux, spirit and matter, are united in one process:

> Flowers and their fruit,
> Man's nourishment, by gradual scale sublim'd,
> To vital spirits aspire: to animal,
> To intellectual, give both life and sense,
> Fancy and understanding: whence the soul
> Reason receives, and reason is her being,
> Discursive, or intuitive.

Again and again in his prose Coleridge argues unities into dialectics, whether he is talking about the structure of the cosmos, the nature of metaphor, or the order of essays in a collection. Such is the way one prepares for imagination as the "reconciling and mediating power." Chapter XIII of the *Biographia,* before Porlock's letter, argues the contraries in rather abstract terms. With the letter, the contraries become Coleridge-Schelling and Coleridge-Porlock, with the third, concluding voice of the famous definitions, philosophical yet natural, borrowed yet original, sententious yet straightforward. Reaching beyond overdetermined, Schellingesque prose, Coleridge finds a new, mediate verbal space. Michel Foucault writes that "between the already 'encoded' eye and reflexive knowledge there is a middle region which liberates order itself." [24] Like Foucault's "middle region," Coleridge's middle voice defines a new freedom—and a new anteriority, restoring in those definitions of Imagination and Fancy what Foucault calls something "more solid, more archaic, less dubious, always more 'true' than the theories that attempt to give those expressions explicit form, exhaustive application, or philosophical foundation." Coleridge's definitions emerge out of and beyond the rhetoric of exhaustive philosophical foundation, and though they borrow from German sources, restore us to a point of origin before philosophic rhetoric.

With the friend's letter and the famous definitions, the chapter and volume are over. Granted that the very abortiveness of the chapter establishes the illusion of an original place, some scholarly demon, if he were to unearth a full hundred-page Coleridge chapter on the imagination, would find no stretch of paradisal prose; its nonexistence is its paradise. As Coleridge presents (or more accurately, does not present) it, the chapter is better left to rest in terms of what Wordsworth would call a "mere fiction of what never was." On the other hand, we could say that if the chapter is a fiction the loss is a real one, and something is always lost when Porlock (here in the form of that genial letter writer) intrudes.

iv

Coleridge's greatest triumph against Porlockian intrusion is *The Rime of the Ancient Mariner*. The planned division of labor between Coleridge and Wordsworth for the *Lyrical Ballads* may be thought to leave the Porlock battles behind, but the supernatural is of interest specifically as a counter to the natural, as a way of redeeming nature into imagination. The antiquing of the poem, first in spelling, later through the gloss, may be said to pre-empt authority for the more-than-natural voice. By themselves, such devices can no more overcome Porlock than can hanging up an old-fashioned knocker keep that spirit of contemporaneity from one's doorstep. Indeed, Porlock does not have to be kept out; he needs to be acknowledged, delineated, and exorcised. I would like to argue that this struggle is to a large extent the subject of the poem. If *The Rime of the Ancient Mariner* is a poem of "pure Imagination," it must achieve that purity as a higher innocence—not an ignorance but a defeat of the person of Porlock. As a poem of imagination it must be concerned with origination, and must come to some sense of its own voice as being more "original," anterior and higher to the genial, natural accents of Porlock. If imagination as a power of origination is the goal, imagination as a "reconciling and mediating power" is the medium in which the struggle takes place.

In its original stasis, the icebound ship marks the fixity of the material—what Blake would call the Ulro—world. Raphael's vision of a greener world contained within it the energy of sublimation to the Spirit of Origins, the One Almighty "from whom / All things proceed":

> Flowers and their fruit,
> Man's nourishment, by gradual scale sublim'd,
> To vital spirits aspire.

The icebound Arctic knows no such aspiration. Far from reconciling the men on the ship to other living things, or mediating between a natural and a supernatural realm, the ice "all between" is a synecdoche for the solid material world unsublimed to vital spirit; far from a sense of voice, of higher spirit interfusing a lower hemisphere with the breath of the Word, this world is marked with the meaningless sounds of matter chafing against matter. The ice "cracked and growled, and roared and howled." Into this unmediated world of nature comes a spirit of mediation: "at length did cross an Albatross," in a line whose internal rhyme emphasizes the crossing between two realms, the Christ-like nature of the intervention. Not itself the polar spirit—which we can interpret not only as the spirit of the pole but the spirit of polarity—the albatross is rather an emissary, a sign of the relationship between realms. The spirit world mingles with the natural world, creating the kind of "interpenetration of the counteracting powers" Coleridge talks about in the *Biographia* before Porlock cuts him off. "As if it had been a Christian soul, / We hailed it in God's name." The change from ice noises to hailing marks the change to interchange, communication between realms, between beings. The communion is symbolized by this not-of-this-world bird eating "the food it ne'er had eat," what the earlier version specifies as "biscuit worms." It is less the worm than the biscuit that marks the mystery here, for what seems new and remarkable is the mingling of something from the human, commonplace world with something wholly other. Language mediates, in the interchange, and the bird, "every day, for food or play, / Came to the mariner's hollo." This communion, like the "mingled measure" of "Kubla Khan," describes an imaginative paradise, broken by àn act that is pure Porlock: "with my crossbow / I shot the albatross."

There is no elaboration, no motivation for the shooting of the albatross, and one does Coleridge wrong to try to turn his tale into a Miltonic account of the story of the fall. Coleridge is not swerving from Milton; he is moving back to a more original relation with the powers behind the story of *Paradise Lost*. The albatross crosses and mediates, the mariner with his crossbow denies that mediation; that is all. Though he wanted to write an epic on the origin of evil, this poem aborts, and in fact fulfills, that desire. Extensity would not do, for it would deflect into story what Coleridge, coming after Milton, desires to restore to an original brevity and simplicity. The resultant poem is about original sin in the sense of "original" that interested Coleridge: "A sin is an evil which has its ground or origin in the agent, and not in the compulsion of circumstances." [25] To return the sense of "original" as prehistorical to the sense of "original" as belonging wholly to the paradigmatic agent—that would be to approach origins the way a poet can. Coleridge suggests how to read his poem by himself abstracting from the Bible and Milton an Eden story that forms a psychological paradigm. "Milton asserted the will, but declared for the enslavement of the will by an act of the will itself." [26] If Milton is understood to have done that, what more could Coleridge do? In *The Rime* he sets about further reducing the "compulsion of circumstances" into "an act of the will itself."

If the mariner has no "character," as Wordsworth thought, if the mariner's act seems abstracted from a particular person into an idea of personality, it is because Coleridge has further emptied the old tale of all but its essential truth, and is presenting his version as more essentially true:

In its utmost abstraction and consequent state of reprobation, the will becomes Satanic pride and rebellious self-idolatry in the relations of the spirit to itself, and remorseless despotism relatively to others; the more hopeless as the more obdurate by its subjugation of sensual impulses, by its superiority to toil and pain and pleasure; in short, by the fearful resolve to find in itself alone the one absolute motive of action, under which all other motives from within and from without must be either subordinated or crushed.[27]

This seems to me appropriate in idea, though perhaps inappropriate in size. Tacking it on *The Rime* may be like hanging an albatross around the mariner's neck. The weightiness of the moral was a problem of which Coleridge was aware, but we do him wrong to exaggerate it. Porlock, after all, is an enlightener, one who would clear the air of these huge flappings on metaphysical wings. We need only the sense that the shooting of the albatross is an act of will, and that this "enlightenment" breaks the spell that bound nature and supernature in mysterious communion.

Immediately we are confronted in the poem with the sun, emblem of the tyranny of the natural world, and with the loss in language, the medium of exchange between worlds. Linguistic repetition mocks the stasis, the failure in the transaction that language could perform. In a stanza that repeats but negates the earlier description we find that no bird comes to the mariner's hollo. The voices of the mariners are equally disjointed. First they aver that a hellish thing was done: "for all averred, I had killed the bird / That made the breeze to blow." When the sun rises, "all averred, I had killed the bird / That brought the fog and mist." Language, and with it moral judgment, is now tied to the weather, that most Ulro of topics of conversation. If the weather is not to be the most "natural" of things in this poem, the usurpation of nature by the forces of the supernatural is prepared by the collapse of language as the communication between realms.

It is often pointed out that the mariner remains passive through most of the poem. After the shooting of the albatross, the first action he takes is a startlingly willful counteraction to the linguistic blight. "Through utter drought all dumb we stood! / I bit my arm, I sucked the blood, / And cried, A sail! a sail!" Again, one may be adding further weight round the mariner's neck in noting that this bloodsucking is a perversion of the communion the albatross brought. But the linguistic events of the poem are so few and so startling that they cry out to be thus invested. Perhaps the burden can be legitimately shifted from critic to mariner here, for in the story he makes this sole and feeble attempt to take salvation in his own hands, to make the restoration of language a restoration of communion. But beyond his single act, the whole of Part III of the poem may be read as the will's effort at imaginative restoration.

If shooting the albatross is the Porlockian act that breaks the relation between realms, we must get back to the *tertium aliquid* Coleridge was talking about in the *Biographia* before the break there. Building this intermediate state is the work of the imagination, and the vagueness of perception at the beginning of Part III is an imitation of that labor. The mariner beholds "a something in the sky," where the "somethingness" marks a step in the direction of imagination. Coleridge writes of the "middle state of mind" being the state of imagination, for the mind must be left "hovering between images":

As soon as it is fixed on one image, it becomes understanding; but while it is unfixed and wavering between them, attaching itself permanently to none, it is imagination. Such is the fine description of Death in Milton:

> The other Shape,
> If Shape it might be call'd, that shape had none
> Distinguishable in member, joint, or limb,

> Or substance might be call'd, that shadow seem'd,
> For each seem'd either; black it stood as night;
> Fierce as ten furies, terrible as hell,
> And shook a dreadful dart: what seem'd his head
> The likeness of a kingly crown had on.[28]

In light of Coleridge's phrase, "as soon as it is fixed on one image, it becomes understanding," we may call to mind Porlock's position on the reason and understanding, his desire to "enlighten" the mystery of Reason by bringing things down to his level of understanding. It is curious that the Porlock of the *Biographia* expresses confusion at Coleridge's terms by citing the same Miltonic passage:

In short, what I had supposed substances were thinned away into shadows, while everywhere shadows were deepened into substances:

> If substance might be call'd that shadow seem'd,
> For each seem'd either!

Porlock, after all, is a friend, and what he wants to do in the *Biographia* is turn the philosophic discussion into a literary *event,* one more happening in an essentially naturalistic narrative. This is not unimaginative but primitively imaginative. It does establish its own indefinite, its own *tertium aliquid,* only failing to recognize the distinction between matters of the spirit and those of the will. *The Rime* is not spoiled by the weight of its moral because the battle over the will is not the mariner's but the poet's. Part III of the poem does have the mariner bite his arm, but the narrative that follows is not due to some willful imagining on his part; it is due to the poet's attempt to write "willfully," to his effort to write the kind of poetry that represents imagination not yet freed from the demands of the will. The section ends with the souls of the shipmates flying away: "and every soul, it passed me by, / Like the whizz of my cross-bow." Each death is a departure of spirit, one more emblem of the break in mediation between realms. It is as if the original act of will were in the air, haunting the events of this part of the poem.

What takes place in the encounter with the ghost ship is a willed imagining, an attempt by the poet to mediate again, to turn definite into indefinite in the manner of the passage Coleridge cites from Milton. The confusion between shadow and substance, Coleridge argues, allows for the imagination in a way that no fixed sketch or skeleton figure could. Like Milton's two indefinites are Coleridge's: "Is that a Death? and are there two? / Is Death that woman's mate?" The surprise here is the mariner's, but we can read the description as a two-willful heightening of dramatic tension. The mariner has further penance to do, and the poem has further to go.

Part IV puts the problem explicitly in terms of communication: the mariner cannot pray. For shooting a bird, the resulting dumbness and isolation is too disproportionate a punishment by any standard. But if we interpret the shooting as a Porlockian interruption, we can read what follows less as expiation for a crime than as education of desire. Porlock has to be arrested so that he can be made to confront the undisturbed "one life" that it is his nature to interrupt. The vision of unity in Part IV, from water snakes up to the moon, is a vision of the continuity of body and spirit, pure and impure, motion and stasis, permanence and flux. Fixed in the still sea, fixated by the stare of his shipmates, Porlock is less punished than he is awed.

In a gesture that itself indicates a restoration of communication between realms, Coleridge provides the most beautiful description as the gloss:

In his loneliness and fixedness he yearneth towards the journeying Moon, and the stars that still sojourn, yet still move onward; and every where the blue sky belongs to them, and is their appointed rest, and their native country and their own natural homes, which they enter unannounced, as lords that are certainly expected and yet there is a silent joy at their arrival.

There is more of Raphael's speech, there is more of Milton here than perhaps anywhere in Coleridge's verse. The stars that "still sojourn, yet still move onward" express the reconciliation between motion and stasis, matter and spirit, that marks the original place in vision from which Coleridge was rapt by recalling himself in Lycidas-like interruption. The paradox of sojourning while moving, if one can use so harsh a term for so gentle a moment, is like the oxymorons that prompted Coleridge to turn to Milton to illustrate the way imagination is kept suspended, kept from falling into understanding. Then comes the seemingly gratuitous comparison, whose excess is like grace, in which the stars are lords. Language is heightened to the point where "native country" and "natural homes" are not terms of intrusion into a spiritual realm but marks of the perfect peace, the perfect integration of nature perceived as the One Life. Nothing in the realm of nature can be said to correspond to the description of lords "certainly expected," and nothing could be more expressive of this vision of harmony of the natural with the supernatural, united by a power that is imagination itself. There is silent joy at the stars' arrival not from an insufficiency of communication but from perfect plenitude, the fullness of relation of star to sky. The stars enter unannounced, yet we are as far as can be from a sense of intrusion. Here is everything that Porlock is not.

Having been made all eye, the mariner must now bring the vision closer, must come to see his own nature participating in that cosmic nature. In this poem, the moon is imaginative vision, the sun physical or all-too-natural sight. The mariner yearns for the journeying moon that goes up "softly." Then the eye turns from that soft whiteness to the redness closer to the self:

> Her beams bemocked the sultry main,
> Like April hoar-frost spred;
> But where the ship's huge shadow lay
> The charmed water burnt alway
> A still and awful red.

The turn inward is repeated in the following two stanzas. The first is closer to the moon vision, and the mariner beholds the water snakes "in tracks of shining white." Are these actually serpentine creatures, or is he watching the moonlight slithering

down wave crescents? The slight ambiguity marks the indefiniteness of imagination not reduced to understanding. The next
stanza makes the necessary move closer to the self. The water
snakes are observed "within the shadow of the ship," where their
beauty overwhelms the mariner. Presumably these are sea creatures, not optical illusions, but this should not deter us from
seeing the ship's shadow as the shadow of selfhood, the water
snakes as images of serpentine Porlock. The difficult reintegration
of the natural man into the One Life is expressed by the visionary
difficulty of including even water snakes in the Miltonic continuum of living forms.

On this point we tend to read the poem too glibly, as though
all one really needed were love, as though *The Rime* were
actualizing Gloucester's invocation:

> Let the superfluous and lust dieted man
> That slaves your ordinance, that will not see
> Because he does not feel, feel your pow'r quickly.

In Coleridge's poem the problem is more a matter of sight preceding feeling. The vision of the journeying moon is a vision
of the One Life, in the context of which the water snakes can
appear beautiful and evoke the mariner's "spring of love." He
had been in something of the state of Coleridge's Dejection Ode:

> All this long eve, so balmy and serene,
> Have I been gazing on the western sky,
> And its peculiar tint of yellow green:
> And still I gaze—and with how blank an eye!
> And those thin clouds above, in flakes and bars,
> That give away their motion to the stars;
> Those stars, that glide behind them or between,
> Now sparkling, now bedimmed, but always seen:
> Yon crescent Moon, as fixed as if it grew
> In its own cloudless, starless lake of blue;
> I see them all so excellently fair,
> I see, not feel, how beautiful they are!

The mariner is made to see, then to feel. The "blank eye" of the
Dejection Ode, the Gloucester eye, the Porlock eye, comes to

see, and in that seeing to sense a re-establishment of the communion that the Porlockian intervention had denied. I emphasize
the order of the progress because Porlock, who suffers from a
failure of vision, is, in his own terms, loving enough. As the
natural will, Porlock must be brought to passivity before the
activity of love is regenerated. To see love being generated from
vision is to see restored the nature of imagination as the power of
origination. Porlock habitually comes too soon. If, as Coleridge
remarked about his own fluency, the Porlock voice comes readily,
it must be hushed or made to appear belated so that the finer
tone can first be heard. The simile of the gloss expresses the
"silent joy" in the sky, and that silence, that recognition of the
inadequacy of the Porlock voice, precipitates the redemption of
the voice: "O happy living things! no tongue / Their beauty
might declare."

Seeing what cannot be spoken, the mariner is now able to
speak: "A spring of love gushed from my heart, / And I blessed
them unaware." The "spring of love" is an original spring, coming
up in contrast to the streams, the continuities of nature, in which
every act, every impression, derives from its immediate physical
causes. "This is the essential character by which *Will* is opposed
to Nature, as *Spirit,* and raised above Nature, as *self-determining*
Spirit—this namely, that it is a power of *originating* an act or
state."[29] At the same time, it seems as if a higher benignity were
flowing into him, as if he were now participating in the continuities of spiritual reality. The "unaware" is the slight but full
recognition of the suppression of the will, the subordination
of one's own power of origination to an inspired one, one that
is breathed into the self. Here is Coleridge in *Aids to Reflection,*
speaking of the coming together of will and submissiveness in a
higher harmony, and using the same metaphor—now literally—of
inspiration:

Will any reflecting man admit that his own Will is the only and
sufficient determinant of all he is, and all he does? Is nothing to be
attributed to the harmony of the system to which he belongs, and

to the pre-established Fitness of the Objects and Agents, known and unknown, that surround him, as acting *on* the will, though doubtless, *with* it likewise? a process, which the co-instantaneous yet reciprocal action of the air and the vital energy of the lungs in breathing may help to render intelligible.

Again in the world we see every where evidence of a Unity, which the component parts are so far from explaining, that they necessarily presuppose it as the cause and condition of their existing *as* those parts.[30]

The mariner perceives the water snakes as part of that Unity, and is impelled to bless them. No longer *ab extra,* he speaks now as part of the continuum of the One Life. Far from interrupting, potency of voice now expresses the continuity of spirit worlds: "Sure my kind saint took pity on me, / And I blessed them unaware." Is it his voice, or some kind saint's working through him? The moment of anti-self-consciousness is the moment of restoration of the relationship between all spirits—in Raphael's phrase—"each in their several active spheres assigned." And the harmony of the spirits' relation is mirrored in the perfect concord of verbal repetition:

> A spring of love gushed from my heart,
> And I blessed them unaware:
> Sure my kind saint took pity on me,
> And I blessed them unaware.

It is as if the single act were approached from both directions in the spiritual world, the human heart reaching up to offer the blessing, the kind saint reaching down, singing the same note, the same poetic line.

v

The restored relationship of the spiritual world means a restored communion between the levels of spiritual being: "the self-same moment I could pray." What more remains? This is the end of Part IV, and the poem is less than half over. The pace of the action changes, as though the poem were approximating the status of the stars that "still sojourn, yet still move onward." With the albatross off, the redemption is sufficiently assured for the poem to afford the tone of sojourning. In terms of the moral action, what follows is more difficult, as though refining the terms the poem has to this point established. No further action from the mariner is required—except that he perceive the poem's further refinement in the conception of the relationship between levels of being. The mariner has been pitied and overwhelmed. If we sense nonetheless that the moment of blessing the water snakes is an imaginative moment, a delicate balance between a giving and a receiving, what remains to be achieved is a firmer sense that one can re-establish relationship from the self upward.

Part V, first, is a resting place where the mariner is refreshed with rain, where we bask, more generally, in the light of a giving from above. Part VI will bring a restored vision of the relation of lower to higher voice, but meanwhile the higher spirits take over. The dead rise in silence, emblem of passive relationship to higher authority. In the sole stanza of human community—or what is, rather, an eerie parody of it—the mariner joins his nephew:

> The body of my brother's son
> Stood by me, knee to knee:
> The body and I pulled at one rope,
> But he said nought to me.

The silence is further emphasized in the first version of the poem, which adds the lines, "And I quak'd to think of my own voice / How frightful it would be!" Why would his voice be frightful? A troup of spirits has taken over the others: the mariner too feels "taken over": "I thought that I had died in sleep, / And was a blessed ghost." Could it be his natural voice that would be frightful to a group of spirits, or frightful to be heard in such a spirited atmosphere? Or does he fear his own accents would be more strange, more ghastly than the silence? In either case he remains silent, while "sweet sounds rose slowly through their mouths." These sounds of birds, of brooks, are most welcome, though their beauty cannot obscure their strangeness. (The disorienting effect of displaced sounds of nature is like that effect sometimes used in contemporary cinema at moments of solipsistic stress, or when one person wants to distress another.) The sounds of nature alternate with "angels' song / That makes the heavens be mute," where that muteness, the "quiet tone" that is sung, marks the desired harmony.

These are harmonies of sounds as sounds. Their strangeness at this point in the poem establishes a distinction between sound and voice. Voices of nature from the mouths of spirits express just the achievement, and just the limitation of the achievement, of the voice of blessing (spirit) in the mouth of the mariner (natural man). The danger is that, though the mariner can pray, the sounds will come from the larynx, worked upon by spirits the way an Eolian harp is moved by the winds. Disembodied sounds, like inspirited bodies, can stand not for communication but for a more subtle, more psychically disturbing disjunction between sound and spirit. Voice is sound and stance, and the poem moves on in Part VI to a redemption of the stance, the relationship between sound-maker and sound-receiver.

In the mariner's trance he hears, and in his soul discerns, two voices in the air. The two voices are a kind of abstraction of the problem of voice, but the relation established between them is the one element of communion not yet achieved. What is their relationship? The first is an inquiring, the second a knowing and answering spirit. They are not voices of nature and grace, of a first and second dispensation, although the knowledgeable spirit has the "softer voice, / As soft as honey-dew." The meaning of their encounter may lie in what it means to be an answering voice. The first spirit inquires a second time: "But tell me, tell me! speak again, / Thy soft response renewing." If this is to be a response to a question, it is also the responsiveness of spiritual reality, the harmonious concord of the One Life. The soft, second voice answers the question about the ocean with what Reeve Parker calls a "virtually Shelleyan myth": [31]

> Still as a slave before his lord,
> The ocean hath no blast;
> His great bright eye most silently
> Up to the Moon is cast—
> If he may know which way to go;
> For she guides him smooth or grim.
> See, brother, see! how graciously
> She looketh down on him.

It will take Coleridge's heir to sustain moments like this—visions of an original grace so frequently sought, so often found by Coleridge himself to be just out of sight. "And still I gaze," he complains in the Dejection Ode, "and with how blank an eye!" What is to keep the mariner from this dreariness, or the condition of the blind old man of "Limbo," who "gazes the orb with moonlike countenance" and "seems to gaze at that which seems to gaze on him"? Parker finds that line from "Limbo" a triumphant encounter,[32] but it seems to me to represent the painful sterility —like that the mariner has already experienced—of the quest for romantic origins reduced to semiotics; there is no Emersonian transparency in the Limbo man's "eyeless face all eye" but the blind confrontation of one sign with another, "seems" staring at "seems." In *The Rime,* on the other hand, the Second Voice apprehends a visionary grace that restores prophetic sight of an originally responsive universe.

What the Second Voice's response about responsiveness means in moral terms is implicit in the master-slave metaphor, "Still as a slave before his lord, / The ocean hath no blast." The moral implication of this metaphor is one Wordsworth inherits in the Intimations Ode; it is also implicit in Gloucester's lines about the man "That slaves your ordinance, that will not see / Because he does not feel." The man who slaves ordinance, who treats the laws that ought to govern the relations between creatures like slaves to be bandied about, must be brought to feel. Because he does not feel love he is made, by an act of poetic justice, to feel power, the force of ordinance. That much has happened to the mariner and is the subject of the prophetic denunciation uttered by Gloucester, who has gained the seer's sententiousness without abandoning his cult of retribution. Returning to a purer morality characterisitc of the mythmaker rather than the prophet caught in bad times, Coleridge's Second Voice reveals love to be the basis of the physical and metaphysical universes, governing the attraction of both persons and planets. "Feeling" in the sense of love is equivalent to feeling the force of ordinance—of the Miltonic hierarchical order of spirits. It takes an act of vision to see that this is vision, not simply a triumph of the moral will; but the essence of vision is learning to read not horizontally— perceiving cause and effect, act and albatross—but vertically —perceiving the harmonious relation of lowly to exalted creature, of the subservient spirit to that, in Raphael's terms "more spir- itous and pure." From the Second Voice's spatially and morally superior perspective, law is love, though Porlock smirk.

Natural affection is the last stronghold of Porlock, whose greatest pride is that, if he interrupts vision, he yet more deeply feels. This special pride must be put in its special place, and the relationship that is love must come to be seen not as natural man's alternative to vision but as the essence of the visionary relationship between all sentient things. The primacy of the natural voice is Porlock's great claim. If the soft response is not a natural man's denial of vision but a higher vision, more of a vision, then imagination has restored the relationship of origina- tion. The relation of moon to ocean is the relation, in this poem, of the imaginative realm to the natural man, who has not an alternative stance (from which he can take potshots at mediating birds) but one acknowledged position in a ladder of being. The vision of soft response is the vision of hierarchy among all spirits, some of whom are more in voice, are more knowledgeable, are more "sublim'd," in Milton's term, than others. Porlock is like an idiot questioner, whose good-natured skepticism would shake every rung. Blake would cast him out; Coleridge finds instead a voice to answer him—finds instead the image of answering voice to represent the relation of spirit to more elevated spirit,

of first to second voice. In the communication of those spirits
is restored stance and restored voice.

"The supernatural motion is retarded," and we step back from
this vision, from the mariner's trance, into the realm of nature.
At last the departing spirits are silenced: "Oh! the silence sank /
Like music on my heart." With a sense of enormous relief we
reenter human community—hermit, pilot, and boy. But the
hierarchy of voices is not destroyed, and the mariner, far from
being now a man among men, visits the human community with
all the aura of otherness with which the supernatural visited him.
The pilot falls into a fit when the mariner moves his lips. The
natural interrupter of the supernatural vision becomes the visionary interrupter of the natural. Then (at that point in the story)
as now (the dramatic time of the poem) he stoppeth one of three.
With "strange power of speech," the mariner assumes his place
in the hierarchy of voices, "Each in their several active spheres
assign'd, / Till body up to spirit work, in bounds / Proportion'd
to each kind." As his business is to help other bodies "up to
spirit work," he goes about seeking out the Porlocks, interrupting
marriage feasts for whatever increase in vision his power of voice
can impart.

How much of an increase in vision is there? The reading I
have been arguing for must seem terribly optimistic to anyone
heeding the visionary voice of the poem, which trembles with
more ominous tones than those taken into account here. Like the
ancestral voices of "Kubla Khan," the prophetic tones of *The
Rime* prophesy a more difficult relationship with the outside
world. Porlock is not to be so easily let in, and to characterize
the change in the mariner from an interrupting Porlock to a
visionary interrupter of Porlocks may seem too shifty a subter-
fuge. Yet in a way the poem licenses such naiveté, and if the
enlightenment of the wedding guest seems to come too easily,
we must realize that such is the nature of enlightenment itself,
lightening for the guest, and ultimately for the reader, the burden
the mariner has assumed. The moral of the poem is to the vision-

ary experience as the interpretation of the poem is to the text. Moralizers and interpreters are Porlocks. As critics we are knockers on the door, and though we invariably intrude, arguing our way into a text, we hope that our voices will somehow be assimilated into the hierarchy and added to the defense against those whom we see as the attacking outsiders.

Poets, like angelic spirits, have their hierarchies too, and a poet stands in relation to his precursor as a first to a second voice. The ancestral voices were right, predicting war. Porlock must be tackled, not ignored or shown the cottage or Xanadu door. As he grows, the younger poet comes to share rather than interrupt the vision of the more knowing, more softly responding voices. The Dejection Ode comes to declare that one does not steal from oneself all the natural man; the voice of the natural man, "a sweet and potent voice, of its own birth," finds itself not standing apart but participating in a harmony of voices. The individual soul's joy gets to be seen *as* the One Life:

> Joy lift her spirit, joy attune her voice;
> To her may all things live, from pole to pole,
> Their life the eddying of her living soul!

Not cast out, the idiot questioner is rather made to listen, to participate in colloquy that binds spirit to spirit. These are the noncorporeal battles of eternity, fought between each poet-as-Porlock and whatever his "abstruse research" can do to make him an ancestral voice. The battle is a subjective one, but as Coleridge says of Milton, "the Objectivity consists in the universality of its subjectiveness": [33] "In Paradise Lost—indeed in every one of his poems—it is Milton himself whom you see; his Satan, his Adam, his Raphael, almost his Eve—are all John Milton; and it is a sense of this intense egotism that gives me the greatest pleasure in reading Milton's works. The egotism of such a man is a revelation of spirit." [34]

We can say the same of Coleridge when he is fighting the Porlock battles. The victory is not in trammeling the natural man, but in finding there the listening ear tuned to the higher harmony. "So I would write," says Coleridge, looking back at Milton, and dreaming of spending twenty years on an epic, "haply not unhearing of that divine and rightly-whispering Voice, which speaks to mighty minds of predestined Garlands, starry and unwithering." [35] Coleridge, haply, was not unhearing of the rightly-whispering Voice, though he did not take years in Miltonic "deep metaphysical researches" preparing to write the great poem. If Coleridge in the Dejection Ode renounces the plan "by abstruse research to steal / From my own nature all the natural man," he nevertheless does find his predestined garland, starry and unwithering.

Acknowledging and arguing with Porlock, Coleridge opens the way, as the gloss says about the stars, to native country and natural home. "They enter unannounced, as lords that are certainly expected and yet there is a silent joy at their arrival." If we keep in mind what a warm, lovable fellow, though a dark, worrisome, and destructive specter this Porlock is, we can picture a gregarious Coleridge opening the door and inviting Porlock in. Porlock interrupts, but since he comes in as the natural man, he polarizes the identity of the poet and makes us see the interrupted bard as a guest already at the party, one of the more original, more inspired company. Commenting on the way man is separated from his contemporaneous (we could say his Porlockian) self, Michel Foucault finds that "amid things that are born in time and no doubt die in time, he, cut off from all origin, is already there." [36] Coleridge the poet is already *there,* preceding and preparing the way for his interrupter and belated successor.

CHAPTER 2

Keats and a New Birth[1]

> Even the wisest among you is only a disharmony and hybrid of
> plant and phantom. But do I bid you become phantoms or plants?
> . . . I conjure you, my brethren, *remain true to the earth,* and
> believe not those who speak unto you of superearthly hopes!
>
> Nietzsche, *Thus Spake Zarathustra*

> To retranslate man back into nature, to master the many vain
> enthusiastic glosses which have been scribbled and painted over
> the everlasting text, *homo natura,* so that man might henceforth
> stand before man as he stands today before that *other* nature,
> hardened under the discipline of science, with unafraid Oedipus
> eyes and stopped-up Ulysses ears, deaf to the lures of the old
> metaphysical bird-catchers who have been fluting in at him all too
> long that "you are more! You are superior! You are of another
> origin!"—this may be a strange, mad task, but who could deny
> that it is a *task!* Nietzsche, *Beyond Good and Evil*

For the poet concerned about inspiration and about his place
in what Keats called "the grand march of intellect," the ordinary
march of nature seems to proceed with enviable regularity. Overlooking the nature of human sexuality and generational gaps, one
sees "out there," in natural history, that season succeeds season,
era succeeds era, without the new having to justify its place and
without the old threatening to occupy more than its place. In
literary history succession is always problematic, both in terms
of the individual poet's progress from one moment of inspiration
to another and in terms of continuity from one poet to another.
The problems are accentuated when one's precursor seems to
have preempted even the awareness of the difference between
natural and intellectual succession.

For Keats, Milton—even more than Wordsworth—was the
great originator of that awareness. Milton wrote the central elegy

about experiential loss and spiritual renewal, and he wrote *the* epic about man falling out with nature. Most important, he represented in his own person the alienation from the continuity of nature, lamenting that "with the Year / Seasons return, but not to me returns / Day" (*Paradise Lost*, III. 40–42). Like Wordsworth, Keats sought a counter to Miltonic discontinuity which would represent inspiration renewed as faithfully as are plants and seasons. The search for or appeal to such a counter-myth of continuity not only underlies Keats's greatest work in the odes and Hyperion poems but justifies a studied lightness throughout the poetry—a lightness all his own—under the auspices of which new bursts of inspiration seem to spring up from the earth.

i

Written first of the five great odes in the spring of 1819, "Ode to Psyche" represents a new spiritual season. This ode not only comes up (crops up) first but is about firstness, about building a fane in some untrodden region of the mind, where the poet will be the new hierophant of a previously unworshiped goddess. Just what is implied by coming first is a question raised in many ways, especially in the central stanzas which announce and sub-vert a belatedness. But it is important that those stanzas are preceded by one that announces a natural origin for the succeed-ing burst of inspired self-proclamation. Cupid and Psyche are discovered on the earth, and as though they had sprung up from the earth. Of course to find a newly emerged infant, a presexual Cupid, would be to find no child of Venus—for whom sexuality is pre-everything; the lovers are sighted, rather, shortly after their sexual *re*generation, after the moment which, in the myth of this poem and in the psychoanalytic myth of the mind generally, substitutes for an original generation. Keats's source for the myth of a reunited Cupid and Psyche is the late classical Apuleius; but the idea that the lovers are united here on earth, not in heaven (and especially the idea that they have just been reunited on earth), is original to Keats himself—or to the realm of nature to which sexual love is here found to belong.

When Pope claimed that Homer and Nature were the same, he expressed an orthodoxy according to which a poet's precursor not only represents an understanding of nature, but is understood to be absorbed into the general body of the given that we call nature. For Keats, the poet and nature are in a sense the same, and the precursor is encountered as a belated version of the same. If one regarded the opening verses of the "Ode to Psyche" as an allusion to or parody of the opening of Milton's *Lycidas,* then *Lycidas* would be an original text and the Ode a belated successor. But Keats's gentle phrasing, "sweet enforcement and remembrance dear," reminds us that Milton's "bitter constraint and sad occasion dear" were bitter and sad because nature had gotten there first and killed Lycidas before the uncouth swain was ready. Unlike "bitter constraint," Keats's "sweet enforcement" suggests a cooperation with nature, for the claims of love precede those of obligation and imply a closer tie to the one who is said to occasion the song—a tie in accordance with which claims of priority are laid aside.

If lovers in general know no first and last, this is all the more true of a poet-lover who is both stricken by the lady he "discovers" and intent on re-creating her. Cupid is appropriately the poet's original because he is traditionally the prime mover in matters of love and is himself victim as well as originator of blind desire for Psyche. In addition there were, in fact, two Cupids: the older god was identified with love in the sense of original motion, the gravitational force that attracts one physical body to another; the second Cupid was the youngest god of the pantheon, and Venus' son.[2] In distinction from the Oedipus story, this bit of lore provided Keats with the material for a myth of originality without anxiety, of a belated youth who can be intellectually identified rather than set in emotional opposition to his original. Like the blinded Oedipus, Milton found himself "Presented with a Universal blanc / Of Nature's works to me expung'd and

ras'd." Like the rejuvenated Cupid, Keats claims in this poem
to "see, and sing, by my own eyes inspired." Is being inspired
by one's own eyes the supreme originality or hopeless victimization by one's sexual nature? If the lure is erotic, Keats seems to
be saying in the Ode, the difference dissolves, for nothing is as
much one's own as one's desire, and to be inspired by what one
sees is to be in touch with both the ultimate priority of nature
—the primacy of eros or Cupid—and in touch with one's powers
of creation—one's Psyche.

The turn on Milton's priority is redoubled, after this little
invocation, by the ensuing narrative of the first stanza of the
Ode. In *A Map of Misreading,* Harold Bloom finds the poet to
occupy the position of Satan, who is not only cast out of heaven,
but who comes upon the already ongoing sexuality of Adam and
Eve and feels belated and excluded.[3] Unlike Satan, who can
speak his seductions in Eve's ear only when her relation to Adam
is held in the suspension of sleep, the poet can sing in the ear of
Psyche without disturbing the relation of Cupid to Psyche. Having no exterior or prior designs on the lovers, he had "wander'd
in a forest thoughtlessly," and so his first thought can be no
voyeuristic sense of exclusion but the pristine, newly begotten
love of Psyche. The semiallegorical nature of Keats's myth gives
him this advantage over Milton's Satan, for "the wingèd boy I
knew" can involve a self-recognition in a way that Satan's sight
of Adam cannot. To find Keats identifying with Satan's sexual
deprivation is to see him doubly removed from the originality
of the paradisal moment; but to see Keats, contra Satan, discovering his own eros is to see one way in which he is by no means
"too late" but has, as far as his psyche is concerned, already
embraced the muse.[4]

In accordance with this anxiety-free reading, the often-cited
original for the middle stanzas, Milton's Nativity Ode, becomes
another text that Keats has preempted. The grand repetition or
represencing that takes place between stanzas two and three
restores a priority not to a pagan over a Christian deity, but to

this poem over preexistent poems. Milton seems like the belated
Christian, while Keats, who claimed to be "more orthodox than
to let a hethan Goddess be so neglected,"[5] reworks the myth
(works it, in a sense, backward) to let in the warm love that
marks the psychological priority of eros and the poetic priority
of Keats.

ii

The gay subversion of Milton's status and that of literary history generally is lavishly extended in *Lamia*. Like the "Ode to
Psyche," this poem begins with an otherwise unnecessary pro-
logue which plants the seeds of an irony about origins; the poem
goes on to tell a story in which the characters' significance is a
function of their relation to this irony. Lost "in the calmed twilight of Platonic shades," Lycius is an idealist, a believer in the
romantic origin of ideas and things, who is lured when he finds
himself outidealized in the subtle pinings of Lamia:

> Thou art a scholar, Lycius, and must know
> That finer spirits cannot breathe below
> In human climes, and live: Alas! poor youth,
> What taste of purer air hast thou to soothe
> My essence? What serener palaces,
> Where I may all my many senses please,
> And by mysterious sleights a hundred thirsts appease?
> It cannot be—Adieu! [I.279–86]

As both lady and text, Lamia makes the "taste of purer air"
something that her admirer must reinvent. In *The Eve of
St. Agnes,* Porphyro accepted an analogous challenge and offered
a banquet for the senses to soothe the essence of Madeline awakening and descending from dreamy romance. Lycius, poor
scholar, needs to be financed by the lady to keep her in the
state to which she claims to be accustomed.

Perhaps on his example the reader borrows a hint from
Lamia and wonders what he ("thou art a scholar") knows
about finer spirits in human climes. If he goes back from Keats

to Burton, Keats's source, he discovers only Lamia as serpent; literary, like biological, sources as such can represent natural origins in the poorest sense, not the riches of imagined pre-existences. On the other hand, if he is impelled to look back to Milton, he finds he knows two things, or two sorts of antithetical things, about finer spirits and their mysterious sleights. In phrasing and ironically in situation, *Lamia* echoes *Comus,* and Lamia herself seems to appeal to Lycius with something of the residual resentment Milton's Attendant Spirit expresses when he first comes onstage. The Spirit belongs, he says, "In Regions mild of calm and serene Air, / Above the smoke and stir of this dim spot." Accustomed to the palace of Jove, he condescends because there are those ("and but for such, / I would not soil these pure Ambrosial weeds") who aspire to the Palace of Eternity. Milton's Spirit thus announces from the start his answer to the question Lamia raises about "what serener palaces" are to be offered in consolation. On the other hand, if we borrow not simply a luxurious resentment but a moral severity from the Attendant Spirit, we recognize in Lamia's question about palaces where all senses may be pleased a greater likeness to Comus than to Thyrsis. It is Comus who claims to be "of purer fire" and who offers to slake a hundred thirsts. Though it is very clear in the masque who is responsible for "fixing," who for liberating the lady, Keats's poem leaves morally ambiguous the power of Apollonius to fix his eye and fix the situation. This new area of uncertainty becomes the untrodden region of the mind—Keats's ground—on which the morally certain Milton seems a heavy-booted trespasser.

A similar ground of uncertainty and originality can be discovered by considering what knowledge *Paradise Lost* offers about the native home of finer spirits. In the most extended source passage, Eve's lament for lost paradise sets the pattern for Lamia's pining over the lost regions of air. Though Adam was created in Eden outside paradise, so that the soil and climate native to man is that of a lower world, Eve bewails the descent from Eden into obscure realms: "how shall we breathe in other air / Less pure, accustom'd to immortal Fruits?" (XI.284–85). Concern about purer air belongs to fallen beings, and re-presents in gentler form an anxiety about origins—about whether the self is continuous with the soul that had elsewhere its home. Belial projects this anxiety forward and takes comfort that though in hell their "purer essence then will overcome / Thir noxious vapor" (II.215–16); Satan turns against the self and is greeted—in a masterful irony—by the "purer air" of paradise (IV.153). The opportunity to conceive of one's native element without anxiety is offered by God when he brings all living creatures to Adam to be named but excepts the fish, who "cannot change / Thir Element to draw the thinner Air" (VIII.347–48). Later, Adam shows how he has internalized this qualification when he deprecates the sublimation of the Babel builder who attempts to climb "where thin Air / Above the clouds will pine his entrails gross" (XII.76–77). That the earth is native to man is a recognition (a re-cognition, something known, repressed, and then remembered) that comes with the fall.

For Keats, a more morally ambiguous forgetfulness or fall accompanies a more startling revelation about what turf one calls one's own. Attempting to undo her belatedness, Eve mistakes her native soil, just as Satan and Comus do. But is Keats's Lamia making a mistake about her history or with prescient strategy misleading Lycius when she challenges the youth to find in mortal experience an adequate counter for romantic origins? "What canst thou say or do of charm enough / To dull the nice remembrance of my home?" Her complaint that she must tread "this floor of clay, / And pain my steps upon these flowers too rough" may be more "charming" than Eve's lament for the flowers of paradise "That never will in other Climate grow." But is this a Comus-like charm of guile or a real feminine charm to evoke a concomitant verbal charm from Lycius and, ultimately, from Keats?

The charm can be broken, or at least understood for what it is, if one poses the riddle of Lamia's origin on the model of the child's question about chickens and eggs: Which came first, goddess, woman, or serpent? Though Apollonius would reply otherwise, Lamia appeals to Hermes with a firm conviction about where true charms lie: "I was a woman, let me have once more / A woman's shape, and charming as before" (I.117–18). In a sense a literary fiction was perpetrated on as well as by Lamia, and one must acknowledge the literariness of the story about origins in purer climes. The point is that either reduction ("Lamia is really a woman" or "Lamia is really a serpent") presents a formulaic demystification of literary fictions and a return to nature.

If statements about what Lamia "is" are antiromantic, reductive versions of statements about what Lamia was first, they could be said to supplant not only the romantic concerns of the opening Lamia-Hermes and Lamia-Lycius exchanges but the romance elements of Milton's poetry as well. Faced with the accusing Deity, Eve fully awakens from her dream of romantic origins, though she does not quite melt away the way Lamia does before Apollonius. Lamia is totally speechless, while Eve, though "with shame nigh overwhelm'd," speaks the single line "The Serpent me beguil'd and I did eat" (*PL,* X.162). For Milton the question of identity must take the form of a question about anteriority: after all, Eve's answer to God was already given in the Bible, and it is equally important for wholly internal reasons that Eve now acknowledge, whether as excuse or plain fact, the anteriority of the serpent. Such answers are defenses against the awesome anteriority of God, as God reminds—has already reminded— Adam before turning to Eve. But what about the answer, or rather the terrible silence, of Lamia when faced with Apollonius? If we borrow from Harold Bloom's *Map of Misreading* the association of defenses with tropes, then in place of Eve's criminal misprison, which makes her an ideological and temporal follower of Satan, we have Keats's literary misprision of Milton, and the conclusion of Lamia can be outlined like this:

The starting point is the recollection of a precursor exhibiting his strength. In *Comus,* Milton represented the Lady's song as being so efficacious "that even Silence / Was took ere she was ware," and Thyrsis is struck by those "strains that might create a soul / Under the ribs of earth" (ll. 555–62). In a mighty reaction formation, Keats conjures up a horrid presence to fill the vacancy left by the absence of Milton, and presents a Silence ravaging rather than ravished: "A deadly silence step by step increased / Until it seem'd a horrid presence there" (II.266–67). Then, in the impassioned cries of Lycius, this original reaction formation is represented as a reversal of the power of Milton's blindness and prophetic insight: the dreadful images of the Gods which "represent their shadowy presences" are invoked to threaten Apollonius with blindness and the isolation Milton bemoaned in the invocation to *Paradise Lost,* Book VII. Though the macrocosm—all the gods—is called down upon this one man, a counterforce is at work in the synecdoche of power—his eyes' ability to make the object of their glance wither. The dominant defense, the one controlling the basic action as well as the language, is the resulting *kenosis,* the isolation and undoing of Lamia. She whose presence filled the room—indeed, whose presence was the palatial room and all its décor—becomes a terrible emptiness. Not only are Lycius' arms "empty of delight"; the contiguity of metonymic language carries the emptied rhetorical structure across the enjambment to "as were his limbs of life." Characteristically, Bloom's map proves most indispensable at this point, guiding us from the limiting psychic defenses of isolation and undoing to the central artistic defense of repression. It may sound a bit weak to label as hyperbole Apollonius' resolution to the ambiguous ontology of Lamia: "Of life have I preserv'd thee to this day, / And shall I see thee made a serpent's prey?" But an otherwise weak identification becomes daemonized in its context, and if we feel the grotesque lowness not only of serpents but of "serpent" as an identity for Lamia, we are shocked simultaneously by the sublime, for these lines elevate the poem to the level of the stars and place it in a line from *Paradise Lost* to *The*

Auroras of Autumn—texts which pose "serpent" as grotesquely low and high sublime central figure. This achievement depends on the crucial repression of the fact that the "killing" irony is the power of the inner eye, or prophetic insight, purchased at the price of plain vision. Whether one believes the heart of repression to be a sexual instinct or a recognizable fact, one could say that what is repressed here is the knowledge of serpent as *ananke*—the body of fate that condemns us all to sexual illusion. More immediately, as far as the rhetoric of the poem is concerned, what is repressed is the knowledge of the priority of the written word. "Serpent" is the Bible's first answer to the question of evil, and "serpent" is the answer Milton has inherited at the beginning of *Paradise Lost* but must "not know" long enough for the poem to grow. "Who first seduc'd them to that foul revolt? / The infernal serpent; he it was" (*PL*, I.33–34). Shifting for a moment from eye to ear, *Lamia* presents the sophist's speech as primary and accords to it the power of demystifying illusion while mystifying or remystifying the charm-breaking word. What is left is quickly told. In a frightfully successful sublimation—the only successful defense, Freud claimed, but that is from the perspective of a reality principle—Lamia evaporates. Then, in a final *apophrades* or return of the dead coincident with the final word of the poem, serpent identity is "projected" on Lycius, "And in its marriage robe, the heavy body wound."

At this point, I realize, the anxiety-free myth of origins from the earth is in danger of being totally overwhelmed by evidence of Keats's engagement with Milton. Perhaps it would not be unfair to say that whereas mere borrowings deflate a myth of natural origins, the purpose as well as the uniqueness of psychic defenses makes consideration of them rather support a myth by which precursors have been ploughed under and the new poetry emerges from the native soil of one's own defenses. But in place of my metaphors, consider Keats's own from a letter concerned with Milton's significance:

What a happy thing it would be if we could settle our thoughts, make our minds up on any matter in five Minutes and remain content—that is to build a sort of mental Cottage of feelings quiet and pleasant—to have a sort of Philosophical Back Garden, and cheerful holiday-keeping front one—but Alas! this never can be: for as the material Cottager knows there are such places as france and Italy and the Andes and the Burning Mountains—so the spiritual Cottager has knowledge of the terra semi incognita of things unearthly; and cannot for his Life, keep in the check rein—Or I should stop here quiet and comfortable in my theory of Nettles.[6]

Even the "terra semi incognita of things unearthly" is imaged as being of this earth, a kind of "back garden" whose relation to a neater front garden would solve problems about cultivating one's originality. And the "theory of nettles" alluded to is a naturalized account of Miltonic power. Here is the passage immediately preceding the above:

I have heard that Milton ere he wrote his Answer to Salmasius came into these parts, and for one whole Month, rolled himself, for three whole hours in a certain meadow hard by us—where the mark of his nose at equidistances is still shown. The exhibitor of said Meadow further saith that after these rollings, not a nettle sprang up in all the seven acres for seven years and that from said time a new sort of plant was made from the white thorn, of a thornless nature very much used by the Bucks of the present day to rap their Boots withall—This account made me very naturally suppose that the nettles and thorns etherealized by the Scholars rotory motion and garner'd in his head, thence flew after a new fermentation against the luckless Salmasius and occasioned his well known and unhappy end.

"Very naturally" he is led to the myth of rhetorical power originating from the earth. What Milton garnered in the meadow was not wholly wasted on Salmasius; newly "fermented" in Keats's brain, the figure emerges in *Lamia* as the crown of thorns appropriate to Apollonius-Milton: "Let spear-grass and the spiteful thistle wage / War on his temples" (II.228–29). From the extrapoetic turf of the letters comes this little confirmation that Keats identified Milton with the sage of cold philosophy. Or better: if we think of Apollonius' final words, "A serpent!" as Milton's opening answer in *Paradise Lost,* Apollonius seems not a redaction of Milton but his precursor. Milton's epic carries the burden of the "past"—of picking up where Apollonius at the end of *Lamia* left off; but Keats and the earth in which he makes his Milton roll—they come before, in his playfully "preposterous" but no less seminal victory over Milton's priority.

iii

If we now turn back from these sophisticated myths of new begettings to Keats's most extended romance, we find there too that all transcendence is preempted by a subtle polemic concerning earthly origins. *Endymion* raises the question of whether it is earthly or no sublunar love that "has power to make / Men's being mortal, immortal." If this question about love is to provide the vocabulary for an argument about poetry, then Keats's answer, "earthly love" (I.843), must seem a swerve from poetic tradition. He asks that we read literary history in two ways: from the established perspective of romance (including Spenser and Milton) we move from Cynthia to Indian Maid, or from the worshipers of intellectual beauty to the worshiper of a particular beauty—in short, from the romancers down to Keats. But from Keats's perspective we begin in some way with the earthly, and if *Endymion* ends by subliming all, it ends where literary history *was*. What preceded in the poem was more "original" in the sense of being both more authentic and, in the poem's chronology, antecedent. A corollary to this argument with literary history is that those who find the conclusion of *Endymion* weak are objecting not to Keats's final touches but to the standard stuff of romance—what comes "after" the music of truth that is more authentically Keats's own.

Like "Ode to Psyche" and *Lamia, Endymion* turns to Milton to shape an antithetical vision. I would like to explore this relationship at some length, and begin by singling out in the following paragraphs a paradigmatic set of contrary moments from the two poets.

At the opening of Milton's *Lycidas,* nature seems to have accelerated beyond her usual pace, and the poet appeals to laurels, ivy, and myrtle—emblems of inspirational achievement taken from nature—to allow him to keep pace. Confronting the death of Lycidas "ere his prime," the poet urges indulgence of a corresponding prematurity, suggesting in his opening words, with the repeated "once more," how the wished-for regularity in the workings of inspiration might match the desired regularity of nature uninterrupted by sudden death. The urgency of the effort at least to match the extraordinary break in nature that occasions the poem is expressed even in the rhythm of the lines: "Yet once more, O ye Laurels, and once more / Ye Myrtles brown." The first three syllables seem to accelerate beyond (certainly they struggle against) iambic pace, impelling one over the enjambment to the autumnal myrtle and ivy.

At the reopening of life in Book II of Keats's *Endymion,* nature seems to have just warmed to springtime pace, and Endymion watches as Adonis, attuned to the season, is awakened from his winter slumber. In contrast to Milton's difficult appeal for poetic voice, Keats pictures natural sounds growing up as easily as nature grows: "Then there was a hum / Of sudden voices." The very rhythm of the appeal spoken by these voices seems to capture the naturalness of the inspiriting they call for: "Rise, Cupids! or we'll give the blue-bell pinch / To your dimpled arms. Once more sweet life begin!" (ll. 505–06). The lines wind down to the continuity of iambic pace, reaching regularity with the springtime call, "Once more."

The difference between the metrical rhythm of Milton's "Yet once more" and Keats's "Once more" may be the smallest token of the different concepts of the relation between natural and poetic rhythm. Milton's urgency in the opening lines of *Lycidas* expresses the tension between inspiration (spiritual energy) and nature (relatively inert object of the energizing). What Milton calls "season due" is disturbed by an occasion that requires inspiration, that requires a shattering of leaves before the mellowing year. The occasion for inspiration has priority over the ordinary workings of nature. Keats, on the other hand, depicts a scene in which the emblematic action seems to be a derivative—an abstraction into myth—of the ordinary workings of nature. With playfulness that seems concomitant with the naturalism, Keats pries under the fictions of the spirit to discover their natural roots. In terms of literary history one could say that the Spenserianism of the whole scene restores us to a pre-Miltonic world, for the realm of Adonis, like that of fairies and incubi according to the Wife of Bath, antedates that of Christian high seriousness.

This little comparison of the two poets may seem as unfair as a juxtaposition of portraits showing one man in formal pose and another caught at play. Yet from the perspective of "Ode to Psyche" and *Lamia,* Keats's playfulness seems to mark no relaxation into light verse but his profoundest responses to the burdens of the literary past and experiential present. He seems to smile knowingly at a high tragedy of the sublime that would alchemize out of nature into purer essence. The passage about the awakening of Adonis does not move up a scale of seriousness any more than it supports an ontological ladder from nature to realms full sublimed and free of space; on the contrary, mythic trappings and philosophical mystifications fall away as the poet approaches a sexual core. Leaning over her awakening lover, Venus charms "A tumult in his heart, and a new life / Into his eyes." Who can separate the "spiritual" element of this inspiriting from "a new life" in the sense of sexual desire kindled in his eyes? Attending the birth of new life here, we approach a moment of origins and confront the creative workings not only of nature but of verse. But moments of poetic origins, like moments of sexual begetting, are embarrassing.[7] The verse becomes self-conscious and breaks off:

> Who, who can write
> Of these first minutes? The unchariest muse
> To embracements warm as theirs makes coy excuse.
>
> [II.531–33]

Calling such a moment "self-conscious," we must distinguish the significance of self-consciousness as embarrassment (present in the most good-humored way) from its significance as poetry's ability to represent awareness of its own implications. On the level of the explicit, rather than the implied, the question "Who, who can write / Of these first minutes?" does not call for an answer—John Milton, John Keats, some "Dear John" to whom the Muse is writing farewell. As a rhetorical question, the lines "self-consciously" evoke another kind of rhetoric, that of more somber dismissals of the power to confront origins. Milton's Adam tells Raphael, "For Man to tell how human life began / Is hard: for who himself beginning knew?" (*Paradise Lost,* VII.250–51). One may legitimately protest that Milton has Adam go on to recount his first minutes, while Keats turns away at this point from Adonis' first minutes. But that mild protest only leads us on to confront the differences between these moments of beginning. While Adam looks back to his creation, Keats glances at Adonis' re-creation, and watches, as it were, the hyphen drop out: Adonis is at his recreation, and Venus his sport. These are not first moments of etherealizing spirit but of sexual love. The temperature in the pleasure thermometer is rising—if one can watch the gauge without the platonizing screen that critics have placed over it. Ostensibly arguing for a hierarchy of soul-delights, Keats offers the image of a device recording degrees of heat from cold pastoral to love forever warm. In the Adonis passage, poetry breaks off not because words have led us up the spirit-scale as far as words can go, but because they have led us back to sexuality, back from literary fiction to the ineluctable fact of nature.

Just as the verse paragraph breaks off, its last words suggest the kind of self-consciousness and the kind of return to origins that Keats has excluded. The last two words, "coy excuse," echo Milton—but with a heavy change. In *Lycidas,* the poet, calling for the Muses to begin, cries, "Hence with denial vain and coy excuse." In *Endymion,* the poet, breaking off, assures us that any muse would at this point make excuse. "The unchariest muse / To embracements warm as theirs makes coy excuse." Both are moments of self-consciousness, when the speaker turns from the story he is creating to his own process of creation. Milton cries, "So may some gentle Muse / With lucky words favor my destined urn," while Keats protests that there are no lucky words to describe lovemaking. Nor is it an accident that Miltonic self-consciousness should take the form of an awareness of the poet's mortality, while Keats stands at one of those moments of coming into being that will more clearly take the form, in the Hyperion poems, of a poetic birth. Self-consciousness for him means in its highest sense attending on, being attentive to, the labor of soul-making, the emergence of identity. The letter writer who exclaimed about Milton, "Life to him would be death to me" more often in his verse exchanged the attributives: moments that in his precursor would imply death and limitation descry for Keats a dawning of consciousness. But we must not overemphasize the presence of questions about the poet in the *Endymion* passage. In *Lycidas* the Muses are asked to dispense with coy excuse and help the poet overcome his sense of unpreparedness. In *Endymion* the coy excuse is blithely unrelated to poetic matters; not incipient poetics but incipient love is the immediate subject, and the change is a fall into nature. Questions about the authority of the poetic voice have been naturalized into concerns with natural rhythms, the "first minutes" of awakened love.

Milton had his own argument with the priority of nature. If one brings to a reading of the opening lines of *Lycidas* the knowledge conveyed in the headnote—that the death of King precedes any attempt to represent death—one sees that the task of the poem is to reassert the priority of the spirit. If we simplify the relation between doctrine, the pastoral form, and Milton's specific achievement, we can call the restored priority that of a Christian scheme of salvation. Consciousness of "Him that walked the waves" takes precedence over consciousness of Lycidas drowned beneath the waves. Perhaps one could say, looking forward to the redemption of lovers Endymion performs in the Glaucus episode, that for Keats the natural renewal has this "compositional" or storylike priority over the myth of resurrection one book later. Within the framewok of the Adonis episode we can take Keats's first draft as emblem of the compositional priority of the natural—a draft which has neither the Miltonism nor the concern with new awakening. The lines as first conceived do express the need to break off: "Away! let them embrace alive! that kiss / Was far too rich for thee to talk upon."[8] The riches of purely naturalistic celebration, perhaps too rich for extended verse of quality, are what come to the poet first. They are the product of the creative "first minutes," modified and made more subtle in revision.

A more famous Keats revision confirms the temporal priority of the naturalistic reading:

> Wherein lies happiness? In that which becks
> Our ready minds to blending pleasureable
> And that delight is the most treasureable
> That makes the richest Alchymy.

Perhaps it is embarrassment at the "blending pleasureable" that makes critics concentrate on the alchemy. Keats himself seems to have shared the embarrassment, and wrote to John Taylor asking that this revision be accepted instead:

> Wherein lies happiness? In that which becks
> Our ready minds to fellowship divine,
> A fellowship with essence; till we shine,
> Full alchemiz'd, and free of space.   [*Endymion*, I.777–80][9]

Some of the naturalism of the first version seems to have been alchemized or sublimated away, for in place of the more solid "blending pleasureable" we have the gaseous "fellowship with essence." The original alchemy may refer to no process of sublimation but to the fleshly realization of the magic of love. The revised desire to "shine / Full alchemized" can better please the platonists.

The passage thus introduced by either the original or the revised lines presents what Keats called "the gradations of Happiness." As long as the senses of touch and smell are presented as but first rungs on a ladder of love, the sensuous grounding presents no problem. Uneasiness about the scheme centers not about the foot but at the top of the ladder—whether it is seen to rest in or transcend sensuous nature. Though Keats protested against his first version of this pleasure ladder that it seemed "a thing almost of mere words," the revised version may come even closer to mere wordage. What is a "fellowship with essence" but words—a near oxymoronic conjunction of implications truer to the nature of metaphor than of mimesis. Perhaps it is a truth about love, or rather about the way love is expressed in language, that for moments of intensity the homeyness of the term "fellowship" and the transcendence implied in "essence" seem compatible. Yet one wonders whether, before approaching what he calls "the orbed drop / Of light . . . that is love," Keats wishes to describe or evade the nature of love. He will grant his readers phrases like "fellowship with essence" (or, in Book III, "symbol-essences") but behind—anterior to—that expression is the knowledge of "blendings pleasureable" gently mocking our need to etherealize.

If the metaphor of alchemization, like the defense mechanism of sublimation, moves away from sensuous nature, nature remains the starting place. Perhaps no Romantic felt that sense of origin so securely or returned to it so vigorously. The history of Keats's career may be regarded as a course in the alchemization not of nature (which seems to be the fundamental view of Earl Wasserman and Stuart M. Sperry)[10] but of passages of naturalism. He seems repeatedly to ask not "How can I transcend nature in this context?" but "How shall I sustain some other movement so that naturalization will appear no failure to get off the ground but a return to real beginnings, a rediscovery beyond cheating fancy?"

Consider the Hymn to Pan in *Endymion,* Book I, which wonderfully balances a sense of orphic mystery against the homeyness of the god. If the god were further alchemized out of nature he would, instead of giving the earth "a touch ethereal," vanish into thin air; if he were further naturalized (demythologized), he would simply disappear into the landscape, and no god, no hymn. After evoking both the more human aspects of his history and the more mysterious aspects of nature that he governs, the hymn moves to the boundary, the "bourne of heaven," just before the breaking point of song:

> Be still the unimaginable lodge
> For solitary thinkings; such as dodge
> Conception to the very bourne of heaven,
> Then leave the naked brain: be still the leaven,
> That spreading in this dull and clodded earth
> Gives it a touch ethereal—a new birth:
> Be still a symbol of immensity;
> A firmament reflected in a sea;
> An element filling the space between;
> An unknown—but no more; we humbly screen
> With uplift hands our foreheads. . . .   [I.293–303]

While Pan's worshipers request continuity with the past (let there be no break in nature) the three *still*s hold the poem still, at the point beyond which it must burst either into epiphany or into self-conscious awareness of its own fiction. Pursued to his symbol-essence, Pan is "a symbol of immensity," hovering in the liminal space betweeen Immensity and our idea of it. The last appositive is significantly "an unknown," and then the hymn breaks off with "but no more." No more of such talk (that's enough hymn for now) or no more than an unknown (that's enough identity for Pan)? Since the nature of the Unknown is a subject for metaphysics, we are, not surprisingly, more sure of the negative than of the thing negated.

According to Haydon, who brought Keats to meet Wordsworth, Keats recited his hymn to the older poet, who "drily said, 'a very pretty piece of Paganism.' " [11] No more of that, Mr. Keats, and I thank you. I risk this colloquial redaction of Wordsworth's sentiment to raise the question of whether the hymn itself, with its "no more," does not preempt his criticism and complicate, or even reverse, the relation of the established to the new poet. We cannot tell, from Haydon's story, whether Wordsworth identified the chanting poet before him with the Latmian chanters of the hymn (what is this upstart—a nature poet?) or whether he thought too playful, too trivial (a very pretty piece!) the distinction between Keats and the Latmians. Wordsworth may have drawn the line peremptorily between non-Christians and Christians (Haydon's own suggestion); between those who profess faith in Pan and those who have the faith in "something far more deeply interfused"; or, most simply, between other poets, the ephebi, and himself, the Poet. Whatever Wordsworth understood of Keats's stance, he made clear his own, as did Haydon in recounting the incident: "This was unfeeling & unworthy of his high Genius to a young Worshipper like Keats." Haydon leaves just a little uncertain whether Keats was a worshiper of the muses or, at this point, for this poem, a worshiper of Pan; most probably he meant that Keats was a worshiper of the inaccessibly apollonian Wordsworth, though that poet took him to be hymning an alien god. If it is preposterous to think of Keats setting up the metaphor by which Wordsworth is the great god Pan, it remains true of Keats that he cultivated the stance of hierophant before the deities, the superhuman Psyches that he half created and half perceived. Finding Keats's to be "the priest-like task," G. Wilson Knight might have it that Keats shared the Latmians' turn from metaphysics to ritual, putting an end to the suspension of disbelief that would, if continued, have taken him beyond naturalism. On the other hand, Morris Dickstein distinguishes the Latmians, who are content with an unknown, from Endymion and his creator, who are intent on imagining the "unimaginable lodge" and exploring the chambers of thought that their predecessors left in darkness.[12]

In the context of *Endymion* one must agree with Dickstein that the poem goes further and defines a stance that transcends the hymn's. But one retains a slightly different impression in imagining the spectacle of Keats chanting the hymn to Wordsworth and breaking off, as it were, by conjuring *him* "to receive our humble Paean, / Upon thy Mount Lycean!" I let fancy dwell on this scene because it helps us distinguish two powers in the hymn—Pan, to whom all is attributed, and the Latmians as singers, whose verse nearly calls a god into being. The power the Latmians attribute to Pan, to give the clodded earth a touch ethereal, a new birth, is the power Wordsworth himself claimed for the poet, who can present objects "like a new existence"; but the sense of new birth, heralded by the Latmians, is like the feeling at the end of *Hyperion* that poetry is witnessing the creation of a new Apollo, capable singer of the poem just sung. The Latmians break off, screening their foreheads so as not to see, not to think, the epiphany of the god. But before breaking off they show how far a poetry of "natural" inspiration can go toward conceiving and almost attending on its own birth.

iv

If the rhetoric of the hymn carries us a little ahead of ourselves, the lines that follow it in *Endymion* restore us to a simpler idea of natural inspiration:

> Even while they brought the burden to a close,
> A shout from the whole multitude arose,
> That lingered in the air like dying rolls
> Of abrupt thunder, when Ionian shoals
> Of dolphins bob their noses through the brine.   [I.307–11]

Unlike Yeats's dolphins which transport to eternity, Keats's are so colloquially and sensuously realized that we are drawn back to nature. Such controlled lightness in verse may be a gift of the god Pan (as opposed to the sublime rhetoric of Apollo), and if its blisses are everywhere manifest in *Endymion* they are characteristic of Keats from the start. Going back from Pan's "bourne of heaven" to the opening of *Poems 1817* we find Keats standing "tip-toe upon a little hill." In this domesticated effort at transcendence he has his feet on the ground, though at the bourne, and "tip-toe" is approximately of the same level of diction as dolphins bobbing their noses. Diction and imagery conspire with the earth itself to restore an innocence that cannot be far from "a new birth." Though Wallace Stevens thought that there never was a place of innocence, Keats repeatedly immerses himself in the pastoral fiction and imagines places of innocence where but to be is to be inspired. The point is not that Keats takes his start in the close observation of nature, but that he imagines pristine nature to be under a magic spell the loss of which makes us call departures from observable nature "fancy" and the pathetic a "fallacy." The 1817 volume is headed by a dedicatory sonnet that recognizes, "Glory and loveliness have passed away," but as the volume proper opens, that recognition is laid aside and something prior to that loss is restored.

Here are the opening lines:

> I stood tip-toe upon a little hill,
> The air was cooling, and so very still,
> That the sweet buds which with a modest pride
> Pull droopingly, in slanting curve aside,
> Their scantly leaved, and finely tapering stems,
> Had not yet lost those starry diadems
> Caught from the early sobbing of the morn.

In the Hymn to Pan the god is requested to hold "still," or released from time, his own liminal status at the bourne of the natural. On this little hill Keats finds in the cool, still air an origin or emblem for the stillness that holds nature suspended before the moment at which one has to give up pathetic fallacy. One might speculate that dew is described as "the early sobbing of the morn" because, like Blake's stars which water heaven with their tears, Keats's morn is prelapsarian. But Blakean innocence depends on the naiveté of a myth of Jehovah, in relation to whom there was once a choice of being rebellious or tearfully repentant; Keatsian innocence seems earlier still, and the poetry is premythic in wantoning with various pathetic investments in nature, indifferently assumed and then dropped.

By the end of the poem Keats moves to a more sustained myth (Endymion); a more sustained pathos ("The Poet wept at her so piteous fate, / Wept that such beauty should be desolate"); and a sustained apostrophe of the goddess ("Queen of the wide air . . . " [ll. 205–10]). But true to the earliness of his myth of inspiration, Keats pauses in the middle of the poem to apostrophize what is no god at all, a human sentiment that antedates the invention of the gods:

> O Maker of sweet poets, dear delight
> Of this fair world, and all its gentle livers;
> Spangler of clouds, halo of crystal rivers,
> Mingler with leaves, and dew and tumbling streams,
> Closer of lovely eyes to lovely dreams,
> Lover of loneliness, and wandering,
> Of upcast eye, and tender pondering!
> Thee must I praise above all other glories
> That smile us on to tell delightful stories.   [ll.116–24]

A glory that smiles on us is close to being a god; a glory that smiles us on is something earlier, a myth of natural inspiration. The only thing transcendent here is the charm of naiveté—if we can picture "charming" before the word wholly loses its magical cast. Lightness of touch and irony guard the charm by which Keats presents the earliest version of natural inspiration: pure love of nature leading to the begetting of a poet. Perhaps because this delicate fiction must be guarded by irony Keats excised a manuscript reading in which men find "An inspiration in a pleasant sound / Or pleasant sight." What he writes instead says as much, but with the disbelieving undertone built in: "For what has made the sage or poet write / But the fair paradise of

Nature's light?" The irony is located between the ostensibly rhetorical nature and the implicitly quite open nature of the question.
As the pseudonaturalism continues, so does the gentle jest at its
expense: "And when a tale is beautifully staid, / We feel the
safety of a hawthorne glade." Milton was not yet blind when he
wrote "'L'Allegro,'" but he need not have seen a hawthorne glade
to write, "And every Shepherd tells his tale / Under the Hawthorne in the dale." Poems are not picked up in glades.[13]

Though the answers to questions of poetic origins are not that
simple, voicing the problem in natural terms can provide a poetic
start. The mistake or misprision is seminal, and gives Keats "I
Stood Tip-toe." A miniature of the process may be observed in
the verse paragraph beginning with the question, "What first inspired a bard of old to sing / Narcissus pining o'er the untainted
spring?" The question is a classicism that really does not call
(despite the "what" rather than "who") for some specifiable
object or event. Whatever the complexities of inspiration, they
are aborted by the direct answer to the rhetorical question. What
first inspired? "A little space, with boughs all woven round." This
naturalized version of genius loci has it that locus itself is enough.
If one smiles at the notion that Ovid received the *Metamorphoses*
on "some delicious ramble," one smiles too observing how Keats
does generate a paragraph of the lush *Endymion* style out of the
attempt to recover the inspiring place.

v

Consider a more sophisticated landscape answer to the question of origins—the "melodious plot" in "Ode to a Nightingale."
Though this special place is another naturalized version of the
muses' haunt, Keats's ambitious ode would seem to have no time
for easy fictions of natural inspiration like those he toyed with in
"I Stood Tip-toe." Yet this is to read too quickly, and to skip
from the initial situation—a real, earthly bird whose priority
is indisputable, who cannot be reached because it will always
stand before the poem—to the high seriousness necessitated by

the voice of ancient days in stanza seven. In fact the easy fiction is there first, disguised only by its urgency: "O, for a draught of vintage! that hath been / Cool'd a long age in the deep delved earth." Here ontogeny recapitulates the phylogeny of Keats's poems, just as the infantile means of ego identification via digestion suggests a line of development that culminates in a more complex attitude towards identification with an imagined "other." Beyond regression to a state preceding self-consciousness, these lines point, via the desired origin of the draught, to the desired myth of the origin of inspiration: the poet wishes his verse to appear to have been, like his wine, gestated in the earth. (It is curious that the very phrases seem to have a "natural" source outside Keats's poetry. The letters speak of the desire for "a little claret wine cool out of a cellar a mile deep." [14]

Fortunately the melodious plot of ground occupied by the nightingale is no locus for the kind of oriental genie who grants a first-uttered wish regardless of one's sobered reservations. The poem gives the poet the chance to revise and refine his expressions of desire. Actually, we must distinguish two revisions, one of which is a comparatively simple overgoing of the original yearning, and the second of which brings Keats to a major statement of earthly inspiration. In the first revision the poet renounces the too somnolent, too deadening vehicle of transport which he first requested and calls instead for the fleeter wings of poesy. It is hard to tell, with the opening "Away! Away!" whether he is at first impelled to cry "away with that slow and slothful alcoholic route!" or "away from the earth! faster!" Whether what he turns from with such energy is the earth itself or his earlier means of transport, the energy of pushing himself away propels him toward what Yeats called "the artifice of eternity."

He does not get very far. Keats's commitment to the earth is too great for him to remain long with an ethereal Pegasus, breathtaking though the flight may be. In a second revision, the poet separates himself from the vehicle of transport and its destination—which seems instantly attained once the rider no longer perplexes and retards the flight:

> Already with thee! tender is the night,
>   And haply the Queen-Moon is on her throne,
>   Cluster'd around by all her starry Fays.[15]

With his feet ever more solidly on the ground, he speculates on the celestial scene that the wings of poesy would attain and that the nightingale—from which he now separates himself—can be thought to have attained. To the bird's superhuman happiness of stanza one is added this transcendent vision of stability and order: the Queen-Moon, perchance encountered while presiding in full state, rules over—while she and her court remain outside of—the world of mutability and death.

Turning from both the fanciful flight and the vision of peace that is its destination, the poet returns to the earth—here, where "there is no light." One can picture the change spatially and say that the ground to which he returns is not the ground he left at the end of stanza three; or one can picture the change emotionally and say that the energy of renunciation—the demystified rejection of transcendent flight—has back recoiled and produced a firmer commitment to the earth. Either vocabulary points to the earth seen anew, as a newly inspired and inspiring place. The groaning earth has become the seminal earth, and the imaginative work of guessing each sweet replaces both the abstracted vision of sorrow and the fancied vision of the moon-court. From this new perspective and this sense of new life the two rejected perspectives may be thought to collapse into one and spell the death he has evaded.

Eamon Grennan has suggested that besides other influences, the ode's impassioned portrayal of the cold earth in stanza three is indebted to Claudio's speech in *Measure for Measure,* III.i.118–32.[16] Terrified of death, Claudio pictures that ultimate displacement as a confinement to a placeless place: "To be imprison'd in the viewless winds, / And blown with restless violence round about / This pendent world." From the perspective of Keats's new stance, the flight on viewless wings of poesy is but an extension of the land of despair and death. Thus Keats may see in the terrified imagination of Claudio an image for what he could have lost had he not separated himself in time. Like Wordsworth's Lucy, rolled round the earth with rocks and stones and trees, Claudio would be eternally coupled with earth— but at an irrevocable distance, forever circling round rather than restored to an original union with the earth.

Keats's commitment to the earth, to borrow a description from Heidegger, is "not to be associated with the idea of a mass of matter deposited somewhere, or with the merely astronomical idea of a planet." [17] Hence even in the vision he rejects Keats substitutes imaginative for real space and finds no senseless astronomical goings-round but the Queen-Moon "Cluster'd around by all her starry Fays." This fictional space seems to provide the condition for seeing the earth anew—in just the way defined by Heidegger: "In setting up a world, the work sets forth the earth. This setting forth must be thought here in the strict sense of the word. The work moves the earth itself into the Open of a world and keeps it there. *The work lets the earth be an earth.*" For "setting up a world" read the fanciful construction of Keats's Queen-Moon and fays; for "letting the earth be an earth" read the extraordinary restoration of the darkling world of stanzas five and six. Thus the cry "Away! away! for I will fly to thee" would constitute the poet's turn to "the Open"—his leap from given to original space—or, more abstractly from the sense of the given to a sense of his own originality. Heidegger says, "To originate something by a leap, to bring something into being from out of the source of its nature in a founding leap—this is what the word origin [German *Ursprung*, literally 'primal leap'] means." Yet I have been arguing that the definitive leap Keats takes is not onto the vehicle of fancy but off of it, so that the space of fancy is a false origin and the earth to which he returns the real "Open." The origin Keats discovers in the earth negates the priority of the flight of fancy and restores the earth to its firstness.

This quarrel over first and second places influences all aspects of Keats's poetic imagination. It determines the belatedness of the poet facing the happy bird whose song forever precedes the poem; and it determines a second place in terms of literary origins—the way Keats's "viewless wings of Poesy" evade the "viewless winds" in his literary ancestry. I do not mean to thrust the whole weight of the argument about place onto the questionable borrowing of some phrases from Shakespeare. But I would like to regard the confluence of turns from birdsong to ode and from viewless winds to poetic wings(from nature to the poet, and from previous poet to present poet) as emblematic of Keats's stance. We can illuminate the turns—and Keats's myth of origins generally—by juxtaposing with the revision of "viewless winds" to "viewless wings" a mysterious turn to the first phrase on the part of Wordsworth.

At the end Book V of *The Prelude,* Wordsworth, having mourned the temporality of greatness and the "poor earthly caskets" of Shakespearean and Miltonic verse, takes comfort from the Nature he finds in the poets:

> Visionary power
> Attends the motions of the viewless winds,
> Embodied in the mystery of words:
> There, darkness makes abode, and all the host
> Of shadowy things work endless changes,—there,
> As in a mansion like their proper home,
> Even forms and substances are circumfused
> By that transparent veil with light divine,
> And, through the turnings intricate of verse,
> Present themselves as objects recognised,
> In flashes, and with glory not their own.   [V.595–605][18]

"Viewless" is an afterthought, a splendid revision of the 1805 line, "Attends upon the motions of the wind." But where are these viewless winds? The "there," the word Wordsworth emphasizes, the place where he locates darkness, is in the specially creative spacings of words themselves—in the voice of the shuttle weaving the fabric of verse. Wordsworth is commenting on the nature of poetry generally, and one could follow his pointer in locating Keats's darkness not in the actual scene (the melodious plot) but in the space opened up by "the turnings intricate of verse" (the plot of melody). Yet Keats insists on the scene, and when he finds himself "in embalmed darkness" he has his feet on the ground in a way Wordsworth does not. Perhaps the difference could be expressed by the distinction that in the Wordsworth passage darkness is a symbol while for Keats it is, first of all, an image; this is to say that Wordsworth is pointing us "there"—in signs, in the space separating signs from significance—while Keats returns us "here"—to the significant earth whence all sign-constructions take their origin.

However one specifies Keats's semiology, care must be taken not to reduce the argument of the ode by picturing the earth itself at war with the signs and symbolic realms abstracted from it. The special status of the earth might better be indicated by supposing the poet, while combating his own primitive thanatos (his desire to "leave the world unseen"), magically renewed rather than defeated by his falls to the earth. The struggle thus would not simply pit nature against an alternative world; rather, in the course of a struggle for poetic voice, nature retains a formal purity, but the Antaeus-like poet (to borrow Hazlitt's term) falls to the ground only to find himself invigorated or born anew.

To give this little Antaeus myth a local habitation as well as a name, consider the ode's seventh stanza, introduced and followed by a fall to the earth:

> Still wouldst thou sing, and I have ears in vain—
> To thy high requiem become a sod.

> ### 7

> Thou wast not born for death, immortal Bird!
> No hungry generations tread thee down;
> The voice I hear this passing night was heard
> In ancient days by emperor and clown:

Perhaps the self-same song that found a path
  Through the sad heart of Ruth, when, sick for home,
    She stood in tears amid the alien corn:
      The same that oft-times hath
  Charm'd magic casements, opening on the foam
    Of perilous seas, in faery lands forlorn.

8

Forlorn! the very word is like a bell
  To toll me back from thee to my sole self!

Between the meaning of the word "forlorn" at the end of stanza seven (distanced, in visionary space) and the meaning of the word opening stanza eight (woeful) the imaginative contraries of the poem may be said to be suspended. From the perspective of stanza eight the first occurrence of "forlorn" is fanciful, the second the powerful expression of one for whom the miseries of the world are misery. At this point one could follow Wordsworth's directive to the "mystery of words" and find, in the "turnings intricate of verse" between the stanzas, that "darkness makes abode." But for Keats the turn is not simply a fall into language but an Antaeus-like fall to the earth. Darkness may make an abode in the pun that marks the turn between stanzas, but it finds a final resting place in the earth to which the poet returns. It is a funerary bell that tolls the poet to his sole self and that leaves the voice of the bird, in the end, "buried deep / In the next valley-glades." From the easeful earthiness of stanza six (the desire to become a sod) to the difficult rightness of a voice not just fled but buried—and not just in another but in the ever-nigh "*next* valley-glades"—is an enormous increase of power.

The turn to stanza seven marks a preliminary but no less striking moment of Antaeus-like strength. In transporting us beyond the melodious plot to ancient days and lands forlorn, the "viewless wings of Poesy" are beating harder than they did in the comparatively fanciful journey of stanza four. Where did this energy come from? Picture a struggle, at the end of stanza six, between capable voice and passive listening, or ecstasy and lethargy. As the turn between stanzas is made, spiritual defeat becomes, rather, degradation to the earth—and renewal from the earth. Voicing the desire to "become a sod," the poet returns to nature and finds his power to return the bird to a realm beyond nature. If the poet exercises Antaeus-like strength, the bird takes the form of mythic rebirth characteristic of the phoenix: "Thou wast not born for death, immortal Bird!" Using the word "born"—in the very phrase that denies natural birth—Keats calls attention to the new birth we are beholding here. A formalist critic might object that the immortal Bird of stanza seven is not the bird of stanza one.[19] Just so; Great Pan has heard the poet's sacrificial prayer of return to the sod and has bequeathed to the poet's symbol "a touch ethereal—a new birth."

vi

Naturalization and new birth assume a different, and ironically a more lighthearted, form in "Ode on Melancholy." Canceling an original opening stanza of gothic claptrap, Keats retained a subtler balance between one stanza of unnatural recourses and one stanza of natural origins for Melancholy:

1

No, no, go not to Lethe, neither twist
   Wolf's-bane, tight-rooted, for its poisonous wine;
Nor suffer thy pale forehead to be kiss'd
   By nightshade, ruby grape of Proserpine;
Make not your rosary of yew-berries,
    Nor let the beetle, nor the death-moth be
      Your mournful Psyche, nor the downy owl
A partner in your sorrow's mysteries;
    For shade to shade will come too drowsily,
      And drown the wakeful anguish of the soul.

2

But when the melancholy fit shall fall
   Sudden from heaven like a weeping cloud,
That fosters the droop-headed flowers all,
   And hides the green hill in an April shroud;

> Then glut thy sorrow on a morning rose,
>   Or on the rainbow of the salt sand-wave,
>   Or on the wealth of globed peonies;
> Or if thy mistress some rich anger shows,
>   Emprison her soft hand, and let her rave,
>   And feed deep, deep upon her peerless eyes.

The stanza of natural origins seems as full of lighthearted demystification as its predecessor, and four lines mock while describing the advent of melancholy like a change in season or weather. Referring to an "April shroud" rather than an April shower, Keats shows how easily darkness can make its abode in the "viewless winds" of metaphor as well as climate. A formalist could say simply that the idea of an April shroud or deathlike spring is paradoxical, and that paradox is a form of playfulness the siege of contraries can take. The readiness with which such observations can be made accounts for the popularity of Keats among the New Critics when having to choose a Romantic: he "teaches best," granted that awareness of irony or the simultaneous presence of conflicting meanings is a primary stage in the appreciation of poetry.

Beyond static contraries, however, is the temporality of natural process and the potentially antipathetic temporality of verse. Isolating the words expressive of mood in the first four lines of the stanza, we find melancholy, weeping, drooping, and the shroud of death. While the fact of death might be said to explain melancholy, weeping, and drooping, Keats's lines mischievously suppose the anteriority of melancholy; it simply "falls and becomes mourning rather than the other (Freudian) way round. The stanza begins in simile: melancholy fits fall like rain; one falling action is compared to another. When we discover not simply "cloud" but "weeping cloud," we meet a poetic equivalent for the anteriority of nature—as though nature knew all about weeping before the poet began looking for things to compare to melancholy fits. Similarly, one comes upon "April shroud" having needed only "April shower," and thus seems to discover the melancholy already there. As the Indian Maid says about Sorrow, "she is so constant and so kind," waiting for us, ready to bestow all we are ready to consume. Hence "glut thy sorrow on a morning rose" (the morning is already mourning; consciousness of ephemerality is caught in the bud) for nature will have anticipated one's appetite for melancholy anyway.

Though one could argue that the presence of an image like "weeping cloud" when we are prepared only for "cloud" points to the anteriority of language (the metaphors seem to have the melancholy before the earth does), language is in fact but figuring the priority of nature. Keats's rhetorical strategy is based on our provisional acceptance of a common synecdoche: if we speak of the earth when we mean nature, then the poet, literalizing "earth," can picture melancholy falling to the earth from a prevenient source in the sky. But no, we say, correcting ourselves, there is no question of temporally distinguishing earth from sky, green hills from clouds, but of distinguishing earthly or natural from supernatural or unnatural sources of melancholy. Thus we come to the earthiness of melancholy with the energy of rejecting a literalism; and, with Antaeus-like strength, we grasp what is, after all, precisely the point: melancholy is of the earth whence joy's grapes grow, and is there not just in the autumn but from the first April shower.

If the poetic desire to invent or discover melancholy is preempted by nature, the desire to personify melancholy is preempted by the appearance of a source of melancholy in facing a natural person. We meet the mistress of stanza two before we encounter the veiled goddess of stanza three. But the question of prevenience is much complicated by the conditional of stanza two ("if thy mistress some rich anger shows") and the discovered eternal presence in stanza three: "Ay, in the very temple of Delight / Veiled Melancholy has [she has had, and she now has] her sovran shrine." To clarify Keats's argument about time, compare this Spenser sonnet, which ends with a figure that looks very much like an "original" in relation to Keats's remarkable variation:

> This holy season, fit to fast and pray,
> Men to devotion ought to be inclynd:
> Therefore, I lykewise, on so holy day,
> For my sweet saynt some service fit will find.
> Her temple fayre is built within my mind,
> In which her glorious ymage placed is,
> On which my thoughts doo day and night attend,
> Lyke sacred priests that never thinke amisse.
> There I to her, as th' author of my blisse,
> Will builde an altar to appease her yre;
> And on the same my hart will sacrifise,
> Burning in flames of pure and chast desyre:
> The which vouchsafe, O goddesse, to accept,
> Amongst thy deerest relicks to be kept.   [*Amoretti,* XXII]

Both Spenser's sonnet and Keats's ode move from a playfully hypothetical situation to a more serious look at a present truth. Spenser begins by setting himself the proposition: if one is going to have to be devotional, let the mood at least take the following form; Keats begins by setting a hypothetical listener the proposition: if one is going to have to be melancholy, let the mood at least take the following source. In the end Spenser moves from the optative to the present tense of apostrophe: "vouchsafe, O goddesse, to accept, / Amongst thy dearest relicks to be kept." In the end Keats moves from the optative through the strong statement of what "is" and what must be to the concluding prophecy: "His soul shall taste the sadness of her might, / And be among her cloudy trophies hung."

The significance of these similarities and differences may be related to Spenser's beginning from the serious perspective of Christian devotion (the Easter season) and coming to apostrophize the new god (the lady, so elevated for the space of this poem). Keats begins with a playful account of the old gods and the old remedies of love (Pluto's lethe, Persephone's nightshade) and comes to divinize Melancholy. In the course of the ode he goes further back than the old devotion (finds a truer source) and goes further than the old mistress-worship to proclaim a prophetic truth of universal experience. If Spenser is a great original for Keats's naturalism, the ephebe must overgo his predecessor at his own game. Spenser's mastery is clearest in the surprising figure. "There I to her, as th' author of my blisse, / Will builde an altar to appease her yre." The "as," at first an indication of likeness, slides out of comparison into causality: since she is author of my bliss (since she, as author, precedes my poetic figurations), she has an anteriority and an autonomy that make her emotional state out of my control; she may well be angry, and need appeasement. This tribute to the extrapoetic lady—bringing with it an acknowledgment of art's limitations—is one of Spenser's most characteristic and most endearing achievements in his poems of courtship and marriage. Keats does not rival Spenser in attributing more "earliness" or more extrapoetic reality to the mistress of stanza two; what he does is to seize on his fiction of an angry mistress and ask that one "feed deep, deep upon her peerless eyes," discovering there, in the energy of that anger, a *source* of animation. By itself the figure of angry eyes is traditional—indeed, it is the central figure of *Amoretti* XXI, the immediately preceding Spenser sonnet. Spenser's mistress can "traine and teach me with her looks"; what she teaches is of moral or social worth. What the mistress of Keats's ode teaches is, simultaneously, the need to take pleasure in an expression of energy—be it a street fight or a lover's quarrel—and the need to take sorrow back to the same transient source.

In the "Ode to Psyche," the poet finds that if he is belated at all he is fortunately belated and can create for Psyche as goddess what history has not provided her. In the "Ode on Melancholy," the poet finds he is fortunately belated in a more difficult sense and can create for Melancholy as goddess what nature has already provided him. The "Veil'd Melancholy" of stanza three is preceded by the mistress of peerless eyes, and the injunction to "feed deep, deep upon her peerless eyes" is causal, rather than simply parallel to "taste the sadness of her might." Both statements are set in a context of mock indulgence, making their Tantalus-like offerings with the knowledge that there is no satisfaction in self-satisfaction. The richness of a lady's anger is an object of aesthetic pleasure only to one detached to the point of melancholy. The lady with her fit of anger and the gentleman with his melancholy fit realizing he feeds alone on the beauty of her eyes—they are having separate fits. Grounded in nature, knowledge of this separation becomes emblemized by the veil of Melancholy that separates her from those discovering her might. The emblem not only transcends but eases the condition of nature. Better one's soul should be the trophy of the unapproachable than the trifle of the reproaching lady. To be sure, a natural lady's anger passes, and that whole image is playfully presented as a source of melancholy. But whatever the degree of woe or play, the relationship between the natural mistress and the mythologized Melancholy is not a parallelism but a redemptive begetting of the mythic from the natural.

If one considers other literary sources as having a hand in the begetting of the final stanza, a similar but richer argument develops about the priority of nature and her spokesman, Keats. Douglas Bush cites *Troilus and Cressida*:

> What will it be
> When that wat'ry palates taste indeed
> Love's thrice-repured nectar? Death, I fear me;
> Sounding destruction; or some joy too fine,
> Too subtile-potent, tun'd too sharp in sweetness
> For the capacity of my ruder powers.[20]

Speaking these lines, Troilus anxiously anticipates the sorrows of love. The speaker of Keats's ode, in advising a hypothesized seeker after Melancholy to "burst joy's grape against his palate fine," approaches him from the perspective of Shakespeare's play, from presumed familiarity with the ways of love. Thus a source of anxiety for Troilus becomes a source of authority for Keats the speaker of this poem, secure in his knowledge of what poetry has come before him.

If we reach further back in literary history, Theocritus' twenty-third idyll offers a more extended though weaker precursor text, and one Keats could be said transumptively to surpass. Though Theocritus is early this idyll is a late, corrupt, pseudo-Theocritus text in which a lover sets about doing just what Keats's ode argues against. Keats's opening line, "No, no, go not to Lethe," could be a response to Theocritus' lover, who announces that he will take the path to Lethe, "where, men say, is the common cure for lovers' ills—oblivion. Yet if I set it to my lips and drain it to the dregs, not even so shall I quench my longing. And now at last I find pleasure at thy door. I know what is to be. Fair is the rose also, yet time withers it." [21] Keats's advice, "glut thy sorrow on a morning rose," comes like an antithetical response. Theocritus' lover is excluded by the indifference and the anger of the boy with whom he has fallen in lover; Keats's lover is advised to feed on anger and by anticipatory knowledge to gain some victory over the evanescence of passion. The poems as a whole are as distinguished as their lovers in their relationship to loss: while Theocritus' idyll is overtaken by its melodramatic conclusion, Keats's poem sets out to find melancholy, and so seems the earlier, less corrupt text. Assurance in Theocritus ("I know what is to be") is purchased at the price of the conjunction of the death of passion (roses and beautiful boys both fade) with the death of the speaker, which he takes upon himself. A greater assurance is achieved in Keats by preempting the mortality of passion for the passion of anger in stanza two—which seems, for a moment, to leave alive the passion of love—and then substituting in stanza three the sure knowledge of evanescence. Finally, Theocritus' lover literally hangs himself in the doorway of the beloved, while Keats's hypothesized lover will find himself hung (a greater reduction than "hanged"? or a metaphoric and therefore easier one?) mid the trophies in the temple of delight. Never penetrating the temple, Theocritus' lover is left at the door, gaining in death a priority over the death of desire as crude as *ejaculatio praecox*. If Keats's lover needed to wait for acceptance and consummation to achieve his melancholy death, he would indeed be belated. But the absurdity of this extension to Theocritus' literalism brings us round to the achieved priority of the ode: even if melancholy can only be "seen" and "tasted" by the experiential lover, it can be sufficiently known by one who knows what the ode knows about melancholy. As a piece of advice the third stanza of the ode seems to argue ambiguously "know this!" or "you need to experience this!" A psychoanalytic reading might find Keats granting poetic priority to the first over the second of these alternatives as a way of countering the priority of biographical fact—lack of sexual experience. But the poem is stronger, and argues that either injunction restores the would-be lover and the poet with him to the original mutability of sexuality in nature as well as human relations, and makes a text like Theocritus' idyll seem belated and in more than one sense corrupt.

vii

Within "Ode on Melancholy," the progress from the injunction "feed deep" to the prophecy "his soul shall taste" makes the lighter, ironic tone appear to generate, to be the natural cause of, the grander rhetoric. Similar gustatory metaphors are of great importance in *The Fall of Hyperion;* and, enlarged from the dimensions of metaphor to those of dramatic action, the path from natural causation to grand rhetoric is the progress of the story. The opening narrative thus marks a beginning place in many ways: it not only itself concerns an originatory action, but it stands before the Hyperion story which concerns a birth of poetic consciousness. In addition, there is this fact about form: language mimetic of an originatory action seems closer to a literal, natural source than speculative language about origins. Simply compare the abstractness (the sense of being "removed") of my sentence, or the metaphoric density of the injunction in "Ode on Melancholy" to feed deep on the mistress's eyes, with the radical simplicity of the announcement in *The Fall of Hyperion,* "I ate deliciously." The context of that statement gives us a dreamer sitting down to feast on the remnants of an Edenic meal—Keats ingesting Miltonic scraps. And the dream vision encourages the sparkling fiction that hunger for status as a poet could be naturally filled. Toasting the living and the dead, the poet drinks and comments on that act with a mixed metaphor (a trope begotten on a trope) that summarizes the myth of the natural origins of poetry: "That full draught is parent of my theme."

Geoffrey Hartman has explored the cathexis of yearnings for muselike nurture and maternal—often specifically oral—gratification in the Hyperion poems.[22] Unlike the complex role reversals of begetter and begotten, nurturer and nurtured, there is a startling naiveté to this line about a "full draught." With the exception of the necessarily cloven "parent" the line itself has a monosyllabic simplicity: "That full draught is parent of my theme." If the genetics of this parentage remain problematic, we know at least that we are close to an essential fiction about origins because the polemical value of the statement cannot be separated from the simplicity of diction and the pure conceit or story-level literalism. We confront something like the essentially childlike evasiveness that replies to the question "Where did you get those words?" with the flat "I ate them." If we pursue this homey redaction and ask "Where did you get the idea of eating them?" two sorts of answers are possible: "It's only natural," and "Everybody does." "Everybody," in the context of *The Fall of Hyperion,* means that initiatory foods and drams are the stuff of romance and epic—in particular that the episode in Keats recalls Adam and Eve eating the fruit of knowledge in *Paradise Lost* and Dante consuming the "special food" that Beatrice offers him in *Purgatorio* XXX-XXXI. But instead of demystifying Keats's myth of originality, these sources confirm Keats's originality. In contrast to Milton, Keats would be himself assuming the burden of his own original sin; in contrast to Dante, Keats would commit himself to drowning the memory of his own sin. On the other hand, "it's only natural" that Keats should take up the "full draught" here because the most immediate predecessor for *The Fall of Hyperion* is his own *Hyperion,* and in that poem Apollo's last words are a recipe for the draft to come:

> Knowledge enormous makes a God of me.
> Names, deeds, gray legends, dire events, rebellions,
> Majesties, sovran voices, agonies,
> Creations and destroyings, all at once
> Pour into the wide hollows of my brain,
> And deify me, as if some blithe wine
> Or bright elixir peerless I had drunk,
> And so become immortal.[23]   [III.113–20]

To be sure, the mysteries of generation are not magically revealed by heralding this "as if" in the last line but two as the forerunner, coming out of similitude and into dramatic action in *The Fall of Hyperion.* Apollo is not immediately translatable into the dreaming poet, nor is the dying into life ending *Hyperion* superimposable on the "cloudy swoon" and waking in *The Fall.* That is to say, translation or superimposition do not work mechanically, and it will take work—poetic work, a large part of the workings of *The Fall of Hyperion*—to make identifications like these. At a certain point in reading or analyzing *The Fall,* it must seem that the poet of the later poem takes over where the god of the former left off. At another point, one comes to see the later poem gaining anteriority and dramatizing the begetting of *Hyperion.* I anticipate the argument here to suggest the onslaught that comes with the "full draught." Realizing that this moment has been anticipated by its Keatsian and non-Keatsian precedents, one could attempt to distinguish: consciousness of other poets would come as a burden, while awareness of *Hyperion* would relieve the tension, given the assumption that a poet and his readers take comfort in being limited to the sphere of the poet's own work. If that is false comfort, and interactions with Keats's predecessors must necessarily be considered, a more immediate comfort is at hand. Against the expansion of allusion outside Keats we can pose the ultimate reduction to the context itself. When the poet says "That full draught is parent of my theme" he means, on some level, *that* draught and not that of any other poem. The potion becomes the poet's first strong emblem of his desire to absorb the role of parent and generate his own identity.

When, in Shelley's *Triumph of Life,* the "Shape all light" offers Rousseau her cup, he obeys an injunction: "I rose; and bending at her sweet command, / Touched with faint lips the cup she raised." In *The Fall of Hyperion,* Keats raises his own cup, offers his own pledge to present humanity and past poets, and brings on his own drowsiness. By a strong offensive he thus defends himself against the burden that falls on one passively seduced by some fruit or cup of knowledge. Of such a one Michel Foucault says, "All these contents that his knowledge reveals to him as exterior to himself, and older than his birth, anticipate him, overhang him with all their solidity, and traverse him as though he were merely an object of nature, a face doomed to be erased in the course of history."[24] In contrast, Keats makes the "contents" he discovers to be "objects of nature," the fruits of the earth that the poet ransacks, when he gathers his Antaeus-like strength from what lay "scattered on the grass." If he is picking on remnants of Milton or what Milton by not writing about the last meal in paradise left untouched, he is nonetheless approaching these leavings as though they were natural remnants. Since no interdicting cherub bars the way, the literary paradises or purgatorial mountains of the past can be approached as innocently as one approaches landscapes unspoiled by signs reading "Private Property."

Milton, and more especially Dante, have become public property, parts of nature as Pope found Homer to be. The possibility for treading guiltlessly on the old poets' ground is further explored in the description of the fresh May breeze. Keats found precedent for this breeze in Dante's *Purgatorio* XXIV, where the poet is directed how to mount beyond the "wood / Whereof Eve tasted"[25]—beyond the sins of gluttony. In Keats's poem, eating deliciously mocks the spiritual authority of Dante's abstract sin. But beyond mockery or insistent innocence is the *naturalization* of appetite and its fulfillment.

We are impelled to see how naturalization is a return to origins if we juxtapose beside *The Fall of Hyperion* the analogous events of the *Purgatorio*. Having passed the tree of abstinence on the terrace of gluttony and felt the refreshing breeze, Dante receives from Statius in Canto XXV an account of human generation beginning with sexual mingling, and considering embryonic growth till the imparting of the soul. Having returned to the scene of fulfilled appetite and glutted himself, the poet in *The Fall of Hyperion* senses the incense as though it were a spring breeze in which "even the dying man forgets his shroud." If he is told no story of biological and spiritual generation, he will find that he stands in a vale of soul-making, attending what is more than description of his "new birth" as a poet.

Were Keats to receive from a parallel authority an analogous tale of soul-making, we could say that the parent draught was the Dante he imbibed in the Cary translation. But Keats has mixed his own drinks using natural ingredients, and no one else has affixed an authoritative label to this home brew. The crucial change in authority-status of the speakers naturalizes the encounters. In Dante, a glowing penitent utters this undisputed injunction:

> "If ye desire to mount,"
> He cried; "here must ye turn. This way he goes,
> Who goes in quest of peace."   [XXIV.137–39]

Compare with this Moneta's first words:

> "If thou canst not ascend
> These steps, die on that marble where thou art.
> Thy flesh, near cousin to the common dust,
> Will parch for lack of nutriment."   [I.107–10]

If the threat is fierce, the authority is gone, and Moneta stands like Shakespeare's Cleopatra resisting to the last the demystification of "No more but e'en a woman." It is a supreme triumph for Shakespeare that Cleopatra's discovery of her womanly creatureliness appears more divine than all her queenly state could make her. Dante too knew how and when to make his figures of poetic authority betray their humanness. The impulse to naturalize is by no means absent, but it is consumed in the reverent but friendly talk of Statius and Virgil—poet with poet, man with man. By the time Dante hears Beatrice, Virgil has been silenced, and there are no qualifications to the austerity of Beatrice's voice. She reprimands Dante and exacts confession from him before the memory of sin can be washed away. In *The Fall of Hyperion* there are no preliminary human encounters, and Moneta, though ostensibly foreboding, proves a very human goddess. It is the poet who interrogates her, gaining authority as he gains audacity, finally compelling her to "shed / Long-treasured tears." Cleopatra's "immortal longings" seem, retrospectively, longings for immortality, while Moneta is an immortal who bursts into the new freedom of acknowledging her everlasting mortal longings. She "breaks down," as it were, or more precisely she breaks out of romance stasis and breaks into life.

Witnessing this new birth, we are taken back to origins, back from a level of mythologization to something more like nature. It is as if we climbed from the third stanza of the "Ode on Melancholy" back to the end of the second and met the real mistress there—met not an abstract goddess but a woman entangled in real frustrations, misunderstandings, ambiguous charms, and a nagging sense of being trapped. Keats limits the humanization by describing her face "Not pin'd by human sorrows, but bright-blanch'd / By an immortal sickness which kills not" (I.257–58). She is, after all, not human, but a muse figure all the more shocking for traces of the human element out of which she has been carved. There remains, as with the angry mistress, only to feed on her peerless eyes and behold, as the poet enjoins her to let him behold, "what in thy brain so ferments to and fro."

The poet's power to stand at his own origins and confront what is fermenting in his muse's brain may have already been suggested by Moneta:

> Thou hast felt
> What 'tis to die and live again before
> Thy fated hour. That thou hadst power to do so
> Is thy own safety; thou hast dated on
> Thy doom.   [I.141–45]

These lines have been read biographically to refer to Keats watching his brother die and enduring that preview of his own suffering. Perhaps less as an antithetical reading than as a statement about correlative poetic knowledge, they might be said to point to the composition of *Hyperion*. *Hyperion* is dead, yet the poet stands in this poem *before* that fated end, watching the Hyperion story through the eyes of Moneta.

At this point, however, *The Fall of Hyperion* does not simply repeat *Hyperion*. Repetition is not "a new birth," and watching the old beginning come round again would be less a confrontation with origins than an evasion of the question "Where did *Hyperion* come from?" From the perspective of a certain kind of literary criticism, such evasion is the only possibility: "The poet can only start his work because he is willing to forget that this presumed beginning is, in fact, the repetition of a previous failure, resulting precisely from an inability to begin anew." [26] But suppose the "inability to begin anew" is faced head on— indeed, suppose the poet chooses for his subject a myth of the failure to begin anew. Re-presenting the tableau of the sunken Saturn, Moneta gives the poet the opportunity to see, in the story of the titans, the story of himself.

In Saturn, Keats beholds not merely a ghost from an unfinished poem come to haunt him in his attempt to begin anew, but a mythologized version of the difficulties with his own myth of origin. Saturn's sleep can stand for the danger that the return to earth will not prove seminal. Watching Saturn "Degraded, cold, upon the sodden ground / His old right hand lay nerveless,"

Keats sees fulfilled with a vengeance the desire in the Nightingale Ode to become a sod. How shall the scene be animated? "Gasping with despair / Of change," the poet despairs of his ability to change a picture or idea for a poem into poetic action. When Saturn does look up and speak, it is to send "Strange musings to the solitary Pan." What has happened to the Latmians' hymn to Pan, the prayer for "a touch ethereal—a new birth"?

Saturn of *The Fall* has lost the energy of Saturn of *Hyperion*. Preempted by the exchange with Moneta is the Keatsian concern with identity, and gone is the grandeur of the hope for an overthrow of the present gods. We are left with a sharpened sense of nature pursuing her course independently of "godlike exercise / Of influence benign." Saturn's last words, recapitulated from *Hyperion* but without the energizing "I will give command!" leave us with a tired and disbelieving echo of the myth of new birth:

> and let there be
> Beautiful things made new for the surprise
> Of the sky-children. [I.436–38]

Like an old uncle who used to bring toys for the children, Saturn returns to that vision of benevolence oblivious to the fact that the children are long grown up and empowered. Such a return mocks the poet's desired return to his origins. Watching Saturn, the poet finds not a recovered "visionary gleam" but the terrible equation of feeble age and childhood innocence. The price for a return to origins is finding oneself not the renewed god—not even a midair Hyperion, flaring onward—but a sick and tired man. Chronologically ripe for an Apollo-like incarnation, Keats is physically and spiritually returning to his fathers.

Has the poet come to disbelieve in his own myth of renewal? Or does he believe and identify all too well, dissolving once and for all the distinction between fathering and returning to one's fathers—to the natural earth? Paul de Man has described the pattern throughout Keats as "prospective": "It consists of hopeful preparations, anticipations of future power rather than meditative reflections on past moments of insight or harmony."[27] By the time Saturn speaks in *The Fall of Hyperion,* the great moment of "future power" has been actualized in the confrontation with Moneta, and Keats has been figuratively absorbed into the ranks of his precursors on whose moments of insight or harmony we reflect with awe, just as he reflects on the vision of the old precursor gods. Throughout his poetry Keats had attempted to anticipate the "new birth," getting behind it in poems or episodes that would *end* with questions like "Was there a poet born?" Now, brought by his Muse back to the womb and witnessing, as it were, the gestation of his old poem—and thus his own identity as a poet—Keats finds that to stand as if a man were author of himself he has to assume more the identity of the father dying in the act of generation than the identity of the newborn son.

Unlike stories about coming of age, the Hyperion poems present the old gods dreaming while the younger generation is already in possession of reality. Against the youth and Herculean strength of the reality principle, what I have been calling the Antaeus in the poet finds an image of the loss of power in the listless Saturn, whose "bow'd head seem'd listening to the Earth, / His antient mother, for some comfort yet." In the end, mother earth will be able only to open her arms and absorb the titans into natural process. Meanwhile an ironic glimmer of renewal is caught in language describing the face of Thea, who looks "As if calamity had but begun." This much of an appearance of origination, truest to the condition of loss, can still be recaptured. But if calamity looks, on the face of it, like a first beginning, the gloom is in fact unchanging, and the burden on the poet is to bear the weight of eternal quietude. He stands under the knowledge of loss, waiting from a vantage antecedent to a moment of origin. "Gasping with despair / Of change," the poet experiences something like the strangling of Antaeus, for the final turn to the earth will be without life-giving reverberations.

Antaeus breathes his last in midair, leaving the wind, as Moneta tells the poet, blowing "legend-laden through the trees." Returning to earth this last time, the giant of imagination is not to be renewed. When Saturn is espied "Like a vast giant, seen by men at sea / To grow pale from the waves at dull midnight," (I.457–58), he becomes, as Wordsworth understood about his old man in the similes of *Resolution and Independence,* a border figure vanishing through metaphor into nature.

To forestall undoing of this charmed moment, this moment of restoration of the mystique of origins, I will let Keats's subtlest demystifier say his worst. Geoffrey Hartman finds the pristine a little too close to the infantile regression and objects that "by the time the second *Hyperion* breaks off, Keats is more of an ephebe than ever: a spectator surrounded by divine cartoons, a child-poet in epic Wonderland." [28] Perhaps there are necessary limitations on the poet who wishes both to represent and to share in a primal scene, but if we focus for a moment on the pathos of the parental figures, we can recapture the magic of the young poet watching as Thea and Saturn "melted from my sight into the woods." The melting *from* marks a victory over the obsession with identity and self-presentation; the melting *into* marks "blendings pleasureable" no less a narrative victory over a Moneta complex than would be their erotic equivalent over an Oedipus complex.

With the word "melted" the myth of renewal by a return to the earth is itself naturalized. Here is no metamorphosis, no Lamia-like magic, but the subtler still trick of descriptive language. Melting into the woods, Thea and Saturn do more than just go away; theirs is what Wallace Stevens called a "green going," and they are left still going as the poem breaks off. They are on their way to the "families of grief, / Where roof'd in by black rocks they waste in pain." Like poetic fathers to whom the misery of the world is misery, the families of grief carry the inheritance of earthly loss even while they are absorbed into nature, becoming woods and black rocks rather than the gods who once inhabited the landscape. The naturalization is the origin of metaphor.

But more; this naturalization defines an energy of origination. The picture of the titans melting into the woods, like the expressed desire in the Nightingale Ode to "fade away into the forest dim," can still capture a resurgence and reorigination of spirit out of the return to the earth. If Antaeus does not get up in the sense that the poem breaks off, we are at least left with this picture of eternal naturalization. As the poet says to the youth on the Grecian Urn, "nor ever can those trees be bare." The final turn to nature does not have to demystify, crying "cold pastoral!" or emphasizing the death of the fiction in finding that the voice of the nightingale is "buried deep / In the next valley-glades." If we stand at the funeral of myth we confront also a point of incipience, watching as Keats images for the last time this prospective stance. The "gathering swallows twitter in the skies." It is important that *The Fall of Hyperion* breaks off before *Hyperion* did, so that even if we think of the titans as already fallen, we know that *The Fall* has yet to recount the divinization of Apollo. As Keats says, closing Canto I of *The Fall,* we remain standing at the origin or "antechamber of this dream." To the end he works the illusion that we are standing before, at a point of origination.[29] As *The Fall of Hyperion* breaks off, we are left forever with a wondrous new birth, the beginning of a poem.

CHAPTER 3

Byron: Troubled Stream
from a Pure Source[1]

> The conception of a *true world,* the conception of morality as
> the essence of the world (these two most malignant errors of all
> time!) were once again, thanks to a wily and shrewd skepticism,
> if not provable, at least no longer *refutable.* Reason, the *right* of
> reason, does not extend that far. Reality had been reduced to
> mere "appearance," and a mendaciously fabricated world, the
> world of being, was honored as reality.
>
> Nietzsche, *The Antichrist*

> I tell you: one must still have chaos in one, to give birth to a
> dancing star.
>
> Nietzsche, *Thus Spake Zarathustra*

In his 1821 diary, Byron waives questions about origins with
the studied nonchalance typical of the narrator of *Don Juan:*
"If, according to some speculations, you could prove the World
many thousand years older than the Mosaic Chronology, or if
you could knock up Adam and Eve and the Apple and Serpent,
still what is to be put up in their stead? or how is the difficulty
removed? Things must have had a beginning, and what matters
it *when* or *how?*"[2] To the poet concerned with history, the prehistorical *when* did matter a great deal—if not in literal, calendar
chronology, at least in terms of the mythic chronology of the
passions, the prohibitions, the guilt. To the poet obsessed with
the divorce between the tree of knowledge and the tree of life,
it mattered *how* these emblems were represented in allusion and
retellings of the myth. Perhaps most of all it mattered that ques-

tions of creation be deflected into awarenesses of the fallen world as we know it. Adam and Eve can scarcely be mentioned without a shift of interest to the apple and serpent, for the creation story remains a distant fiction while the Fall is a present truth. "With a characteristic ellipsis," writes Michael Cooke, "Byron blanks out the supposedly historical perfect world and shows the certified world going from bad to worse."[3]

What Byron "blanks out" remains as much a presence in his poetry as the materials of repression are presences in the psyche generally. In *A Map of Misreading*, Harold Bloom suggests that a poet's greatest moments are related to his powers of repression, and his verse seems daemonized with special energy when presences the poet would rationally or consciously dismiss are given voice while an inner censor sleeps. Calvinist in temperament but no Christian in belief, Byron thought that an undisguised faith in a paradise was at the root of intellectual and social error. Whether out of rivalry with Shelley on the subject of evil or simply in pursuit of the satirist's antimask, Byron implies that the history of inauthentic poetry—and the progress of the world at large from bad to worse—may be the responsibility of those who have failed to forget the belief in an anterior, perfect world. No doubt he would mock the idea of deep repression as much as he did the failure to put radical innocence out of mind, for Byron makes public the gesture of assigning nostalgias about an unfallen condition their proper place. What for others are the hidden workings of the psychic defenses and tropes of representation are often for him the surface subject or plaything of his verse. Remarkable always is the way he gets us to discard commonplaces about the traumatic or scandalous stuff of repression and to see sexuality and fallen experience as what we find acceptable to expose, while innocence and its priority need to be hidden.

i

Cain, Byron's most successful reworking of Genesis myth, announces from its very title the decentering of myth or the differentiating deferral from prelapsarian origins to fallen experience. Early on, the drama also makes clear a concomitant reversal of our ordinary sense of belatedness: radical innocence, not sexuality or a fall, is what we cover. Oblivious of the loincloth of Christian theology, Cain points to what seem to him to be unaccommodated facts:

> The snake spoke *truth:* it *was* the tree of knowledge;
> It *was* the tree of life: knowledge is good,
> And life is good; and how can both be evil? [I.i.36–38]

In hushing him, Eve asks Cain to content himself with what is, and let the innocence of his perspective be relegated back in history—and to the back of the mind. Bringing to the surface what Eve has repressed, the devil offers Cain knowledge, leading him to a different sort of statement than the one with which he confronted Eve: "It was a lying tree—for we *know* nothing" (II.ii.366). It is hard to be a devil of stature in the devil's presence, especially when Lucifer is contriving to accentuate his epigone's sense of creatureliness. The full daemonization of Cain depends on Lucifer's being gone, and Cain seems closest to the spirit whose presence he disdains when, away from Hades, he insists grandly on his innocence of the Fall and shares Lucifer's revaluation of temporal and moral priorities.

Byron shares them too. Before the drama proper he prefaces a note that ostensibly belittles a demonic stance: "The assertion of Lucifer, that the pre-Adamite world was also peopled by rational beings much more intelligent than man, and proportionably powerful to the mammouth, etc., etc., is, of course, a poetical fiction to help him make out his case." The particularities of this preexistence may be a "poetical fiction," but the interest in upsetting the priority of the received account is for Byron a most authentic business of poetry. In the play proper Byron dismisses the primacy of the Genesis creation and has Lucifer present visions of anterior worlds. At the same time, he images his own belatedness by centering on a fall after the inherited one, not on Adam but on Cain. References to earlier creation seem designed not for the assertion of temporal priority by itself but for the pressures they place on Cain to bear the burden of new anteriorities, and stand as the focal point on which the turn from the received to the new myth can pivot:

> Cain: Where dost thou lead me?
> Lucifer: To what was before thee!
>   The phantasm of the world; of which thy world
>   Is but the wreck.
> Cain: What! is it not then new?
> Lucifer: No more than life is; and that was ere thou
>   Or I were, or the things which seem to us
>   Greater than either.   [II.i.151–56]

If we read just the first two sentences of this exchange, we could entertain, with justified suspicion, the notion of a time machine. And "the phantasm of the world" seems a Luciferic reduction to the level of claptrap of Shelley's magnificent fiction of a shadow world in *Prometheus Unbound*. But contempt for such machinery is undermined when the word "world" is replaced by the word "wreck." If past glories are not as such to be recaptured, ruins of the past can still be very much present; if other worlds are the business of romancers turned science-fiction visionaries, still the belatedness of this world has an authentic ring. Thus, while we can hardly make a significant imaginative gesture toward recapturing the purity of origins—which belong somewhere back in God's country—we can come to recognize that we stand at a significant distance from such things, and can come to see an external Hades or a dark region of the mind haunted by the phantasms of anterior creation.

When Lucifer tells Cain that they are on their way to view shades of pre-Adamite beings, Cain's surprise, "What! is [the world] not then new?" presents the newness of the world balanced, as it were, on the tenuous point of the interrogative. For the moment Cain holds the world up on one questioning finger. Lucifer's casual shrug, "No more than life is," topples that world from its fragile axis. Though the action and reaction are verbal, "In the beginning was the Word," and this verbal exchange seems to demand priority over what is to be seen in space. "Language is properly the medium for this play of presence and absence," writes Derrida: "Is it not within language—is it not language itself that might seem to unify life and ideality?"[4] For Lucifer and for Byron language rather separates present life from preconceptions of ideality, and a particular verbal exchange constitutes a particular victory over both the presence or givenness of spatial reality and the possibility of past spaces and times. At this point in Byron's drama the verbal exchange precedes the sight of anterior creatures and precludes the sight of alternate worlds. Lucifer does not take Cain to other planets but passes them by: "The lights fade from me fast, / And some till now grew larger as we approach'd / And wore the look of worlds" (II.i.167–69).

The experience of passing by these worlds preludes the experience of confronting shadows of the past and introduces the perspective from which dismissals prove more authentic than actual confrontations with preexistents could be. Indeed, Cain finds the trip he does take no match for his anterior and superior desires. But the attitude cultivated in outer space extends to contempt for priority more generally. Lucifer tells Cain,

> Many things will have
> No end; and some, which would pretend to have
> Had no beginning, have had one as mean
> As thou. [II.156–59]

Beginnings are mean things, and sublimity is to be sought not in the dawning of days or worlds but in what Nietzsche called the twilight of the gods—in grand dismissals of the past. Lucifer is thus educating Cain to the indifference toward beginnings that Byron expressed in his diary entry. Or perhaps more precisely, Lucifer is abetting the process that Byron's diary witnesses by which the sense of creatureliness (of feeling what Milton's Adam felt when he first woke and knew himself *made*) goes under-

ground and is covered by indifference to origins and the postur-
ings of a fallen angel.

Brought back to his own postlapsarian world, Cain finds the
price of his proclaimed freedom from the past to be a radical
naturalism, knowledge of mortal nature's nothingness regardless
of (or repressing knowledge of) its Creator. When Cain's offering of fruits is scattered on the earth, he exclaims, "From earth
they came, to earth let them return." This is *radical* innocence
because rooted in the earth, ignorant of the fact of human death
that lies hidden in the phrase as it lies hidden in Cain's effort
to cast down Abel's altar and return it too to the earth. If Abel's
piety leads him to acknowledge God as spiritual source, Cain's
knowledge of the earth makes him stick to his earthy vision of
origins.

"There may be always a time of innocence," Wallace Stevens
tentatively proposes in *The Auroras of Autumn:* "There is never
a place." [5] Dismissing Jehovah as a bloodthirsty God who delights
in sacrifice, Cain could be said to claim both "There never was
a time of innocence" and "This must be the place." Insisting on
the present time, the present place, he exclaims to Adah before
Abel comes on the scene to make his sacrifice, "Why, *we* are the
innocent." To make this a place innocent of sacrifice, sublimation, and all experiential orderings of the world into higher and
lower, spiritual and earthy, Cain proposes leveling Abel's altar.
He asks Abel to "Stand back till I have strew'd this turf along /
Its native soil." The intended physical deconstruction of the altar
and metaphysical deconstruction of the hierarchies it acknowledges may be taken as an emblem of Byron's lifelong efforts to
reduce spiritual pretensions and fictions to their "native soil."

To challenge prevenient mythology, Byron needed to do more
than inherit the dichotomies of good and evil, God and Satan,
and choose the other side. Nor could he simply adapt the dual
vision of man as both creation of God and creature of dust who
to dust returns and create a protagonist who is wholly committed to one of these Biblical statements of origins. The conflict

between Cain and Abel, while it concerns two views of man's original substance, subsumes an argument between two views of what constitutes original action. For Abel and for the Bible one discovers one's originality in relation to the Originator. For Cain and for Byron one does not discover one's originality in relationship to the Author of Evil; nothing can be thought "original" till it separates itself from relationship to sources. So Byron argues about his Cain in a letter to John Murray:

Cain is a proud man: if Lucifer promised him kingdom, etc., it would *elate* him: the object of the Demon is to *depress* him still further in his own estimation than he was before, by showing him infinite things and his own abasement, till he falls into the frame of mind that leads to the Catastrophe, from mere internal irritation, not premeditation, or envy of *Abel* (which would have made him contemptible), but from the rage and fury against the inadequacy of his state to his conceptions.[6]

If Cain's action is to be his own, not Satan's, it must be motivated by "internal irritation," not a larger dialectical quarrel with God in which he would be a victim, and no originator. Even envy would not have been sufficiently his own, depending directly as it does on awareness of the priority of the envied. To the scene of the murder Cain brings a preexistent sense of infinite things and a preexistent sense of abasement, of dust-to-dust, both of which have been abetted by Lucifer. Impelled toward both awarenesses, he is now on his own; and if the glory seems a vision borrowed or imposed, the naturalistic dismissal of preexistent sublimity is something experienced as original to the self.

From his flight with Lucifer, Cain returns to his natural existence, his existence as natural man—a paterfamilias, a man of the earth, one who feels his littleness far more native to his consciousness than his memory of "extinguish'd worlds." The glory he could call his own would come from the possibility of transcending memory, transcending the givenness of the past, and striking (if need be, with a deathblow) a point for the originality of the self. Writing of Proust, Gilles Deleuze voices a kind of credo for the mind unextinguished by its immersion in preexistent materials: "It is no longer a matter of saying: to create is to remember—but rather, to remember is to create, to reach that point where the associative chain breaks, leaps over the constituted individual, is transferred to the birth of an individuating world."[7] Blake repeatedly finds this point; Byron repeatedly discovers it to be an illusion. His Cain is disappointed in the possibilities of breaking the chain of the past and attending the birth of an individuating world; he is confronted instead with the natural birth of an individual—his flesh-and-blood son—a birth which, in Byron's telling revisionist chronology, antedates the slaying of Abel. When Adah berates Cain, "Do not whisper o'er our son / Such melancholy yearnings o'er the past," she voices the simple demystification that would put all hankerings for romantic origins in their place. It is the kind of rebuke Byron himself makes of Cain's weak desires, and of his own moments of soft romanticism from the lingering over childhood scenes in *Hours of Idleness* to the moments of innocence in the Haidée episode of *Don Juan*. Adah continues with cheerfulness she seems to have picked up from the end of *Paradise Lost*: "Why wilt thou always mourn for Paradise? / Can we not make another?" But the awareness of death intervenes and keeps Cain (to borrow Byron's own term from the letter) "depressed."

This depression is not simply sadness but the reduction of man to his earthy origins and first nothingness. Tiller of the soil, father of an earthly creature who is overshadowed by cypresses and the fact of death, Cain finds that the awareness of man's grotesque lowness is the concomitant of his sublime ambition to stand original and free. "Nota," says Stevens's rejuvenated Crispin: "His soil is man's intelligence. / That's better. That's worth crossing seas to find."[8] Cain has crossed vast seas of space and thought with Lucifer to find this soil the sum total of his intelligence and knowledge. In a terrible irony, even the soil is alienated from Cain when it absorbs Abel's blood; as a vagabond, Cain will be estranged from the earth he had thought most truly his own.

In Genesis, Cain protests that his burden is too great and that whoever finds him will slay him. In Byron, Adah voices these objections while Cain himself asks to be allowed to die. The visual brand on the forehead is thus all the more imposed and is accompanied by a verbal brand: "Stern hast thou been and stubborn from the womb, / As the ground thou must henceforth till" (III.i.503–04). These signs of separation magically rouse Cain into authentic voice, for he speaks now with Shakespearean power and Miltonic resonance, but comes into his own:

> After the fall too soon was I begotten;
> Ere yet my mother's mind subsided from
> The serpent, and my sire still mourn'd for Eden.
> That which I am, I am; I did not seek
> For life, nor did I make myself; but could I
> With my own death redeem him from the dust—
> And why not so?   [III.i.506–12]

Truer than the plain fact ("I did not seek / For life") is the extraordinary imaginative independence that comes precisely in the diminished idea of causality—the narrowed sense of priority that nevertheless aggrandizes the self. The opening lines of this speech are like those of Shakespeare's Edgar saving for himself what little imaginative freedom is left after the wheels of causality have rolled to this catastrophic point: "The dark and vicious place where thee he got / Cost him his eyes." Asserting the metaphor-making power (the power of localizing a symbolic topos or a time) over the catastrophe from which the need for metaphor springs, these speeches leave the imagination triumphant yet. Byron's Cain seems to surpass Edgar in moving from slender to full-fledged self-assertion: "That which I am, I am." If the power of this seems limited by our awareness that it is borrowed from Milton's Satan (Tennyson's Ulysses will be similarly threatened), it becomes all the more Cain's and Byron's own when compacted with a new, unsatanic—indeed, Christ-like—impulse. Even if it does come from despair, the wish to redeem Abel by sacrificing himself seems to contradict everything Cain

stood for in opposing Abel and the sacrifice-loving God Abel
worshiped. But instead of a capitulation, these lines, so summarily
dismissed by the angel, represent a final fictiveness, a last emblem
of the mind's capacity to transcend its circumstances and create
its own vision of things.

The power given to the branded Cain is like that Byron gives
his Prometheus: "Thou art a symbol and a sign / To mortals of
their fate and force." Turned into signs, Cain and Prometheus
have restored to them a purity of figuration which asserts both
the individual origination of their actions and their special connection with ultimate origins. One's act is divine, one's demonic,
but branded forever they share the fate of having their daemonized power abstracted from their persons and made a sign of
the human condition. We do not worship, but we "read" or
recognize the sign, point to it and say:

> Like thee, Man is in part divine,
> A troubled stream from a pure source;
> And Man in portions can foresee
> His own funereal destiny,
> His wretchedness, and his resistance,
> And his sad unallied existence.
> To which his Spirit may oppose
> Itself.   ["Prometheus"]

ii

The idea of a "pure source" can be safeguarded from both the
assaults of experience and the jibes of the worldly satirist by
appearing to be translated from this earth to some imaginatively
anterior one. In the diary entry quoted at the beginning of this
chapter, Byron speculates on an original innocence: "I sometimes
think that *Man* may be the relic of some higher material being,
wrecked in a former world, and degenerated in the hardships
and struggle through Chaos into Conformity." The stipulation
of *material* being guards the innocence of the idea of preempting
the satirist's ammunition and imagining man's faded spirit to
have the form, originally, of a more fulfilled natural man. In

the context of his satirical poems, Byron makes the anterior world that of sexuality which, he loves to protest too much, he has long renounced. Man's "original" moments, to be recalled but not recovered, are moments of satisfied love:

> No more—no more—Oh! never more on me
> The freshness of the heart can fall like dew,
> Which out of all the lovely things we see
> Extracts emotions beautiful and new.   [*Don Juan*, I.ccxiv]

As an addition to the manuscript of *Don Juan*, this little nostalgia for innocence appears mid the flamboyant posturing with something of the air of an aria mid recitatif telling the story of decay.

A similar tone is struck when Byron explains his treatment of Contessa Guiccioli to the Countess of Blessington: "I am worn out in feelings; for, though only thirty-six, I feel sixty in mind, and am less capable than ever of those nameless attentions that all women, but, above all, Italian women, require."[9] (The man who could no more resist adding that last particularizing slur than he could resist sexual objects of any sex, any nationality, was not to be worn out.) Blessington records Byron's myth of imaginative independence as that of an antecedent world from which the imagination, like a Son of God, emerges never to be capable of feeling quite at home with a single, belated Daughter of Man:

The way in which I account for it [my boorishness, or the "something . . . in the poetical temperament that precludes happiness"] is, that our *imaginations* being warmer than our *hearts,* and much more given to wander, the latter have not the power to control the former; hence, soon after our passions are gratified, imagination again takes wing, and finding the insufficiency of actual indulgence beyond the moment, abandons itself to wayward fancies, and during this abandonment becomes cold and insensible to the demands of affection. . . . It is as though the creatures of another sphere, not subject to the lot of mortality, formed a factitious alliance (as all alliances must be that are not in all respects equal) with the creatures of this earth, and, being exempt from its sufferings, turned their thoughts to brighter regions, leaving the partners of their earthly existence to suffer alone.[10]

Depicting the imagination as a "creature of another sphere," he grants it priority, so that turning away from a particular alliance and letting one's fancy wander back to the brighter regions becomes a matter of visionary loyalty to the mind's original place. Whether the marriage is that of man's spirit to his natural being or more literally the entanglement of a man with an actual lady, the marriage metaphor allows for both the legitimate pull into nature and the legitimized resistance to that pull on the grounds that spirit would be pulled down into unequal alliance. The concept of "factitious alliance" provides a vehicle for the conflicting ideas of origin: spiritual preexistence and demystified naturalism.

Obviously the concept of "factitious alliance" was attractive to Byron the man, allowing him to turn biographical facts into a kind of personal fall myth. The concept also has much to do with the structure of *Don Juan* and the way originality is regained in the love encounters. But let us turn, rather, to a poem whose more muted tones give the romantic alternative to naturalistic origins a better chance.

iii

The advertisement to the 1814 edition of *Lara* seems to play coyly with the nature of the "factitious alliance" of the hero and heroine of the poem: "The reader of *Lara* may probably regard it as a sequel to a poem that recently appeared: whether the cast of the hero's character, the turn of his adventures, and the general outline and colouring of the story, may not encourage such a supposition, shall be left to his determination." If we follow these suppositions, Lara and Kaled are Conrad and Gulnare of *The Corsair* now caught in the unequal alliance of preoccupied man and devoted lady. What these identifications tell us about either poem is more difficult to determine. Byron seems to be toying with the concept of origin, as though seeing *Lara* as sequel to *The Corsair* answered questions about the genesis of the poem or about the mysterious preexistence of its hero. But the plot of *Lara* seems to be neither dependent on nor significantly clarified by the story of *The Corsair,* and it is not immediately apparent what insight we gain into one dark hero by the suggestion that he is to be identified with another, equally mysterious character.

The story of *Lara* may be briefly stated. After a long absence, Lara returns to his feudal seat accompanied by his faithful page Kaled. At a party some time later, Lara is recognized by Ezzelin, who, before he can challenge Lara or reveal Lara's past identity or crimes, mysteriously disappears. Hostility to Lara grows, and in an all-out battle Lara is mortally wounded. He is attended in his dying moments by Kaled, whose grief reveals her identity as a woman.

As Byron himself commented on the tale, "it is too little narrative, and too metaphysical to please the greater number of readers." [11] The "metaphysical" quality needs to be discussed, though we may dismiss Byron's habitual protestations that his poetry was carelessly composed and insignificant. There is too little narrative in *Lara* for the "metaphysical" cast not to be a conscious goal, and one belies the work by seeming to discover, as critics have done, the obvious clanking of gothic machinery and the overt resort to mysterious silence.

In general, Byron's fondness for mystery is almost as great as his delight in satiric demystification. The poet of *Don Juan,* for example, toys with the penchant for the secret, protesting that he will, rather, be perfectly open. Introducing Haidée and Zoe, he declares, "I'll tell you who they were," as if to forestall dark conceits about their nature. "Besides, I hate all mystery, and that air / Of clap-trap which your recent poets prize" (II.cxxiv). More than an incidental laugh at his own "clap-trap," the dismissal of mystery underlies the genuine effort at the pristine. Not simply gothic trappings but the sophisticated joking about trappings must be gotten out of the way if the Haidée episode is to glimpse an unsophisticated simplicity. Later in *Don Juan* the demystification is less gentle, and it is worth recalling the last episode of that poem to keep in mind how much of what came easiest to Byron had to be laid aside in cultivating the "meta-physical" in *Lara*.

Here is Juan reacting to sounds of the Black Friar ghost's reappearance:

> Were his eyes open?—Yes! and his mouth too.
> Surprise has this effect—to make one dumb,
> Yet leave the gate which eloquence slips through
> As wide as if a long speech were to come.
> Nigh and more nigh the awful echoes drew,
> Tremendous to a mortal tympanum:
> His eyes were open, and (as was before
> Stated) his mouth. What open'd next?—the door.
>
> [XVI.cxv]

The listing of opened apertures prepares for the openness of the full naturalistic disclosure to come: the phantom is "her frolic Grace," the very much flesh-and-blood (though not too much flesh, indulged taste makes Byron pause to note) woman. The revelation of Fitz-Fulke is a veritable apotheosis of naturalism, defeating once and for all any pretenses to possible sublimity. What is banished for good is not simply the ghost-as-mystery, but more particularly the Black Friar ghost, the ghost that recalls a lost patrimony and, by extension, betrayed spiritual paternity. It is just those suggestions that *Lara* would explore, raising the metaphysical speculation of whether "some higher material being" and not simply some natural woman may lie at the origin of the story and the center of its mystery. But let me delay our return to *Lara* a little longer to glean from the *Don Juan* stanza a symbol and theme central as well to the earlier poem.

Caught with his mouth open, unable to speak, Juan is com-ically but significantly restored to an innocence that would fit him not for the degenerate Fitz-Fulke but for the more primary beauty (whose very name suggests beginnings), Aurora. Throughout *Don Juan* speech is the mark of the fall, and the hero's ease at social pleasantries betrays his distance from "higher material being." Aurora disdained Juan's talk, but "approved his silence" (XIV.cvi). "The ghost at least had done him this much good / In making him as silent as a ghost" (XVI.cvii). Insofar as the ghost in this ghostly silence is man's ghost or *geist*, his spiritual nature, Juan finds revived in him "the love of higher things and better days," glimpsing thus the vision of preexistent sublimity that haunts Byron, though not usually his hero in *Don Juan*. Aurora herself seems to come from such another world, and is preserved from degeneration by the outward manifestation of spiritual quietude:

> The worlds beyond this world's perplexing waste
> Had more of her existence, for in her
> There was a depth of feeling to embrace
> Thoughts, boundless, deep, but silent too as Space.
>
> [XVI.xlviii]

From her perspective we can look back at the several ladies of the epic and find them measured by their talk. Julia, who has the priority only in terms of biography or biology in Juan's life, falls into the poem's longest speech when first discovered by Alfonso. If nature is thus victorious in Canto I, the Haidée episode images a prenatural sublimity in portraying the lady coping with the pleasing restraint of a language barrier. That Edenic possibility closed, the poem moves to a parody of the speech problem when Gulbeyaz expects Juan to melt by her "merely saying, 'Christian, canst thou love?'" (V.cxvi). From the still more depraved Catherine we get no direct words.

Keeping in mind the Haidée episode, where the language problem is recognized and valorized, we may return to *Lara,* where master and page share memories of a preexistent state under the cloak of a foreign tongue. "Cloak" belies the innocence of their speech, however, for the magic of the former language is that it is spoken not behind doors but in all openness, entrancing its uncomprehending auditors. *Lara* is perhaps Byron's most silent poem, and we stand in relation to it as do the retainers or antagonists of Lara when the communication with Kaled is not to be shared. What Byron says of his hero can thus comment on or forestall what others could say of Byron here: "His silence formed a theme for others' prate" (I.xvii). We cannot dismiss *Lara* as a simple tale overlaid with mystery, because silence is theme, story but the setting in which the central silence can be examined and admired.

As the poem opens it presents in setting what I have described in theme. Lara is returned, and "The gay retainers gather round the hearth, / With tongues all loudness and with eyes all mirth." The gathering round of loud-tongued retainers is pictorially representable as a magic circle, and it describes in social terms what Wordsworth might have called a central silence at the heart of endless agitation. The potential is all there at this point for a tale like Keats's *Eve of St. Agnes,* or, a little later, *Lamia.* But Byron deliberately suppresses narrative and gives mystery its barest background.

One fact seems both to call for and strangely to defeat further explanation. Since Lara is returned, he does not descend into the poem like a Christ figure into earth, trailing clouds of pre-existent glory from the soul's home. The land to which he returns *is* home, and the otherworldliness has been acquired elsewhere, in a place not native to him. In a way this simple story-fact captures all that story can do to dramatize the conflicting claims of natural and supernatural origins. The fatherland seems less one's own than some other land one has made one's own, for natural and spiritual paternities seldom correspond. The question of priority is complicated by the question of whether the father-land is a place to live or a place to die. Corresponding to the sense that *Lara* has "too little narrative," that the story is essentially over before the poem begins, would be the hero's sense that his life has really been lived elsewhere. He is now but the shadow of himself, a death-in-life figure,[12] or, more accurately, the remains of a figure of spiritual life returned to the death that is natural life.

The conflict between spiritual and natural paternities, or perhaps more accurately between the alternate voids of both failures of relationship, is expressed in the second stanza's description of Lara, "Left by his sire, too young such loss to know / Lord of himself—that heritage of woe." As Byron discovered biographically and dramatized in stories of absent or hostile father figures, one is not simply left to oneself by a father's death; to take the self as one's domain one must both abandon a natural patrimony and seize or create a realm elsewhere. To discover in the self a "heritage of *woe*" one needs to conceive of experiential possibilities as exhausted and one's futurity burdened by belatedness. With all but the woe spent from the self-heritage, Lara returns to the patrimonial heritage, almost knowing, perhaps, that that too will be shortly spent.

In the years away was the domain of self conquered or squandered? One could retreat to the pun on a life "spent" and say simply that the gaining is the spending. Byron gives the two actions just a little more space than they would have in a pun and depicts self-knowledge as the waking from self-indulgence. A manuscript reading, "for his feelings sought / Their refuge in intensity of thought," is corrected to read, "his feelings sought / In that intenseness an escape from thought" (I. viii). "Escape" suggests that self-consciousness surrounds indulgence, preceding and following it, and evading questions about anteriority. In lines that follow, however, experience becomes not the void between moments of heightened awareness, but the height from which awareness of the soul's home can spring: "The rapture of his heart had look'd on high, / And ask'd if greater dwelt beyond the sky." Does the question signify assurance and satisfaction, challenging heaven to provide greater pleasures than those enjoyed? Or does the question, disdaining all earthly achievement, point via the appetite's insatiableness to the soul's infinity? The glimmer of ambiguity provides a glimpse at the mystery of *Lara,* the dark relationship between past experience and the kind of alternate celestial worlds Lucifer and Cain passed by.

The mystery is intensified (one cannot really say "explored") in the stanzas that follow. In the portrait gallery, "where his fathers frown'd," Lara's attendants heard "The sound of words less earthly than his own." What or whose words these may be, if they be, "must not be known." To say that mystery here is serving its own purposes is to be on precisely the right track, though to say that mystery without communication is gothic claptrap seems to me to avoid both the intention and achievement of such episodes. Parody of such moments will come soon enough in *Don Juan;* and exploitation of such moments requires more narrative—the kind of mystery that provides significant or misleading clues, not the deliberate paucity of detail we find here. We are given simply the suggestion of voices, "the sound of words" without the words, and the single descriptive detail— always ready, in gothic literature, to turn from adjective to verb—of frowning fathers in the portrait gallery. If those portraits were to respond to Lara, would their frowns or voices be the communication of dead fathers to their heir, or would they be protesting the intrusion of another ghost, another voice out of the past that belongs to Lara alone and not to them? The moment is too tenuous to permit such speculation to take hold, but again a manuscript revision points to Byron's care with suggestive ambiguity. "The sound of words less earthly than his own" was originally written,"The sound of other voices than his own." The original line is closer to claptrap, allowing suggestions of a general communication with the dead or, for possible naturalistic solution, voices of the living; the revised line properly focuses the ambiguity on communication "less earthly" because spoken by a spirit of the earth's past or a spirit from other realms and other skies.

A similar ambiguity attends a fearful call one night when the palace occupants hear a sound that rouses them from their sleep and confronts them with preoccupied Lara's bad dream—or what may be the pre-occupied palace's ghostly Presences:

> 'Twas midnight—all was slumber; the lone light
> Dimm'd in the lamp, as loth to break the night.
> Hark! there be murmurs heard in Lara's hall—
> A sound—a voice—a shriek—a fearful call!
> A long, loud shriek—and silence; did they hear
> That frantic echo burst the sleeping ear?
> They heard and rose, and tremulously brave,
> Rush where the sound invoked their aid to save;
> They come with half-lit tapers in their hands,
> And snatch'd in startled haste unbelted brands.   [I.xii]

As in Coleridge's *Christabel,* question and answer suggest the disparity between spiritual quest and the declarative nature of the world we know. When Lara wakes with (or is it "to"?) a shriek and fearful call, the sound of words puzzles his attendants, for the delirious prince speaks in what seem to be "accents of another land" (I.xiii). Neither attendants nor readers discover what those words are, though it is not difficult to say that they have more to do with the "sound of words less earthly" than with anything explicable in "his native tongue." At this point we are given what comes closest to being a narrative thread to seize on. Lara's words were "meant to meet an ear / That hears him not—alas, that cannot hear!" If we are tired of mystery, we can use this thread to weave the connection between *Lara* and *The Corsair.* Lara would thus have had a dream of his dead love Medora, who "cannot hear," and would be comforted by Gulnare-Kaled, who knows of Medora, can speak her language, and at least quiet the spirit of the man she cannot distract into love.

To say that such are the identifications behind the "mystery" is less to resolve than to deny the mystery and its richness. If we turn back to the dream night we can discover more from the setting, the poetry that lies just outside narrative:

> It was the night, and Lara's glassy stream
> The stars are studding, each with imaged beam;

> So calm, the waters scarcely seem to stray,
> And yet they glide like happiness away;
> Reflecting far and fairy-like from high
> The immortal lights that live along the sky.   [I.x]

A small but not insignificant contribution to the air of romance may be noted in the identification of the stream as "Lara's." The country too is called "Lara's" rather than by any national name, and in general the paucity of proper names or properly externalized events makes one view what story there is as belonging more to the psyche than the person of Lara. The commerce between external and internal nature seems imaged in the lines about reflection. It is not that the mind, like the stream, receives images of external nature; rather, the stream for the moment seems to image a higher spiritual reality represented by the stars. Waters that "glide like happiness away" are easily enough separated from the human emotion they are said to represent. But "The immortal lights that live along the sky" are not so easily divorced from the anthropomorphic, the inspiriting humanization of the verb "live." The adjective "immortal" moves the description into a realm of higher being, thus insulated, as it were, from assaults of self-consciousness about such projections. The riverbed seems a little Eden, complete with flowers and waters "mazy like the snake." To Lara, who feels he is already fallen, such Eden vision is best left alone, for its unadulterated perfection but "mock'd such breast as his." This mockery takes the place of the ordinary mockery satiric naturalism directs at visions of "higher spirit," and at the myths of organized religion generally. Here, where any potential demystifying mockery would have to be spirit's scorn of flesh, "You scarce would start to meet a spirit there."

What kind of spirit? Some daughter of God come down to mingle with the sons of men? Or some ghost of a daughter of man, haunting the consciousness of Lara as fallen son of God? To rephrase, would one imagine such a spirit come from man's mythic, idyllic past, or Lara's biographical, actual past? The alternatives, for the moment, mingle. If stars in water are a visual illusion and spirits in nature a romantic fantasy, the mingling of mythic and personal past is nonetheless a real mingling. Lara is painfully reminded "of other days, / Of skies more cloudless, moons of purer blaze." By itself "other days" most properly belongs to his personal past, while the purified scene belongs to imagination's ideal or anterior world. One can neither scorn Byron's fancied "higher spiritual being" as the delusion of young love nor scorn young love as an inadequate vehicle for the sense of spiritual being. Scorn is preempted by this fallen spirit who remembers what he was yet must endure the descent into nature or the nature of loss.

In a stanza Byron added to the original manuscript, Lara's relationship to his Luciferic literary ancestry is made explicit:

> As if the worst had fallen which could befall,
> He strove a stranger in this breathing world,
> An erring spirit from another hurl'd;
> A thing of dark imaginings. [I.xviii]

Taken by themselves, either the implied satanism or the naturalistic pity for lost love would seem self-indulgent. Tenuously identified, the spiritual potential of each is given a local habitation in the other. In *The Corsair*, Conrad is a little too good to be thought capable of grand satanic crimes. *Lara* taints its hero with just a suggestion of something less than sweet. Aloof from others, his mind dwelling "in regions of her own," Lara is capable of fixing himself upon others' memory like a serpent round a tree. The detail may be there to prepare for Ezzelin's recall; more significantly, it keeps the suggestions of spirit menacing as they are attractive. Lara himself is the most menaced, victim of his own power to defy forgetfulness.

The introversion of this power is dramatized in the encounter with Ezzelin, who points to Lara at Otho's party the way Keats's Apollonius stares down the no less serpentine Lamia. These demystifiers would clear away all but memory of the actual, historical past. Yet an incomplete exposure only mystifies further, and

Ezzelin leaves Lara with the cryptic warning, "O! never canst thou cancel half her debt, / Eternity forbids thee to forget" (I.xxiii). Is the debt memory's debt to Eternity or Lara's debt to a specific lady? The abstractness or absence of the antecedent for "her" only heightens the thematic mystery concerning antecedence and forgetting. Though the encounter with Ezzelin is as spare of detail and information as was Lara's dream, its very silence tells us more than details of the past could. Ezzelin's questions, "how came he thence?—what doth he here?" (I.xxii), seem not to demand an account of the slings and arrows of Lara's outrageous fortune but to strip away the accidents of fortune and confront Lara's romantic origins. Robert Gleckner calls the Ezzelin encounter "a transparent device to dramatize the presentness of all the past and the inescapability of one's self, one's inner world." [13] Ezzelin's own mysterious disappearance, while teasing the fancy into inventing story explanations arouses the imagination to confront Ezzelin as a specter of Lara himself. Instead of asking, "What did they do with Ezzelin?" we are directed to more Wordsworthian intimations: "Whither is fled the visionary gleam? / Where is it now, the glory and the dream?" Not that Ezzelin embodies glory and dream, but his presence marked the presence of the question to Lara. As voiced by the poet, the question asked the next day about Ezzelin teases us out of thoughts about visionary gleam: "But where was he, that meteor of a night, / Who menaced but to disappear with light?" (II.vi).

At a moment of visionary failure, Wordsworth looks around him and finds "waters on a starry night / Are beautiful and fair; / . . . But yet I know, where'er I go / That there hath past away a glory from the earth." If we turn back from the night of Ezzelin's disappearance to the night of Lara's dream, we can find in the waters of the starry night reflections of glory past. Lara is a fallen star, and Ezzelin, "meteor of a night," an image of star's fall—its fading into the light of common, naturalistic day. Inasmuch as these star references are images, they suggest that an experiential loss is being treated, under the license of romantic hyperbole, as a Lucifer-like fall from heaven. But in a poem so spare, where these few images are so much the light and the life of the poem, we are thrown back into the romance element with the conviction that story details, experiential losses, can only represent the "starry connaissance" that makes metaphoric language closer to reality than narrative plain song. While the story lasts, the relative claims of starry and earthy realities, spiritual and natural origins, must be kept in balance. The ambiguity is represented, for example, by the description of Lara leaving Otho's party with Kaled. "His only follower from those climes afar, / Where the soul glows beneath a brighter star" (I.xxv). If "climes afar" describes the ordinary territory of romance, the extent to which this distance is natural or supernatural depends on whether one emphasizes "beneath" or "star." Nature lovers flourish beneath their star, but the star represents all that transcends nature and connects man to primeval glory. Love is, the poet says in *The Giaour*, "A spark of that immortal fire / With angels shared" (ll. 1132–33).

Only after Lara's death does the poem return to the night of the encounter with Ezzelin, as if to record that the stars shine still though the flesh is mortal. With the death of Lara the character, the poem can dispense also with the ordinary bounds between man and man or mind and mind that keep one literary figure an antagonist rather than a projection of another. In terms of the story, the demystification of Lara—when our hero is reduced from the ambiguous element Byron elsewhere calls "fiery dust" and is returned to dust—is followed by the demystification of Ezzelin's death. But whether we are wholly in the realm of nature now remains a further mystery. The story of Ezzelin's death is separated from the main narrative by being presented as a peasant's tale. Within that tale comes the poem's most startling detail, all the more prominent if the peasant's tale is read beside Byron's source, where the detail is not to be found.[14] The Serf watches the stream into which a body has been cast:

He caught a glimpse, as of a floating breast,
And something glitter'd starlike on the vest;
But ere he well could mark the buoyant trunk,
A massy fragment smote it, and it sunk:
It rose again, but indistinct to view,
And left the waters of a purple hue,
Then deeply disappear'd.   [II.xxiv]

If one wishes to see the star here merely as Ezzelin's badge of knighthood, one's desire for naturalistic reduction receives this final dousing. If one sees instead an echo of the night of Lara's dream, one finds Byron approaching, in muted tones, the kind of imaginative triumph Shelley more flamboyantly executed at the end of *Adonais*. For Shelley, the star beacons from on high, while for Byron—building into the image itself its insurance against demystification—the reflection of the star glimmers for a moment from below. If Ezzelin was a pursuing specter to Lara, his death here shadows forth the life of the hero. The mysterious Lara returned to his fatherland is the star "indistinct to view" at second and final remove from its prelapsarian state. In terms of the peasant narrative, the star sinks; in terms of romantic narrative, the star image outlasts Lara's life in nature.

The mystery of *Lara* lies in the strange relationship between narrative and preexistent sublimity revealed at the end. If one believed in the temporal priority of a prenatural state, the fall into narrative—telling the story of a man's loves and losses on earth—would be a fall into nature. In itself, the Byronic speculation about an anterior spiritual state has the same fictive status as naturalistic narrative. But a narrative true to one's sense of fall restores the spiritual sublimity that lies "behind" and thus anterior to the story. Not that romance comes first, satiric reduction next. Byron's revisions, whether on the scale of individual lines of *Lara*, the addition of the romantic stanzas at the end of Canto I of *Don Juan*, or the major reworking of Act III of *Manfred*, show that often the impulse to reduction came first and had to be purged or laid aside to allow for a possible sublimity. Within the achieved fiction, however, one can find restored the primariness of the higher spiritual state and the belatedness of nature. An account of a fall contains no assurance that the prelapsarian condition will convincingly represent a higher spiritual state; neither does satire insure the anteriority of the serious. But if a narrative has earned its emblems of spirit, the degradation of those emblems can authenticate what they once were.

As the poem draws to a close, the very story seems a degradation of the spiritual into the literal. It is one thing to sense that a pure adventure tale is being embroidered by sophisticated innuendos and images, or turned into embroidery by having narrative detail cut out to leave a delicate, lacelike story-fabric. But it is something very different to sense that the literal level has itself descended from the metaphysical and darkly reflects a purer literary origin. With the battle lost, Lara's faithful soldiers see that "One hope survives, the frontier is not far, / And thence they may escape from native war" (II.xi). To cross that border would be (or once would have been) to become border figures and haunt the ambiguous geographical spaces that used to be more than geographic. They would "bear within them to the neighboring state / An exile's sorrows or an outlaw's hate." These burdens are theirs proleptically, for the exile's sorrows are the inner sorrows of alienation regardless of where one stands; and the outlaw's hate grew from the mind's war with nature before the war became that of Lara and Otho, or before it could become the war of outcasts and citizens. The geographic border seems a descendant of a temporal one and reminds us of Lara's exile from an original, *un*native home, for which a new exile could be but a literalizing repetition.

In abstract terms the significance of such a new border crossing is figured by Foucault, who speaks of the "recession of the origin . . . on the far side of experience."[15] Picture the "far side of experience" literalized geographically; imagine the retreat of origins turned into a military retreat, and one sees Lara's forces traveling backward across the border to the dynasty of archaic or arcadian imaginings, under the government of which the mysteries of life and the simple patterns of life peacefully coexist. But does Byron's "recession of the origin" reach the "dynasty of its own archaism"? Lara and his men look more closely and discover not arcadia—the mythic land of prelapsarian pastoralism—but Otho's men, who have *preempted* the border ground and cut off Lara's forces from retreat. Byron's poised verse matches one preemption with another, first descrying the romantic or "preposterous" perspective of Lara's men, then the realistic fact of Otho's ambush:

> It is resolved, they march—consenting Night
> Guides with her star their dim and torchless flight.
> Already they perceive its tranquil beam
> Sleep on the surface of the barrier stream;
> Already they descry—is yon the bank?
> Away! 'tis lined with many a hostile rank.
> Return or fly!—What glitters in the rear?
> It is Otho's banner, the pursuer's spear!
> Are those the shepherds' fires upon the height?
> Alas! they blaze too widely for the flight.   [II.xii]

The star misguides, the *already*s mistake, and those wonderful shepherds' fires come to be seen with greater clarity as fires from the enemy camp.

The plaintive, gentle music of the questions and answers in this stanza forms an equivalent, in narrative voice, of the undertones in Shakespeare's *Antony and Cleopatra,* the sad music of the god Hercules leaving Antony before that star falls. The effect in Byron's stanza is also more particular, for the misprision in the last two lines quoted does more to create a sense of the lost pastoral than could any extended description of shepherds in the beyond-the-border land whence Lara came. These two lines express a further loss, the absence of the particularity in the lines that precede them. By themselves, the last two lines would capture ordinary delusion, the defeat of expectation when an envisioned land of escape turns out to be the enemy's camp. This is what any such loss might be. The lines before, however, depend for their resonance on all that stars and streams have come to be in this poem. The expectation that reflected starlight will appear prelapsarian tumbles when the lights are more clearly descried. Whether or not a prelapsarian state was a tenable myth, the loss of that topos, that expectation, is a real loss, authenticating the imputed anteriority of the preexistent spiritual state. For the moment we are caught expecting stars of redemption—or at least a battle of angels in which the stars throw down their spears and become the fallen angels. But the spears are simply Otho's spears, and the war is not heavenly but corporeal. The weight of allusion is lost; simultaneously, and consequently, the anteriority of the "higher spiritual state" is assured.

As far as the narrator of *Lara* is concerned, "The secret long and yet but half conceal'd" (II.xxi) is the sex of Kaled. By itself this revelation is so meager that the aura of mystery maintained throughout the poem would be no more than what the *Quarterly Review* found the dream episode to be, "a mere useless piece of lumber."[16] Is the secret wholly demystified one must ask, when we extrapolate from the revelation of Kaled's sex that she is Gulnare, and that Lara-Conrad has been pining over Medora (first love of the hero of *The Corsair*)? By itself the turn from one set of literary facts to another avails naught. Yet the very inadequacy of such information proves instructive and leads to the recognition that the specific identity of Kaled, like the sex of Kaled and sexuality in general, are not the secrets of poetry but the cover for the mysteries of love, of innocence, and of the priority of spiritual life.

Byron's admission that the secret of Kaled's sex has been but half concealed all along makes public the kind of half concealment characteristic of the workings of repression. In a sense Kaled's devotion to Lara is founded on forgetfulness of Lara's preoccupation with Medora, and Kaled's mystification figures that of the reader. Yet as revelation, the baring of Kaled's breast is as poor a thing as would be the baring of plain facts of past experience to one undergoing psychoanalysis. To represent the fact that nothing has really been revealed, Kaled is seen ever silent while all around demand facts: "Vain was all question ask'd her of the past, / And vain e'en menace—silent to the last." What she has to reveal is love, and that is a significance that has just found public sign, though in an important sense the signs were there all along. What she has to conceal is the daemonic or transcendent rather than purely sexual nature of love, and that is something no physical unveiling could destroy. The preexistence of this bond between Lara and Kaled preempts the status of organized religion's bond between God and man. Dismissing the special sanction of churches, Byron presents Lara resting as much at peace as man could be: "Nor is his mortal slumber less profound, / Though priest nor bless'd, nor marble deck'd the mound." Yet these lines mystify as much as they demystify, for while denying special status to church or fame, they grant special status to the emotions of Kaled, which add to the burial of Lara a special grace.

The literary kinship between *The Corsair* and *Lara* confirmed at this moment also encourages the renewed mystification. We are drawn not to the sexual facts that bind the stories but to the fact of love, which, transcending the single poem, seems to transcend natural life as well and image a source purely "literary" and therefore purely spiritual. The one-sidedness of love—Kaled-Gulnare loves Lara-Conrad who loves Medora—keeps the line of transcendence looking pure, and while ostensibly confronting the fact that Lara is really the old disappointed lover of *The Corsair*, we remember also that Conrad was as much a fallen angel there as Lara is in this poem. "The relic of some higher material being," Byron specified, "wrecked in a former world." One could say that the very entrenchment of the myth of pre-existence in nature authenticates it. More accurately, the entrenchment is not in nature but in a previous poem. If Conrad is not Lara but Lara's literary precursor, then the reference *Lara* makes to a preexistent state is both natural (equal fictions represent states on the same plane) and supernatural (the reference to another fictional framework represents the movement outside nature). The preexistence is real, while the knowledge that this realm is but another fiction safeguards such poetry from further demystification.

iv

Granted Byron's enormous skepticism of any romantic assertion, some solution like that discovered in *Lara* is necessary to protect the authenticity of the representation of a higher spiritual state. Unless the poet were to undertake a more strenuous career of poetic remaking—as does Wordsworth, for example, in *The Prelude*—the technical solution found in the relationship of *Lara* to *The Corsair* is a device available only once. What are other possibilities?

Perhaps closest to the play between fictions in the *Tales* is the play with the reader's knowledge within a given fiction. Byron's dramas, in particular, catch the reader in his tendency to draw premature conclusions. When the false prematurity is exposed, one is embarrassed or persuaded into accepting some other figure or story as prelapsarian. *Werner; or The Inheritance,* in which degeneration is literalized (the son *is* more a demon than the father) may be a successful melodramatic representation of achieved anteriority. Act III, Scene iii takes place in a "secret passage" between Werner's and Stralenheim's chambers, as though spatially representing the mysterious and morally dubious paths between the generations. We are tempted into believing the Gabor's soliloquy precedes the murder of Stralenheim. When we discover later that the murder has already been committed, that the scene of anticipation is in fact belated, the degradation of our sense of time and judgment makes us more willing, in turn, to accept glimpses of fallen angel in Gabor and Werner. Though the terms are those of melodrama, the internal argument is that of, for example, Wordsworth in *Prelude* VI, confronting the fact that he has crossed the Alps before he was aware of it and finding, retrospectively, an unfathered vapor of imagination. Perhaps *Werner* remains, ultimately, the story of a too clearly fathered heritage of woe; but perhaps the very blatancy of the family romance leaves some room for intimations of spirit redeemed from the general curse.

More thematic and less technical solutions to the problem of representing the anteriority of a higher spiritual state may be discovered in Byron's stories of individual or governmental tyranny. If the present state of oppression can be seen as having degenerated from a purer form of nature, then our sense that demystification would parallel or participate in the degeneration helps forestall demystification. In the song at Haidée's banquet in *Don Juan* III, the hypothesized poet sang—or would have sung —of past glory and past song, bemoaning how the lyre "degenerated" into hands like his. "The voices of the dead / Sound like a distant torrent fall," more a part of nature, and for the moment more real, than the artificial aestheticism of the banquet or the lighthearted attitude of the poet of the surrounding stanzas. Having stood for the moment with Lambro discovering what has happened to his island home, we extrapolate on the basis of the degeneration of this paradise from our first view of it to the larger sense of paradise lost in the degeneration of historical Greece. In *The Two Foscari,* Marina exclaims that "this crowd of palaces and prisons is not / A paradise" (III.i.147–48), a remark that has only the pristine perspective of understatement to counter the weight of Venetian corruption and unhappiness. Less ladylike is the Doge's myth of preexistence: "Methinks we must have sinn'd in some old world / And *this* is hell" (II.i.364–65).

Byron's grandest adaptation of imputed anteriority based on a sense of present fallenness is *Manfred*. In other dramas and the tales the myth of preexistence is generally safeguarded by being grounded thoroughly in nature, so that to the skeptical eye there are only two geographies, or two historical periods, or, at most, two poetic fictions. In *Manfred* the concept of an anterior spiritual state is further guarded by the distinction drawn between Manfred's spirit and the world of other spirits, whose authenticity is ultimately denied when their power over Manfred is denied. The kind of ambiguity about spiritual or biographical past, so necessary in *Lara,* is still there: Manfred's longed-for lady is Astarte, her very name suggesting an otherworldly attraction as much as a flesh-and-blood lure. Ultimately the drama distinguishes between Manfred's quest for spiritual originality and the questionable primariness of the supernatural personae.

In his first approach to the "mysterious agency" of spirits, Manfred conjures unsuccessfully with "written charm" and magical signs. Denying the primal quality of this writing scene, the spirits respond rather to a spell "Which had its birthplace in a star condemn'd / The burning wreck of a demolish'd world" (I.i.44–45). The song of the Seventh Spirit would imply that this is Manfred's star, though he seems both to operate under its influence and to operate its influence. The question of whether the power to raise spirits is Manfred's own or is merely lent him, as the Seventh Spirit claims, "but to make thee mine," is one of a number of questions about the past which need to be demystified rather than simply answered. Another such question concerns forgetfulness "of what—of whom—and why?" as the First Spirit asks. To give particulars about the "what" and "who" is to answer the question—perhaps a necessary stage in the demystification, and one Byron relegates, not without tact, to the confrontation with the Witch of the Alps in Act II. Beyond answers, however, the whole concept of forgetfulness needs to be exposed and perhaps discarded.

Byron was all too fond of the stance urbanely versified in the 1805 poems "To Caroline": "Not let thy mind past joys review— Our only hope is to forget." The passion for forgetfulness marks the turn to more postured romanticism in the opening of Canto III of *Childe Harold.* Perhaps poems like *Lara* sophisticate the

efforts to suppress the past or escape victimization by it. Biographically, the call for forgetfulness seems more self-indulgent.
Memory had no pleasure for him, he was fond of confessing, and
he expressed the wish "for insanity—anything—to quell memory,
the never-dying worm that feeds on the heart, and only calls up
the past to make the present more insupportable."[17] It would
be too easy to walk away from *Manfred* as from a portrait of
man under the weight of his personal burden of the past. Nor
can we simply say that forgetfulness is dismissed in the drama.
Perhaps the desire for forgetfulness is purged, but only when it
is demystified or shown to be a misdirection or a misapprehen-
sion of the object of desire.

Already in Act I, Manfred discovers the powerlessness of
supernatural agency in his search for oblivion. "I lean no more
on super-human aid, / It hath no power upon the past"
(I.ii.4–5). At this point the path of the superhuman and the
path to power over the past divaricate. Manfred does not immediately pursue either of these paths, however. He turns instead,
whether by conscious redirection or the accidents of external
nature, to the scene around him, and discovers the beauty of
nature. "Why are ye beautiful?" is another misleading question,
however, and it takes suicidal thoughts to confront him with the
importance of nature: its primariness. Part sublime, part pastoral, the scene is through both attributes primordial, in touch
with the sources of power because in touch with the past in a
way that has nothing to do with personal memory. "Here,"
Manfred notes parenthetically, "the patriarchal days are not / A
pastoral fable" (I.ii.310–11).

If it would be too radical a dismissal to say that incest is not
Manfred's crime, we could at least say that incest only makes
literal a perverted relation to paternity and the past. The scene
on the Jungfrau mountain less indulges than purges Byron's
tendency to bemoan the burden of experience, and self-drama-
tization as fallen angel is aborted when Manfred is rescued by the
Chamois Hunter. The literalized, dramatic height of the Alps

permits the momentary fiction that a suicidal plunge would be a Luciferic fall. This fiction confronts us with a greater truth, that Manfred literally unfallen cannot so melodramatically impute to himself the state of fallen angel. Literally unfallen man is also spiritually unfallen in some sense not yet fully recognized by the abortive suicide but implied in the grand injunction of the hunter: "Stain not our pure vales with thy guilty blood!" (I.ii.372). Not acquiescing to Manfred's self-abnegation, the hunter calls Manfred's blood "guilty" only proleptically. The blood would be guilty of staining the vales which are yet pure. Just as the vales retain the stamp of the primeval, Manfred himself retains contact with the unfallen element of human nature.

"Power upon the past" was a misapprehended object of desire, and questing for it is like the child's questioning whether God could build a mountain he would be unable to move. I compare a quest to a question not for verbal play but to suggest that this is the kind of play Manfred himself is engaged in. When the Witch of the Alps retires, Manfred claims he has one resource left: "I can call the dead / And ask them what it is we dread to be" (II.ii.271–72). Has he himself confused his quest with a question? He needs to learn that the object of his own quest is not power over past or future; the real desire is to be able to approach, in the future, the power *of* the past. The mountain scene was a first contact with the primeval; the colloquy with the spirits in Act II is the second.

When the phantom of Astarte answers Manfred—and she answers only him—she gives not the information Manfred requests, but knowledge nonetheless that he will translate into power. Questions of forgiving or forgetting were misdirected questions, betraying—regardless of their answer—a subjugation to the past. With the information given by Astarte, that he will die the next day, Manfred is forced to analyze or deconstruct into its components the desire to redeeem his relationship with Astarte: on the one hand, guilt at violating another can be erased only by passive resignation to the will of another; "forgive me!" is something only the *you* can do for the *me*. On the other hand, the desire to be forgiven or to forget is the desire to restore the primariness of one's own will, the desire to feel one's "original" power unburdened by the past. The component of resignation baffled, Manfred asserts the full power of original will.

The mystification dispelled by the act of will involves the relationship between the past and the supernatural. In a confusion about primariness and power, the supernatural personae had been appealed to; but if they could not dispel the past, Manfred learns that he can dispel them. His was the spell that conjured them, and his is the power to deny their primacy. One's past belongs to one's self, not to any other powers, and demons are de-mans, spirits who come from man and not parental figures who bequeath power to students of the past. Manfred identifies his present power with his skill:

> In knowledge of our fathers when the earth
> Saw men and spirits walking side by side
> And gave ye no supremacy.   [III.iv.377–79]

In this vision of primordial times man is not degenerated from the spirits but an equal with them. Thus dispelling Byron's myth of degeneration, Manfred restores the primariness of his will and lifts the burden of the past. When the "original" in the sense of what took place originally is distinguished from the "original" in the sense of manifested originality, the original moment is no longer in the lost *then* but in the present *now*. Making an end of the demons, Manfred stands like God in the primary act of imagination asserting "I am" and silencing the deep. The mind becomes "its own origin of ill and end."

CHAPTER 4

Shelley: From the Caverns
of Dreamy Youth

> In the ages of crude primeval culture man believed that in dreams
> he got to know *another real world;* here is the origin of all meta-
> physics. Without the dream one would have found no occasion for
> a division of the world. The separation of body and soul, too, is
> related to the most ancient conception of the dream; also the
> assumption of a quasi-body of the soul, which is the origin of all
> belief in spirits and probably also of the belief in gods.
>
> Nietzsche, *Human, All-Too-Human*

It is a commonplace of psychology that dreams are born from
desires unacted or unrealized in conscious life. It is a theme
common to a whole range of Shelley poems, on the other hand,
that conscious desire is born from the unrealized images of
dream life. Shelley is variously subtle, profoundly skeptical, or
playfully indifferent on the question of the natural or extra-
natural origins of dreams themselves. But he is always energized,
as if from a spiritual center, when he posits dream vision as the
source of ideal quest objects.

The taking of dreams for origins is, throughout Shelley's
poetry, a literary taking, a fiction about the workings of consciousness and not a representation of an extrapoetic idealism
or belief in a world of spirits. Yeats, who thought spirits brought
metaphors for poetry but who did not always believe spirits to
be themselves metaphors of poetry, offers a strong standard
against which one may test Shelley's wavering skepticism on
matters of dream vision. In his essay "The Philosophy of
Shelley's Poetry," Yeats announced his own conviction that
"imagination has some way of lighting on the truth that reason

has not, and that its commandments, delivered when the body
is still and the reason silent, are the most binding we can ever
know."[1] Such would be the faith of the Poet in Shelley's *Alastor,*
but the faith does not seem to be shared by the narrator of the
story or the author of the Preface. *Alastor* is Shelley's first extended treatment of dream vision as source, and already every
rift is loaded with the *or* of ambiguity about origins.

i

Alastor tells the story of a Poet whose infancy was nurtured
"By solemn vision, and bright silver dream" and whose life of
romantic quest is shaped around a questionably numinous center: "A vision on his sleep / There came, a dream of hopes that
never yet / Had flushed his cheek" (ll. 149–51). In Yeastian
terms this is the story of a poet who, when his reason is silent,
receives the most binding command from a power called Imagination—a power not to be reduced to the influence of childhood's "bright silver dream" or the day-residue of adolescent
eroticism. The important words are "never yet," and what is
given a romantic origin here transcends erotic context to become
a form of Emersonian "newness" or imaginative power. Assessing critical perspective on the ambiguous origins of the Poet's
vision, Bryan Cooper writes, "The vision is, and must remain,
basically a vision, a dream, which comes mainly from within the
Poet rather than specifically from any outside realm."[2] The three
qualifiers, "basically," "mainly," and "specifically," remind us
of the characteristically Shelleyan ambivalence about both the
authenticity of vision and the possibility of love transcending its
narcissistic roots. Norman Thurston helps us beyond a picture
of an immature poet—one who has not resolved his uncertain-
ties—by suggesting that *Alastor* develops in a clear temporal
sequence from one attitude to the other: "The narrator is
unable to sustain his sympathy with the Poet at this point [the
Poet's indifference to a real Arab maiden]. The narrator does
not in fact believe that a visionary woman is more desirable than

a flesh and blood companion. The Poet's reality seems suddenly unreal to the narrator." [3]

Focusing on this turning point of the poem, Thurston discovers a natural origin for the lines that appear to assert the supernatural origin of the Poet's vision: "The spirit of sweet human love has sent / A vision to the sleep of him who spurned / Her choicest gifts" (ll. 203–05). Partly psychological, partly rhetorical, Thurston's explanation demystifies the concept of an Alastor or avenging spirit. The narrator's realization of the discrepancy between his character's visionary perspective and his own earthly one shocks him into commenting on the absurdity of vision, and that comment takes the form of inventing the fiction of "the spirit of sweet human love." Capitalizing on the poet's dreaminess, the narrator appears to add the capital letters to the Spirit of Love, and creates a fiction of the transcendent out of his defensive distaste for the transcendent. But only the Poet and readers deluded by the image of Shelley's identification with the Poet misread the word "spirit" as though it were spelled with a capital *S*. "His phrase about the 'spirit of sweet human love' does not, as Gibson and Wasserman have realized, inject a new allegorical or metaphysical power into the world of the poem. Instead it expresses, metaphorically, in lower case letters, the narrator's analysis of the Poet's vision." [4]

One may object that Thurston tells but half the story, for though a critic can trace spiritual events back to natural causes, the poet also claims the vitalizing power of tracing natural events to spiritual causes. The real Shelley would thus appear to be half naturalist, believing in the reality of love for real human beings, and half dreamer, believing in the reality of vision—or at least the reality of a poetic beginning from the hypothesis of dream origins. This would be the view of Earl Wasserman, who identifies the narrator with the speaker of the Preface and finds the two perspectives of the poem—the narrator's and the Poet's— upheld like two columns of an arch by their continued pressure against one another. [5] The origin of the poem, like the origin of an individual, is traceable to a point where the generational line forks and two parent ideas (say, the narrator as child of the World Mother, the Poet as child of an otherworldly father) can be discerned. This picture Thurston finds too static. Believing that skepticism is not a matter of alternatives held in atemporal equipoise but the narrator's experience of uncertainty, he is led back to the view that there are three positions—the Preface-writer's, the narrator's, and the Poet's—and that the boundaries between them are subject to adjustment. Instead of granting that Thurston is half right to focus on the turn away from the Poet's dream, we might say that he is one-third right to focus on one of a crisis poem's three turning points.

My model is the map proposed by Harold Bloom, which I would apply to *Alastor* as a whole, including the Preface as its first section. Since our concern is with romantic origins rather than with natural, biographical ones, whether the actual writing of the Preface preceded the composition of the poem matters less than the fact that Shelley chose to publish the poem with the Preface. Though some have thought *Alastor* a poem descriptive of the divided structure of the poetic mind not yet softened by irony, the Preface may be understood as pure irony in the sense that, like many an opening of a Romantic lyric, it shows the poet saying exactly what, in his truest self, he does not mean. Freud used the term "reaction formation" to describe defensive behavior like showing extreme affection to disguise hostility. Here the hostility or moral harshness of the speaker provides a cover for the intensity of the poet's involvement with the psychic conditions for love. The images concern the presence and absence of light, love, and life, and offer Shelley an opportunity to express, under the disguise of antithetical imagery, the continuity of actual and ideal passion. Thus, quoting Wordsworth, he concludes that "those whose hearts are dry as summer dust / Burn to the socket." They are the poor scholars of one candle who never kindled the fading coals of imagination into more brilliant light. To be fully alive to the possibility of love is to be a luminary stricken with sudden darkness by an excess of brightness, by "too exquisite a perception" of the workings of Love. The irony is the experiential one that such intensity cannot be sustained and is awakened only to be extinguished. Irony cloaks the Shelleyan truth that love is a "generous error" perhaps inseparable from the daemonized poetic imagination. Falling in love with an Ideal Other or another human being both involve a generous suspension of disbelief—a willingness to identify an ego-ideal with another (real or fictive) person and a willingness to free oneself of the urbanity and skeptical naturalism with which we fence in our affections. Perhaps the central irony is that Shelley must call "error" what the word "generous" betrays: the high truth of *caritas* which allows a self to transcend itself.

Mr. Bloom calls the second stage of the crisis lyric *tessera*, after the broken piece of pottery by which an ephebe would demonstrate the fact that he is part of a greater whole. As *Alastor* proper begins, Shelley invokes "Earth, ocean, air, belovèd brotherhood." At this stage he is not countering the claim of Nature's firstborn, Wordsworth, by claiming to be a visionary fire-child in a way Wordsworth never was; his concern is not with overgoing others but with overleaping the wall that separates the would-be poet from the established brotherhood. He identifies himself not as a child of the Spirit of Love—the Lord who comes as a consuming fire—but as a child of the "great Mother" whose presence is felt as a form of gentleness, helping the inspired soul to accommodate itself to the earth and "modulate with murmurs of the air."

"The narrator starts out speaking the language of a first generation romantic," Thurston comments.[6] But to see Shelley turning against himself and posing as a Wordsworthian is to see beyond the simple division of the speaker into Preface-writer, narrator of the poem, and Poet. Those divisions are static, and obscure the development of the single ego from defense to defense or from one rhetorical stance to another. By identifying the invocation of *Alastor* with the second stage of the crisis lyric, we can understand the narrator's naturalism as Shelley's reversal of his own metaphysical idealism. We can see also that Shelley has faced—or rather outfaced—a crisis of election by imagining himself a dutiful son and worshiper of the Great Parent Nature.

Leaving behind the "Thou" whom he addresses directly and turning to his subject (the career of a third-person Poet) Shelley as poet incarnate is in something of the position of the Son as he turns from heavenly communion to incarnate himself in the object or "It" world. Borrowing the term from St. Paul, Mr. Bloom might call this the *kenosis* of the poet, and the departure from this allegorical heaven has its parallel in the earthly career of the youth who leaves "His cold fireside and alienated home / To seek strange truths in undiscovered lands" (ll. 76–77). Isolating and undoing his faith in the supernatural, the poet regresses to the childlike faith in the contiguity of nature. The figure of the mother is, as it were, spread out over the face of nature, so that animals are "Lured by the gentle meaning of his looks" (l. 101) and share in what might be called a metonymic paradise, where to be close to nature is to be part of nature. Is this the state of total fullness or of a divine nature emptied of its essence? The Poet who gazes and gazes "till meaning on his vacant mind / Flashed like strong inspiration" (ll. 126–27) is himself vacant and, in the most spiritual sense, filled.

Shelley now approaches the turning point on which Thurston concentrates, the point that Bloom calls the crisis of solipsism. From a naturalistic perspective there is no such thing as turning into a daemonized spirit, one of the "luminaries of the world" on the other side of this crossing. There is also no real crossing ground or liminal space between nature and the transcendent because natural events have natural causes and "romantic origins" is but a mist thrown over a source in nature further back. The Poet has been preoccupied with the search for origins, "poring on memorials / Of the world's youth" (ll. 121–22). In addition there is the day-residue from his encounter with the panting Arab maiden. Nothing could be more "natural" than that his dreamwork should turn to the origins of sexual love in his own mental memorials of youthful dissolution into a maternal embrace. Psychoanalysis, in one sense the strongest opponent of romanticizing origins, provides a vocabulary for understanding the "generous error" at the poem's core. Thomas Weiskel, who carried the psychoanalytic reading of Shelley's sublime as far as it could go, offered this explanation: "At just the point where 'objects cease to suffice,' the insatiate mind responds to the anxiety of deprivation (appropriately rendered as thirst) by projecting and consolidating a 'single image' of the Other."[7]

To the questions "Whose insatiate mind?" and "Which image of the Other?" there are three possible answers. There is Shelley's insatiate mind consolidating a single image of the Other into the form of the Arab maiden; there is the Poet's insatiate mind unsatisfied with—or oblivious to—the Arab maiden and turning instead to the dream vision of the Other; there is finally the mind, not satisfied with the fleeting dream vision, that goes on to imagine a Power behind the shadow—a Spirit of Love who manifests herself in shadowy form as a vision sent "to the sleep of him who spurned / Her choicest gifts" (ll. 204–05). From a reductionist point of view the Poet who "eagerly pursues / Beyond the realms of dream that fleeting shade" (ll. 203–05) is really pursuing a memory of the Arab maid. From a visionary point of view the Poet is really pursuing the shadow of a Power beyond the realm of shadows. But either way the violation of place opens up a new place, the place of "newness" or the origin of power. The same may be said for the gap separating one verse paragraph from another and separating the natural maiden who "to her cold home . . . returned" from the Poet's wanderings on to a more eastern, more romantic place elsewhere whence "a vision on his sleep / There came." These gaps free a daemonized consciousness from its roots in immediately antecedent nature. Rhetorically, Shelley has left behind the realm of metonymic contiguity where the Poet began his quest, but does not yet approach the metaphoric imagination by which the Poet will repeatedly attempt to read the landscape as a projection of his mental state. In the heights between these two plains, rhetoric centers on the hyperbole of the dream vision, modified tangentially by the grotesque or bathetic awareness that the vision is but an empty dream.

Like the influx of power characteristic of the daemonized poet speaking in the first person, the influx of sexual power experienced in dream by the character the Poet is founded on a repression. If one imagines the content of repression to be sexual, one might say that the dreamwork luxuriates in infantile sexuality and represses aggressive sexuality when it represents the Poet submitting to the overwhelming lady who "Folded his frame in her dissolving arms." Alternatively, one could describe the repression as that of an ego-instinct (an instinct for survival, for maintaining one's indissoluble individuality). Most important, one can describe as a force of repression the demystified knowledge that this fulfillment is but a dream. While the narrator sees through the illusion by which he finds the Poet bound, the narrator himself represses any awareness that the Poet's dream brings to a climax the narrator's own yearning for and belief in a transcendent, though immanent, "great Mother."

For poets as men, a crisis of solipsism means that one feels in danger of lapsing into solipsism. But for poets as poets the crisis of solipsism means just the reverse—the point where vision threatens to dissolve into illusion—where the power of the sole self looks like a poor disguise for loneliness. In *Alastor* the Poet's crisis of solipsism is successfully—indeed outrageously—negotiated when he remains oblivious to the Arab maiden and wanders on to be rapt into a vision of a transcendent Other. But the narrator's crisis of solipsism may be distinguished as the hypothetical point at which he was in danger of giving up his own sole self and identifying by way of sympathy with the Poet. The narrator's victory is Shelley's: remaining aloof he takes on daemonic power—the power to create, and perhaps himself to incarnate the *alastor* or Spirit of Solitude.

To read the moralism of the **Preface**, the Wordsworthian naturalism of the invocation, and the visionary stance of the Poet as various psychic defenses of a poetic ego is to privilege the *daemonization* section as the section of romantic origins. In other crisis poems the poet is daemonized into abandoning his sense of reality and speaking as though a man were author of himself— and his own transcendental realm. The peculiarity of *Alastor* may lie precisely in the fact that the narrator appears most him- self and most powerful when he distances himself from the Poet's visionary perspective. Though at the center of the poem, the *daemonization* separates itself from antecedent causes and seems to generate the whole poem—as though the whole character of the narrator were begotten at this point in reaction to the Poet. At a minimum the daemonization section gives Shelley the re- mainder of *Alastor*, for what follows is a long *askesis* or purgation as both Poet and narrator attempt to sublimate the quest for the origins of desire into a geographic quest for some landscape that will metaphorically represent the Poet's mind.

To the crossings of election and solipsism must be added the crossing of identification by which the Poet can turn to something outside, something he comes upon, and say "that I am he." Per- haps it is a measure of how strong—or how elusive—a "generous error" lies at the heart of *Alastor* that the *askesis* section of the poem must be so long. Among the repeated efforts to identify himself with the forms of external nature are the beautiful swan passage (ll. 272–95) and the verse paragraph beginning with the word *as* and exploring the very nature of the metaphorical "as if" (ll. 316–51). The question of identification with an imaginary Other reaches a crisis point when the Poet regards "two eyes, / Two starry eyes, hung in the gloom of thought" (ll. 489–90). These are the reflections of the Poet's own eyes, the narrator believes, though to the Poet's mind "A Spirit seemed / To stand beside him." For the narrator, the crisis of identification involves the terrible recognition that the Poet's journey toward death represents his own Wordsworthian natural- ism which is no different from death. In the envoy the narrator discovers—or rather fails to discover, as Earl Wasserman points out—that "despite his belief that he is of the community of nature, he is, as merely a child of the World Mother, just as solitary as the Visionary, as alone as the incarnate death of the Wandering Jew."[8] If in the end it seems a vain illusion to project the life within outward onto the face of nature, it is a resolution of some sort to discover oneself identifying inner death (death of the visionary spark, or death of the Poet whose story one has been telling) with the death in nature—barren earth, imageless ocean, and "senseless wind" (l. 705).

ii

It has been objected against Harold Bloom's distinction between the stages of *daemonization* and *askesis* that these newfangled terms only mask a very traditional distinction between illusion and disillusion or idealism and skepticism. But if it is correct to identify the daemonization of the narrator of *Alastor* with his turn from the Poet and his repression of desire for communion like that enjoyed by the Poet in dream, then dreams cannot be dismissed as mere illusions or representations of an idealism that the urbane Shelley rejects. Rather, the Poet's dream appears to him as the origin of his desire endlessly to pursue his romantic quest for the shadow of the Power that visited him; concomitantly and most significantly, the episode of the dream emerges as the romantic origin of the narrator's voice. Retrospectively this daemonic desire to exorcise the visionary element from his own perspective seems to have impelled the tone of the Preface, the reactionary transcendentalism of the invocations (antithetically claiming kinship with a Spirit of Nature rather than the numinous Power of Love) and the mysterious return of the dead—of that quasi-Wordsworthian stance at the conclusion of the poem.

Approaching other poems by Shelley from the perspective of *Alastor,* we must be prepared not only to find Shelley using dreams as vehicles for the daemonization of consciousness, but to

find skepticism at the core of—rather than in purgatorial retreat
from—the daemonized poetic consciousness. *Mont Blanc* is a
poem everywhere concerned with origins, with what it means
to find the sources of thought to be "secret springs"—in the water
imagery of *Alastor,* "inaccessibly profound." If further specified,
sources would become fixed places or fixed stages in a process
of thought; sources would be naturalized into points on an endless line of antecedence—just as, on another level, the image of a
water-source can be "naturalized" by considering the endless
antecedence of a water-cycle. Evading fixity of place and the
danger of reducing all to natural causes is one of the functions
of dreams for Shelley, and so section III of *Mont Blanc,* one of
the greatest achievements of the daemonized Romantic consciousness, begins with the possibility of dream vision: "Some say that
gleams of a remoter world / Visit the soul in sleep."

In *Alastor,* the Poet "wandered on" after the episode of the
Arab maid so that the dream vision can conceivably be said to
stand detached from the natural cause of erotic day-residue. In
Mont Blanc, the speculation "some say" provides the distance
between the overwhelming presence at the end of section II
("Thou art there!") and "Mont Blanc appears" (l. 61). While
appearing to stake out an area of indifference (some say this,
but others say otherwise) the equivocation about dream visitation from a remoter world intensifies, in the process of expressing
uncertainty about, the quest for romantic origins. A central
skepticism or evasiveness points to an original place:

> Is this the scene
> Where the old Earthquake-daemon taught her young
> Ruin? Were these their toys? or did a sea
> Of fire envelop once this silent snow?   [ll. 71–74]

Like the dialogue between two spirits in *The Rime of the Ancient
Mariner,* this gleam of a remoter world takes the form of a scene
of instruction all the more primary, all the more "original" for
the uncertainty about a prime mover in a natural world. The
power to question the origin of Mont Blanc becomes the power

to confront the origination of a new poetic voice. The equivocation is first followed by plain silence: "None can reply—all seems
eternal now." If one did reply we would be in the realm of
scientific fact and natural causation, and we would be answered
in terms of natural history, not poetic origins. Instead, the silence
of none replying becomes a place for the generation of poetic
voice, and the wilderness is found to have "a mysterious tongue."
The poet's pentecostal power manifests itself as Imagination
descends upon the mountain in the form of a tongue of flame,
a miniature epiphany of the consuming fire that devastates the
work of idolators: "Thou has a voice, great Mountain, to
repeal / Large codes of fraud and woe." Returning to "the lone
glare of day" the poet confronts reduction to bare nature not
unlike that the narrator of *Alastor* discovers when he imagines
the dead Poet's "divinest lineaments / Worn by the senseless
wind" (ll. 704–05). If the daemonized poet comes into his own
voice in attributing voice to the mountain, the more reality-
oriented observer of the dead world of nature returns in the end
to find in the wind a motion without sound, a current of air and
no holy spirit: "Winds contend / Silently there, and heap the
snow with breath / Rapid and strong, but silently!" (ll. 134–36).

Section III of *Mont Blanc* ends the way Wordsworth's vision
on Mount Snowdon has been said to end: the poet comes upon
Imagination and calls it Nature:

> The wilderness has a mysterious tongue
> Which teaches awful doubt, or faith so mild,
> So solemn, so serene, that man may be,
> But for such faith, with nature reconciled;
> Thou hast a voice great Mountain, to repeal
> Large codes of fraud and woe; not understood
> By all, but which the wise, and great, and good
> Interpret, or make felt, or deeply feel.

The "gleams of a remoter world" have taken the dreamy form
of a fantasy on the origins of Mont Blanc, and this return to
origins—with a skeptical equivocation at the center—seems to

generate the voice of the wilderness. Like *Alastor, Mont Blanc* discovers that the hypothesis of gleams from a remoter world cannot "prove" a transcendent realm, but can prove efficacious in generating a rhetoric of sheer imaginative power. In a sense Shelley recapitulated the close of *Alastor* when he ended Section III of *Mont Blanc* with the thought that "man may be / In such a faith, with nature reconciled" (Boscombe manuscript). That mild faith is the one invoked and in the end retreated to by the narrator of *Alastor*. Perhaps the skeptical Shelley found his own voice by emphasizing the possibility of such faith as something Wordsworth might have believed: man *may* be reconciled to nature in such a faith, if he is willing to pay the price of possessing no fuller a consciousness than that of the narrator of *Alastor* at his most deluded moments. But in changing "In such a faith" to "But for such faith" Shelley moved beyond the equivocations of *Alastor* to a stronger voice more truly his own.

iii

If we keep in mind the relationship between equivocation and the generation of voice in *Mont Blanc*, we can better understand the relationship of dream vision to its context in *Julian and Maddalo*. The madman does come "To give a human voice to [his] despair," and voice is similarly derived from a speculation about a source of power:

> What Power delights to torture us? I know
> That to myself I do not wholly owe
> What now I suffer, though in part I may. [ll. 320–22]

The extent to which one is personally responsible for his suffering is precisely the issue Julian and Maddalo have been debating. Julian has voiced the unironic side of Shelley's own position: "it is our will / That thus enchains us to permitted ill," and Maddalo has thought to counter this optimism with the spectacle of the madman. The madman's own voice takes over, and the friends' urbane argument is silenced. The poem itself is silenced too, for it breaks off with a gentle refusal to divulge more of the madman's story, so much has the effect of his voice triumphed over what seems in the end like extrapoetic detail.

The madman is mad the way the Poet of *Alastor* is—pursued by the specter of solitude or selfhood which is given an ambiguous origin in dream vision. The difference is that where the *Alastor* Poet dreams the form of his emanation, and then wakes to bemoan her loss and seek her through the world, the madman has encountered his lady in the historical past, which he retrospectively regards as a dreamlike state. The result is a more self-conscious despair, for the past is even more inaccessible than are dreams, and so the desire associated with romantic quest is replaced by passive resignation. Knowing the limitations of action in the postdream world, the madman knows too the special status of speech that is coupled with awareness of loss. He describes past awakening in a way that seems to call forth his present mode of address: "as one from dreaming / Of sweetest peace, I woke, and found my state / Such as it is" (ll. 335–37). If the "as" indicates the purely metaphoric nature of the past dream state, this account of breaking one fiction introduces another. He turns to his lost love, whom he addresses as if she heard—or rather, with pained consciousness that she is being addressed fictionally, and cannot, should not hear:

> O Thou, my spirit's mate
> Who, for thou art compassionate and wise,
> Wouldst pity me from thy most gentle eyes
> If this sad writing thou shouldst ever see—
> My secret groans must be unheard by thee,
> Thou wouldst weep tears bitter as blood to know
> Thy lost friend's incommunicable woe.   [ll. 337–43]

From the pieces of story we are given, there would seem to be more evidence that pain is his shadow than that the lady is a compassionate "spirit's mate." But the desire to speak words that could evoke compassion from the emotionally dead "inspires" these words and makes the speaker turn from incommunicable woe to communication.

The plain burden of misery, as Julian senses it later, is enough to silence any spirit. What calls forth the madman's monologue is rather the replacement of one fiction with another. He seems, in the words that describe past waking, to be waking now from illusions about past fidelity to the illusion of present responsiveness in the lady. Hence the speculation "If this sad writing thou shouldest ever see"—giving his oral ravings the substantiality of written communication—is coupled with this safeguarding of the illusion: "My secret groans must be unheard by thee." The gentler fiction that the lady could see what is in fact unwritten covers the harsher truth that even if his groans were heard she would not weep.

For Maddalo the origin of the madman's high language of grief is simply and painfully clear:

> Most wretched men
> Are cradled into poetry by wrong,
> They learn in suffering what they teach in song.
>
> [ll. 544–46]

Experiential wrong—the experience of having been wronged by an individual or an illusion—has this much in common with the dreamlike fictions we entertain about the past. Wrong and fiction are opposed to truth—or, more accurately, both lie anterior to and are generative of the truths plain to demystified consciousness. In *Alastor,* where there is some ambiguity about whether the poet has wronged the spirit of love or whether the spirit, posing as more than a fiction of consciousness, wrongs him, either mystification precedes the state of mind represented in the cold Preface. In *Julian and Maddalo,* the "sweetest peace" dreamt by the madman in his period of infatuation has generated the real nightmare of his conscious life. The idea of being "cradled into poetry by wrong" is Shelley's notion of a Byronic myth of origins; but the idea of a mystified dream state preceding present consciousness is a centrally Shelleyan fiction.

iv

Unlike the way Shelley uses the dream state to represent the nebulous origin of the idealisms in *Alastor* and *Julian and Maddalo,* his use of dreams in *Prometheus Unbound* is bold and unequivocal. Here Shelley allows an extended look at the kind of vision previously guarded closely by the ironies attendant on dream form: and here dream vision comes without baleful consequences to dreamers who must awake in a world of loss. Of *Mont Blanc,* Earl Wasserman wrote, "The transcending capacity of dream has granted insight into that transcendent Power, unknowable in normal experience or in terms of the idealistic definition of existence."[9] While this is a problematic reading of *Mont Blanc,* where a dream state may be a momentarily entertained alternative to the revelation of transcendent power, there can be no question of the positive revelation dreams bring in Act II of *Prometheus.*

Two large-scale features of the poem may seem to be at variance with Shelley's use of dreams as sources. Dreams are more properly the mode of revelation of Asia rather than Prometheus, the first mover of the action, and dreams are most important in Act II, whose action temporally follows that of Act I. But in moving from the world of Prometheus on the precipice to Asia in the vale we do move back, away from the external manifestations of conflict between good and power and toward the wellsprings of saving grace. By the end of Act II we have moved, with Asia, further back from the world of time and decay as we know it. The act opens with Asia awaiting the coming of spring, which she addresses in terms that suggest the dream visions of *Alastor* and *Julian:*

> Thou dost awake, O Spring!
> O child of many winds! As suddenly

> Thou comest as the memory of a dream,
> Which now is sad because it hath been sweet. [II.i.6–9]

The spring she awaits will bring a sweetness not to be turned to sadness because not subject to the fading characteristic of dream visions in a fallen world. In the course of this scene "the memory of a dream" will become more than a comparison to something natural, and Asia will, by restoring the memory of a dream, advance the state of redeemed innocence beyond that of recollected gladness. Panthea enters enraptured by "the delight of a remembered dream" and the sense of having dreamed a second, unremembered dream.

This little failure of memory is coupled with another sweet lapse: just as Panthea's consciousness stumbles under the burden of the visions she has had, so do her words. It is left to Asia to restore the second dream and to restore the vitality of both visions which is seen to lie behind, rather than within verbal translation. As Panthea begins to recount her experience, Asia says, "Lift up thine eyes, / And let me read thy dream." Presumably she will thus be able to see into Panthea's soul, and thus receive the dream in less mediated fashion. It is important that her metaphor shifts the medium from hearing to sight, and "read," which implies writing—still words, but to be seen—helps arrest and emphasize the transition away from voice. In general, Shelley has used the attribution of voice to voiceless things to represent the furthest reach of man's fiction-making powers. In *Alastor,* the poet first receives something "like strong inspiration" from the meanings he reads into or out of the "mute thoughts on the mute walls around." When he hears, in dream, a voice "like the voice of his own soul," he is on more dangerous ground. The *Hymn to Intellectual Beauty* distinguishes suspect "hopes of high talk with the departed dead" from the more modest, more mediated visitations of a shadow of a power. In *Mont Blanc* the attribution of voice to the mountain is the furthest reach of the mythmaking mind. And in *Julian and Maddalo,* when the madman would protect himself by the fiction that he is writing, he retreats to that final expression of despair, "How vain / Are words!"

Voice is precisely what Asia must valorize and recover, making her task a parallel to, perhaps a purer form of, Prometheus' task in Act I. There he recovers voice literally when the words of his curse are returned to him. Asia must find the limits to the projection of voice outside the self, and in that discovery, cleanse voice of its deleterious powers of mystification. We may note in advance that Act II ends in song, Asia's voice responding to a pure "Voice in the Air," each enkindling in the other the breath of voice. The power of origination is restored in such spontaneous generation, and the song itself properly moves back from death and birth into a realm of shapes whose only form is the melody they chant. "The act thus ends by returning us to the music of its beginning," notes Stuart Curran, "as the love duet replicates the dream." [10]

That is where Act II will end. Meanwhile, Asia is properly suspicious of the power of voice, and she denies to Panthea's words the power of unmediated revelation:

> Thou speakest, but thy words
> Are as the air: I feel them not: Oh, lift
> Thine eyes, that I may read his written soul!   [II.i.108–10]

One unsympathetic to such raptures might say that what Asia could "read" in Panthea's eyes—all that one ever hopes to read in another's eyes—is love. Far from demystifying the metaphor, however, that would bring us closer to its essence. Besides, Panthea herself seems to forestall demystification when she asks Asia, "what canst thou see / But thine own fairest shadow imaged there?" This could be a failure of insight if it were to mean simply that the eye were acting as physical reflector and a lady is regarding her miniature in a convex surface. On another level Panthea is exactly right. What Asia reads in Panthea's eyes is the form of love, allowing the physical image the ambiguity that ordinarily belongs to "one's love"—one's own emotion or the object of that emotion.

This exchange between Asia and Panthea about the mode of transmission of Panthea's vision lies between Panthea's account of her first dream and Asia's evocation of the second. Since the first dream and the discussion of its mode of apprehension concern the form of redeemed love—the rejuvenated Prometheus— we would do well to recall the discussion about the form of love in Act I. There too Panthea loses voice, though Ione exclaims of the spirits, "their beauty gives me voice." The chorus asks, "Hast thou beheld the form of Love?" and the Fifth Spirit describes the passing of "that planet crested shape" whose "footsteps paved the world with light." Now, in Panthea's dream, Prometheus appears in his redeemed form, "and the azure night / Grew radiant with the glory of that form / Which lives unchanged within." What follows is complicated by the extraordinary gesture of having Prometheus achieve voice in the dream and herald Panthea as "Sister of her whose footsteps pave the world / With loveliness." One imaged form of love verbally rebegets the other, heralding the total communion to come. But if we keep in mind the evocation of the form of love in Act I, our expectation is aroused about what must immediately succeed it in the dream sequence of Act II.

In Act I, the Fifth Spirit says, "His footsteps paved the world with light; but as I passed 'twas fading, / And hollow Ruin yawned behind" (I.767–68). That much is the condition of the experiential world we know, and we can recognize in the way Ruin dogs the visionary form of love just the pattern of *Alastor* and *Julian and Maddalo*. The Chorus, however, sings to Prometheus the prophetic hope of redemption: "Though Ruin now Love's shadow be, / Following him, destroyingly . . . Thou shalt quell this horseman grim." In the dreams of Panthea what faintly resembles a repetition of the shadow pattern becomes a break in the cycle of repetition, and Ruin no longer follows love destroyingly.

Were Panthea's dreams merely to bring to Asia what the spirits bring Prometheus, then a first dream of the form of love paving the world with light might be followed by a second dream of destruction. This is almost what happens, but the difference is crucial. For the moment Panthea has forgotten her second dream, and Asia, looking into Panthea's eyes, is revoicing the first dream. The form of love is descried as Prometheus, whose very smile spreads radiant light. From the passive position of beholding an image, Asia is daemonized into voice, and addresses Prometheus directly:

> Say not those smiles that we shall meet again
> Within that bright pavilion which their beams
> Shall build o'er the waste world?   [II.i.124–26]

The dream may be said to have been not fully spoken until it has moved Asia to speak to it. With her question voiced, Asia proclaims, "The dream is told." But voice proves seminal, and instead of those four words enclosing the dream as separate entity, they *generate* a further interrogative and a further power of vision: "What shape is that between us?"

Though brought into being at this moment, the shape has its own history, or preexistence, in dream. Shelley's myth of origins thus makes what is perhaps its subtlest and most suggestive appearance. Without the device of having Panthea dream and forget her dream, the shape could seem one more thing of air. As it is, Panthea recalls her dream in a parallel but ultimately more radical sense than that in which Prometheus recalls his curse. The curse is recalled in that it is brought back to consciousness and—once given voice again—revoked. The dream is recalled in that it is brought back to consciousness and given a voice which heralds apocalyptic revocation of the order of nature: it says "follow, follow," pointing the way beyond repetition toward redemption. Here, as in *The Triumph of Life* more problematically, concern with origins is the specific counter to the curse of repetition. The pattern described by the spirits in

Act I consists of a form of love, and then Ruin, "Following him, destroyingly." Now the form of love reappears in dream form, and a reoriginated dream of ruin follows, itself crying "follow!" The almond blossoms—emblem of apocalyptic haste[11]—have been blown down, but their destruction heralds renovation. What was previously simply the ruin attendant on the forms of love (whether objects of sexual desire or literal flowers) has become a gentle intimation of the kind of ruin Shelley heralds in the "Ode to the West Wind." The rude-haired shape Asia sees is a form of wild wind, which in Panthea's dream "swept forth wrinkling the Earth with frost." As the Chorus of Spirits describes it to Prometheus, the wind is now seen "Trampling down both flower and weed . . . Like a tempest through the air." In the form of the second dream, however, the wind impels not another natural cycle but the redemptive journey back "through the caverns hollow," the caverns of dreamy youth, to diviner day and more original weather.

Responding to Panthea's dream, Asia is herself brought to remember forgotten dream images, and there is an increased credibility in the power of words written and oral. Panthea presents the almond leaves as stamped with the word "follow," while Asia recalls cloud shadows spelling out, and "Low, sweet, faint sounds" voicing, the same message. These renewed sensibilities mark the seminal nature of dream vision. As long as man looks to external agency he will be vulnerable to the tyrannies of the future; as long as man does not challenge and take more seriously the implications of verbal signs he will be subject to the tyrannies of the past. The appearance of the dream shape before Asia fulfills the stipulation that apocalyptic energy, however externally represented, come from within, and the injunction of the dream to "follow" heralds the confrontation with the limits of words.

In following the dream, Asia and Panthea are reprieved from the kind of fate that attends the *Alastor* poet when he pursues his vision "beyond the realms of dream" and "overleaps the bounds." Asia and Panthea do not take a dream vision beyond the caverns of dreamy youth, but rather pursue those caverns till dream divulges its essence. Their path is outlined by the Echoes into which the dream—diminishing its externality—has evolved:

> In the world unknown
>   Sleeps a voice unspoken;
> By thy step alone
>   Can its rest be broken;
>   Child of Ocean!   [II.i.190–94]

All the originating power of dream vision seems contained in these compacted lines, which are not fully reducible to the idea that there is a being who has a voice which he has not yet used and which Asia can evoke. The words "Sleeps a voice" allow metaphoric language to represent the absence of a being whose existence is even more metaphoric. If we expand "Sleeps a voice" to read "Demogorgon sleeps, and he will have a voice," we elicit from the phrase the conditions for the scene of confrontation between Asia and Demogorgon. But the phrase also implies the limitation of that confrontation: as Demogorgon will say to Asia, "I spoke but as ye speak," for in fact "a voice / Is wanting, the deep truth is imageless" (II.iv.113–16).

Dreams awaken images and give voice to otherwise senseless and shapeless impulses. In Act I, the Third Spirit identifies a dream which "had kindled long ago / Pity, eloquence, and woe." The spirit rides the dream, as Asia follows hers, both seemingly dependent on the metaphorical nature of dream motion: if dreams "move the world," Asia and the Third Spirit can move with dreams. The Fourth Spirit in Act I takes still more seriously the kindling or originating power of dreams, and it is therefore appropriate that this spirit come from a dreaming poet. From dream shapes poets create "Forms more real than living man, / Nurslings of immortality." The Fifth and Sixth Spirits appear as such nurslings, as does the dream of Panthea and—playing on the child-shape of nurslings—the Spirit of the Earth in Act

III and the Earth and Moon of Act IV. Even "that fatal child" who is Jupiter's dream belongs to this category of dream-generated images, though he remains, in Shelley's version of the myth, unrealized. All these forms may be said to inhabit a world unknown where sleep voices unspoken. Or, more accurately, all these forms may be said to originate in such a world unknown, and to move into voice when embodied in poetic language.

A full analysis of voice in *Prometheus Unbound* would have to consider every scene, perhaps every speech, in the poem.[12] But the place of dream vision is most properly the domain of Act II, and the act concludes with an exchange of pure voice that transcends dream origins only to recur to dream imagery. After Panthea reminds Asia of her own origins and of the power she manifested at her "uprise" to arouse love, a "Voice in the Air" sings of Asia's undiminished power to kindle responsive love wherever she is. Asia responds in kind with a song begotten, as it were, upon that of the Voice in the Air. The metaphor "My soul is an enchanted boat" engenders the extended conceit, "And thine doth like an angel sit / Beside a helm conducting it." Lulled by the soft reciprocal motions of wind and correspondent breeze, or voice and answering voice, the soul is rocked to sleep and seems to float on the waves of song. The journey described in Asia's song is thus a dream journey away from day cares toward a diviner day of personal and perhaps cosmic prehistory. More primordial than Elysium or Eden, the paradise described is the domain one is led to by Dante's Matilda, who also walks upon the sea while beautiful chanting expresses the yearning to purge oneself of experience and regain a higher innocence. Asia's song ends the act with the dreamlike vision of such spiritual return to paradisal origins, as though the chariots of sleep were being restored to the caverns of dreamy youth after a strenuous day's excursion.

v

The dream vision of *Epipsychidion* extends in complex ways two themes of Asia's song: in both poems the movement toward a prophetic future is heralded by intimations of a return back to a lost diviner day; and in both concern with poetic voice is the medium through which redemptive awareness is developed. Asia sings in response to the sweet singing of a Voice in the Air; in *Epipsychidion,* the visionary voice is recalled in response to a problem in the speaker's voice.

To read *Epipsychidion* one must accept two literary conventions about responsiveness. One is the extended address to an idealized beloved or muse, an absent Other regarded as a representative of an eternal Presence. The drama of such a poem depends on the element of suspense in unfolding the past and future of this illusion of presence, including the moments of intermission when the poet addresses his larger audience ("She met me, Stranger," l. 72) or only himself (ll. 123–29, and in a sense the whole history recounted in ll. 160–344). The drama concludes with the moment of reconciliation to absence when the poet speaks to the words that mediate between himself and his fictional Other ("Weak Verses, go, kneel at your Sovereign's feet," l. 592). The second convention is that, popularized by Dante, of regarding a youthful vision as the romantic origin of a transcendent one. The poet is surprised to find "Youth's vision thus made perfect" in Emily (l. 42), and as readers we are repeatedly surprised to find that what seems largely a convention about youth's vision ("the words / Of antique verse and high romance," ll. 209–10) can produce the possibility of beginning anew. To appreciate *Epipsychidion* one must pursue the relation of these two literary conventions about presence or absence and about the belatedness or romantic earliness of dreamy vision.

In *Alastor,* the dream vision of an idealized beloved represents the suspiciously daemonized consciousness of the Poet, reacting against which the narrator himself is daemonized into something like an Alastor or vengeful spirit—an analogy to, or parody of, the fully empowered poet. In *Epipsychidion* the passage corresponding to the dream vision of the idealized beloved occurs relatively late—after two passages which, retrospectively, appear to have revealed feminine forms destined to occupy no place closer to the heart of the poet of *Epipsychidion* than did the Arab maiden to the Poet of *Alastor*. The third passage brings the poet to something like the dream vision in *Alastor* from the Poet's point of view:

> Soft as an Incarnation of the Sun,
> When light is changed to love, this glorious One
> Floated into the cavern where I lay,
> And called my Spirit, and the dreaming clay
> Was lifted by the thing that dreamed below
> As smoke by fire, and in her beauty's glow
> Was penetrating me with living light. [ll. 335–41]

The idea of light being changed to love represents an extreme extension of the Miltonic idea of sublimation by which grosser matter is transformed into purer spirit. The rhetoric is hyperbolical because this vision marks an achieved moment of the sublime, a moment when the poet seems most clearly empowered to create out of nothing what the character he represents is said to have merely beheld.

In both *Alastor* and *Epipsychidion* descent from rhetorical height takes the form of a romantic quest. If we say that the major dream passage in ll. 190–216 of *Epipsychidion* corresponds to the central vision of *Alastor* (ll. 140–91), then the whole attempt in *Epipsychidion* to find in mortal forms "the shadow of that idol" corresponds to the long journey of the *Alastor* Poet in pursuit of "that fleeting shade" beyond the realms of dream. But if we see the crossing of solipsism—the definitive turn to the high rhetoric of the sublime—delayed in *Epipsychidion* till the episode cited above (ll. 335–44), then the dream passage of ll. 190–216 appears rather as an elaboration of the prehistory of poetic consciousness described in *Alastor* in the lines, "By solemn vision, and bright silver dream, / His infancy was nurtured" (ll. 67–68). The importance of this correspondence is that it helps us see Shelley lingering over the prehistory of the soul in love to the end that the new soul at its birth or romantic origin ("Then, from the caverns of my dreamy youth / I sprang," ll. 217–18) comes appareled with celestial light.

Like the myth of preexistence which Wordsworth revised as background for the experience of loss in his Intimations Ode, Shelley's history of the soul "in the clear golden prime of [his] youth's dawn" poses as a true spiritual beginning, a dream world elsewhere from whence the soul descends into nature. Though it is crucial to see the soul in line 217 making a new beginning when it springs forth from the dreamy background of the preceding verse paragraph, it is no less interesting to inquire what in the poem impels the appearance of the dream vision of preexistence. Looking at the verse paragraph which begins "There was a Being whom my spirit oft / Met," one is tempted to think of narrative verse paragraphs of *The Prelude* which seems to spring forth without apology for appearing at a given moment in the poem. All the difference between Shelley and Wordsworth might be caught in the juxtaposition of the incident beginning "There was a Being" to Wordsworth's incident "There was a boy" (*Prelude,* V.364–425). Yet there remains something essentially Wordsworthian about presenting dreamy youth as though it were an incident, a single spot of time to be revisited.

The three preceding paragraphs, under the veil of being Emily's wisdom, deliver a polemic against exclusiveness, moving from explicit vituperation against marriage to more abstract argument about division in emotional and intellectual commitments. These verse paragraphs thus concern on a thematic level (in terms of the structure of human relationships) what on a structural level Mr. Bloom calls the romantic lyric's stage of *tessera* or antithetical completion. The third paragraph, immediately preceding the dream vision, ends in a vision of what the Kabbalah calls *tikkun* or restitution of broken rhetorical figuraitons and a broken world:

> Mind from its object differs most in this:
> Evil from good; misery from happiness;

The baser from the nobler; the impure
And frail, from what is clear and must endure.
If you divide suffering and dross, you may
Diminish till it is consumed away;
If you divide pleasure and love and thought,
Each part exceeds the whole; and we know not
How much, while any yet remains unshared,
Of pleasure may be gained, of sorrow spared:
This truth is that deep well, whence sages draw
The unenvied light of hope; the eternal law
By which those live, to whom this world of life
Is as a garden ravaged, and whose strife
Tills for the promise of a later birth
The wilderness of this Elysian earth.   [ll. 174–89]

What seems like a rather careless profusion of value words in the first four lines may have been influenced by the argument against the narrow mind which limits its contemplation to one object. A mind not narrowly set in one frame of reference can associate with the idea of a limited object evil, misery, the base, the impure and frail. The next two lines suggest a hypothetical program for making the defects of the object world of nature easier to bear. One can no longer stick to the marriage referent, which would make dividing suffering and dross sound like a plan of social concern in which everyone spends a small number of hours with the sick, the ugly, or the poor in spirit so that no one is long bound to them. But one need not trouble oneself specifying why such a plan would prove impracticable; the speculation remains vague, in the realm of what "may be." On the other hand, the two lines suggesting the division of positive pleasures are extended and move out from the realm of what may be into imagined futurity. Spreading the kingdom of love, Shelley gathers into his fold the sages and believers in orthodox religious accounts who look forward to a time of *tikkun olam*—the restoration of a broken world when the dross of experiential loss will be redeemed under the reign of a God of Love.

Shelley distinguishes himself from the orthodox, "to whom

this world of life / Is as a garden ravaged," by posing an alternative, personal myth of shared love. *Epipsychidion* will end in an extended vision of an island paradise, replacing the Christian millennium. It proceeds, at this point, to an alternative to Christian Eden. Perhaps for this reason the last line before the dream-vision passage describes the post-Edenic world as "The wilderness of this Elysian earth." The adjective is a counter to the Christian myth, and marks Shelley's isolation from a mainstream of visionary orthodoxy. In Christian terms, or in the metaphor adopted by Mr. Bloom, this stage might be called *kenosis* or the putting off of manifest divinity in the service of this earth. Like the narrator of *Alastor,* who lays aside a transcendentalism and regresses by recounting the Poet's childlike faith in the continuity of nature, the poet of *Epipsychidion* undoes his visionary metaphysics by regressing to the childlike "clear golden prime of my youth's dawn" (1. 192).

Both poems depend on our ability to distinguish the softer antithetical vision of dreamy youth from the radical daemonized vision of the sublime. In *Alastor* Shelley identified the regressive stage with the faith in a Wordsworthian "natural piety," the faith in the metonymic contiguity of nature which allows the face of the earth to be explored the way an infant explores his mother's face. In *Epipsychidion* the *kenosis* of the poet does not exactly return him to a Wordsworthian earth, for the "visioned wanderings" of a spirit met by a Being on faery isles and imagined shores is a far cry from the wanderings lonely as a cloud of a poet whose encounters are wholly of and in the realm of the natural. Shelley regresses not to the romanticism of an earlier generation but to the gentler romanticism of a hypothetically earlier Shelley. The "caverns of dreamy youth" are caverns of Shelley's own dreamwork, birthplaces of the self-generated spirit who, fully awakened to his powers, will return to make those caverns his haunts. Here is the verse paragraph in its entirety:

> There was a Being whom my spirit oft
> Met on its visioned wanderings, far aloft,

In the clear golden prime of my youth's dawn,
Upon the fairy isles of sunny lawn,
Amid the enchanted mountains, and the caves
Of divine sleep, and on the air-like waves
Of wonder-level dream, whose tremulous floor
Paved her light steps;—on an imagined shore,
Under the gray beak of some promontory
She met me, robed in such exceeding glory
That I beheld her not. In solitudes
Her voice came to me through the whispering woods,
And from the fountains, and the odours deep
Of flowers, which, like lips murmuring in their sleep
Of the sweet kisses which had lulled them there,
Breathed but of her to the enamoured air;
And from the breezes whether low or loud,
And from the rain of every passing cloud,
And from the singing of the summer-birds,
And from all sounds, all silence. In the words
Of antique verse and high romance,—in form,
Sound, colour—in whatever checks that Storm
Which with the shattered present chokes the past;
And in that best philosophy, whose taste
Makes this cold common hell, our life, a doom
As glorious as a fiery martyrdom;
Her Spirit was the harmony of truth.   [ll. 190–216]

The Spirit sighted here is lost in—or rather at one with—a metonymic sea in which all names, all specificities of time and place, are washed together. "The caves / Of divine sleep" and the "waves / Of wonder-level dream" are not two locales but two attempts at representing a visionary landscape. "Her voice came to me through the whispering woods," less from nature than from the rhetorical effort of personifying nature. Even if we grant that woods and fountains are conventional haunts of nature spirits, we must see that the odors are autocthonically Shelleyan, and the extended simile they inspire (causing her, in this metaphor within metaphor, to be expired or breathed forth) evokes the spirit of love with a power suggestive of songful soul-creation in *Comus*. The impression of richly literary language of creation fades when the next four lines, each beginning with the words "And from," emphasize what look like natural origins. Until one has sorted the parts of the sentence one is perhaps more aware of the "from" than of the voice coming from breeze, rain, birds, and sounds. There is a temptation to rest in the very inquiry after origins—a temptation increased by the fact that one of the *froms* has been elided and we must expand the last line to read, "And from all sounds [and from] all silence." But that last line of ten about the origins of voice confronts us with the largest possible diffusion: all sound and all silence divide between them all possibilities, making of inclusive nature not a source but the general medium of voice. Thus *from,* like the opening *in* or the following *through,* really points to a mediating sense of place, and like the four *ins* of the next sentence leads us not to an original singleness but to shared—what the previous verse paragraph called "divided"—pleasure and love and thought.

The rather abstract line concluding the dream-vision paragraph summarizes the diffusion of Her Spirit and makes of the verse paragraph less a search for origins than a conglomerate original vision. The following lines make this clearer: "Then from the caverns of my dreamy youth / I sprang." With these words the preceding paragraph as a whole comes to represent the caverns of dreamy youth, and the generalized period of life called dreamy youth replaces a more specifiable source in dream visitation. The substitution retains the form of dream experience, however, for the words "I sprang" better describe being roused from a dream than they do the ordinarily gradual process of maturing. What springs forth at this point, as if from a dream rather than from any source in nature, is the first of several increasingly mature versions of the daemonized poetic spirit. As a poet, Shelley represses the distinction between mythological and actual past—just as Wordsworth repressed the distinction between the visionary gleam of childhood and that of mythological preexistence.

For Wordsworth, the substitution by which natural forms stand in a place said to have been originally above nature takes the form of metaphoric language barely noticeable as personification:

> —But there's a tree, of many one,
> A single field which I have look'd upon,
> Both of them speak of something that is gone:
>> The pansy at my feet
>> Doth the same tale repeat:
> Whither is fled the visionary gleam?
> Where is it now, the glory and the dream?
>
> [Intimations Ode]

Tree and field speak of the vanished dream—of what was more than nature—but they "speak" in wholly natural terms. Shelley risks more:

> A voice said:—'O thou of hearts the weakest,
> The phantom is beside thee whom thou seekest.'
> Then I—'Where?'—the world's echo answered 'where?'
> And in that silence, and in my despair,
> I questioned every tongueless wind that flew
> Over my tower of mourning, if it knew
> Whither 'twas fled, this soul out of my soul. [ll. 232–38]

If the questions concluding these two passages are not the same, the difference can only emphasize Shelley's determination to have his myth of loss a personal one. "This soul out of my soul," though it could be called a "visionary gleam," could not be said to come "From God, who is our home." For Shelley the soul is ultimately its own home, though the sense of loss requires a vocabulary of otherness. In place of Wordsworth's mild investiture of the landscape with voice, Shelley boldly appropriates the mechanism ("A voice said") and then demystifies what looks like supernature when voice is reduced to echo. In miniature this passage repeats the exchange *Epipsychidion* carries out between the passages of vision and those of natural quest. In the paragraph of dream vision, "Her voice came to me through the whispering woods"; in the paragraph of loss, the winds are "tongueless." Voice is power, and the search for voice is the quest of the whole poem.

If *Epipsychidion* ended shortly after this point, it could restrict vision to dreamy youth, and like Alastor picture experience stretching downward toward death from the occasion of dream vision. *Julian and Maddalo* gains subtlety in summarily recounting how the dream lady returns for a space to her enraptured love. And in *Prometheus Unbound* the recalled dream, like the resurgent Spirit of the Earth who runs up to Asia in Act III, stands for the ethic and the prophetic vision of recall that form the very subject of the poem. *Epipsychidion* might have been schematically easier with just the one period of dreamy youth, but Shelley required a myth of memory in which both the past recaptured and the moment of sublime presence would be dream visions having no part of nature. The appearance of Emily at the daemonized center of the poem purifies as it restores the concept of dream. Here again are the lines I identify as approaching the apex of the sublime, the point where the history of the past breaks off into apostrophe and eternal presence:

> This glorious One
> Floated into the cavern where I lay,
> And called my Spirit, and the dreaming clay
> Was lifted by the thing that dreamed below
> As smoke by fire, and in her beauty's glow
> I stood, and felt the dawn of my long night
> Was penetrating me with living light.   [ll. 336–42]

The cavern image, important to the prophetic analogue for such experience,[13] recalls "the caverns of my dreamy youth" and makes of life generally, as Plato did in the famous myth, a cave but occasionally visited by light. Almost magically, the passage manages to retain its reservations about the externality of transcendental experience in the very phrases that describe it. The illumination is not from above but from below—internal, as it were—and "the dawn of my long night" is a dawn as much the

property of as an interference upon the night of life. The passage
ostensibly records that which surpasses and redeems one from
dream; but dreamy clay is lifted by "the thing that dreamed
below," and dream vision remains the source of transcendence.

Like *Prometheus Unbound, Epipsychidion* ends with an extended celebration of prophetic vision that circles round and sees
in redeemed time "echoes of an antenatal dream." The paradisal
place, which is given an origin "in the world's young prime,"
returns in a way to the visionary space of the dream passage,
"In the clear golden prime of my youth's dawn." It returns also
to the source of poetic voice and represents in extended narrative
the fluency that marks poetic power. Restored too is the vision of
power transcending particular voicings, the vision emphasized
in the original dream passage by having the list of sources of
voice culminate in "all silence." In the new place talk will be
empowered

> until thought's melody
> Become too sweet for utterance, and it die
> In words, to live again in looks, which dart
> With thrilling tone into the voiceless heart,
> Harmonizing silence without a sound.   [ll. 560–64]

Until such time, however, the voiceless heart is too closely
allied to vacancy, and words must be the vehicle of all images
of the soul's transcendence, just as they prove ultimately "The
chains of lead around its flight of fire."

vi

Approaching *The Triumph of Life* from consideration of
dream vision elsewhere in Shelley's poetry, one is in a position
both privileged and precarious. The danger, as Harold Bloom
has shown in surveying some eminent readings of *The Triumph*,[14] lies in the temptation to impose one poem on another.
Having seen a number of shapes all light from Cythna to Emily,
or having observed the hierarchy of luminous bodies in *Epipsy-*

chidion, one may unguardedly let associations substitute for con-
textual explications. The privilege, on the other hand, lies in
education to the deceptiveness of dream spirits, coupled with
awareness of the compulsion to seek for embodiments of that
which transcends the light of common day. Having seen the
Alastor poet or the madman of *Julian and Maddalo* haunted by
their recollections of idealized maidens, one is suspicious of any
visionary lady offering the nepenthe love. At the same time, the
reader of *Laon and Cythna, Prometheus Unbound,* and *Epipsychidion* will resist the temptation to see in *The Triumph of Life*
only a radical demystification of all "light diviner than the common sun." Ironic awareness of delusion may triumph over
daemonized poetic consciousness; life may triumph over that
which is glimpsed in dream vision. But these triumphs—the same
triumph—are at least as ambiguous as that of Apollonius in
Keats's *Lamia,* and closely allied to death.

What is certain, amid the attractions and risks of seeing the
pattern of other poems repeated in *The Triumph of Life,* is the
fact—indeed the subject—of repetition itself. The poem's most
expansive vision concerns the repeated triumph of life over individual experience and aspiration; its form—vision unfolding
within vision within vision—suggests the internalization of a
pattern of repetition. Its dominant incident involves the experience of Rousseau spoken as a warning against repeating the
dance of death. And the Induction already presents vision
entangled with an awareness of repetition:

I knew

> That I had felt the freshness of that dawn,
> Bathed in the same cold dew my brow & hair
> And sate as thus upon that slope of lawn
>
> Under the self same bough, & heard as there
> The birds, the fountains & the Ocean hold
> Sweet talk in music through the enamoured air.
> And then a Vision on my brain was rolled.   [ll. 33–40]

Though it is the dawn's freshness that the poet recognizes, awareness of déjà vu overrides any mystique about freshness or an
original time. The irony—the opening irony which allows Shelley
to make a fresh beginning—is that one expects an antithesis
between repetitious nature, on the one hand, and, on the other,
visionary experience as a departure from or transcendence of
diurnal pattern. Instead, it seems that nature itself is perceived
in apocalyptic terms while dream vision confronts the specter of
repetition. When the Induction opens by comparing the sun to
a spirit hastening to his task, the sun seems energized like a newly
conscious Prometheus, and the mask of darkness falls as if for
a final revelation; when the trance opens, the dreamer confronts
a "perpetual flow / Of people" as bound to Life as gnats or
leaves are bound to cyclic nature.

The exception to those so bound are the few who shunned
the cycles and compromises of experience and "Fled back like
eagles to their native noon." A retreat to native noon, all involved in self and self-destruction, cannot be more than an
exception; Socrates and Jesus may be worthy of admiration, but
they are not examples which call for repetition of their patterns.
Though Christians may wish to imitate Christ, they only mock
in the worst sense when they have in mind the death instinct of
their hero. Even if Socrates and Jesus are singled out not because
they were suicides but because they did not write, because they
left to others the task of stereotyping moments of original Presence, the fact remains that to imitate someone's originality is to
fall further victim of a repetition compulsion. Nonetheless "they
of Athens or Jerusalem" help identify the avoidance of repetition—or avoidance of awareness of repetition—with the return
to sources of power. Socrates and Jesus represent the good
daemons of the world who, from the vantage of their native
noon, preside over the daemonization of poetic consciousness
when Shelley and his surrogate Rousseau repress awareness of
repetition and achieve their highest moments of rhetorical power.

There are three moments in the poem where Rousseau's claim

to originality is urged by sheer rhetorical gesture. The first finds him distinguishing himself from others who battled Life and were conquered by her:

> "In the battle Life & they did wage
> She remained conqueror—I was overcome
> By my own heart alone, which neither age

> "Nor tears nor infamy nor now the tomb
> Could temper to its object."   [ll. 239–43]

In colloquial terms he "did himself in," but if one attempts to pursue the figure of speech to a meaning beyond figuration, one may be at a loss to specify precisely what he did or did not do. Suicide is not the literal referent and origin of the figure; neither is it easy to understand by "my own heart alone" Rousseau's sensual appetite as revealed in his autobiographical writing. Rousseau is asserting the power of his own romanticism—the power to repress awareness of the reality principle and be overcome by the limits of one's desire rather than the limitations the world presses on one. In the battle with death-in-life his defense of repression proved stronger than Voltaire's and Kant's defenses of sublimation; "I am a hero of the daemonized romantic consciousness," he appears to assert, "while the eighteenth-century figures I mentioned are victims of the reality-orientation imposed by Life's *askesis of* the spirit." Whatever the historical validity of this claim, it is given poetic validity in that Shelley is moved to reject, with Rousseau, the idea that the Enlightenment brought anything more than an illusion of something new:

> "Let them pass"—
> I cried—"the world & its mysterious doom

> "Is not so much more glorious than it was
> That I desire to worship those who drew
> New figures on its false & fragile glass

> "As the old faded."   [ll. 243–48]

In a poem so haunted by the specter of repetition and the dis-
illusioning light of common day, it is notably safer to assert one's
own imaginative prowess by rejecting others' newness than by
flaunting one's own. Like the suspicious daemonization of the
Poet in *Alastor*, Rousseau's romantic dream may be summed up
in the phrase, "I was overcome / By my own heart alone." Like
the narrator's antithetical daemonization in *Alastor*, Shelley's
(Shelley the narrator's) daemonization may be summed up in
the rejecting gesture, "Let them pass!" He half assumes Rousseau's stance in rejecting what Rousseau rejects. But he puts on
Rousseau's power without committing himself to the same
illusion about being self-begotten and self-betrayed.

A second rhetorical climax follows hard upon the first when
Rousseau identifies the repression on which poetic strength is
based (repression of "the mutiny within," l. 213) with the self-
control of the "bards of old who inly quelled / The passions
which they sung" (ll. 274–75). As a gesture of self-pity rather
than the repetition in a finite mode of the infinite I AM, Rousseau's assertion comes as something of a Byronic parody of
daemonic consciousness. Rousseau reaches outward rather than
soaring upward at this point, and he is met by Shelley's brief
but sufficient gesture of support:

> "—I
> Have suffered what I wrote, or viler pain!—
>
> "And so my words were seeds of misery—
> Even as the deeds of others."—"Not as theirs,"
> I said—he pointed to a company. . . .   [ll. 278–82]

In the first exchange Shelley overlooked Rousseau's statement
about himself in order to share with Rousseau the powerful
prophetic stance of rejecting others. This time Shelley responds
more specifically to what Rousseau says about himself, and by
reaffirming Rousseau's uniqueness reunites speaker and auditor
into a single identity, the separate projections of which are cap-

able of assuming the stance of the high sublime. Though the sublime may be defined as language that seems almost to create the object or addressee it contemplates, language that evokes response from an actual other belongs to the middle, conversational mode. Here it forms a critique of the first climax in Rousseau's speech, and marks the distance ahead till the third and definitive claim made by Rousseau for his own power.

In *Poetry and Repression,* Harold Bloom identifies the lines from 412 on as the *apophrades* or return of the dead.[15] Mr. Bloom is interested in the return of Wordsworth; we may note that Rousseau also returns in that he repeats, in a finer tone, the high rhetoric of his own assertion of individuality:

> "I among the multitude
> Was swept; me sweetest flowers delayed not long,
>   Me not the shadow nor the solitude,
>
> "Me not the falling stream's Lethean song,
>   Me, not the phantom of that early form
> Which moved upon its motion,—but among
>
> "The thickest billows of the living storm
> I plunged, and bared my bosom to the clime
>   Of that cold light, whose airs too soon deform.—"
>
> [ll. 460–68]

If we again pose the light-of-day question, "Just what is the difference between being swept away by death-in-life and plunging into the (ironically labeled) 'living storm'?" we may respond, with all the more conviction, that the less difference it seems to make the purer the rhetorical stance. Having no meaning (no precise meaning) in terms of the natural history of the man Rousseau, this statement of attitude escapes the mimetic function of language; it escapes being a repetition, and comes as pure daemonization.

As always, Bloom's map of the romantic crisis lyric serves the purpose of alerting us to what distinguishes a given poem

from the repetition it would be if it fit too neatly into the pattern
of the map. Dependent on Rousseau's repression of awareness
that the end is the same whether one falls or plunges into the
stream, this rhetorical climax in the sixth or *apophrades* section
of the poem captures a power properly mapped at stage four,
the *daemonization* section. If the sublime style rises to the point
where it seems to create the object or addressee it contemplates,
Shelley's question, "Then, what is life?" at the end of the poem
marks Rousseau's achievement of a rhetorical height not equalled
by the earlier moments to which Shelley responded with "Let
them pass!" (l. 243) and "Not as theirs" (l. 281). More important, what Bloom identifies as the fifth section, the *askesis* of
the poem (ll. 300–41) takes on the tone and function of the
kenosis section ordinarily preceding and calling forth an anti-
phonal daemonization. We have seen, in *Alastor* and *Epipsychidion,* that the *kenosis* of the poet involves a descent into
Wordsworthian nature; the poet lays aside the sense that he is
a supreme spirit, and entertains the faith in the metonymic
contiguity of the face of nature, the faith that one can go anywhere, encounter anything, and discover the sense sublime of
something "deeply interfused," the maternal Presence. In *Alastor*
and *Epipsychidion* the *kenosis* sections included prehistories of
the (Wordsworthian) soul not yet born into fully daemonized
(Shelleyan) power. In *The Triumph of Life* the prehistory of
the soul is recounted by Rousseau in what Bloom calls the *askesis*
section. Here then, in structural terms, is a key to the "originality" of *The Triumph of Life*: in this poem about repetition the
askesis returns us to a *kenosis,* and the *aphophrades* returns us
to a *daemonization.* The only escape from "this valley of perpetual dream," as Rousseau calls it, is further dream—or rather
antecedent dream, dream about mythical antecedence or the
romantic origin of one's battle with death-in-life. In *Alastor* we
find out early and relatively briefly about the "solemn vision,
and bright silver dream" by which the infancy of the Poet was

nurtured. *Epipsychidion* expands the dream state into something of a Wordsworthian incident or spot of time. *The Triumph of Life* returns to dream origins of romantic consciousness in a section that is at once the *kenosis* of Rousseau (who lays aside his sense of himself to recount this Wordsworthian myth) and the *askesis* of Shelley the narrator (who learns the bitter truth that whether or not a moment of daemonization succeeds, the glories of solipsistic consciousness are washed away in the onslaught of death-in-life).

Shelley's critics have noted the poetic justice of having Rousseau, father of state-of-nature romanticism, appear first in the totally naturalized form of "an old root." The greater poetic justice seems to me to lie in having Rousseau, who understood the delusiveness of all accounts of origins, represent for the last time the kind of dream vision Shelley has repeatedly used as a point of origin. The question "How did thy course begin?" (l. 297) calls for a spiritual, not a biological, history of the self, and so it is understood by Rousseau when he begins to discover to the poet whence he came. When the "sacred few" were described as fleeing "soon / As they had touched the world with living flame," touching the world did not mean entering life as newborn infants but entering the world of experience. Rousseau's account likewise concerns soul-birth at a stage in developing consciousness:

> In the April prime
> When all the forest tops began to burn
>
> With kindling green, touched by the azure clime
> Of the young year, I found myself asleep
> Under a mountain which from unknown time
>
> Had yawned into a cavern high & deep.   [ll. 308–13]

Like the images of "the clear golden prime of my youth's dream" and "the caverns of my dreamy youth" in *Epipsychidion,* these lines depend on the accessibility of landscape phenomena as metaphors for consciousness. An easy commerce between the natural and the transcendent permits budding leaves to be spoken of as burning—an image representing, in Moses's vision, that which is beyond nature. Similarly, the mountain yawns into a cavern, as though the sleep metaphor and its implications about the growth of the unconscious could be registered in landscape terms. Like the caverns of dreamy youth, this cavern appears to be the source of a fountain whose waters' sound brings a new sense of presence. The *Epipsychidion* dreamer felt "Her voice came to me . . . from the fountains"; Rousseau hears sounds with the power of an "oblivious spell."

If the forgetfulness induced by the sound of these waters were forgetfulness of a prenatal state, the narrative would soon exhaust the metaphor of childbirth. If what were forgotten were a realm of childhood innocence, Rousseau would be presenting a paradigmatic psychology of adolescence in which certainty about stages could take the place of the indefiniteness of childhood encounters with forms of desire. But insofar as the forgetfulness is a Lethean forgetfulness of his historical self, the narrative concerns an afterlife of interest in that it repeats and re-presents the stages in the growth of consciousness in this life.[16] The examples in ll. 318–30 suggest that what is forgotten is the historical world we know, the world of experience and loss. To die, perchance to dream—and be condemned to repeat eternally the awarenesses and anxieties of life? To imagine a death of the old self, rather than a literal death and bondage to eternal repetition, one must presuppose a kind of forgetfulness so that one may be laid asleep in body to become a living soul. A certain obliviousness to the world is a precondition for being awake to transcendent visitations, and one necessarily represses or lays to sleep one's knowledge of the world in approaching a given encounter as otherworldly. The point is clearest in, though not confined to, sexual terms: to approach a given lady as though she were what the *Epipsychidion* poet calls "veiled Divinity," one needs to be oblivious of what one knows about the loss of previous illusions, sexual or otherwise.

"How did thy course begin?" the poet asks, and if Rousseau's account focuses on the origins of sexual illusion, it is because there one has most illusion of being able to locate the beginnings of the course of repetition. To be drawn by the chariot of life is to be bound on a wheel of desire, condemned to repeat the cycle of intellectual or libidinal attachment, disillusion, forgetfulness, reinvestment in a new visitation, and new disillusion. *Epipsychidion* detailed a number of libido attachments and disillusions, but hoped to discover in Emily the visitation that would lead the poet centrifugally from the wheel of desire into a world elsewhere. In *The Triumph of Life,* Shelley pursues more relentlessly the forms of repetition, and presents a "Shape all light" who stands for all the psychidions of his poems and others'. The Shape may have been suggested by Dante, by Wordsworth, by Rousseau's *Nouvelle Eloise,* in the climactic chapter of which St. Preu says of Julie, "elle aime les promenades sur l'eau," which could be Englished out of its common idiom by a relentless pursuer of the origins of metaphor into the water-walking lady. The question is not, however, the source of the Shape but what the Shape has to offer in the quest for source—for a point of origins which will transcend repetition.

Rousseau repeats to the Shape the poet's question to him:

> If, as it doth seem,
> Thou comest from the realm without a name,

> Into this valley of perpetual dream,
>   Shew whence I came, and where I am, and why—
> Pass not away upon the passing stream.   [ll. 395–99]

In an unpublished essay on *The Triumph of Life,* David Quint notes that the illusion-inspired desire, "Pass not away!" contrasts with Shelley's enlightened gesture of resignation in line 243, "Let them pass!" Rousseau associates the Shape's "non-representa-

tional imaginative origins ('the realm without a name') with
some kind of divine or eternal order of truth; he wants to believe
in the neoplatonic myth which the poem is at pains to deconstruct." Similar to the process of mystification by which one
representational Shape is elevated beyond sign into ultimate significance is the mystification by which one dreamy realm is
projected beyond the leveling designation of "perpetual dream"
into the status of true source. The mythology in which Shelley's
Rousseau would believe is not simply neoplatonic, or that of the
historical Rousseau's presumed idealizations of love, or that of
Wordsworth's idealizations of nature; it is also that which Shelley
himself projected in earlier poems—the romantic origins any
poet must hypothesize whether as object of belief or object for
the imaginative work of demystification. One can represent the
fact that the ostensible deconstruction of a neoplatonic or Rousseauistic myth is for Shelley an act of imaginative self-curtailment
by asking other Shelleyan dream visions to stand the test of these
lines. What Shelley represented as the caverns of dreamy youth
in *Epipsychidion* have been transformed in the phrasing of
Rousseau's question into "this valley of perpetual dream."

If there is no answer to the "whence" that Shelley and
Rousseau inquire about but a further view of the cycle of
repetition, this does not mean that there is no "deep truth," or
that "the deep truth is imageless"; the truth—or rather half the
truth—is precisely that each request for the "whence" of origins
invites mystification. The attractiveness and inevitability of our
idealizations are apprehended in the poet's images and Shape
of repetition. In *Prometheus Unbound*. Demogorgon elides the
distinction between the world and representations of it when he
asks Asia, "what would it avail to bid thee gaze / On the
revolving world?" When the Shape offers Rousseau the cup of
nepenthe, she takes him out of the role of gazer or spectator and
makes of him a participant in or victim of these shaping fancies.
He finds another form of oblivion, and another metaphor for the
vanishing forms of desire. As the fair Shape wanes in the coming

light, Rousseau becomes like a stargazing lover who hopes "That his day's path may end as he began it / In that star's smile" whose morning-star–evening-star identity really does stand for constancy, but ironically that of the repetition pattern, not of one love's devotion: every Venus is a Lucifer, and every enticement of love a further tie to a cycle of mystification, loss, and de-mystification.

When he sees "a new vision, never seen before," the extended simile introducing that vision belies the idea of newness or an approach to origins except as a further image of repetition:

> And suddenly my brain became as sand
>
> > Where the first wave had more than half erased
> > The track of deer on desert Labrador,
> > Whilst the fierce wolf from which they fled amazed
>
> > Leaves his stamp visibly upon the shore
> > Until the second bursts.   [ll. 405–10]

In *Prometheus Unbound,* the Fifth Spirit describes a form like the Shape all Light, one "whose footsteps paved the world with light"; the Sixth Spirit describes Desolation treading "with lulling footsteps" and soothing "to false repose" as Rousseau has been soothed. In *The Triumph,* the moment isolated between wave cycles finds one set of footsteps already fading and another soon to be effaced. The waves will come again, and even the image of a fading form of desire will be replaced by a new oblivion and new images of desire and desolation.

When the waves subside in the Genesis account of the Flood, the rainbow establishes God's promise that the world will not be again visited by such desolation. But while God's creation endures, man's created forms of desire are condemned to repeated floods, and the appearance of the rainbow "arch of victory" in *The Triumph of Life* comments ironically on all efforts to transcend the cycles of illusion and disillusion. With a truly Dantesque touch of pride, Rousseau attempts to distinguish himself as one who was not captivated by the elements of illusion but recognized destruction's inevitability: "Among / The thickest billows of that living storm / I plunged." Yet it makes less and less difference, as vision unfolds upon vision, whether one identifies oneself "finally" as a prophet of illusion or of disillusion. *Alastor* represented the daemonization of the disillusioned narrator as following hard upon the dreamy daemonization of the illusioned Poet. *Julian and Maddalo* gently suggested something of an alternating current flowing between, and energizing the representatives of, illusion and disillusion. Though there is throughout Shelley's career a desire to envision a more linear psychic history—historically tempered in *Laon and Cythna,* insistent in *Epipsychidion,* daemonically frenzied in *Adonais,* preeminent in *Prometheus Unbound*—he returns in *The Triumph of Life* to the awareness that even the poetic forms of mystification and demystification appear in cycles. An *askesis* can be hard to tell from a *kenosis,* and another limitation can produce another representation of daemonized poetic consciousness, only to fade again before the light of common day. Yeats, who understood so well what it meant for a poet like Shelley to discover the primal scene of his secret life and recur to it, historicized to some extent in his own poetic development a single path through increasingly complex images of worldly disillusion and transcendental escape to increasingly this-worldly images of reality. For Shelley the caverns of dreamy youth more decidedly belong not to the poet's actual youth but to a repeatedly reimagined place of origin from which the poet springs again and again.

As *The Triumph of Life* reaches its point of breaking off, Rousseau pictures a creative process sadly juxtaposed to natural process. Forms of desire turn into shadows of desire, "And of this stuff the car's creative ray / Wrought all the busy phantoms that were there" (ll. 533–34). Only the most blatant irony could make that ray look creative. But it is more than irony, and ultimately more than metaphor, which recalls "the joy which waked like Heaven's glance / The sleepers in the oblivious valley." Joys die. A Shape all light may prove to be what *Epipsychidion* calls a "cold chaste moon"; another may retain "a gentler trace / Of light diviner than the common sun." But "Heaven's glance" has for Shelley no reality which joys mock; in their morning the joys *are* heaven's glance. And each glance is a return to the dawn of dreamy youth.

CHAPTER 5

George Darley:
Buoyant as Young Time[1]

> O Zarathustra, thou stone of wisdom, thou sling-stone, thou star-destroyer! Thyself threwest thou so high, but every thrown stone—must fall! . . . I ascended, I ascended, I dreamt, I thought—but everything oppressed me. A sick one did I resemble, whom bad torture weareth, and a worse dream reawakeneth out of his first sleep. But there is something in me which I call courage: it hath hitherto slain for me every dejection. This courage at last bade me stand still and say: "Dwarf! Thou! Or I!"
> He who hath ears to hear, let him hear.
>
> Nietzsche, *Thus Spake Zarathustra*

In 1840, George Darley wrote to a friend complaining about poor reception of the drama *Thomas à Becket* and bemoaning his inability to achieve recognition as a poet: "Why have a score of years not established my title with the world? Why did not 'Sylvia', with all its faults, ten years since? It ranked me among the *small* poets. I had as soon be ranked among the piping bullfinches.[2] The ranking has not much changed over the years, and even the very beautiful *Nepenthe* has received little notice. Reading Darley's poems and prose pieces, one is less surprised at the status of his reputation than at the conscious and unconscious ways he cultivated the implications of being a "small poet." *Thomas à Becket* and *Ethelstan* are deliberately written as closet dramas, and struggle against their lyricism as if asking to be ignored. *Nepenthe* was not only privately and badly printed; the poem itself hides behind obscurity and the pretense of being a fragment of a more "humanitarian" whole. The pastoral drama *Sylvia*, like Darley more generally, is remembered—when remembered—not for larger designs but for the small, sometimes exquisite lyrics buried in it.

Darley's smallness is not merely a judgment of literary historians or a painful realization in the history of the poet's own consciousness; it is a *seminal* theme—a major aspect of the search for generative origins. Underlying Darley's best work is what we might call a myth of weakness: that the poet is of diminutive scale, and that he stands a minor to the major or full-grown poets before him. Can one wish to be small? Can the image of diminutive stature impel, and not merely mark a diminishment in, creative process? Before extending this argument to Darley generally—and by implication to all poets struggling for a place in literary history—one must confront the frustration Darley expressed in the 1840 letter, the frustration that must attend, or that must motivate, the search for images of diminutiveness.

i

Perhaps it is no accident that the disappointment often expressed in Darley's correspondence should achieve its most open form in a letter about *Thomas à Becket*. He looks back to *Sylvia,* but it is *Becket* whose failure brings out the frustration and anger. Darley complains that the few who read the play disliked the grotesque dwarf Dwerga. "To me it seems, of course, the highest creation in the work."

Malicious as Iago, insightful as the fool in *Lear,* Dwerga haunts Darley's most realized attempt at Jacobean theater as a specter of all that is dwarfish in man. Herself a fiend of energy, she embodies what makes others conniving rather than grand, small-minded rather than heroic. She calls the queen in whose service she is employed "grandam"—much to the queen's distaste—and explains that having been fed for years on the delicacies of a witches' brew, she has been nursed into deformity:

Dwerga: What made me, pray you
            All that I am, but this fine food? Thou art,
            Then, my creatress; and I am thy creature.

Queen: My creature, not my offspring.
Dwerga: Oh, thou thought'st
        I meant thy very babe. [I.ii]³

Though distinguishing between the order of nature (mother and
child) and the order of politics (master and slave), this interchange does not distance the queen from the nastiness of having
Dwerga her "creature." Dwerga is attached to Queen Eleanor
as Eleanor is attached to mischief, as—in a comparison only
Dwerga could suggest—a horse leech is fond of blood. Dwarfishness becomes not simply a matter of diminished form but a form
of the power of diminishment, the power to feed on the life of
others.

   Besides being responsible for most of the action in the Eleanor
subplot of the play, Dwerga is specifically a demystifier. Like a
deconstructionist critic facing the privileged objects and moments
of others' symbol-schemes, she becomes at her best a prophet of
negativity whose energy exceeds what one might have thought
the context could inspire. Her final achievement is to penetrate
the embowered labyrinth of Rosamond—who is more a mythical
emblem of chastity, a literary symbol that needs to be demystified,
than a mistress of the king. Perhaps Dwerga's most awful appearance is in the scene where Eleanor is consulting a conjurer,
trying to discover the identity of her rival. Just as the conjurer
invokes Eleanor's double, Dwerga comes forth and "the fiend-
shape flies." Substituting her own presence for what she reveals
to be a theatrical device of the conjurer's (one of his "familiars"
coming up from the trap door), Dwerga appears like "a real
devil" banishing the fantasy one. Though personified as a character, she represents the real devil in Eleanor, and she makes no
secret of the relationship between her mistress's thoughts and the
external action. Dismayed at having been played upon, Eleanor
asks, "And am I / The dupe of such poor tricksters, then?"
Dwerga answers, "No, grandma; / Of thy own folly rather!"
Not only the conjurer but Dwerga herself is Eleanor's own folly.

   Darley recognized his greatest dramatic power to lie in such revelation of man's dwarfishness. Besides taking grotesque form, as with Eleanor and Dwerga, smallness could appear in more genial form, as with Rosamond and Prince Richard. The clear slate the dramatist could not give Henry II he is able to accord his son Richard I—in his minority. Having chased "the fiend" Dwerga off stage, young Richard is rewarded by the fair Rosamond with a choice of titles:

> Shall I call you
> Herculean Cupid, for thy beauteous strength,
> Or, for thy generous courage, Coeur-de-Lion?   [V.ii]

The rejected, more oxymoronic epithet expresses the paradoxical nature of human achievement: nobility can be actualized only in a context of limitation, in a world of cupids, not among real and adulterous lovers. Uncaged—outside this bower of cupid and fair lady—the lionhearted prove diminished by political actuality; the young cub is the only possible image of nobility.

The major plot of *Thomas à Becket* involves the tragedy of a man impelled by his conscience or his pride not to accept diminished status. In refusing to stoop to the king, Becket necessarily arrogates to his physical being a Goliath-like eminence bound to tumble before the slings and arrows of outraged Fortune. It is, to be sure, the office, not the physical person, that Becket would elevate to heights beyond the king's reach, but when he is attacked in Canterbury Cathedral, more than the bishop's robes are run through by the king's swordsmen. In a sense it is hard to separate the fall of the character from the fall of the play. So sure is Darley of the exclusive authenticity of littleness that the effort at heroic martyrdom seems bound to fail. Perhaps the dramatist simply did not resolve to his own satisfaction the conflicting moral statuses of vaunting ambition and stubborn heroism. Or if Becket actually grows from one to the other, we could say that whereas the larger-than-life hero is rather crudely destroyed, the earlier ambitious Becket is more subtly undermined by his own rhetoric. Contemplating the dizzy heights of his ambition, he actualizes in speech what Darley called, in the title of another poem, the errors of ecstasy:

> To our minds
> Alone, we may—by custom of great thoughts,
> By venturous deeds and versancy with power,
> Ambrosial food of books, august discourse,
> By every straining towards some height from which
> Our former selves look little—to our minds
> We may add stature, cubit upon cubit,
> Until in them we become Anakim,
> Nobler than earth e'er form'd!   [II.iii]

The means betray the end, which is not inner nobility but the appearance of grandeur. What "to our minds" may be added are not the heights of romantic satanism but the dwarfed desire to appear great. At his most "sublime" Becket feels his "very frame grown gigantical," but unlike Milton's Satan he never questions externality, and rather mourns the absence of pre-eminence of form than exults in preeminence of independent mind. He contemplates ways in which his "mien and move-ments" could signify grandeus of soul and sets down as a rule of conduct that "giant-minded things / Disclaim the pigmy natural to most men." The qualifier "most" stands ready to ensnare the man who would aspire beyond his own pigmy nature. In a sense the fall has already taken place when giant-mindedness is con-ceived as snobbery rather than solipsism.

With *Thomas à Becket*, Darley hoped to gain recognition not as a giant poet but as a small voice capable of stirring his readers into dramatic recognition of the "pigmy nature" of all men. Among Darley's major works, *Becket* was the one most available for popularizing his theme. Small wonder the failure of recogni-tion, even from his friends, roused his anxiety about his "right to be called 'poet.'"

ii

Let us return to the questions Darley asked in his letter: "Why have a score of years not established my title with the world?

Why did not 'Sylvia', with all its faults, ten years since?" Questions about fame, like fame itself, are best pursued indirectly; I should like instead to explore how *Sylvia* itself pursues a more difficult myth of minority.

The induction to *Sylvia* (1827) could be taken from these lines introducing another poem, "Harvest Home":

> Dreamer, wake up!—and with me hie
> Thither!—Thine Elfin Genius I,
>   Soul of thy fitful mirth!
> No sprite who mid the starry spheres
> Spends all his angel time in tears
>   Over unhappy Earth.
>
> Half earth is dark, but half is bright;
> If darkness thee, and the demons, delight,
>   Keep to thy bower still;
> There, in sad triumph, cypress-bound,
> Like statue in his own fountain drowned,
>   Sit darkling if thou will.[4]

The enchanted valley in which *Sylvia* takes place is divided, like the earth in pastoral miniature, between dark and bright, shade and sunlight, and the two realms are presided over respectively by fiends and fairies. Darley is the "Elfin Genius" neither inspired by a heavenly muse nor concerned with the kind of tragic recognition that would call forth tears such as angels weep. The pastoral poet, soul of mirth, not only sides with the fairies rather than the fiends—or, in terms of mood, with "L'Allegro" rather than "Il Penseroso"; he also diminishes the level of tension between the opposing moods or moral sides.

Throughout *Sylvia* the music continues sweet, the plot drawn out by the mildest of entanglements. It is astonishing how the elements of tension—which might distinguish the giants of Elizabethan pastoral from lesser practitioners—are so studiously diminished. Finally, in Act V, Sylvia strays into shady (demon) territory, and it is time for the little elfin battle over her soul.

Morgana, queen of the Fairies, cries "War be the word, and Battle be the cry!"

With this line the scene breaks off, and we are treated not to a diminutive war in heaven but to an invocation of Milton in which Darley confronts his own diminutiveness. What Milton meant to Darley is illuminated by this passage in Darley's Introduction to *The Works of Beaumont and Fletcher:*

Milton seems to have been our first bird of untireable pinion, who could sustain himself for a long flight through the loftiest empyrean without almost one descent from his sublime level—in truth a "mighty Orb of Song," which power so divine projected, that it could swerve but little out of its course till completed. But our earlier poets are heteroclite beings, half giants, half dwarfs; their genius is at perpetual suicide and self-resurrection; here they crawl as awkwardly as land-crabs, there they swallow the ground with noblest swiftness like warhorses; we might assimilate their works to pantomimes, wherein a Sylph springs out of a wheelbarrow, or *hey presto!*—and a throne sinks, leaving its occupant seated on the bare floor.[5]

As a dramatist and lyric poet Darley attempts to regain some of the power of "our earlier poets," perhaps even mythologizing their capacity for genius "at perpetual suicide and self-resurrection" in the figure of the phoenix of *Nepenthe.* Milton's status he never questions. But when he concludes his Introduction by noticing *The Faithful Shepherdess,* yet insisting "a fine English Pastoral Drama remains to be written," his own ambition is clear. He cultivates the virtues of the Elizabethan lyricist and Jacobean playwright, hoping not merely to reproduce their "heteroclite being," but, by not aspiring to be "half-giant," to perfect the half dwarf.

In the *Sylvia* Invocation to Milton, Darley makes his most explicit statements about poetic stature. Since the text is not readily available, I will quote in sections the first eighty lines.

> O thou dread Bard! whose soul of fire
> Moved o'er the dark-string'd Epic lyre,
> Till brightening where thy spirit swept

> Lustre upon its dimness crept,
> And at thy word, from dull repose
> The Light of heavenly Song arose!

Milton's sublimity is dramatized by having images of power precede, and seem to call into being, images of beauty. Noticeably
absent at this point is direct reference to Milton's blindness, for
Darley is concerned not with the corporeal man but the idealized, almost abstract idea of the poet. The darkness in the second
line is the obscurity in which origins are necessarily shrouded,
for no tracing of a poem to its tradition or machinery can ultimately "illuminate" the process of its generation. One can only
mythologize origins, and so Darley uses the metaphor of angelic
visitation, which is all the more authenticated as a version of
spiritual beginning because of the corporeal or literal contradiction in having the shadow lighten rather than darken where it
sweeps. (The figure reverses Milton's moon, which "o'er the dark
her Silver Mantle threw," *PL,* IV.609.) Darley's lines do not
simply refer back to Milton's power the way Milton refers his
own power back to the inspiration of the Holy Ghost. "At thy
word" seems to reverse the priorities as assumed in Milton's own
invocations and to make the poet awaken or beget the heavenly,
not the other way round.

At this point, touching the poet's greatest ambition, Darley
turns from Milton to himself:

> O that this lyric shell of mine
> Were like thy harp, Minstrel divine!
> With thunder-chords intensely strung,
> To chime with thy audacious song
> That scorned all deeds to chronicle
> Less than the wars of Heaven and Hell:
> O that this most despised hand
> Could sweep so beautifully grand
> The nerves Tyrtaean!—I would then
> Storm at the souls of little men,
> And raise them to a nobler mood
> Than that Athenian Master could!

That the longing is to share divine Miltonic power—rather than to stand with Milton, receiving divine power—is specified by the second line. If one were to add a comma after "Minstrel," Milton would be subordinated to the divine and the poets could together stand as aspirants. Darley is, however, far more concerned to put Miltonic grandeur out of reach. The lines that follow specify Milton's power as that by which wars of heaven and hell may be told in verse. Ostensibly, that power accounts for the presence of the invocation at this point in *Sylvia*. Darley had reached the juncture in his story Pope reached with the cutting of Belinda's hair in *The Rape of the Lock* and it is time for a miniature war in heaven. But Darley is writing pastoral, not mock heroic, and the war must be avoided. He wishes to be small, but not comic; wise in his weakness, not sparkling in playfulness.

At the same time that Milton's power to depict war in heaven is acknowledged, the threat posed by his power is limited to the heroic rather than the pastoral. Darley invokes the Milton of *Paradise Lost* VI, as though making that giant visible lured us from considering the Milton of *Paradise Lost* IV. A similar preemption of place occurs later when Darley confesses himself no swan and bemoans the anticipated bitter fate of perishing Lycidas-like, "Amid this lone deserted stream . . . And for my hollow knell shall teem / Its dittying waters over me." Not only does he diminish the "whelming tide" to "dittying waters"; by not attempting heroic voice he eschews the angry revenge of Milton who might "to avenge the deed / . . . blast me, impious." He thus leaves the hypothetically angered Milton in something of the position of St. Peter, while the pastoral voice superbly Milton's in *Lycidas* seems unthreatened when Darley takes it up as author of *Sylvia*.

Simply claiming the pastoral while leaving Milton the heroic would not suffice as a defense mechanism, and Darley shies further away from power by supposing that, if it were his, he would "Storm at the souls of little men." The comfortable implication is that with power, littleness would still be his sphere, even granted the ambition to make little men noble. When he then goes on to reject the power he would use, this double distance from Miltonic greatness permits one of his most open and most moving statements about smallness:

> But no!—the spirit long has fled
> That warmed the old tremendous dead,
> Who seem in stature of their mind
> The Anaks of the human kind:
> So bright their crowns of glory burn,
> Our eyes are seared; we feebly turn
> In terrible delight away,
> And only—"Ye were mighty!" say.
> We turn to forms of milder clay,
> Who smile indeed, but cannot frown,
> Nor bring Hell up nor Heaven down.

The lament for lost power is a theme echoed from the death of Milton through Collins's "Ode on the Poetical Character." If we recall Collins, we see how much more guarded, how much more defensive is Darley's depiction of lost power. Collins would aspire; he confesses, "My trembling Feet his guiding Steps pursue," and he confronts his own myth of exclusion reworked from the early part of the ode—that one, only one, can make it: "In vain—Such bliss to One alone / Of all the Sons of Soul was known." Where the myth of one follows Collins's exclamation of disillusion ("In vain!"), the myth of many follows Darley's "But no!" He diminishes the power of the threatening precursor by re-presenting lost power as that of the plural "tremendous dead." Collins misreads Spenser and assumes only one could wear the magic girdle. Darley (perhaps sliding into the plural from talking about audiences—the little men of today vs. Milton's readers) seems actually to multiply the wearers of "crowns of glory."

If multiple Anaks of old seem less threatening than a single giant, the rhetorical gesture of multiplying the weak further protects as it diminishes the "I" of the poet. "We feebly turn" and "We turn to forms of milder clay" are phrases that bury the individual poet under the intellectual current of the day. In between these two "turn" statements the little quotation "Ye were mighty!" stands as a feeble voice, the voice of minority confronting the major achievement of the past. Though Darley buries his identity under the cloak of plurality, we are witnessing not a moment of death but a kind of birth, the *generation* of poetic voice. The turn from the mighty to the mild is a generational turn, embodying Darley's myth of his own genesis. He derives his originality from this posture of weakness and makes it his "virtue"—his power—to confront smiling rather than frowning forms.

Throughout Darley's work beauty that hath terror in it has the terror removed. This radical emptying runs its risks and can produce something closer to insipidity than the explosive vacancy Wordsworth achieves, for example, in the Lucy poems. Anxiety always remains in Wordsworth, and a poem may be emptied of story content only to leave the anxiety more profoundly naked. Darley's lyrics and his short stories—generally emptied of even that minor anxiety, suspense—seem to be generated by the desire to rework richer, more traditional materials into more benignant form. Consider the one Darley lyric that has achieved some repute, "It Is Not Beauty I Demand." Not simply the traditional attributes of beauty but the threatening aspects are rejected. He reacts, as it were, not as much against the blazon tradition (cataloguing the mistress's corporeal riches) as against Keats's injunction to feed deep on the mistress's rich anger. Substituting comforting smiles for features that make adventurers perish, Darley achieves one of his purest expressions of desire.

Having confronted the center of weakness, the Invocation to Milton moves away, diminishing the contrast between past greatness and present mildness by excepting a modern "mighty":

> One gloomy Thing indeed, who now
> Lays in the dust his lordly brow,
> Had might, a deep indignant sense,
> Proud thoughts, and moving eloquence.

It is curious, though characteristic of Darley's evasion of great-ness, that Shelley and Keats, far more important to him at his best, should go unmentioned, and that he should single out Byron here as upon other occasions.[6] Whatever Byron's virtues, he was not one meekly to acknowledge "Ye were mighty!" in relation to anyone. Thinking of Byron, Darley finds he misses the lowly wisdom of the modern, just as he misses the "high poetic strain" of Milton. Recognizing Byron's limited achieve-ment, Darley with his low wisdom joins the aspirants to sublime heights in resisting the satirist's demystifications. Outlining what Milton had that Byron has not, Darley sketches as well his own romanticism:

> But oh! that high poetic strain
> Which makes the heart shriek out again
> With pleasure half mistook for pain;
> That clayless spirit which doth soar
> To some far empyrean shore,
> Beyond the chartered flight of mind,
> Reckless, repressless, unconfined,
> Spurning from off the roofed sky
> Into unciel'd Infinity;
> Beyond the blue crystalline sphere,
> Beyond the ken of optic seer,
> The flaming walls of this great world,
> Where Chaos keeps his flag unfurled
> And embryon shapes around it swarm,
> Waiting till some all-mighty arm
> Their different essences enrol
> Into one sympathetic whole;
> That spirit which presumes to seize
> On new creation-seeds like these,
> And bears on its exultant wings
> Back to the earth undreamt-of things,
> Which unseen we could not conceive,
> And seen we scarcely can believe;—
> That strain, this spirit, was not thine,
> Last-favour'd child of the fond Nine!
> Great as thou wert, thou lov'dst the clod,
> Nor like blind Milton walk'd with God–

Since the desire to soar is not merely recalled but impelled, as it were, in reaction to Byron's limitations, the passage seems to generate romantic aspiration as well as to restore its primacy. Milton wrote about creation; Darley, writing about writing about creation, seems to discover his own creative power. Straining to seize "On new creation-seeds like these," he participates in the myth of origination.

To say that Milton "walk'd with God" is to attribute to Milton not only power or righteousness but priority. Enoch and Noah, who "walked with God," walk not too far from the beginnings of Genesis. In Darley's description Milton seems to move back in time as he moves up in stature:

> Him who dared lay his hand upon
> The very footstool of Jove's throne,
> And lift his intellectual eye
> Full on the blaze of Deity:
> Who sang with the celestial choir
> Hosanna! to the Eternal Sire;
> And trod the holy garden, where
> No man but he and Adam were;
> Who reach'd that high Parnassian clime
> Where Homer sat as gray as Time,
> Murmuring his rhapsodies sublime!
> Who from the Mantuan's bleeding crown
> Tore the presumptuous laurel down,
> And fix'd it, proudly, on his own!
> Who with that Bard diviner still
> Than Earth has seen or ever will,
> The pride, the glory of the hill,
> Albion! thy other deathless son,—
> Reigns; and with them the Grecian one,
> Leagued in supreme tri-union!

The dialectic of early and late is superimposed on that of great and small in such a way that Milton's belatedness in relation to the Bible or the classics is overcome. Milton seems to approach Virgil from anterior distance, coming from Adam, from Homer "gray as Time," and less establishes a new hierarchy than restores an indisputable right. The trinity of poetic giants looks not like the triumvirate as latest constituted, but like a holy trinity the persons of which are immemorial.

When the early and late dialectic is brought into focus, into coincidence with the terms great and small, it restores to view a third dialectic of active and passive. Milton did not kneel to accept his laurels but "Tore the presumptuous laurel down, / And fix'd it, proudly, on his own." He preempted not only the signs of glory but the sphere of activity. Defining himself as the contemplative acknowledger of Milton's active virtue, Darley argues that writing a battle scene in *Sylvia* would be out of character. Yet this extraordinary return to context does not merely forgo the grandeur he has tarried with. Resignation is mingled with newly achieved strength when Darley explains, "Wise in my weakness, I forego / The deeds of fell contest to show." He has earned the humble wisdom Michael enjoins Adam to seek upon exile from paradise. Yet if the poet, exiled from aboriginal place, returns to his weakness, it is with a new sense of where he has been—where his own poetic identity has discovered its origin.

The "modern poet," Darley understood, for better or worse, invariably writes into his works "Contributions to the Memoirs of Myself." [7] When the Invocation to Milton concludes and the pastoral action of *Sylvia* resumes, the drama seems to carry over from overt discussion of the poet's status the sense of new beginnings. Like angels hymning the first day of creation, the Chorus of Spirits chants, "Victory-Lo! the welkin clears! / Victory-Lo! the sun appears." In asking that we suppose the battle between fiends and fairies to have taken place offstage, Darley shares, in the remotest way, the wisdom of the Christian expositor who supposes a battle of heaven and hell to have preceded the opening of Genesis. The spirits' song concludes, "The Powers of Darkness yield the Glen / So breathe sweet harp and trump again." In miniature—and magically therefore, with an added sense of being close to new birth—chaos has been dispelled and a world of innocence newly created.

It has been thought of Darley that his critical insights are not sustained by his original composition, and it could be argued that *Sylvia* as a total composition does not equal the myth of origination Darley constructs about his own weakness in the Invocation. Whatever the final literary judgments are, Darley must at least be read in terms of the story of his own weakness— his best, and perhaps his most basic, theme. In the Introduction to *Thomas à Becket* he acknowledges the antidramatic quality of romantic subjectivity, providing an important guide to readers of *Sylvia* as well—and to readers of romantic drama generally:

Subjective composition is . . . the natural tendency of our refined age, and on this postulate founds itself an argument I fear convincing against the probable regeneration of Acting Drama. Can we restrain that tendency? or *should* we, if we could? Though fatal to the drama, it may be vital to something else as desireable.[8]

iii

The subjectivism at the core of Darley's poetry is very much on the surface in his prose. The stories in *Labours of Idleness* (1826) are radically innocent reworkings of romantic subjectivity, which, if they seem at their worst child-versions of the quest for ideality, manage, at their best, a pure lyricism costing not less than everything. Their originality lies in their naiveté, as though older or more common tales were stripped of detail and psychological sophistication, and emptied as far as possible of all extraliterary meaning. What the stories may be said to contain, surrounded by self-indulgence and sentiment, are images of pure spirit, either in the form of the actual lyrics (it may be the prose serves merely as "context" or false origin of the lyric impulse) or in moments of highly lyrical descriptive prose. The solitary of "The Enchanted Lyre," for example, discovers in his paradisal bower something more than earthly. "I bent over the waves, and saw clearly, in the reflected bell of one of the lilies, something cradled up like an infant asleep; rocking to and fro as the wind moved the flowers."[9] It is no sublime epiphany, but a visionary glance at what Darley calls elsewhere "Adam's pigmy sperm," the redeemed spiritual form of man not yet spoiled by or grown into his illusions of grandeur. When Darley concludes the paragraph with pedestrian doubt, "Again, I say, this may have been a dream," he closes the little vision as Keats closes a major ode—but with no grand tension locked in. The vision insists on remaining minor, and thus all the more essentially about minority.

Even granted the conscious or unconscious desire to banish tension, one would find difficulty telling a weak story from a story about weakness. But the one story which cultivates narrative as well as dream vision so remarkably dramatizes Darley's myth of the small poet that the weaknesses become strengths.

"Pedro Ladron, or The Shepherd of Toppledown Hill" is a story about a storyteller whose diminutive physical stature belies his powers of spellbinding an audience with his tall tales. Pedro, whose first name suggests *pedrea* (falling of stones) and whose last name suggests *ladrar* (to bark, clamor) seems partly a parody, partly a wish-fulfillment image of his creator. Throughout his life Darley was tormented by a stammer he found to be so great an obstacle to social intercourse that he not only dreaded new acquaintances but habitually excused himself from dinner engagements with friends who would have happily borne with him. The "infinitely communicative" Pedro who is "seen in all places of amusement" embodies Darley's yearning for fluency and social success. At the same time, this little man, equipped with "a Toledo of intolerable dimensions" and boots and gloves of the same outlandish scale, cuts too comic, too grotesque a figure to threaten the writer with an image of what he is not.

Writing about subjectivism in what he understood was an age of autobiography, Darley elsewhere warns that "the confessor wishing to acquaint us intimately with his several perfections, unwarily, at the same time, lets slip some pretty broad hints of his weakness." [10] In "The Shepherd of Toppledown Hill" the pretty broad hints become the basis of some pretty broad humor, under the cover of which Darley can shape his myth of weakness into perfected form. Pedro is invested not only with fluency and a predilection for self as topic but with a "faculty likewise of giving to stories, which he had repeated several times over, a freshness and a novelty on every new occasion that rendered them almost as good as if they came that moment from the mind." Under the guise of fancy Darley thus represents the most mysterious and most cherished power—the power of originality. Pedro's skill in heraldry is another demystifying expression of originality, as if the invention of family trees, which wins Pedro something like patronage, could absorb the poet's desire for creating his own sources. Like Chatterton, whose genealogies launched a career of fabricating antiquities and who became for the generation of Wordsworth more a figure of a poet than a poet actually read, so Pedro becomes, in the course of the story, an artist more interesting for the figure he cuts than for the collected fictions he is supposed to have woven.

True to Darley's seminal stipulation that tension be banished, Pedro is seen as threatened, but not really threatened, by the appearance of a rival storyteller. If the rival could be said to represent Darley's conscious fear that his speech impediment would make him lose audience, the representation itself soothes, for the loss of a few auditors to another speaker is a mild failure compared with the object of unconscious fear: total loss of (poetic) voice. In any case Pedro, responding to the challenge, recounts "with measured phrase and voice sonorous" the story that assures his continued status as "magnus Apollo."

It is a story about little Pedro encountering big things under circumstances which deprive size of its awesomeness. If Darley's distaste for his own poetic smallness inspires this story in which size does not matter, his distaste for the representation of anxiety inspires the reworking of folk materials into gentler form than they usually receive. Shipwrecked during a monstrous storm, Pedro finds himself lying on a beach, pecked at by giant vultures. Thus wounded, he brandishes his great sword, sending the vultures back to the carcasses of his shipmates. Further to protect himself against the birds Pedro makes a dwelling of a cave, loosening the dirt around an overhanging boulder so that it falls and blocks the mouth of the cave, leaving only a little space through which he, but not the birds, can pass.

To measure the diminished peril in which our hero stands, compare the circumstances of Ulysses and his men in the cyclops' cave of *The Odyssey,* Book IX. A giant shepherd will make his appearance in Darley's story too, but in a separate and less terrible incident than Homer's. Pedro is in his cave, protected by a boulder too big to move but past which he can worm his way in and out. Ulysses is trapped in a cave with the giant, and his way is barred by a stone only Polyphemus can move. Ulysses faces the preliminary task of getting the cyclops drunk on the wine he has brought along; Pedro finds his thirst pleasantly quenched by a cask of claret which has been dropped by one of the vultures scavaging the wrecked ship. For his gift of the wine Ulysses is promised that he will be eaten last of his men; Pedro's worries about being devoured take the milder form of hunger pains gnawing at him.

When his supply of food and drink is nearly exhausted, Pedro (who has "a taste for the sublime") confronts the lofty cliffs that enclose Vulture Bay, and the seemingly endless staircase, each of whose risers presents a sheer rock face several times a man's height. Fear is somewhat tempered by aesthetic appreciation of this Burkean delight, and while Pedro claims "I seemed absolutely to melt in my boots, from the mere sense of my own insignificance," he continues to climb, surviving for days on bits of leather from those same boots. Like the poet in *The Fall of Hyperion,* Pedro does not doubt that his only salvation lies in mounting the stairs, and yet he is not troubled by a Moneta voice threatening imminent decay. What he does hear is a sound like the braying of a herd of asses.

One can hardly overemphasize the significance of having Pedro hear that giant sound before confronting its less threatening source. Darley's story recapitulates not only the turn from a gigantic burden of literary tradition to this lighthearted tale, but the whole movement from figurative language—conceived as firstborn—to belated literalism. In a famous passage on the anteriority of metaphor, Rousseau established the pattern:

> Upon meeting others, a savage man will initially be frightened. Because of his fear he sees the others as bigger and stronger than himself. He calls them *giants*. After many experiences, he recognizes that these so-called giants are neither bigger nor stronger than he. Their stature does not approach the idea he had initially attached to the word giant. So he invents another name common to them and to him, such as the name *man,* for example, and leaves *giant* to the fictitious object that had impressed him during his illusion. That is how the figurative word is born before the literal word, when our gaze is held in passionate fascination; and how it is that the first idea it conveys to us is not that of the truth.[11]

The givenness of others and the challenge they necessarily pose to the power and independence of the individual mind are thus countered by the imputed anteriority of one's verbal re-presentations.

Darley's story literalizes and turns into pure naiveté something like the birth of figurative language that Rousseau describes. The comic elements of his carefully staged scene on top of the giant plateau are not to be distinguished from the forms of gentleness appropriate to a new birth. If the sublime is always marked by a dialectic of high and low, Darley's specialness can be localized in the way he explores the implications of the imaginatively childlike coincident with soarings to imaginative heights. Purging himself of meliorating sentimentalisms and domesticities, John Ashbery expresses the literary desire actualized in Darley when Pedro stands on the giant's green land:

> To reduce all this to a small variant,
> To step free at last, minuscule on the gigantic plateau—
> This was our ambition: to be small and clear and free.
> ["Soonest Mended"][12]

It may be that poetic originality always lies in the "small variant" one makes in the ratio of the literal to the metaphoric. The literalness with which Darley conceives of the small and the gigantic is part of his original turn on a tradition of the sublime.

Days after Pedro first hears the giant sound, he discovers that sound to be the thunderous voice of a giant shepherd who, in the green land atop the enormous cliffs, pastures his elephant-sized sheep and sings his "amoroso pastorale." Unlike Homer's Polyphemus, Darley's giant has a countenance "not at all ferocious, but extremely good humored." Equally important to the extraordinary emptying of his narrative, Darley's giant does not see and does not address Pedro, who espies him only from a distance, and who covers his ears tight as he can to hear the thunderous voice as muffled as possible.

In this vision, the ordinary desire of a daydreaming youth—or, more particularly, of a belated poet—to stand where Ulysses stood, is now fulfilled in a manner characteristic of and "original" to Darley. Pedro does, in a way, stand as Ulysses stood, but with the sublime distilled from the dangerous. Of the cyclops Ulysses says,

> Nor was he
> Like any man that food could possibly
> Enhance so hugely, but (beheld alone)
> Shewd like a steepe hil's top, all overgrowne
> With trees and brambles, litle thought had I
> Of such vast objects.

And when the cyclops speaks,

> Feare from our hearts tooke
> The very life, to be so thunder-strooke
> With such a voice and such a monster see.[13]

Pedro gets to see and hear without feeling threatened by the "vast object" of the giant. And what he sees is a shepherd as much at harmony with his pastoral landscape as he is at peace with—and rather fond of—his own huge body. What he hears is a voice so tuned to nature that when the shepherd sings the rocks fall down in chorus.

Discussing such pleasing continuity of nature, in the face of which the individual consciousness seems an interruption, Michel Foucault points to the way anxiety is relieved by imagining new half-human forms. He discusses the psychological "necessity of introducing monsters into the scheme—forming the background noise, as it were, the endless murmur of nature." [14] Just such a monster is Darley's giant, who rather mediates than menaces the relation between mind and landscape. Since the giant's involvement is with nature, rather than with Pedro, he appears to be not a model of authoritative voice which threatens the would-be poet, but a dreamlike fulfillment of the poet's own desire for voice. Like Darley, who achieved his greatest fluency in lyrics of an Elizabethan cast, the giant is imagined to be singing a song of Damon and Delia, which, though it thunders in tones "amazingly sublime," works within the limitations of pastoral convention. One detail toys with as it confirms Darley's allegory of the poet. When the recitatif is halted for what might be called Pedro's great aria, "The Giant's Song," the song Pedro sings is not exactly presented as the giant's, since Pedro cannot duplicate the words but only the melody. He sings a song of his own in place of the song of the giant.

. . . Of course I am unable to give you the words, or even the sense, of what he sang, but the tune I can never forget; it sounded in mine ears for a whole twelvemonth after. If you are contented to hear some verses of my own composing, Signiors, you shall have them; they are such as (with all humility I say it) might do no discredit to the Shepherd of Toppledown Hill.

Here there was of course a murmur of approbation, and Pedro immediately gave vent to the following stanzas, which he asserted were the fruits of his own genius, but which were found after his death in the handwriting of a young canon belonging to the church of San Pablo, a great friend of his and the Muses.

> Browse on, my gentle flock! the while
> A roundelay I sing:

And quake, ye meads, for many a mile,
   Ye solid mountains ring!
Green-bearded valleys, club your echoes all!
   Groan, ye loud hollows! Every deep cave whine!
Topple down, rocks, and thundering as ye fall,
   Bear hearty chorus to this chant of mine!

(*Chorus of falling rocks*)

Hurrurah!—
Crumble down!—hurrurah!
Tumble down!—hurrurah!
Rattle down! brattle down, still!
   Crag, flag,—hurrurah!
   Block, stock,—hurrurah!
   Roll! bowl! clatter! batter!
   Hurrurah! hurrurah!—
Topple down, rocks, from the hill!

Though I am sore opprest, opprest,
   With love's almighty pain,
And in this (ah! too faithful) breast
   Soft pensiveness doth reign;
Yet while there's hope, there's life (they say) in love,
   And therefore, since I've nothing else to do,
I'll sing my passion whersoe'er I rove,
   And make the rocks roll me a burthen too!

Hurrurah!—etc.

When Delia on the plain appears,
   The streams forget to flow,
The groves are dumb, each flower rears
   Its head to kiss her toe.
The pretty lambkins round her frisking skip,
   And amorous breezes wanton in her hair,
For a red rose the bees mistake her lip,
   And come in crowds to gulp the honey there!

Hurrurah!—etc.

Ye purling rills repeat my grief!
   Ye Zephyrs breathe my sighs!

> Tell her to yield me quick relief,—
>   Or else poor Damon dies!
> Then if the cruel fair one shall relent,
>   And with one smile bless her dear shepherd boy,
> I'll sing her praise till all my breath be spent,
>   Whilst hill and dale shall echo to my joy!
>
> > Hurrurah!—etc.

After having sung this song (continued Pedro), which indeed he appeared chiefly to like for its chorus, he laughed heartily, and, to swell the applause, struck his huge palms together so as to produce a sort of thunderclap each time.

The joke seems compounded when we recognize this lyric, ostensibly an uninteresting poem greeted with undue enthusiasm, as in fact a most curious piece. The shepherd's blundering lament is a genre unto itself with significant precedents in Theocritus (Idyll XI) and *Don Quixote* (I,xiv); but most unusual is the way this poem appears to grow in conventionality while it becomes increasingly bold in figuring the poet's dilemma. Stanza one projects giant figurations onto the landscape: "Green-bearded valleys, club your echoes all!" Stanza two shows the burden of the past totally diffused into carefree fancy: "since I've nothing else to do. . . . " Stanza three figures the threat of stuttering or of silence absorbed by the responsive groves, while the troublesome image of pigmy man is transformed into the genial image of pigmy nature—the little flowers under Delia's toes. "Words do not originate like flowers," cautions Paul de Man in explicating the structure of the Romantic image: "They need to find the mode of their beginning in another entity; they originate out of nothing, in an attempt to be the first words that will arise as if they were natural objects, and, as such, they remain essentially distinct from natural entities." [15] In this poem the flowers, reared up out of pure responsiveness to Delia, assume the burden of poetic language, absorbing into their very figurativeness the responsibility for autogenesis ordinarily borne by words. For the mellifluous, honey-tongued bard of the past substitute Delia, whose power of speech could hardly be imagined to be abetted by the bees' mistake. (This misprision of the lip—*bilbul svatayim*, it is called in Hebrew—would make Delia's face, like Falstaff's, more a "table of green fields" than she could babble about.) For the last stanza one need only contrast Darley's *Nepenthe,* where Antiquity is intent "To crush our souls with that dim frown." Darley's lines figure a pastoral smile that obliterates the disapproving authority of the past, and the poem ends released of the threat of silence when silence is envisioned to be not imposed but achieved by the sufficient self: "I'll sing her praise till at my breath be spent." The last line, with its still-present "whilst," images ongoing responsiveness and the atemporality that knows no anxiety.

The prevenient apology for the lyric calls attention to the theme of representation or re-presentation of something as one's own. In the lyric, "Hurrurah! / Crumble down!" like expletives stand for the sound of the rocks, which stand for nature responding to Damon, who stands for the giant singing his love, who is "stood in for" by Pedro, who stands for Guy Penseval, who stands, pseudonymously, for Darley, who—we can say—stands for any poet confronting the power of voice—the power to represent rocks, Damons, or Darleys as speaking. If such circularity seems playful, it is the central playfulness of literary discourse, of language whose "stand for" quality exceeds mimesis. (Wittingly or not, Darley compounded the self-referentiality with the misleading parenthetical "continued Pedro" in the sentence following the song.) The seemingly infinite regress of what stands for what points us back, like a psychological regression, to an early cathexis of authorial desire, or what we may specify as three desires: the desire to make something stand for something else (the basic desire to write; the desire to be "stood for" (to have something one writes deeply image the self); and the desire to "stand for" something greater than oneself, so that the self can be lost or transcended through the guise of representation. That these desires are at their origin conflicting and yet innately conglomerate may be better seen by employing other terms: the poet desires power of voice—the power himself to originate representative language and to call forth images of the self. At the same time he senses his own voice to be weak, stuttering, or silent, and desires to be infused with a voice that will speak *through* him (as the ancient Greek actors spoke through masks) and thus give his voice "per-sonality," the sense of being spoken through. The poet wishes to be original (to feel that his voice is really his own) but also to stand close to origins (to feel that a more original power is being diffused through him). Like Wallace Stevens's giant "Beau linguist," something in the poet wants to exteriorize the power and grace of poetic speech, "As if the language suddenly, with ease, / Said things it had laboriously spoken." [16]

Darley's Pedro, singing verses "of [his] own composing" in place of those of the giant, aims at originality in both senses. On the one hand, the verses are his own, original to him (Pedro claims); on the other hand, the giant speaks through him, and so Pedro's voice has giant power. In his Introduction to *The Works of Beaumont and Fletcher,* Darley presented as the power of origination just the quality that Pedro presents as "original" to the giant—the rhythm, the melody of the shepherd's song:

Rhythm I should maintain was chiefly valuable as an *inspirer,* and needful to the *poet* rather than the poem. We must all have remarked the inspiring nature of note-music—what numberless ideas, visions, emotions, passions it suggests; what *creators* it makes us! Every true poet has a *song in his mind,* the notes of which, little as they precede his thoughts—so little as seem simultaneous with them—do precede, suggest, and inspire many of these, modify and beautify them.[17]

Now if the vision of the singing giant-shepherd captures the desired power of voice, the remembrance of rhythm and melody captures the desired power of a source beyond the self.

Darley's story protects its vision by seeming to mock it. Not only does little Pedro cut a ridiculous figure croaking out for his

willing audience the giant's song and its "Crumble down!—
hurrurah!" chorus in which the earth trembles and the stones
fall; the narrator adds a further demystification, claiming that
the stanzas Pedro sings as his own "were found after his death
in the handwriting of a young canon belonging to the church of
San Pablo, a great friend of his and the Muses." As the vision
of power of voice is made nonthreatening, so the challenge to
poetic originality is deprived of its sting and given this gentlest,
most whimsical form.

The challenge to poetic originality is disarmed on both sides:
singing his own—or the canon's—song, Pedro neither rivals nor
detracts from the giant; singing to himself, the giant in Pedro's
story neither challenges nor even confronts Pedro. We can better
understand the significance of this bilateral disengagement if we
once more juxtapose the story of Ulysses and Polyphemus.
Homer's thundering cyclops is unobtrusively challenged by
Ulysses when he gives as his name "Noman." Emptying himself
only in terms of name, Ulysses gains a strategic advantage over
the giant, who appears to his fellows self-tormented or tormented
by a still higher authority: "If no man hurt thee and thy self
alone, / That which is done to thee by Jove is done." But it is
Ulysses' character to challenge where he does not have to, and
to name himself in exultation over his enemy. Straining his vocal
cords to trumpet his message from his ship in the sea—ironically
the territory of Neptune, Polyphemus' father—Ulysses brings
down on his head the curse of Polyphemus that will cost the hero
all his men.

If Polyphemus' curse makes the reestablishment of hierarchical
relations between man and giant, ephebe and god, a theme of the
ensuing narrative, Polyphemus' outburst before the actual curse
reestablishes those relations in verbal terms. Polyphemus says he
expected a challenger, a mighty conqueror, "when now a weak-
ling came, a dwarfie thing, / A thing of nothing." That is just
the sort of contempt Darley might have experienced but would
never depict. It is interesting that Chapman elaborates the de-

scription of the expected conqueror as a "great and goodly personage," one with "vertue answerable," thus leaving Ulysses' supposed merits ambiguously physical or moral. The cyclops as Homer conceived him seems to reassert hierarchy in purely physical terms: this small, weak man was not at all what he (giant cyclops) expected. Besides the descriptive deprecation, there is the hierarchical restoration in the cyclops' voice itself. Chapman renders—or rather elaborates—Polyphemus' first reaction to Ulysses' words thus: "At this he braid so loud that round about / He drave affrighted Ecchoes through the Aire."

In Darley's story the pretensions of Pedro risk no confrontation with hubris, whereas Ulysses' exultation seems almost to invite one. Moreover, Pedro's weakness and smallness is pitted against the giant stairs, which he can master, not against the giant himself. Whereas Neptune, behind the sea, personifies the most invincible opposition to Ulysses, the sea for Pedro, who has climbed to staggering heights, becomes less a thundering threat than an object of aesthetic contemplation: "Although the waves were flowing high, they appeared to fall without noise; and, if I may so express myself, I could only *see* them roar." (The fastidiousness about figurative language here points to the Wordsworthianism.) Most important, the braying of the cyclops—the Greek word actually means simply a cry of grief—is diminished not in volume but by association. Pedro hears unintimidated a sound like the braying of a herd of asses, since many grazing animals are less troublesome than the consolidated voice of one malevolent giant. In place of the gulf between giant and dwarf, thunderous voice and stammering man, Darley substitutes a de-generated sibling relationship. Pedro looks around contentedly and concludes, "There was nothing here to annoy me, neither wild beast nor vultures; as for the asses, I had always a brotherly affection towards the race."

To some extent Pedro must be an ass if Darley is to present an image of dwarfishness which threatens neither by being more grand than its creator nor by too seriously embodying the tragedy of smallness. But Pedro himself may be meant to imply, by this "brotherly affection," not something about his own identity but something about the nature of the auditors he is befriending with his storytelling gift. The mockery of his own size is, in any case, not to be distinguished from the general comedown: a small man who puts his arms on the shoulders of his fellows in a circle makes all shoulders stoop.

Pedro punctuates his narration of the heroic stair-climb with the rallying cry, "Courage! exclaimed I, where asses are to be found, men, I am sure, cannot be far distant." Talking to himself he may be talking most about others. On the other hand, talking about others he comes closest to revealing himself. The sound of the giant shepherd's voice, he says, is not to be imitated: "No, though you all brayed your very best (and some of you, I know, have a wonderful knack in that way), you could not equal the softest note of his wind-pipe!" Besides—or perhaps under the cover of—repeating the joke, these remarks about asses represent Pedro's, and ultimately Darley's, victory over their diminutiveness. Their small voices capture the big ears.

The very desire to win audience may be seen as a form of diminished desire. Ulysses' interest in self-revelation is vis-à-vis not his men but the giant. For Darley the poet, concern about audience may be a diminished anxiety about his status in relation to the poetic giants. The narrator of "The Shepherd of Toppledown Hill" suggests as much when his gentle tolerance of Pedro and his rival is outflanked by his mockery of their auditors. The rival, Captain Rovedillo, has two winning topics, giants and the land of gold. "Whilst employed in describing this treasure of a city, like Midas, every thing he touched became precious; and like Midas too, or rather more fortunate, he had for his reward a great many pairs of asses' ears presented to him daily."

Two little transformations caught in this passage sum up Darley's Ovidian power to change tensions into tableaux. Midas physically touched the objects he turned to gold; Rovedillo "touches upon" things in El Dorado, gilding all in his descriptions. Describing precious things, he creates descriptions held precious by his auditors, holding them astonished (turned to stone) and turning the tension of rivalry into a matter of who can most actualize the desired image of stasis: spellbound ears. To hold others' attention, to hold them still, is to achieve a Midas-like, or more truly an Ovidian, victory over mutability in matters of voice.

Rovedillo is also like Midas, "or rather more fortunate," in his ears—the "asses' ears presented to him daily," for the burden of sporting such appendages is shifted. Valorizing the audience relationship, and then identifying the auditors as the asses, Darley grants Rovedillo some status. Further valorizing audience relationships Darley grants Pedro more status by picturing him as a successful transformer of an experiential anxiety into literary event; the herd of asses becomes the shepherd-giant. Seen as the creator of his giant forms rather than the dwarf combatant with giants, the poet triumphs over his diminished stature.

iv

So intertwined are the substance and slightness of "The Shepherd of Toppledown Hill" that one contemplates with trepidation—as Darley must have done—the prospect of a major literary work built on the myth of weakness. *Nepenthe* (1835) is Darley's major poem, suggesting in the high romanticism of its quest both Shelley's *Alastor* and Keats's *Endymion*. Against the giantism of attempting to rival those achievements Darley defends himself by converting high romantic quest into a search for images of poetic diminutiveness. In the Preface and in several letters to friends he outlines a scheme that would further safeguard the poem from anxiety about poetic stature. While publishing two cantos of *Nepenthe* in a very small, poor issue, he claimed that there was originally to be a third canto, containing "my modicum of the humanities; as the first and second shew the extremes of Aspiration and Dejection with their evil effects, so the third was to shew the medium, contentment with our human lot, and its effect, happiness." [18] Whether Darley believed in that third canto (whether he believed he would write it, or, more simply, whether he believed in its designed "message".) is less significant than the role played by advertising it. The designed "medium, content-ment with our human lot," pulls the romantic achievement of the first two cantos down to size.

The idea of dwarfing his poetic strengths was not new to the author of *Nepenthe*. In *The Errors of Ecstasie* (1822) he had reworked Keats's *Endymion* into an extraordinarily degraded form by which the young hero is a raving "Mystic" and the Moon is a spokesman for the golden mean and good common sense. Chastened from vaunting ambition back to his small, sole self, Mystic acknowledges his error: "I thought—deceptible, ah! too deceptible— / The true Elysium lay within the mind." The achievement of the poem is an ironic perspective on its own antiromantic sentiment, so that in place of deflating Keatsian romanticism the poem seems to contract into itself, forestalling readers' rejections by having the Moon reject her worshiper. If the diminishment takes place in the story of *The Errors of Ecstasie,* it is absorbed by the *plan* of *Nepenthe,* leaving the poem proper to soar.

Darley's ordering of the two cantos and his labeling their themes "Ambition" and "Dejection" further mislead or protect. Canto I pursues a path of sublimation by which weakness takes the form of lightness. The existence of a second, more sobered canto safeguards the buoyancy of the first, and only a min-imal tribute to corporeality keeps the quester from vaporizing altogether:

> Light! for the ardour of the clime
> Made rare my spirit, that sublime
> Bore me as buoyant as young Time
> Over the green Earth's grassy prime,
> Ere his slouch'd wing caught up her slime;
> And sprang I not from clay and crime,

> Had from those humming beds of thyme
> Lifted me near the starry chime
> To learn an empyrean rhyme.   [I.35–43]

The single rhyme sustains a protracted flight, characterizing not only this introductory passage but the whole canto. Here is sublimity less of great than of first things, ethereal because not yet weighted by experience. "As buoyant as young Time," the poet appears like a newborn Homunculus, unburdened by the past and unaware of the sorrows that temper romantic passion. Lightness or buoyancy becomes less a mood than what Blake would call a state, permanent in itself though the passing individual may change. The state of lightness is the original state, the state of "young Time" freed from anxiety by the dispensation according to which weakness and diminutiveness are but signs of the newly born, confirmed rather than challenged in pristine romanticism. Fit emblem of the state is the phoenix, who is always close to birth or rebirth and whose relationship to the sun is that of happy weakness to benignant strength: "Steadfast she gazed upon his fire / Still her destroyer and her sire."

If the relationship between phoenix and sun in Canto I can represent the tensionless reciprocity between "young Time" and its powerful, invigorating source, Canto II may be said to explore that reciprocity by superimposing on the dialectic of early and late Darley's habitual concern with great and small. The first line of Canto II apostrophizes "Antiquity, thou Titan born!" and the first two hundred lines explore the relation between the giant Antiquity and the poet's small, young time. Unlike the giant in "The Shepherd of Toppledown Hill," Antiquity is a threatening power whose capacity to topple is no mere Orphic harmony of voice and nature:

> Still thou rear'st thee in thy scorn,
> Antiquity, thou Titan-born,
> To crush our soul with that dim frown!
> Strong Son of Chaos! who didst seem

> Only a fairer form of him,
> Moulding his mountainous profounds
> To fanes and monumental grounds.   [II.15–21]

The frown of Antiquity is precisely the sign of displeasure the poet of *Sylvia* sought to avoid in turning away from the monumental past: "We turn to forms of milder clay, / Who smile indeed, but cannot frown."

The might which Darley apprehends in *Nepenthe* by not turning away may be gauged by comparing these lines on the same topic from a poem Darley seems to have read:

> Nature o'erwhelms the relics left by time;—
> By slow degrees entombing all the land;
> She buries every monument sublime,
> Beneath a mighty winding-sheet of sand.[19]

These four lines consistently picture nature as the entomber and the mighty achievements of the past as dead remains. Darley's Antiquity, on the other hand, is ambiguously the sum of past achievements and the sum of past decay, and the frown is not exhausted in contempt of past monuments but continues in scorn of modern puniness. Not simply the power of degeneration, Antiquity is personified as generated and generating. Titan-born, Son of Chaos, and one who

> look'st with dim but settled eye
> O'er thy deep lap, within whose span
> Layer upon layer sepulchred lie
> Whole generations of frail man.

The lap of generation and the span of earth in which generations are buried are the same place.

"Frail man" is further protected in his weakness by the knowledge that the might of Antiquity stands against generations of frail men, who together experience the power personified into singleness—"one same Power, enorm, sublime." Collectivity keeps the poet from being discovered no David to Antiquity's Goliath, and he can, instead of challenging, beg for power—if only the power of recognition—to be diffused among men:

> Enlarge our little eyeballs still
> To grasp in these degenerate days
> Marvels that shewed a mighty will,
> Huge power and hundred-handed skill,
> That seek prostration and not praise
> Too faint such lofty ears to fill!

But the poet is not simply one among many. Though he shares with the other possessors of "little eyeballs" the awe of the past, he holds a special relation to history. If the power is "from antique clime to clime / Eternal stumbling-block of Time," the inspired poet finds his spirit bounds through temporal ages and geographical sites of past magnificence, "with rainbow leap sublime / Vaulting at once from clime to clime." His lightness lets him soar over the stumbling block of time into special relationship with antiquity. As the invocation closes, the poet's romantic buoyancy is clarified into the image of ecstatic flight directed by and tied to Antiquity portrayed as giant falconer:

> I
>
> Can Egypt's hollow realm descry
> Whence my extravagant wing did bend,
> Where at one swoop my soar shall end,
> Blind falcon! towering to the sun
> Ever, till thou entreat me down,
> With magical voice, Antiquity!
> More proud thy bird than Jove's to be,
> Creature sublime, beside thy knee
> Perched, and for aye in life's disdain,
> 'Mid the great stillness, thy reign,
> Sitting with Solitude and thee.

These lines supremely fulfill the ambition of the mythologizer of weakness. Unlike the phoenix, who is first consumed in towering to the sun, the poet-falcon is comfortably—unapocalyptically—brought home again, happy in the might of Antiquity's "magical voice." The gentle paradox of the last line creates just enough tension to toll the death of the fiction that Antiquity is a personified third accompanying the poet and Solitude. Thus the statement of weakness or subservience becomes also a closing challenge to Antiquity. At the same time, it rather introduces than breaks off the vision of redeemed weakness, for what follows in Canto II may be analyzed into two overlapping movements, in the first of which the poet comes into reconciled relation to giant Antiquity, and in the second of which he confronts his ultimate solitude.

First the poet confronts a pair of giant images, addressing them even before explaining who they are:

> Save me! O save, ye mighty Twain,
> Arbiters here twixt Sin and Pain!
> Tho' Angels still of Judgment, be
> Angels of Mercy now to me!
> Bend down your level looks, or raise
> One iron finger from the knee.

Having made this appeal he then explains that there were two mighty forms, two giant sculptures, that looked like "Umpires of my doom." Left curiously indefinite is the nature of the threat—just how a spatially realized hell images the "sorrow of Sinfulness" the poet feels. Against the background of that indefiniteness—itself an expression of the prime difficulty in materializing a romantic quest-poem—the definite sculpture forms with their iron-fingered posture come as both mediators and menacingly realized antagonists.

Were one of these giants to address the poet at this point, Darley would be forced into the kind of awesome confrontation Keats represents with Moneta in *The Fall of Hyperion*. Darley allows the myth of weakness greater sway and has the giants play out or reenact the poet's relation to his past rather than jointly confront him with his own inadequacy. The poet faints at their feet, but for a while they remain dumb, "like the symbols of the world to come / Immutable, inscrutable!" If we borrow from Harold Bloom's *Map of Misreading* the figuration of apophrades (the return of the dead), we can note that this symbol-making is "preposterous," for emblems of anxiety about the past are projected outward and forward into less troublesome figures of futurity. Ostensibly the poet's prostration is the sign or pictorial emblem of a crisis, but since the inscrutability of the world to come is less threatening—and less figurative—then the inscrutability of the past, the crisis is met with a remarkable defense mechanism.

There is a verse paragraph break, and when our hero's sense of life—and the poem—resume, one of the giants is discovered to be Memnon, the statue that according to tradition emits musical sounds at the coming of dawn. These sounds Darley interprets as Memnon's yearning matin song to his mother Aurora, generative and diurnal originatrix. Hegel described the special fascination of the Memnon statue when he called it more than a mighty form—"a living, significant and revealing thing, albeit the mode of revelation is purely one of symbolic suggestion."[20] Darley's Memnon is all the more awesome a living thing because he "signifies" to his mother in a symbol system closed to ordinary ears. But for the moment the poet is reprieved from his doom—from the sickness of excessive self-consciousness, excessive concern about *his* doom—and he breathes anew in the relaxed space of a spectator, where he can witness this splendidly realized relationship between the goddess and "her monumental Son." There is, at least on the surface, no question of guilt concerning romantic self-consciousness (how diminutive the intrapersonal concern seems beside this "interpersonal" one). Comfortably laid aside is the question of the poet's own diminutiveness vis-à-vis these giant forms or the giant forms of his poetic precursors. All interest is centered on Memnon *as son,* eternally involved in that relationship of giving voice and receiving light and life. In place of the iron-fingered stoniness of the statues as viewed by the awed poet there is the geniality of this immortal filial devotion:

'Twas Memnon here
Sat gazing with a mournful cheer
Still at his mother! Still with smile
Fond as her own would fain beguile
Her sorrow! Still each matin rise
Welcomed her bright tears with his sighs!

Unlike Keats's poet in *The Fall of Hyperion,* who, watching
Saturn, Thea, and Moneta silent, is himself challenged to sit still
and bear "the weight of eternal quietude," the poet here is passive witness to the emotional constancy which is the new meaning
expressed by those three *still*s. The setting of Keats's poem challenges the ephebe to take up where relationship between the
titanic forms has failed. In *Hyperion,* shortly after the old god
is specifically compared to Memnon, Keats enjoins his Muse to
abandon the titans, "For thou art weak to sing such tumults
dire." Yet the titans are abandoned only for the more awesome
task of describing Apollo, whose divinization is an apotheosis of
the poet. Darley will go on to image a weaker form of the self-
investiture Keats describes in the Hyperion poems, but not yet.
For the moment the lines of force run between Memnon and
Aurora, "By sighs responsive to each other known." Memnon
does mourn the fact of separation, crying "Leave me not, Mother
beloved! from your embraces torn, / For ever here forlorn."
But this is the eternal loneliness of Memnon, not the poet, who
is disburdened of self-consciousness while watching the giant
assume the position and voice of small, begotten man.

At the end of Memnon's song, the poet becomes more than
an outsider or auditor and assumes something of the mediatory
role Keats assumed in the "Ode to Psyche" when he moved
from spectator to priest. Though himself a figure of antiquity,
Memnon has been heard to sing, sonlike, a lyric of desire to be
back at the source. He remains, in the last stanza, yearning: "O
could my Spirit wing / Hills over, where salt Ocean hath his
fresh headspring." While stony Memnon cannot wing it, the
poet can, and he senses the winds echoing his desire to be

"away," taking that echo to be an inspired injunction. The giant is fixed in time and place, while the poet journeys onward to the "fresh headspring." If Memnon remains, like Shelley's Prometheus, liberated by his own words yet still bound, the poet is like Asia, urged in songful journey back to origins.

He confronts, on his eastward journey (the traditional direction for a journey to origins), not the giants of the past but the absence of giants. In Thebes the "denizen giants" are no more, and in Apis, "Giant thing inhabits none, / But vast Desolation!" Darley's wish to avoid confrontation is respected, almost pampered, when the poet's weakness, more gently expressed as his sense of his own desolation, is mirrored in the desolate landscape. If the mighty of the past are gone, the poet discovers not simply artifacts of canceled times but the "womb of sublimity," seemingly more aboriginal. He discovers as well something like the womb or generative center of his own poem. In what looks at first like a circular journey back to the entombed spirit of Memnon, Darley pictures a further easterning or journey to "fresh headspring," and a place that will prove more womb than tomb. It seems that "there were two statues of Memnon: a smaller one, commonly called the young Memnon . . . and a larger and more celebrated one, from which, when touched by the rays of the morning sun, harmonious sounds were reported to have issued." [21] I take it that having been auditor of the music of the larger statue, the poet is now faced with the less threatening "young Memnon." The small poet is to liberate the spirit of the small statue by performing a ritual ablution. Hearing a groan that (metaphorically, of course, but now no longer a dead metaphor) makes the dead turn in their graves, the poet is directed to an engraved prescription according to which the liberator of Memnon's spirit is to mingle "A cup of darkness here with one of light, / Fit opiate for Life's fever." Recall that the announced seminal idea of overall conception of *Nepenthe* was one canto of ambition, one of dejection, and a medium of contentment. Happily the prescription is filled symbolically, for in purging the desire to pour a mingled balm, Darley leaves us with a beautiful two-canto poem—a better poem than what the recipe for Canto III would seem to predict.

If in following the engraved directions the poet symbolically reworks the recipe for *Nepenthe,* he reworks as well the ambition to turn the tables on the giant without actually confronting him. He does approach the giant—at least a lesser image of a giant— only there is no danger, no heroic act of courage or endurance, just the simple act—ludicrous, did it not so symbolize the relation between the small and the great—of pouring the mingled balm in the statue's "cleft and hollow crown." Especially comforting is the fact that this "embalming" of the past requires no verbal exchange. No thundering words threaten the poet; neither is he called upon to speak. In response to his efforts the air, not the statue as such, "Grew vocal for a moment there, / With out-flown shriek of joy." In place of imaging his own coming to voice, Darley pictures the silencing of giant voice once and for all: "Memnon from that day, by the shore / Of Nile, sits murmurless evermore."

With all the limitations on the poet, this act nonetheless represents far more of a confrontation with the giant of the past than the mere acknowledgment of past greatness Darley wrote into the invocations of *Sylvia* and *Nepenthe,* or the mere glimpse of the pastoral giant in "The Shepherd of Toppledown Hill." As if to purge the act of its hubris, or at least to externalize guilt at the element of violation implicit in the act, the poet is now overwhelmed by the blackening wind and clouds of a monsoon: "O'er me the hard sky, massy-paven, / Seemed to be dropping crags from heaven." If the chorus of rocks in the short story represented an Orphic harmony of voice and nature, this torrent gives the poet—the *little* Orpheus—a little taste of maenadic fury. Not stoned to death, he is brought down to size, and he acknowledges his weakness in images that identify diminishment with placid dejection. He desires "like the poor minnow from the shark . . . [to] plunge into deepest abysses dark." All of

Darley, life and work, seems involved in this plunge. He finds
that heroic heights are fundamentally alien to the soul, which
returns to its origins when it returns to its sense of smallness:

> Chasms with cragged teeth beset,
> Swallow me deeper, deeper yet!
> Lowliest path is least unsure,
> Most sublime most insecure,
> Fond Earth, within her parent breast
> Finds us, weak little ones, safe room
> And thither pain or care opprest,
> Sooner or later, as their doom,
> All creep for refuge and for rest.

If the first line of this passage images the threats of a vagina
dentalis, the succeeding lines discover the safer path back to the
womb in the sense of maternal comfort. Unlike those whose
closeness to primeval nature implicates their greatness and fall—
"huge aboriginal sons / Of Earth,"—the poet draws back to his
status as diminutive offspring. "Shall Adam's pigmy sperm /
Think to reach that sacred sphere[?] . . . Then hie on to
humble lands!"

A problem—and ultimately a special pleasure—in these climactic passages of poetic diminution lies in the great precedents
for the renunciation of great exuberance. In rhythm, occasional
turns of phrase, and in overall plan of the two parts, "One of
melancholy gladness, / One of most majestic sadness," *Nepenthe*
recalls Milton's "L'Allegro" and "Il Penseroso." When the poet
welcomes "Caverns in whose dripping cells / Hermit Sadness
sits alone," solitude is mitigated by the welcome presence of
Melancholy and Milton. The "dim cathedral walks" that now
please his fancy were the setting for dissolving into ecstasies in
"Il Penseroso." When he is impelled away from fame and sublimity, he distinguishes his wise passiveness from that last infirmity of noble minds so guarded in "Lycidas." And as he comes to
renounce both privileged fruit and cosmic vaulting, he seems to
call down on his own shoulders the injunction of Milton's

Raphael to be "lowly wise." What remains is to make his own shoulders not seem to bear the whole weight of the tradition of chastened spirit. The small poet must escape having his smallness seem sacrificial or his sadness seem a mode of Byronic posturing.

To guard himself from the blast of thunder that might strike the aspirant to emblematic humble dejection, Darley works one supreme transformation. The poet stands aside and beholds externalized, at inviolable distance, the emblem of desolation—the unicorn:

> his lonely pride
> To course his arid arena wide,
> Free as the hurricane, or lie here,
> Lord of his couch as his career!

The diminished poet retains his prime identity as derivative: he is "Desertion's only child," while the unicorn, no offspring but wholly *sui generis,* is acclaimed "wondrous Creature, of no kind." The poet keeps his loneliness while the animal absorbs the burden of emblematizing "lonely pride." The poet remains subservient to the winds and tides that rush him from place to place, while to the unicorn accrues a purified romanticism of the mind's being its own place: "Lord of his couch as his career." To be sure the "as" does not primarily mean "for" (able to fill his heart with Wordsworthian pleasure though oft on his couch) but rather "just as" (lord of both pleasures, active and contemplative). But whether the unicorn enjoys his flight imaginatively or actually, he is master of it. While he is singled out as the emblem of chaste vision, the poet (to use the emblem Collins adopts) escapes being tested by the girdle only one can wear.

The escape from greatness has been the theme, and a final escape concludes the poem. Even the vehicle of return from romantic lands back to the limitations of civilized nature is true to the myth of weakness in displacing anxiety. The poet espies a camel "Mourning his fallen lord that dies," and, as if that death took the place of his own, he lets the camel bear him, secondary rider, back to his native home. *Nepenthe* ends with a renunciation of romantic quest which, lightly skirting the subject of poetic stature, rests more easily in a statement of diminished breadth:

> Why leave I not this busy broil,
> For mine own clime, for mine own soil,
> My calm, dear, humble, native soil!
> There to lay me down at peace
> In my own first nothingness?

Spiritually as well as physically, the poet's "first nothingness" is his "original" state, from which his buoyancy carries him as far as it will and toward which his new sense of limitation draws him home again.

Darley's work may be regarded as a series of flights which substitute buoyancy or escape to humble lands for more strenuous wrestlings to the earth. But at his best he works some wondrous returns to the mysteriously self-transcending awareness of man's pigmy nature, and that awareness distinguishes poetry about weakness from weak poetry.

CHAPTER 6

Re: Generation in Blake

Altered is Zarathustra; a child hath Zarathustra become; an awakened one is Zarathustra: What wilt thou do in the land of the sleepers?

Nietzsche, *Thus Spake Zarathustra*

At a certain point in the history of psychoanalysis, Freud discovered that the physician's effort to recover the facts of a forgotten trauma was misdirected.[1] Some patients heard the facts that they or others had revealed to the analyst and remained wholly unaffected by such revelations. Others sought external or their own approval by inventing the kinds of trauma the analyst or they themselves wished to hear. However conscious or unconscious such invention, progress toward the psychic regeneration of the patient seemed unaffected or even impeded by the attempt to uncover the natural history of what had in fact been reconstituted in the mind. Freud came to see the analyst not as a researcher into the true histories of his patients but as an interpreter of their resistances and reworkings.

For Blake, prophet of psychic regeneration, the attempt to discover natural causes of mental states is likewise a misdirection. The traveler on the path from generative nature to regenerated human nature must leave behind him the figures and events of his biographical past, or at least come to distinguish their historicity from their reconstituted presence as phantoms of the psyche. In a letter to Thomas Butts, Blake depicted himself as such a traveler, met by an admonitory Thistle: " 'If thou goest back,' the thistle said, / 'Thou art to endless woe betrayed.' "[2]

Instead of going back or continuing on his way burdened by the actual past, "With my father hovering upon the wind / And my brother Robert just behind," Blake strikes the thistle, separating it from its "delving root." This defiance results in apocalyptic sight: "My brothers and father march before; / The heavens drop with human gore." Whatever the precise meaning of that apocalyptic gore, some visionary resistances have been overcome, and this personal poem draws to a close with renewed power: "Now I a fourfold vision see, / And a fourfold vision is given to me."

Insofar as biography offers natural rather than spiritual history, it misleads as well as impedes. Attempts to locate the origins of psychic phenomena outside the psyche are attempts to naturalize—to reduce man to nature, and the productions of inspiration to natural causes. In *All Religions Are One,* Blake distinguishes the spiritual journey from the search for sources. "As none by travelling over known lands can find out the unknown, so from already acquired knowledge Man could not acquire more. Therefore an universal Poetic Genius exists." Stylistically, this argument discovers the inspiration it announces, imitating the energetic unbinding of genius through the suddenness of that "therefore." If we sense a slight gap—the kind of gap an original, rather than a methodically reasoning, mind would make—between the first sentence and the second, we are experiencing in little the work of poetic genius. Searching for the natural causes of genius in "already acquired knowledge" would be denying genius, or the power to originate. One may borrow trappings—names, myths, meters—but all things that have sources outside the self remain just that—trappings for genius, externals employed by genius, and traps into which genius can fall. "The true man is the source, he being the Poetic Genius."

In contrast to the true man, author of his own sense of transcendence, the father of falsehood is the Devil, the "Mind of the Natural Frame." To such a mind no man can be understood to be a source or image of God as First Cause; every man in mind and body is the son of his natural mother, with a body moved by natural needs and a sciential mind busied in searching after second or natural causes. Against this Blake fulminates: "He who says there are Second Causes has already denied a First. The Word Cause is a foolish Word" (Annotations to Bacon). True causes for Blake are spiritual, though their consequences are to be read in the natural world. The refusal to reduce to natural causation becomes the basis of moral vision, which knows no ameliorating circumstances of the natural world. For this reason, there is very little phenomenal (as opposed to phenomenological) circumstance in Blake's poetry, which insists on placing the full burden of consequence on every mental affect. Every act of kindness is a little death, and every act of selfhood is a little fall—or better, Death and Fall in little. The whole history of consciousness seems at stake at every conscious moment.

Consequences are everywhere. The problem for the poet is to make a little clearing, a fictional space where a story can *seem* to begin. Recognizing the misdirection of natural causation, the true poet speaks of his work as being given or dictated to him. He knows the fictionality of this as of all myths he makes. But he knows that stories of inspiration are at least true to the fictionality of myth, and he knows that his stories must express this truth. The authors of scripture, for example, true poets that they were, composed an "original derivation from the Poetic Genius." What they wrote was a *derivation,* a fictional form, a secondary container of God as Word. But what they wrote was *original,* not to be reduced to Ugaritic or Sumerian sources but to be taken itself as The Source, itself poetic genius.

Blake's myths of origin are "original derivations" too, more original because more suspicious of the idea of derivation and more concerned with the sense of internal derivation—with the interior consequences of ruminating over a version of origins. To use the terms Blake prefers, we can say that we are directed to questions of regeneration rather than generation. In what follows I would like to consider Blake's central myth of origin and how the successive retellings of this story of generation—the way things first came to be the way they are in this world of Generation—move to regeneration.

I count seven major tellings: five in *The Four Zoas*, two in *Jerusalem* (plates 43, 80). There are prefigurings in the minor prophecies and lesser allusions in *Milton* and elsewhere in the two poems that offer full recitations. Significantly, the story loses its centrality after *The Four Zoas*, for the first version in *Jerusalem* is brought in tangentially from *The Four Zoas* III, while the second is a corrupt one spoken by the most unreliable of voices, and seems to move the poem to a different salvific myth by antipathetic reaction. But *Jerusalem* is a poem about forgetting and forgiving, for which Blake necessarily puts aside or decenters the story of remembered origins. I turn to the five versions in *The Four Zoas*.

i

Since getting to a beginning point behind a given beginning point is as much Blake's technique as his theme, it is no surprise that the earliest written version of the myth in *The Four Zoas* is to be found in Night II:

> Albion called Urizen & said: "Behold these sickening spheres!
>
> . . . . .
>
> Take thou possession! Take this sceptre! Go forth in my might.
> For I am weary, & must sleep in the dark sleep of death."
>
> [p. 23]

These lines probably marked the actual beginning of *Vala*, the ur-text of *The Four Zoas*—a point that is of far more than purely bibliographic interest. An epic mythology cannot be described from its genesis; the poet must plunge *in medias res*. In this traditional sense, as well as in a personal, psychological sense,

Blake could not invent, he could only reinvent, an epic poem, and so the stark assertiveness of these lines ("this is how things got started!") is countered by the poet's knowledge that he is not really beginning but borrowing from an earlier fragmented poem whose end—and more especially whose beginning—was left uncertain.

The essential fictionality of a declared origin is a point summarily articulated by Foucault: "It is always against a background of the already begun that man is able to reflect on what may serve for him as origin. For man, then, origin is by no means the beginning—a sort of dawn of history from which his ulterior acquisitiveness would have accumulated. Origin, for man, is much more the way in which man in general, any man, articulates himself upon the already-begun."[3] In the context of *The Four Zoas*, I would want to rewrite that last sentence this way: "Origin, for Blake, is much more the way in which man in general—Albion—articulates himself upon the already-begun." Though this would be true of the larger relation of the "Albion called Urizen" lines to all that precedes, something of this "articulation" can be observed even grammatically by comparing the peremptory "Albion called Urizen" (the simple past involves a determination to begin) with "Behold these sickening spheres!" (the ongoing action indicates the already-begun). If Albion is already sick, then calling upon Urizen to take possession can only be a belated response to a given situation. By projecting sickness on the spheres, the Fall is caught in the present act of falling away. I take it that the healthy Zoas are the cherubim that impel (and in some sense constitute) the wheels of the chariot of Divine Vision. If health is visionary "forwardness," the ability to impel the chariot onward, then sickness is self-revolution—like the motion of a wheel caught in a rut, spinning without engaging the other three.

Albion's cry, "Take thou possession," pushes into the position of cause an activity or state of mind ordinarily conceived as the effect of fall. Blake cannot begin, as he thought the Bible began, with a Urizenic possessor of the spheres. Possession is a fallen condition, possessiveness is diseased love. But he can begin with a voice crying, "Take thou possession," a defensive cry that causes or hastens the fall by hurrying over the fictionality of this first motion. Writing about Freud's myth of extrapsychic origins, David Carroll suggests that "to arrive too fast is probably not to penetrate deeply enough, to take what is only a symptom, a replacement for the origin, for the origin itself."[4] If we reconceive of Albion's hasty cry as "a replacement for the origin," we realize that what may be a false beginning is a real defense against beginnings. Albion cites his weariness as his reason, thus making spiritual sloth the antecedent of possessiveness. Energy is the consequence, indolence the original sin. Lavater aphorism 487: "If you ask me which is the real hereditary sin of human nature, do you imagine I shall answer pride? Or luxury? or ambition? or egotism? no; I shall say indolence—who conquers indolence will conquer all the rest." Blake notes in the margin of his copy of the *Aphorisms:* "Pride fullness of bred & *abundance of Idleness* was the sin of Sodom. See Ezekiel Ch xvi 49 ver." Blake's agreement with Lavater is indicated by his emphasis on idleness in a passage that, in context, seems rather to be pointing to pride. But the works of pride and the energetic activity of ambition are seen as consequence in *The Four Zoas,* results of Albion's spiritual sloth; this first sleep marks a turn from consciousness of the human form divine to the vegetable or generative state.

The concept of Urizen's energetic activity as consequence is enforced by the statement of motivation a little later: "and if perchance with iron power / He might avert his own despair." Already Blake seems to have come closer to the origins of his mythic action than he did in *The Book of Urizen,* where simple possessiveness, the desire to hold still, motivated Urizen: "I have sought for a joy without pain, / For a solid without fluctuation." In eternity one does not so seek. "He who kisses the joy as it flies / Lives in eternity's sunrise." Fearing evanescence, Urizen seeks a permanence Blake identifies with spiritual death. According to *The Four Zoas,* Albion's sleep, his going to "eternal death," impels Urizen's fear and flourish of activity.

In *Beyond the Pleasure Principle,* Freud announces the discovery that in addition to—anterior to—the instinct for pleasure is the instinct to restore things to an earlier state of inorganic quiescence.[5] Freud seems to delight in this little victory over his own theory that sexuality has absolute priority, and he speculates on lower forms of life with the happy thought that sexuality is itself a belated arrival in the course of natural history. Since the death instinct is, by his own admission, a variety of the pleasure principle, one is never sure whether *this* late arrival in his theory is accorded priority because of new discoveries about the nature of the mind or new needs to reapproach origins. At least as far as a particular patient is concerned, we make more therapeutic progress in supposing a given indolence to be a defense mechanism rather than an original instinct reasserting itself. For Blake the "sleep of nature" is no original state but the condition man falls into when he falls out of Eternity. Some decision about the sleep of Albion as a reaction formation seems to have been reached by Blake between the *Vala* version of the lines under consideration and their reappearance in *The Four Zoas.* The omitted line I have indicated by spaced dots reads "Whence is this Voice of Enion that soundeth in my Porches?" Adding this line Blake exteriorized Albion's decision in the way characteristic of this most dramatic poet: what is at first arbitrarily taken as an original action is, in revision, seen to be a response to another voice. (Voice retains this priority even in *Jerusalem,* where the sight of Jerusalem in Vala makes Albion fall for Vala; but it is Jerusalem's speech [plate 20] that is attempting to establish the priority of mediated desire and sight.) This general principle about the priority of voice in Blake is emphasized here by the "whence," which shifts questions about origin from the given encounter to another—another set of voices—further back.

Exactly what Albion has heard (which cry of woe) is not
specified, but we can distinguish two senses of "whence" each of
which tells us something of Blake's procedure. If we interpret the
"whence" literally—in terms of the letter of the poem—Albion
makes us question just where in the poem Enion's voice comes
from. From page 4, 5, or 7 in what becomes Night I? From
pages 17–18, which Stevenson places in Night II, Erdman in
Night I? Any of these lamentations would be enough to sicken
Albion, as would most especially Enion's grand song of experience which comes at the end of Night II. In one sense the "sickening spheres" could refer to the circularity of this poem, and
this Night in particular, which finds its beginning in its end. An
analogous mystery about origins is approached if we leave aside
such literalism about the "whence" and consider the meaning
of Enion and her voice. Blake opens the action of *The Four Zoas*
with the cry, "Begin with Tharmas, parent power, darkening in
the west: / 'Lost! Lost! Lost are my emanations. Enion, O
Enion!'" (p. 4). As the emanation of Tharmas, Enion is properly
the idealized expression of "parent power." Her cries of protest
that Tharmas is harboring Enitharmon are the jealous cries of
a fallen, natural parent over a child's preemption of her place.
Schematically, Blake's myth represents Enion as the emanation
of Tharmas, and Enitharmon as the emanation of Urthona-Los.
This we can call the schema of romantic origins, or things as they
are conceived from the perspective of Eternity. From the contrary
perspective of natural origins, Enitharmon and Los are born
from Enion. To begin his poem Blake must begin "with Tharmas, parent power," and a story of natural origins which is for
a while taken to antecede all else. The two perspectives are thus
like those in a Freudian scheme for conceptualizing the origins
of neurosis. The analyst must begin with the equivalent of
"Tharmas, parent power," and the exploration of natural origins
or trauma of extrapsychic sources. At some point, however, the
trauma as re-presented in the mind comes to have its own

"original" unity, and to be seen to have been composed of many "divisions" of sundry experiential roots.

The alternate anteriorities that the nature of Enion makes us confront are also represented in her name. "Enion" and "Tharmas" are said to be derivatives of ENItharmON. But the anteriority of the sign (the name Enitharmon and its Greek roots) opposes the anteriority of its significance in Generation: as the child of Enion, Enitharmon represents Tharmas caught in Enion —a "literal" sexual intercourse of alphabet letters as a sign of female possessiveness. Thus, though it is possible etymologically that Enion comes from Enitharmon, the "natural" story represents Enitharmon as Enion's child. The conflict between romantic and natural origins, between the letter and the litter, is represented in the story action by having Enitharmon first find her way into the bosom of Tharmas (this is pity, an element of high romance, and a derivative of the story of Albion's fall); she is then "taken in" by Enion (this is the possessive love represented as pregnancy, an element of natural origins, and a derivative of the story of Tharmas' fall).

Before leaving this first account of first things, we must note where it divides between the origins it presumes to be in the past and the original action that constitutes its present tense. In revising the story from *Vala* for *The Four Zoas,* Blake added two lines after those already quoted: "Thy brother Luvah hath smitten me; but pity thou his youth, / Though thou hast not pitied my age, O Urizen, prince of light." Acknowledging the smitings of Luvah as past, but calling for the reorganization of the psyche under Urizen, Albion stands at a point he takes as the origin of his own neurosis: between the sexual events—the natural origins of the past—and the displacement of the libido that he calls into being. To be sure, as Freud insisted, the unconscious mental processes "are not ordered temporally"; [6] but in granting consciousness and a conscious decision to Albion, Blake represented poetically a point of origin that can only be hypothesized by the analyst.

ii

The manuscript of *The Four Zoas* leaves uncertain where our second account of Albion's fall is to be placed. In the Erdman-Bloom text it is the one placed first in the poem, in the middle of Night I; in the Stevenson-Erdman text this account forms the opening of Night II. By either reckoning it was, though composed later, intended to come earlier in the poem than the first account we have examined.

This version is sung by Enitharmon:

> "Hear! I will sing a song of death; it is a song of Vala.
>
> The fallen Man takes his repose: Urizen sleeps in the porch.
> Luvah and Vala woke & flew up from the human heart
> Into the brain; from thence upon the pillow Vala slumbered.
> And Luvah seized the horses of light, & rose into the chariot
> of day.
> Sweet laughter seized me in my sleep; silent & close I laughed,
> For in the visions of Vala I walked with the mighty fallen one,
> I heard his voice among the branches, & among sweet flowers:
>
> " 'Why is the light of Enitharmon darkened in dewy morn?
> Why is the silence of Enitharmon a terror, & her smile a
> whirlwind?
> Uttering this darkness in my halls, in the pillars of my holy
> ones,
> Why dost thou weep as Vala & wet thy veil with dewy tears,
> In slumbers of my night-repose, infusing a false morning,
> Driving the female emanations all away from Los?
> I have refused to look upon the universal vision;
> And wilt thou slay with death him who devotes himself to
> thee—
> Once born for the sport & amusement of man, now born to
> drink up all his powers?'
>
> "I heard the sounding sea; I heard the voice weaker and
> weaker.
> The voice came & went like a dream—I awoke in my sweet
> bliss."

> Then Los smote her upon the earth. 'Twas long ere she
>   revived.
>
>   .   .   .   .   .
>
> Then Enitharmon reddening fierce stretched her immortal
>   hands:
> "Descend, O Urizen, descend with horse & chariots."
>
> [pp. 10–11]

The setting is important and not to be separated from the song.
Just as Albion, according to the first account, establishes a point
of origin by declaring a certain event past and calling down
another, so Enitharmon establishes her own role in originating
the fall. She begins by reciting an account of the past and ends
by calling for the same event as Albion did—the descent of
Urizen. By telling this story and herself bringing about the reign
of Urizen, she challenges the priority of the account Blake wrote
first. This challenge is not simply a function of the revision in
the myth she recounts or the fact that Enitharmon's account is
placed earlier in the poem. It is itself the subject of the argument
between Los and Enitharmon that provides the setting for Enitharmon's story. As generated children, Los and Enitharmon are
aware of not standing at their own origins. Los acknowledges
their derivative nature and points to the fact of generation—the
fact of the Fall: "O, how our parents sit & mourn in their silent
secret bowers!" Perhaps it is Los's prophetic nature that lets him
identify with the condition of the parents, knowing as he does
that every child is but a proleptic parent, every parent but a
belated child.

Enitharmon wants no part of such knowledge and insists instead on the bitter facts of *storge* or parental love: parents
depend on the uneasy devotion of their children, who in turn
require an incessant flow of affection, feeding on all they can
get with insatiable "storgous appetite, craving" (p. 61). "If we
grateful prove," she warns, "they will withhold sweet love, whose
food is thorns & bitter roots" (p. 10). Such is natural love, rooted

in the bitter facts of guilt and dependency. Los's "soft" attitude toward parents relaxes the tension in the line that binds generation to generation. Enitharmon accuses Los, "Thou in indolence reposest," and transposes this lethargy to the usurpation story in which Albion's generated offspring revolt against their father. The Song of Vala she sings begins with double indolence, double trouble: "The fallen Man takes his repose: Urizen sleeps in the porch." Thus her own conflict with Los provides the context— the natural cause—for the story of an original sleep. Were she innocently recounting the events of the past, they would have imaginative priority over the quarrel between herself and Los; but her narration is by no means innocent, and behind the ostensible "let me tell you how things were," we hear "let me fabricate a tale that will re-present the past in a way that will alter your present subservience to it, Los."

One tribute to Enitharmon's revisionary power comes from manuscript evidence. Just as Enitharmon is revising the myth of Albion's fall, Blake is revising this Song of Vala, evidently written earlier for another purpose, to suit Enitharmon as speaker. The manuscript shows that the story originally concerned Luvah and Vala directly, and that revision transformed the episode into a vision of Enitharmon. Thus Albion's cry that Enitharmon says she heard in the vision of Vala, "Why dost thou weep as Vala," was originally Luvah's direct address to his emanation, "Why dost thou weep, O Vala." The revised "as" has two mutually reinforcing meanings. Enitharmon is seen by the Albion of her own song to weep as (in the character of) Vala. She also weeps as (while, when) Vala weeps, because this song is a history of the present state—a tale of the genesis of the tale and, as such, an extraordinary victory over the priority of the past. The self-referential nature of her literary achievement stands as a counter to Los's reverential humanism.

We shall see (we have already seen, if we follow Stevenson's ordering of the manuscript pages) that in the standard account of Albion's fall presented by the Ambassadors from Beulah, Vala's seduction of Albion was not quite the first event. But it is the one Enitharmon presents as first—before challenging the whole notion of anteriority by having Vala slumber, and Albion, in Vala's dream, address Enitharmon as Vala. We could say that when Albion, by Enitharmon's own account, asks "Why dost thou weep as Vala," the recognition seems to be given to him that Enitharmon is occupying Vala's place, that she is repeating, in her relation to Los, a fundamental error of possessive, Vala-like love. The only thing wrong with such a formulation is that it makes use of the temporal assumption of repetition, whereas it is precisely that which Enitharmon is challenging. Is this challenge deliberate, or does she see no more than her own story—can she read the old myths only as referring to her and literally addressed to her? The alternate answers to this question deserve separate attention.

If we attribute to Enitharmon consciousness of her own revisionism, we see her reworking of the Albion myth as an aspect of possessiveness: she makes even the myth her own, and presumably out of an intention to thwart or arouse Los. She cannot, we are told, herself "weave a veil of covering for her sins," but she can use a ready-made veil, the Song of Vala, for her purposes. The result is a kind of neurotic behavior whose scenario we can clarify by supposing, for a moment, that it takes place wholly on the level of domestic quarrel. An antirevisionist husband, eager for family reconciliation, is at odds with his wife, who finds her husband's interest in relating to their parents a threat to his absolute involvement with her. She tells a story that exposes her selfishness, and he strikes her. She cries for help, and in rushes Your Reasonable Parental Authority—be it policeman, actual parent, or nosy neighbor who has been listening at the door and just waiting to interfere anyway. Breaking the conjugal scene, this interferer leaves the husband, previously concerned about a diminishment in his wife's love, now worried about losing his wife altogether. He repents not only having hit her but having crossed her in any way, and, like the fifth husband of the Wife of Bath, willingly reasserts his dependence on her good will. Back to Blake:

> Los saw the wound of his blow; he saw, he pitied, he wept.
> Los now repented that he had smitten Enitharmon; he felt love
> Arise in all his veins; he threw his arms around her loins
> To heal the wound of his smiting.   [p. 12]

But there is the other possibility we must consider—one that offers an alternative to the bad taste of the first, or at least exposes an unwarranted limitation there. As is often the case in criticism of Blake's "characters," it is the attribution of consciousness to Enitharmon that leads one to domesticate the scene. Yet if we take more seriously Blake's statement of Enitharmon's restriction, that she "had no power to weave a veil of covering for her sins," we come up with a different relationship between her motivation—now unconscious—and the story she tells. Suppose we read that statement as "she had no conscious power to weave a veil of covering." Conscious power to rework the Albion myth would depend on an awareness of the difference between the way the myth is remembered and the way it is reformulated and presented to Los. With a demystified sense of the relation of memory to the "real" past, Freud noted that "it may indeed be questioned whether we have any memories at all *from* our childhood: memories *relating to* our childhood may be all that we possess." [7] On this model we would need to distinguish a time of memory formation (the time of the fall into nature in which Los and Enitharmon are generated as the mutually hostile children of Enion) from a fictional time, a mythic childhood (the time of Albion, the time in which Albion could find Enitharmon weeping as Vala). Personal, like national, memory uses materials from the mythic past, but it dates from, "originates in," a more naturalized historical consciousness. Freud gave this idea a beginning by naming it: "A recollection . . . whose value lies in the fact that it represents in the memory impressions and thoughts of a later date whose content is connected with its own by symbolic or similar links, may appropriately be called a 'screen memory.' " [8] Blake could be saying that Enitharmon had not the power to construct a screen memory, and that despite herself she tells the past as it happened, bringing about consequences unforeseen by her. But the idea of an unadulterated tale of origins is so remote—though all versions expose, through their separate adulterations, real truths—that we more accurately reflect the relation of Enitharmon's Song of Vala to other accounts by reading her restriction as the impossibility of weaving anything *but* a screen memory for her sins.

There seems to be special warrant for citing Freud in a discussion of Enitharmon's version of first things because there is a psychoanalytic orthodoxy about an account which has sex as both center and origin. Equally Freudian—though perhaps only more recently appreciated as such—is the implied relation between a hypothesized ur-text belonging to the unconscious and any given text or conscious transcription. If we consider the Albion story as an unconscious text, re-presented in the various versions, then Jacques Derrida can sum up what Enitharmon's account tells us about re-presentations of the myth:

The text is not thinkable in an originary or modified form of presence. The unconscious text is already woven of pure traces, differences in which meaning and force are united; a text nowhere present, consisting of archives which are always already transcriptions. Originary prints. Everything begins with reproduction. Always already: repositories of a meaning which was never present, whose signified presence is always reconstituted by deferment, nachträglich, belatedly, supplementarily. [9]

"Always ready!" is an exclamation a reader can make opening to any Blake text, though the burden of belatedness is especially keen in the first books of *The Four Zoas*. And the coupling of "meaning and force" can refer us not simply to the urgency of the Albion story that will out, whatever the circumstances or level of understanding of the speaker; it can stand for the energy everywhere manifest in Blake that we are learning, through successive readings, to find more truly coupled with meaning because more truly concerned, whatever the context, with the meaning of origination.

iii

There is something very moving about the circumstances surrounding the account of Albion's fall presented by the messengers from Beulah. Though the whole idea of a "saving remnant," to whom this version is recounted, has been criticized as extraneous to Blake's myth, such harshness only helps us see their supplementarity as itself salvific, and the story they hear as delayed but divine. Coming on the scene at the end of Night I, the messengers from Beulah offer the reader as well as the Remnant a Beulah-like repose from the complexities of *Nachträglichkeit* and the perspectivism to which they have already been introduced through other speakers and chronologically later events. By the Stevenson reckoning this would be the first account of first things—a kind of "rest before labor," to borrow Blake's aphorism preceding the whole work. By the Erdman ordering we have already heard Enitharmon's version, and this one straightens things out. Either way it has a claim to corrective definitiveness. We should note that the story the messengers tell is preceded by the exclamation "Shiloh is in ruins." Bloom, observing that Shiloh is a name for Christ, the bringer of peace, explains: "That Shiloh is in ruins accounts for the contentions in war between Luvah and Urizen."[10] But we must neutralize the implied causality and temporal sequence. The Christ myth, like the saving remnant which is an aspect of it, has not priority but authority; it offers a parallel, and perhaps a superadvenient, mythology like the counterplot Milton shadows forth at the end of *Paradise Lost* I. Thus to state "Shiloh is in ruins" is to offer neither cause nor effect of Albion's fall; and if it seems, in a phrase, a definitive

formulation of origins, this is only from the perspective of a
preempted end.

What the messengers have to say about origins they say through
the detail of their account:

> The Eternal Man wept in the holy tent. Our brother in
>   Eternity,
> Even Albion, whom thou lovest, wept in pain; his family
> Slept round on hills and valleys in the regions of his love.
> But Urizen awoke, and Luvah woke, & thus conferred:
>
> "Thou, Luvah," said the prince of light, "behold our sons
>   and daughters
> Reposed on beds. Let them sleep on. Do thou alone depart
> Into thy wished kingdom where in majesty & power
> We may erect a throne. Deep in the north I place my lot,
> Thou in the south. Listen attentive. In silent of this night
> I will enfold the eternal tent in clouds opaque, while thou,
> Seizing the chariots of the morning, go outfleeting, ride
> Afar into the zenith, high bending thy furious course
> Southward, with half the tents of men enclosed in clouds
> Of Tharmas & Urthona. I remaining in porches of the brain
> Will lay my sceptre on Jerusalem the emanation,
> On all her sons and thy sons, O Luvah, & on mine.
> Till dawn was wont to wake them. Then my trumpet sound-
>   ing loud,
> Ravished away in night my strong command shall be obeyed.
> For I have placed my sentinels in stations: each tenth man
> Is bought and sold, & in dim night my word shall be their
>   law."
>
> Luvah replied: "Dictate to thy equals: am not I
> The prince of all the hosts of men, nor equal know in
>   Heaven?
> If I arise into the zenith, leaving thee to watch
> The emanation and her sons, the Satan and the Anak,
> Sihon and Og, wilt thou not, rebel to my laws, remain
> In darkness building thy strong throne, & in my ancient night,
> Daring my power, wilt arm my sons against me in the Atlantic,
> My deep, my night—which thou assuming hast assumed my
>   crown?

I will remain as well as thou, & here with hands of blood
Smite this dark sleeper in his tent; then try my strength with
    thee."

While thus he spoke his fires reddened o'er the holy tent;
Urizen cast deep darkness round him, silent brooding death,
Eternal death to Luvah. Raging Luvah poured
The lances of Urizen from chariots; round the holy tent
Discord began, & yells & cries shook the wide firmament.
              .   .   .   .   .
But Urizen, with darkness overspreading all the armies,
Sent round his heralds, secretly commanding to depart
Into the north. Sudden with thunder's sound, his multitudes
Retreat from the fierce conflict, all the sons of Urizen at once
Mustering together in thick clouds, leaving the rage of Luvah
To pour its fury on himself, & on the eternal Man.

Sudden down fell they all together into an unknown space,
Deep, horrible, without end.   [pp. 21–22]

In their useful summary of the action of *The Four Zoas,* Mary
Lynn Johnson and Brian Wilkie attribute the clarity of the messengers' account to their concern for the origins rather than the
outcome of the Zoas' action: "The messengers see the fall in
terms not of its symptoms but of its causes, not in terms of
stunned instinct or confused imagination but as a conspiracy and
power struggle between Luvah and Urizen, . . . the two . . .
powermongers in man."[11] Though the last two words of that
sentence acknowledge what must always be taken for granted
in talking about Albion, we can approach the uniqueness of the
messengers' account by considering how they elide the interiority
of the action. If Enitharmon offers an orthodoxy of psychoanalysis, the messengers offer an orthodoxy of political science: the
will to power is the original will, and other formulations (like
sexual will or the death instinct) represent belated, decadent
efforts at accounting internally for what can be observed first
externally, between two warring principles or parties. Stevenson
calls the messengers' account "the usurpation story in its standard

form," an identification we can valorize by interpreting *standard* not simply as "normative" but as an ensign or emblem of a political movement.

What makes this account so public or political—without diminishing its authoritativeness—is its emphasis on rhetoric. Not in a thought behind a speech but somewhere between speeches is the origin of the Fall to be sought now. Other accounts leave Albion's sleep suspect; but as the setting of this verbal exchange, Albion's sleep is not itself an Original Flaw but a given—like that of similar nocturnal encounters in Homer, Virgil, Milton, down to Wagner's *Götterdämmerung*. (The epic conventionality of the scene is part of its public nature.) We are directed instead to the exchange between speakers, and precisely to something that occurs between the two speeches. For hearing first Urizen's plot and then Luvah's response, one cannot tell who had the thought first. Was Luvah plotting the death of Albion, and is he angry to find Urizen ambitious too? Or is it Urizen's suggestion that moves Luvah into anger and conflict? "Who first?" expresses the standard question about origins. But this account would imply that if we wish a definitive answer we had best define (set a limit to) the question by rephrasing it, "Who spoke first?" Rhetoric questions whether antecedent thought—if, indeed, that can be posited—should be considered action. From Luvah's passional viewpoint, priority is a desideratum, and the sequence works like this: Luvah had a thought, Urizen spoke that thought, Luvah is impelled into action. From Urizen's cerebral and political perspective, the goal is to impel action without appearing to be himself the first mover, so that he can be thought the right counterrevolutionary force to call to power. The sequence works like this: Urizen broods, Luvah rebels, and Urizen remains "silent brooding death." Both Zoas offer technical solutions to the problem of origins by suggesting in different ways that the first action is a reaction.

We can better confront the relation of rhetoric to the politics of the messengers' account by substituting for the limited vo-

cabulary of action and reaction the more suggestive terms of
Shakespeare:

> Between the acting of a dreadful thing
> And the first motion, all the interim is
> Like a phantasma or a hideous dream.
> The Genius and the mortal instruments
> Are then in council; and the state of a man,
> Like to a little kingdom, suffers then
> The nature of an insurrection.   [*Julius Caesar,* II.i.63–69]

In the first reading (to the extent that such origins are recover-
able or imaginable) the crucial words in the opening line could
be misread. If one takes "acting" to mean the actual doing, and
"first motion" to mean a deliberation of a political caucus not
yet seconded, the result is a temporal confusion—a "hideous
dream" like that into which Urizen's strategy casts Luvah. If one
corrects oneself and reads *acting* to mean "enacting" (deciding)
and "first motion" to mean the actual doing, the result is a
"hideous dream" like that in the lines of the messengers' account
that I have omitted and indicated by spaced dots. Here are the
missing lines:

> Beside his anvil stood Urthona dark, a mass of iron
> Glowed furious on the anvil prepared for spades & coulters.
> All his sons fled from his side to join the conflict. Pale he
>   heard
> The eternal voice. He stood; the sweat chilled on his mighty
>   limbs.
> He dropped his hammer. Dividing from his aching bosom
>   fled
> A portion of his life, shrieking upon the wind—she fled
> And Tharmas took her in, pitying. Then Enion in jealous fear
> Murdered her, & hid her in her bosom, embalming her for fear
> She should arise again to life. Embalmed in Enion's bosom
> Enitharmon remains a corse—such thing was never known
> In Eden, that one died a death never to be revived.
> Urthona stood in terror, but not long; his spectre fled
> To Enion, & his body fell. Tharmas beheld him fall
> Endlong, a raging serpent rolling round the holy tent.
> The sons of war, astonished at the glittering monster, drove
> Him far into the world of Tharmas, into a caverned rock.

In the sleepless night of resolution and rebellion that Blake describes, the moment between the acting (the debate between Urizen and Luvah) and the first motion (Urizen's, like the Miltonic God's, primordial uncircumscribed retirement) is the "phantasma or hideous dream" presented here. Broadly, it is the phantasma of Night I—for the gruesome events that the Night recounted are redreamt here. Particularizing, we could say that the phantasm that rises is the Spectre of Urthona, who is divided from Enitharmon at this point of insurrection in the state of man's mind. Urthona (Earth owner) is like Shakespeare's mighty Caesar, about whom Brutus remarks, "I have not known when his affections sway'd / More than his reason." If, suddenly, Luvah rages, we must remember that Urizen (his very name sounds like "your reason") holds superior sway. Behind these identifications is a plain political fact: as Brutus discovers when he tries to reason the desire for rebellion into being, no rebellion can take place till a withdrawal of reason lets affection rage. When reason returns, it is to justify what has been decided in the interval of choice for which ordinary temporality and temporizing rationality have been suspended.

Because the dialogue between Luvah and Urizen precedes and establishes the conditions for Urthona's deliberation and despair, Blake's myth, like a more orthodox one, could be said to affirm that "In the beginning was the Word." Yet in the politics of divine temporality, questions of origin refer not to the anterior intentionality of God but to the begetting he publicly reenacts when he declares, "This day I have begot mine only Son." Just as, for Milton, creation could take place because God the Father himself retired, so for Blake creation and fall take place in a revisionary sense of retirement—Albion's sleep. And, just as Milton's Satan challenges the anteriority of God's brooding—"new Laws thou see'st impos'd; / New Laws from him who reigns (*PL,* V.679–80)—and goes on to make his own withdrawal to the north, so Blake's Urizen localizes a time and place for the beginning of fallen time. I turn to these literary parallels here to emphasize just how literary, how much a function of poetic narration, is the displacement of questions of origin from a first motion to a space between motions, a poetic space opened up in the messengers' account between their representation of Luvah's speech and their return to Urizen. In this space all the events of Night I are newly "presented" or made present. The sense of stasis provides the new beginning, and it is altogether appropriate that the new character discovered at this point is Urthona—the one who, in making a beginning, becomes the form of the temporal poet, Los: "Pale he heard / The eternal voice. He stood; the sweat chilled on his mighty limbs. / He dropped his hammer." A few lines later Blake repeats the verb of stasis before announcing Urthona's actual fall: "Urthona *stood* in terror, but not long; his spectre fled / To Enion, & his body fell." If the search for historical beginnings is futile, poetry still can create the illusion of real beginnings by opening up such spaces—"not long," but long enough—and seeming to impel action out of them. Not the Daughters of Memory but the Daughters of Beulah are Blake's muses, and their work is "creating spaces."

iv

In Night III, Ahania re-creates the story of the original Urizen-Luvah conflict and creates just such a space. Psychologically, Urizen is already damned, but the interval of her narration allows for the separation between Urizen's anxiety and a first motion, making the action he goes on to take, when it comes, seem an originatory one. After Ahania's speech, Urizen castigates her: "And thou hast risen with thy moist locks into a watery image / Reflecting all my indolence, my weakness and my death" (p. 43). The indolence was already there—indeed, it is the subject of Ahania's story. But the distance between indolent Urizen and the reflection of his indolence is a blank in nature, a space in which consciousness grows and seems freshly impelled.

Here is her vision of first things, which we need to examine
by itself before considering its very beautiful and complex setting:

> The darkening Man walked on the steps of fire before his halls,
> And Vala walked with him in dreams of soft deluding slumber.
> He looked up and saw thee, prince of light, thy splendour
>   faded,
> But saw not Los nor Enitharmon, for Luvah hid them in
>   shadow,
> In a soft cloud outstretched across; and Luvah dwelt in the
>   cloud.
>
> Then Man ascended mourning into the splendours of his
>   palace;
> Above him rose a shadow from his wearied intellect
> Of living gold, pure, perfect, holy; in white linen pure he
>   hovered,
> A sweet entrancing self-delusion, a watery vision of Man,
> Soft exulting in existence, all the Man absorbing.
>
> Man fell upon his face prostrate before the watery shadow,
> Saying, "O Lord, whence is this change? Thou knowest I am
>   nothing."
> And Vala trembled and covered her face, and her locks were
>   spread on the pavement.
>
> I heard, astonished at the vision, and my heart trembled
>   within me;
> I heard the voice of the slumberous Man, and thus he spoke,
> Idolatrous to his own shadow, words of Eternity uttering:
>
> "Oh, I am nothing when I enter into judgment with thee.
> If thou withdraw thy breath I die and vanish into Hades;
> If thou dost lay thine hand upon me, behold I am silent;
> If thou withhold thine hand I perish like a fallen leaf.
> Oh, I am nothing, and to nothing must return again;
> If thou withdraw thy breath, behold I am oblivion!"
>
> He ceased: the shadowy voice was silent; but the cloud hov-
>   ered over their heads

In golden wreaths, the sorrow of Man, and the balmy drops
   fell down.
And lo! that son of Man, that shadowy spirit of the fallen
   one,
Luvah, descended from the cloud. In terror Man arose.
                                                [pp. 39–40]

In contrast to the psychoanalytic and political accounts offered
by Enitharmon and the messengers from Beulah, Ahania's perspective could be called that of the history of religion. Or,
acknowledging that all accounts are versions of the workings of
the mind, we might say that whereas Enitharmon could have
been reading *The Interpretation of Dreams,* Ahania seems to
have mastered the opening chapters of *The Future of an Illusion.*
As a representation of the origins of religious consciousness,
Ahania's myth shares with others of that sort a special relationship to the idea of beginnings based on an ambiguity in referent:
the individual mind, or some historical memory on the part of
the race, or one attributed to primitive minds generally. The
individual (or collective) religious consciousness senses its belatedness and attributes its own origin to a preexistent divinity.
Myths like the one Blake represents here begin challenging such
attributive priorities through their very generality: before an individual or a people invented its divinity, there was this pattern
of inventing divinities—this pattern which is as characteristic of
the mind generally as it is of anthropological history. If "slumberous man . . . idolatrous to his own shadow" is man creating
God in the image of man, then a remark of Nietzsche could sum
up the universality of such self-made origins, transcending distinctions between conscious and unconscious, individual and collective mythologies: "What we do in our dreams we also do in
our waking hours; we first invent and create the man with whom
we are dealing and then—we forget immediately that we have
done it." [12]
   If we anticipate ourselves for a moment and consider the
drama of Ahania addressing Urizen, we might imagine her

rewriting Nietzsche's aphorism in the form of an injunction: "What we do in our dreams we must not do in our waking hours!" But leaving aside for a while the drama and its hortatory intentionality, we can note in her presentation of her vision a fictional equivalent for the self-begetting her story concerns. She introduces the story by asking Urizen to heed "The vision of Ahania in the slumbers of Urizen," and the very line with which I began the excerpt from her account is no doubt prefixed (Blake's manuscript is unpunctuated, but this arrangement makes best sense) by the subordinate clause, "When Urizen slept in the porch and the Ancient Man was smitten . . ." Since Ahania's vision is "in the slumbers of Urizen," it is, she would claim, Urizen's vision; and since Albion's trouble originates in his "soft, deluding slumber" which in turn originates in Urizen's sleep, Urizen has but to wake—to come to consciousness of Ahania's story as history—and the future of the religious illusion will be in his hands.

It seems especially appropriate that Ahania should present religious history if we consider her association with the Kabbalistic Chochmah or the Christian Holy Spirit. Harold Bloom notes that "Ahania is like the Wisdom of Jehovah that played before him in the Book of Proverbs, and helped him to his creation."[13] Speaking in Proverbs 8, Wisdom claims the "originality" of having been created before Creation: "Ages ago I was set up, at the first, before the beginning of the earth." Her priority is not simply historical but psychological, for the Wisdom who "was daily His delight" embodies the pleasure of creativity before anxiety was known. Proverbs goes on to envision the lady Wisdom repeating the religious theme of the whole book: "The fear of the Lord is the beginning of wisdom." By Ahania's less orthodox account, "fear of the Lord" is the beginning of the end of wisdom, for when man addresses God, "O Lord, whence is this change?" the change from psychological health is reified.

Ahania's demystification of orthodoxy—or, more precisely, of the orthodox prestige of origins—furthers her role as inspirer, the form of Intellectual Pleasure that attends poetic, if not cosmic, creation. This is important to observe in its particularity, for if unorthodoxy is ordinarily late—a falling away from a pristine state—deconstructed orthodoxy can earn the right to be thought itself early and originatory. Milton evoked the Heavenly Muse who "from the first / Wast present," and who, as the Holy Spirit, "Dove-like satst brooding on the vast Abyss / And mad'st it pregnant." Ahania's story demystifies this by distinguishing what from the first was present from the "watery shadow" that broods over slumbering Man. The Idea of the Holy is originating: "Above him rose a shadow from his wearied intellect." But there is already a shadow there, a cloud in which Luvah hides Los and Enitharmon. When Milton prays, "What in me is dark / Illumine," he asks for unobstructed vision of first things. In reminding us that Los and Enitharmon, generated offspring of the Original Zoas, are already *there,* Blake preempts the very idea of first things and lets us see that only a blindness to some aspect of the story can allow the story to seem to begin.

In a sense such disenchantment with origins is always predicated, for every account of beginnings is a repetition, and only some distinction about levels of fiction allows for each beginning to maintain its authority. By Northrop Frye's account one escapes circularity in distinguishing planes. Thus "Albion's fall began with his adoration of a separate female will in Beulah, and was completed in Generation, the world of Luvah and Vala." [14] Yet the temporal terms (began, completed) nag at the scheme, and the problem is accentuated when Vala is identified as both the original object of adoration and the result of a divided, fallen consciousness. Similarly, Urizen is faded but also about to fade, and even within Ahania's story Albion is worshiping Urizen in the role of an Old Testament God before Urizen falls into that role. Milton could easily distinguish the temporality of Satan's fall from that of Adam's, but for Blake the commitment to internality requires that the illusion of origins be predicated on a blindness to one aspect of what remains, after all, the same tale. Such is the wisdom of Ahania.

Though it is possible to read Ahania's story as a history of religious consciousness generally, certain aspects of it suggest a specifically Christian myth as its original. Perhaps the greatest conceptual difficulty in Ahania's story ("mystery" would be the appropriate term within religious vocabulary) concerns the identity of the enclouded figure, and this uncertainty would be specially charged if set against a Christian background. The passage in which man is seen creating his own god is preceded by the suggestion that Urizen is in the skies; man "looked up and saw thee, prince of light." After the passage of god-creation there is no further reference to Urizen within the story, and we are told only that Luvah "descended from the cloud." Since, for Blake, all deities reside in the human breast, the elements of parody are built into a scheme of vertical transcendence that conceives of God as above and man below. The line "Above him rose a shadow from his wearied intellect" forms its own critique of man's self-lowering: "Man fell upon his face prostrate before the watery shadow." And the very speed of directional transformations mocks the idea of transcendence when we read in a single line, "Luvah descended from the cloud. In terror Man arose."

The more specific attack on Christian temporality has two foci: For one thing, the first god figure perceived as "there" before man's projection is Urizen, "prince of light, [with] splendour faded." As such he is more like Lucifer the morning star than the God of Light. For the Christian, man's awareness of the living God is primary, while Ahania's account leaves the idea of God a consequence of some awareness of fall projected onto the universe at large. Not so did Milton describe Adam waking in paradise; but religious educators ever since the Fall have followed Ahania's scheme anyway. Put simply in terms of existents rather than awarenesses, Christianity has it that Satan himself is later than God; his fall is consequent to the elevation of the Son, and man's creation follows third. To Christianity's ordering—God, Satan, Man—Ahania's story responds with this revision: Man, Satan, God.

The other focus for this radically elliptical reworking of Christian time is the point of identification of Luvah and Christ. The temporality of the Son is a Christian mystery, and though Milton placed the Son in time, orthodoxy has him coeternal and thus an actualization, as well as an image, of generational reconciliation: there is no generation gap between the Father and the Son. Blake's Luvah, hiding Los and Enitharmon, makes a mystery of the fact of generation and the state of Generation. When he descends it is not as Son of God but as "son of Man"—in a very unchristian sense of that term, signifying something like "conception of God (generated) by man." (Staying wholly within a religious vocabulary one could say that Luvah makes a mystery of regeneration, but the meaning of this separateness is clarified by considering its equivalent in the naturalistic terms of parents—Tharmas, Enion—and children—Los, Enitharmon.) Equally unchristian is the sense in which Luvah is God of Love. As sexual desire, Luvah preempted the mind of Man. And, while sexuality in the world of Generation can find its proper outlet, a Luvah in the clouds—idealized form of sexual desirability—constitutes a genuine pornography and calls for the imagining of a great censor. In Freudian terms, the ego, to protect itself from the demands of the id, projects an ultimate superego. If such terms seem to preempt religious history, that is because Ahania's account acknowledges the reordering of the events of psychic hitsory and suggests that sexual physics has priority over religious *meta*physics.

Johnson and Wilkie describe Ahania as "a combination of Desdemona and a Near Eastern princess, and in Night III Urizen is a jealous Othello, a base Indian who throws away a pearl." [15] Seeing Ahania's Luvah as a revision of the Christian Son of Man, we might recall that the line from *Othello* alluded to by

Johnson and Wilkie is a textual problem in Shakespeare, and can alternatively be read as referring to a base Judaean who throws away a pearl that is Christ. Ahania mourns the "throwaway" she claims is past history: "Why didst thou listen to the voice of Luvah that dread morn / To give the immortal steeds of light to his deceitful hands?" (p. 39). She also asks, implicitly, "Why don't you listen to me instead?" To understand how the turn she desires to effect influences the account of first things that she gives Urizen, we need to move from the account as religious history to the dramatic situation and the "character" of Ahania as Urizen's emanation.

There is ample reason to think of Ahania's relation to Urizen as that of loving wife to hopeless husband. If she errs in assessing Urizen's powers of control, "that is the kind of dutiful wife she is," write Johnson and Wilkie, and if her fears and ignorances stand in her way, she has done all she could: "Ahania's loving and sensible advice produces the same response that Desdemona's intelligent and well-meant advocacy of Cassio does: Urizen feels jealous rage." Harold Bloom is more stringent and dismisses Ahania's account because she is "a faithful but misled wife in assuming that Urizen must have been seduced by Luvah, but as readers we have learned better."[16] We have, to be sure, learned otherwise, or—if we can accept Ahania's account too and make of Urizen's fall a single event not yet completed—we have learned later ways. Her account does not so much refute the story of Urizen's usurpation as it antecedes it, reworking his possessive insecurity into a reaction to her speech. As we have heard the account up to now, Urizen grew power-hungry. As we hear the account now, a failure to assume his proper powers produced the weakness that makes Urizen (hearing about his failure and reacting against hearing about it) power-hungry. In saying this, I risk the accusation that I am confusing what was with what is to come. But so much of Blake depends on challenging our ordinary assumptions about temporal sequence in mental history that the risk seems a necessary one.

Let us clarify the alternatives. If we assume that there is a single time sequence to the past, then Ahania may be misled in believing Urizen was seduced by Luvah; she may, alternatively, be not misled but misleading, telling the history in a nicer, more guilt-free way (giving the present the most romantic origins) for the purpose of luring Urizen into using what she believes is still his best potential; or she may be neither misled nor misleading but overtly, though subtly, acknowledging Urizen's part in the rebellion and exposing both his weakness and his will to power disguised as the Shadow from man's wearied intellect. Thus when she turns from second person ("saw thee, prince of light") to third person ("Above him rose a shadow") she is expressing not the illusion of man seeking an ultimate I-Thou relationship but the machinations of Urizen who incarnates himself as the Ultimate Thou. Ahania may be exposing what Urizen has hidden from man, or she may be exposing what he has repressed, hidden from himself as well. This last alternative leads to the further possibility that the straightforward temporality of the past is questionable and that Urizen's unconscious, not "true history," is the subject of her tale. "With the alterity of the 'unconscious,' " writes Derrida, "we have to deal not with the horizons of modified presents—past or future—but with a 'past' that has never been nor will ever be present, whose 'future' will never be produced or reproduced in the form of presence." [17] The "past" of the unconscious never was present in the sense that the history, as Ahania reveals it, was never before seen that way by Urizen (or, for that matter, by the reader). It never will be present because the representation in her story does not simply reproduce the past but involves Urizen in a new present situation, and his relationship to the history of consciousness remains distanced by new defenses and resistances.

Derrida helps us focus on the *différance*—the temporal deferrals and reorganizations of material characteristic of the work of the unconscious and, I want to argue, of Blake's narrative structures—rather than on the mere *difference* between accounts of Albion's fall. Ahania's account does more than shift the psychology one step back. It finds a new beginning in an error of perception, a mistake which separates things as they are from things as they are taken to be and acted upon. It does not matter who thought first of Luvah taking over Urizen's steeds of light. We have had one account in which Luvah simply seized them, one in which Urizen made the suggestion to Luvah. Now Ahania suggests Urizen heeded the "voice of Luvah." In pleading with Urizen to heed *her* voice, the vision she now unfolds, Ahania shifts the concern away from the misplaced search for origins to the failure of perception responsible for Urizen's troubled state at present. For all the sweet pathos of her voice, the vision she presents is prophetic, preaching the renunciation of concerns with origin, the renunciation of fears for futurity, and the acceptance of vision as redemptive. If Urizen could see himself as he is now, he would be redeemed.

Such seeing is not easy, and is just what Urizen will refuse. But Ahania's attempt at persuasion is an important episode in the confrontation of Urizen's blindness as blindness. Ahania's method is to present past history as the politics of perception rather than the politics of power. Lay aside—she asks—the question of who did the *seizing* and look at what Albion was *seeing*. Vala walked before him, diverting attention from the Divine Vision to this limited sexual sight. Turning further away, so that he focused on a figment rather than a fragment of the imagination, "He looked up and saw thee, prince of light, thy splendor faded." Never mind the *Nachträglichkeit* (belated retranscription of memory traces) that may have occurred on the part of Albion, Urizen, or Ahania herself and produced this possibly proleptic fading; what matters for the moment, she insists, is not how things came to be so perceived but that they were so perceived. Spoken without the anguish she knows ("Why didst thou give the immortal steeds of light?") and without appeal ("Resume thy fields of light!"), her version concentrates on Albion's perception—on what he saw and what he could not see. By reaction, the mind shapes more clearly the form of the unseen—just as, if one stares hard at a red object, one turns away and sees green. If Albion saw not the Divine Vision, the possibility comes to mind of his still seeing the Divine Vision and acting in accordance with the reintegrated faculties. If Albion saw Urizen's splendor faded, the possibility comes to mind that Urizen's splendor was not diminished—*is* not diminished—but obscured. Albion "saw not Los nor Enitharmon, for Luvah hid them in shadow, / In a soft cloud outstretched across; and Luvah dwelt in the cloud." Adding these lines to the *Vala* manuscript, Blake emphasized the failure of perception beyond its causality. Repeating the word "cloud" and turning the activity of usurpation into a stasis, "Luvah dwelt in the cloud," Ahania creates a space free from questions of the Zoas' temporal sequence or causality. Indeed, her tale seems to be generating its own temporality as it generates its own scenic spaces: Albion walks "on the steps of fire before his halls." He looks up, and ascends "into the splendours of his palace." He falls prostrate before his shadow, and arises in terror. These simple spaces and sequences give the aura of a new beginning, independent of Luvah's and Urizen's striving, aided by the language of description of the following new spectrous form: "Above him rose a shadow from his wearied intellect."

"From" is the deceptive word, ignoring as it does the history and the nature of this shadow. Is the shadow itself or the "wearied intellect" the slumberous Urizen? Or is it impossible to conceive of this phantom of orthodoxy without presupposing that Luvah has preempted the domain of Urizen, that Urizen himself could not turn into this Shadow of Man? Or should we say further that the shadow is neither Urizen, nor Luvah in Urizen's place, but Luvah Tyrannos, figment of the indolent or slumberous man's wish fulfillment: it is easier to confront the energies of Luvah as an outside threat than as one's own impulses one is responsible for expressing. None of these alternative definitions of the shadow is quite true to Ahania's vision, because she momentarily presents the shadow independent of Zoa names.

With "shadowy voice" Albion venerates a "shadow from his wearied intellect"; then "that shadowy spirit of the fallen one, / Luvah, descended from the cloud." With the return of the Zoa name, the story returns to the psychology of power and what Albion now perceives as a "dark deceit," Luvah—who should be the capacity for love—seeking dominion. In the interim, however, man has been free to generate his own fall, bringing down upon him the god created in his own image, the shadow of Luvah generated as the "Son of Man."

Ahania's vision of man's moral responsibility for his fall is intended to awaken Urizen into responsibility. Urizen does see the terror of man contemplating his shadow, but seems to mistranslate the vision. Calling Ahania "the indulgent self of weariness," he identifies her with the vision she presents to him that reflects all his indolence. In one sense he is right—she has reflected his indolence, though she has exposed not what he *is* but what he was and might still be. Mistaking her, he mistakes himself, and substitutes anger and rejection for interpretation and insight. Ahania had provided the possibility of regeneration; now Urizen, whatever the previous psychic history may have been, whatever role Urizen, as the name for a psychic faculty of Albion, may have played—Urizen, a character reacting to the voice of Ahania, generates his own fall. The story generates the point of its own origin.

In all this, I have given Ahania a great deal of credit. But her understanding has been challenged by Bloom, by Johnson and Wilkie, and most probingly by Thomas Weiskel, who finds Ahania's attempt to forestall Urizen's ruin doomed "by her own naiveté"—by her failure to see Urizen implicated in the story of man worshiping his shadow, and by her refusal to see Urizen hopelessly victimized by his defenses and beyond free choice. I have suggested that Ahania is not necessarily unaware of Urizen's involvement; but based on the outcome I must acknowledge some shortcoming in her tactics whatever her knowledge. The point is best explicated by Weiskel:

Ahania hopes that Urizen will reject the idolatry perpetrated while he "slept in the porch," but unknowingly she has exposed his project. (All of her vision may of course be understood as Urizen's moment of self-recognition, but so deeply is the original Urizen split, that this further reduction has only theoretical significance at this point.) Urizen is dismayed at her vision (41:5–9, 18; 42:7–8) not because it recapitulates the fall, but because it reveals a countermyth to his own version of the fall—a myth which highlights his own role with an ingenuous clarity the more dangerous for being unconscious. In Urizen's view, Man fell because he became intellectually lazy and his "active masculine virtue" succumbed to Vala, "the feminine indolent bliss. The indulgent self of weariness"—what he hopes to avoid by casting out Ahania. Pleasure undermined self-discipline; in short, Man failed to sublimate. But Ahania's account of the fall suggests that sublimation is itself a creation of intellectual weariness (40:3), which in turn results from Man's commerce with Vala "in dreams of soft deluding slumber." From this point of view Urizen's myth of the fall is totally incoherent because it proposes as a saving alternative the very sublimation which is the idolatrous result of mental failure.[18]

We may specify the "naiveté" of Ahania's hope as the beautiful faith that man has only to see clearly the nature of his intellectual weariness in order to be freed of the burden of the past. It is a psychoanalytic faith, or more precisely the faith of early analysis before the mechanisms of defense and the death instinct came to be recognized in all their complexity. More than a wife, Ahania is like a physician treating the victim of a repetition compulsion. Her plea to Urizen, "Leave all futurity to him; resume thy fields of Light," may be doomed to failure the way the less elegant injunction "Stop worrying!" would be. But we must also see behind the attractiveness of her appeal the desire to return his powers to Urizen by focusing his mental energy toward memory rather than futurity. Freud says of the physician: "He is prepared for a perpetual struggle with his patient to keep in the psychical sphere all the impulses which the patient would like to direct into the motor sphere; and he celebrates it as a triumph for the treatment if he can bring it about that something the patient wishes to discharge in action is disposed of through the work of remembering."[19] In Ahania's case the treatment must be deemed a failure; what the physician would have discharged through the work of remembering gets discharged in action. (Ahania's failure is the poet's success, for thus the action of the poem continues.) The physician is also "discharged," her advice rejected as the female wiles of Vala. What Ahania had to tell Urizen looks very much like the classic stuff of analytic revelation: the shadow from wearied intellect is yours, Urizen; it came to be worshiped because its origins were concealed from consciousness, though they are revealed in my account—which you ought to listen to, Urizen; and the basic roots of the neurosis are sexual, in Albion's dalliance with Vala, though all that was screened by the memory of a power struggle. These revelations do not themselves need to be qualified, and what follows in *The Four Zoas* is not a correction of the perspective of Ahania. But like an analysis aborted by premature revelation (let alone injunction, an analytic sin at any time), Urizen's confrontation with the story of first things has only furthered his defenses against regeneration.

Looking from Night III at the extensity of the poem ahead and at the failure of Ahania's account to prove definitive (at least in the sense of providing finite limits to the fall), we might conceive of the problem of repetition from the perspective of Ahania and Urizen as analyst and victim of repetition compulsion. Urizen's hostile rejection of Ahania provides the clue, and Freud the formulation: "If, as the analysis proceeds, the transference becomes hostile or unduly intense and therefore in need of repression, remembering at once gives way to acting out. From then onwards the resistances determine the sequence of the material which is to be repeated."[20] For both psychoanalysis and the literary analysis of Blake, Freud's notion of the new "determination" does not really provide a hope of definitive understanding of sequentiality; it does offer a permanent challenge to the idea of distinguishing the original from the reoriginated in psychic history.

v

It is possible to approach the special character of the version of first things in Night VIIA by projecting back on the author of this extraordinary episode something that the student of it must feel. If one has read through *The Four Zoas* one knows that the version in Night VIIA is the temporally definitive one—in the sense that the remaining Nights, VIII and IX, do not offer still another version. On the other hand, the perspectivism of previous versions challenges the very idea of a definitive account, and the larger problem—how to bring so continually climactic a poem to a single climax—finds a focal point in the repetition of the story of Albion's fall.

That a final turn to beginnings should bring the poem to its climax and help precipitate the end suggests the critical approach (and the attempt to discover its equivalent for the creating poet) called "deconstruction." The term implies climactic, if not destructive, finality, while actually referring to the project of searching out underlying or originatory metaphysical assumptions on the basis of which a literary or philosophical work has been built. Derrida writes of Husserl's phenomenology that the whole system is based on the categorical distinction between primordial presentation and representative re-production: "Properly speaking, Husserl is not *led* to recognize this heterogeneity, for it is this which constitutes the very possibility of phenomenology. For phenomenology can only make sense if a pure and primordial presentation is possible and given in the original."[21] The categorical distinction that Derrida "comes to" is the point that Husserl may be said to "come from." I turn to this illustration because it seems to me more than an analogy or metaphor for poetry. Blake's work cannot be reduced to a pure phenomenology; and not enough sense can be made of Urizen, Luvah, and Urthona if their actions and stances—let alone their emanations—are simply the constitutive elements of a transcendental psychology. Blake is in the position of Husserl's critic, exposing the "absolute heterogeneity"—or rather expanding the heterogeneity of presentation and representation to fill the space of his poem.

To be sure, it is impossible to recapture the burden of awareness Blake assumed in revising Night VII of *The Four Zoas* and presenting the poem's story of first things for the last time. But to represent the retrospective consciousness that surveys the heterogeneous presentations of the past and sets out to re-present the story in a way that will free it from first-and-last, I borrow from Derrida this summary of his argument with Husserl: "Perception does not exist . . . what is called perception is not primordial . . . somehow everything 'begins' by 're-presentation' (a proposition which can only be maintained by the elimination of these last two concepts: it means that there is no 'beginning' and that the 'representation' we were talking about is not the modification of a 're-' that has *befallen* a primordial presentation)." [22] We could call such critical insight the fruit of what Blake terms, in Night VIIA, "The Tree of Mystery," for in taking it in one's eyes are opened, one's illusions about the primordial are demystified, and the nakedness of the text's assumptions is exposed. What Blake finds left to do is to reconstruct on the basis of such a deconstructive awareness, to reimagine his Giant Forms in terms of a story that will express the consciousness of illusion otherwise burdensome. He requires both a recovery and a re-covering: a return to imaginative health (finding a medium for expressing the otherwise oppressive consciousness of illusion) and an act of covering once more (as Adam and Eve did their generative parts, as Wallace Stevens finds the poet must do to the primordial rock) by refictionalizing the story of original generation.

Consciousness of fictionality may be expressed in terms of an original fiction by transforming the literal and figurative elements of an old tale. In Night VIIA, Blake goes back to the Genesis story of a tree of knowledge and, by a triumphant displacement, makes the undermining of that fiction stand for the consciousness of his own fictions about first things. "Undermining" is perhaps not quite the right word because it is not quite literal enough. Blake gets to the ground of the old fiction by re-presenting his old characters *on the ground* of the old fiction, "Beneath the Tree of Mystery among the leaves & fruit." Genesis describes fallen Adam and Eve hiding *bitoch etz hagan* (within the tree[s] of the garden), which the Vulgate preserves in the singular (*in medio ligni paradisi*). Literalism in the reimagining of this event leads to such imaginative achievements as Milton's banyan tree and Chaucer's pear—with Damian and May up in it. Blake no doubt draws on the tradition when he conceives of the tree of knowledge—like Jesus' cross, said to be of the same wood—as a synecdoche for the world of nature in which the fallen imagination is bound. But he goes further in questioning the ground of these imaginings and returning his characters to the literal ground in which these metaphysical trees take their root. More precisely, he does not return the old characters to the newly literalized ground but reimagines the old characters in terms of shadows that represent them and whose very reimagining stands for consciousness of representation. In place of Los and Enitharmon we find, beneath the tree of mystery, the Spectre of Urthona and the Shadow of Enitharmon. These two shadow forth their counterparts in the world above, and when they present the story of Albion's fall once more they not only "present it" in the sense of making it present to one another and to us; they re-present it, for they are characters whose very existence and whose setting acknowledge the fact that there is no presenting but in re-presencing.

The Shadow of Enitharmon and the Spectre of Urthona tell the story to one another, in itself a fact that acknowledges fiction because conversation or dialogue demystifies the potentially absolute status of myth as revealed by one speaking voice. The phenomenological aspect of previous versions of Albion's fall depended on the transcendent dignity of the individual voice. Derrida points out that the special status of voice for phenomenology depends on "the fact that the phenomenological 'body' of the signifier seems to fade away at the very moment it is produced; it seems already to belong to the element of ideality."[23] When Blake presents two speakers, for neither of whom individually the original myth has the "immediate presence" it gains in their dialogue, the "body" of the signifier seems to be apprehended not in the fading but in the making. The limits of phenomenology are transcended because dialogue ventures "outside ideality, outside interiority of the self-present life."[24] Previous versions have taken into account the situation of speaker and auditor—in Night III particularly, where what Ahania has to say about Urizen is intricately dependent on the fact that she is speaking to him and registering his reactions while attempting to change them. Nevertheless the story has at that point a self-presence to Ahania that it does not to the Shadow of Enitharmon in Night VIIA.

Here are the portions of the exchange that together constitute the new version of our story. First the Shadow of Enitharmon to the Spectre:

> Among the flowers of Beulah walked the Eternal Man, & saw
> Vala, the lily of the desert: melting in high noon
> Upon her bosom in sweet bliss he fainted. Wonder seized
> All Heaven: they saw him dark; they built a golden wall
> Round Beulah. There he revelled in delight among the
>   flowers.
> Vala was pregnant & brought forth Urizen, prince of light,
> First-born of generation. Then behold, a wonder to the eyes
> Of the now fallen Man, a double form Vala appeared!
>   A male
> And female, shuddering pale: the fallen Man recoiled
> From the enormity, & called them *Luvah* & *Vala,* turning
>   down
> The vales to find his way back into Heaven—but found none,
> For his frail eyes were faded & his ears heavy & dull.

Urizen grew up in the plains of Beulah. Many sons
And many daughters flourished round the holy tent of man,
Till he forgot Eternity, delighted in his sweet joy
Among his family, his flocks & herds & tents & pastures.

But Luvah close conferred with Urizen in darksome night
To bind the father & enslave the brethren. Nought he knew
Of sweet Eternity: the blood flowed round the holy tent,
    & riven
From its hinges, uttering its final groan all Beulah fell
In dark confusion. Meantime Los was born & Enitharmon,
But how I know not; then forgetfulness quite wrapped me up
A period, nor do I more remember, till I stood
Beside Los in the cavern dark, enslaved to vegetative forms,
According to the will of Luvah who assumed the place
Of the Eternal Man, & smote him.   [p. 83]

Forgetfulness covers part of the story (precisely the facts of Enitharmon's generation), but the Spectre recovers and re-presences
the tale of generation. Los, Enitharmon, and the Spectre of
Urthona emerge as the de-generated components (degenerate,
and one generation later) of the original Urthona:

                        One dread morn—
Listen, O vision of delight—one dread morn of gory blood
The Manhood was divided, for the gentle passions, making
    way
Through the infinite labyrinths of the heart & through the
    nostrils issuing
In odorous stupefaction, stood before the eyes of Man,
A female bright. I stood beside my anvil dark; a mass
Of iron glowed bright, prepared for spades & ploughshares:
    sudden down
I sunk, with cries of blood issuing downward in the veins
Which now my rivers were become, rolling in tubelike forms
Shut up within themselves, descending down I sunk along
The gory tide even to the place of seed, & there dividing
I was divided in darkness & oblivion. Thou an infant woe,
And I an infant terror in the womb of Enion.   [p. 84]

As dialogue, this exchange suggests that the myth recounted has been naturalized, or recast in terms of the way people talk about their backgrounds. David Wagenknecht says of the Shadow and the Spectre here that "they while away the time before coitus like young people at a dance, telling each other where they come from." [25] But I doubt whether young people at a dance often get this much "into" one another's histories, for as dark and self-serving as these characters are they appear to be conversing with, not just talking at, one another. It is a common history they speak, dividing between them the recitation of its parts. The Shadow's account expands on other versions of Albion's dalliance and outlines the events given by the messengers from Beulah in Night I, lines 179–213 of Stevenson's text. The Spectre follows with the equivalent of lines 214–229.

Some of the differences between the messengers' account and this one need to be specified. In Night I, the Spectre is a minor meteor breaking off from the celestial body of Urthona, and so the difference between "Beside his anvil stood Urthona dark" (I.214) and "I stood beside my anvil dark" (VIIA.280) is more than a shift from third to first person—even acknowledging the dramatic re-placing of the mysterious adjective. One could say that in Night VIIA the speaking "I" is proleptically the Spectre of Urthona, or simply that the Spectre identifies himself with his unfallen form. Both these formulations belie the way the Spectre's account belies his generation. The difference between the "I" identified with Urthona and "I an infant terror" is unlike the temporal difference between the "I" I was yesterday and the "I" I am today. Memory connects my past with my present self; but when the Spectre remembers himself as Urthona, he re-members the self that has been broken apart into separate members—Los, Enitharmon, and the Spectre. Urthona has been dismembered; he is not yet re-membered and only anticipates such union: "then shall we unite again in bliss." As a sign of this union to come, Enitharmon and the Spectre embrace now. The pre-coital conversation thus must be seen as a sign of a sign, with the fitting

together of their narrative parts standing metaleptically for the
more corporeal fitting together to come. That, in turn, stands
for the final, less corporeal fitting together—the reunification of
Spectre and Los which in time stands for and works toward the
ultimate union of Spectre, Los, and Enitharmon to reconstitute
Urthona.

The number of *in turn*s necessitated here points to the episode
as a turning point. Surely we approach a nadir reading about
the Shadow of Enitharmon, "Bitterly she wept, embracing fervent / Her once-loved lord, now but a shade, herself also a
shade." But this literal apophrades or return of the dead has
these shades, at the same time, shadowing forth the apocalyptic
union to come. Here is one of Blake's shadiest episodes confronting itself as such, playing with all senses of shade (*le jeu des
différences*) and discovering in such self-consciousness about how
one episode shadows forth another a point of regeneration.
Derrida writes, "If language never escapes analogy, if it is
indeed analogy through and through, it ought, having arrived
at this point, at this stage, freely to assume its own destruction
and cast metaphor against metaphor. . . . It is at the price of
this war of language against itself that the sense and question of
its origin will be thinkable." [26] We can say of Spectre and Shadow
that they are metaphor cast against metaphor. The product of
their union (a metaphor for metaphor confronting itself) is a
form of Vala, who is Veiled Meaning or Analogy (Nature as
metaphoric vehicle) incarnate.

Two details help authenticate the revelations of the Night
VIIA version as more than play with the idea of language. One
is that Vala is not named as such when Enitharmon brings forth
"a wonder horrible." When this wonder is named later in the
poem it is renamed Rahab. Error is thus consolidated, not left to
the mild mistakes of metaphoric language and the circularity of
coming up with (coming back to) Vala. The other detail is that
Vala *is* named in the Shadow's account, which literalizes the
doubling nature of analogy when Vala is seen splitting into

Luvah and Vala. From the psychologizing perspective of previous accounts we could say that "a double form Vala appeared" refers to the doubling of the mind in the presence of a sexual object. More precisely, in response to an object of desire absent to the mind because *out there* in external nature, a man (or a woman, mutatis mutandis) creates the Form of Desire present to the mind—an imago-vision of the ideal (to which no lady can match up) or a vision of the external object as metaphoric (no lady can threaten *as* a lady). Such Presences are forms of Vala. But one also idealizes oneself as desirable and desiring, and one can be dwarfed by this shadow's superior form and purity of desire. We encountered the creation of such an overshadower in Night III: he is Luvah, who appears when Vala splits, when sexuality alienates Albion from the basic self-presence in which one recognizes one's desire and one's object of desire as one's own.

Yet at the center of this version of first things we are beyond psychology—or rather at a core of pure psychology we might better label semiology. The turn from Albion "saw / Vala" to "a double form Vala appeared" is a return from the interpersonal possibilities of sexuality to intrapersonal sign creation. The Shadow's account concerns the way we make shadowy presences and signs that do not simply refer to external reality but differ from it, defer our involvement with it, and finally debar us from it. When Adam named the animals he knew a creative power that preceded fall. But when Blake's Albion "called them Luvah & Vala" he read the signs, as it were, that barred his way back to paradise. The Shadow's account insists on this primordial relationship between metaphor-making and sexuality. Her opening lines present sexuality in especially literary, even biblical, terms: "Among the flowers of Beulah walked the Eternal Man, & saw / Vala, the lily of the desert" (The fall into metaphor is the fall into Generation—the equation of sexual attraction with the forms of generated nature.) Any freshness accompanying the turn to such metaphors is dispelled by the haste and the deadness of the metaphors that follows: "melting in high noon / Upon her bosom in sweet bliss he fainted." Time (noon) is distempered, place (bosom) displaced in such language, and the distance implied by language is literalized in the building of a wall around Beulah. But semiology is not simply topology—metaphors do not simply substitute one place for another; they temporally displace meaning, and the Shadow's greatest variation on the story of the Fall involves a reworking of the fall into time.

It has the ring of the pristine, almost a Biblical genealogy: "Vala was pregnant & brought forth Urizen, prince of light, / First-born of generation." We have met other acts of generation in which one of Blake's Giant Forms "takes in" and gives birth to another; Enion, for example, harbors Enitharmon and Los and delivers them into this world of Generation. But this is the first time one of the "original" four Zoas is imagined as generated, and the lines challenge the idea of an original, atemporal state. Derrida says of speech that what distinguishes it from other modes of signification (like pictures) is its temporality: "And this temporality does not unfold a sense that would itself be nontemporal; even before being expressed, sense is through and through temporal." [27] The situation in Night VIIA of one disembodied shadowy voice addressing another focuses on the nature of their account of first things as speech and reminds us that sense itself is temporal, that the forms that Shadow and Spectre re-present make no sense outside time, and that an unfallen Urizen is (as yet) inconceivable. Out of this awareness the fallen Urizen could be said to be "conceived."

Psychologically, the fallen Urizen appears to be something like the superego, so that one idea of a deferred or generated Urizen rather than an original Zoa could correspond to the generation of an internalized authority figure out of the confrontation of the id with externality. But the semiological cast of Night VIIA suggests that we reformulate the temporal difference in terms of what Husserl calls the phenomenology of internal time consciousness, and consider Urizen not as a parental Presence but as the arch denier or evader of the present. Husserl calls our awareness of the present "primal": "The primal impression is the absolute beginning of this generation [of the sense of time]—the primal source, that from which all others are continually generated. In itself, however, it is not generated; it does not come into existence as that which is generated but through spontaneous generation. It does not grow up (it has no seed): it is primal creation."[28] That is just what Urizen cannot recognize and cannot "be." All anxiety and futurity, Urizen must now be conceived "as that which is generated." The Shadow's account continues, and Urizen's collusion with Luvah in rebellion against Albion takes on something of the quality of the Freudian primal scene: it reminds us of the first sons' tribal slaying of the father. This reminder tags the fall, for the very turn to psychology marks a falling away from purer concern with signs. The account of the Shadow of Enitharmon makes manifest the nature of Generation by naturalizing the story, turning the Zoas, who ought to be seen as faculties of the individual psyche, into children rebellious against a parental authority. This naturalization is a central error within a Blake story, just as nothing could be more invidious than the mode of interpretation that would argue Blake's interest in regeneration to be a displacement based on the failure of Blake-the-man to generate biological children. Biographical criticism *naturalizes,* and finds not first things but fall, not even psychology—the study of the soul—but biology, the study of the world of nature. Los and Enitharmon, children of the fall, may be said to be generated when they are mentally (and, in terms of the myth of Enion, physically) conceived as children. Yet confronted *as metaphor,* biological generation is essential. Night IX will rejuvenate the parental metaphor, and rejuvenate man: he will "rise from generation free," but in an innocence expressed or organized into generational terms. And to rejuvenate the generational metaphor is to see generation as image of regeneration.

That formula (Blake uses it in the opening of *Jerusalem*) discovers something not just about the nature of a generational image but about metaphoric language generally. In Night VIIA, to see Urizen as generated is to see that our "primary" sense of time—the one that "pre-occupies" us most—concerns the anxiety produced by the presence of shadows of the past and the fore-shadowed presence of the future. "I think, therefore I am" may be true in the sense that my "first" thought is logically the thought that I am thinking. But that was no child's first thought, and no functioning adult's most stimulating (generative) thought. We live in and think about not a world of what Husserl calls "the spontaneous generation of the awareness of presentness," but a world of Generation, a world of delayed gratifications and de-layed symbol-making. We learn to describe our world metaphor-ically, knowing that the very use of metaphoric language marks a falling away from presentness.

The tree of mystery, beneath which these revelations take place (are given a place in Blake), could thus be called the tree of metaphor-making. God planted many trees and one big metaphor in the first garden—or, more precisely, two metaphors, a metaphor of metaphor-making (the tree of knowledge) and a metaphor of presentness (the tree of life-without-the-temporaliza-tions-of-metaphor). In Blake's revision of the Biblical archetype, the fruit of the tree of knowledge still opens the eyes to an awareness connected with sexuality, but now the knowledge could be said to concern just how metaphoric "tree," "opening the eyes," and sexuality itself really are, and how dependent on covering, delaying, and hiding in the tree we really are. The lure of knowledge posed in the Biblical story by the serpent properly belongs to the Spectre in Night VIIA, and like the serpent the knowledge he has must first be seen as a piece of psychology or psychological strategy before it can be abstracted into knowledge about the nature of representation.

By presenting Urizen as born from the union of Albion and Vala, the Shadow of Enitharmon suggested that parental pos-sessiveness may be basic to sexual desire. Ending her speech with that tantalizing note of obscurity and fascination about her genesis

("Los was born & Enitharmon, / But how I know not"), she gives the Spectre his cue for the parental reading of the history of psychic division. In his account, Albion's sexual fall causes a division felt as a descent into generation: "I was divided in darkness & oblivion. Thou an infant woe, / And I am infant terror in the womb of Enion." Perceiving that the fallen female is attracted to the image of a father, he comes up with just the history that makes him seem, though "so horrible a form," sexually attractive:

> My masculine spirit scorning the frail body issued forth
> From Enion's brain, in this deformed form leaving thee there
> Till times passed over thee; but still my spirit returning
>   hovered
> And formed a male to be a counterpart to thee, O love.
>
> [p. 84]

I do not know what authority that last line has as history of the Eternals, but its effect on the Shadow of Enitharmon is clear. Claiming to be Los's "father," the Spectre presents himself as what the lady really wants. The sexuality is nasty but incisive, and might be deemed the counterpart of the pedestrian nastiness which sees a man as being really attracted to the Mother Nature he sees in potentia in a given lady; woman is attracted to that in a man which seems not of woman born. Something in a wife not only prefers her father-in-law (spiritual form of man of whom the son is de-generated shadow) but desires the destruction of the natural husband who stands in the path of spiritual union with that idealized form. I may look like deformity and lust, the Spectre argues, but "I am as the spectre of the living," and will take you beyond natural appearances back through the "gates of Eternal life." [29]

That much is Spectre psychology, and like Milton's Satan, who takes his clues from Eve, the Spectre depends for his knowledge on the Shadow's blindness to the fact that her tale of generation contains the seed of the answer the Spectre elaborates. But what begins as psychology or a naturalized drama of sexual temptation emerges in our eyes—and, more especially, in the eyes of Los, who "reads" this episode—as a drama about the nature of metaphoric representation. The Shadow cannot remember the facts re: generation; the Spectre re-members and re-generates the Zoas, and re-presents the present confrontation in a stark I-Thou relationship that, incidentally, shows just how much Blake can do with his dramatic verse: "Thou an infant woe, / And I an infant terror in the womb of Enion." What seems nothing less than miraculous is that this literal or biological regeneration points the way to spiritual regeneration. Their unified story of generation—of themselves as infants—which "stands for" and impels their union and generation of an infant horrible, leads to the regeneration of Los and Urizen. Night VIIA closes triumphantly with a metaphor of generation as Los comes to see Urizen aright: "he beheld him an infant / Lovely."

The Night VIIA version of first things is thus distinguished not only by its subtlety but by the way this narration moves us closer to the return to Eternal life. The old story is regenerated (refurbished for the occasion); it now concerns re-generation (seeing the Zoas reemerge as infants, the next generation); and it regenerates the poem (giving Los, and ultimately the poet, the burst of energy to fabricate embodied semblances). Though the rebirth of Luvah as Orc and the rebirth of Vala as Rahab are not themselves redemptive reworkings, they increase the momentum of regeneration that produces the vision at the end of Night VIIA of Urizen as an infant, and, ultimately, in Night IX, of Tharmas and Enion as little children. More immediately, the recitation of the story of the fall sends reverberations into the larger plot stalled at that point. The labor pains of the Shadow of Enitharmon produce sighs and groans each of which "bore Urthona's Spectre on its wings." Pity, which divides the soul, also humanizes its spectrous forms, turning them from objects of fear and distance into objects of identification.

One can summarize the achievement of the Night VIIA account of first things by pointing to the relationship of a story re: generation and one of regeneration, or by noting that a story about origins becomes a story about originating stories about origins—a story about originality. But such formulas belie the *poetic* achievement of Blake and the way metaphoric language transcends any statement language can make about metaphor. Consider the wondrous innocence of the Shadow of Enitharmon as she declares herself in the dark about her origins: "Meantime Los was born & Enitharmon, / But how I know not; then forgetfulness quite wrapped me up / A period, nor do I more remember." Such little oblivions are the special province of poetry and help it to the same transcendence of formulaic thought that the whole creative mind has over pure consciousness. Forgetfulness covers not just the birth of Enitharmon but the relationship between Enitharmon and the Shadow of Enitharmon speaking. When the Spectre hails her, "Listen, thou my vision, / I view futurity in thee," he collapses in the appositive "my vision" just the temporalizing difference that is allowing this whole episode to take place. "My vision" could be said to mean, literally, "she whom I now see." It also means "she in whom I foresee," or "she with whom I foresee." If the Spectre made clear just what would he would lose through clarification, his statement might go something like this: "You are the one through whom (granted the awareness I have but can lay aside that you are 'lovely / Delusion') I can create."

Stalled on the level of Los and Enitharmon, the narrative has plunged beneath the tree of mystery to confront shade with shade. This expressed awareness of metaphoricity is no stumbling block but almost a condition of creativity, which so often in Blake—and in revisionary poetry generally—depends on taking what was literal metaphorically or vice versa. When this awareness of metaphoricity is projected on the Shadow herself it produces this beautiful pause: "Bitterly she wept, embracing fervent / Her once-loved lord, now but a shade, herself also a shade." When the awareness of metaphoricity is projected back on the spatialized distinction between Enitharmon and her shadow in the world "below," it produces the vision Los sees: "She lay the image of death, / Moved by strong shudders till her shadow was delivered." In some literal or pseudoliteral way these lines describe two characters, one so in sympathy with the other that one's labor pains are felt by the other as deathly agonies. While metaphoric language is being used the effect of perceiving Enitharmon as the "image of death" seems to be to make—for a moment—Death a reality with Enitharmon Death's shadow, and the Shadow of Enitharmon the Shadow of a shadow. But this is a mistake of metaphor-making, for the "reality" taken away from Enitharmon in making her an "image" belongs not to Death but to the Shadow, whose woes Enitharmon is reflecting. What is required to separate these terms more clearly is not a topology of upper and lower worlds, not a spatial but a temporal distinction, which is precisely what Blake offers in describing Enitharmon as the image *till* her shadow was delivered. Blake's subject is less immediately the delays of gratification needed for any labor (genetic or literary) than it is the deferral needed for any sign to perform the function of representation by giving as "present" something not (yet) there.

Blake dismisses the Shadow of Enitharmon, which has done him good service (foreshadowing and bringing about the regeneration of Enitharmon) but which he no longer needs; he puts the Shadow (the Shadow's child?) far off—giving it charge over the world of the dead till the time of the resurrection. Metaphoricity is replaced by the mutuality of present affection, and we have only to contrast with the complexities of the account we have heard the radical simplicity, "Enitharmon told the tale / Of Urthona" (ll. 334–35) to see how far we have come. Summarily, the events of generation are recounted from the perspective of regeneration, and not only recounted but redeemed. "The whole *proprium* or self-hood of man," wrote Swedenborg, "is in the will, and this *proprium* is evil from his first birth, and becomes good by a second birth."[30] The search for origins—the curiosity about natural or first birth as such—is for Blake the indulgence of the selfhood. Perhaps for this reason Blake leaves Los blind to the birthpangs of Enitharmon's Shadow, sympathetic to the agonies of Enitharmon but oblivious of the actual facts of generation: "nor could his eyes perceive / The cause of her dire anguish." Los's business will be to "see" generation as an image of regeneration, and for such prophetic vision a little literal blindness is a help.

A new understanding of the nature of image or metaphor is a new burst of imagination. Los sees the Shadow-Spectre union shadowing forth the integration of self that is spiritual regeneration. What must be *first* expressed in external, natural terms comes to be understood in its deferred or metaphoric form as the inner life. Los announces:

> Even I, already, feel a world within
> Opening its gates, & in it all the real substances
> Of which these in the outward world are shadows which pass
>   away.
> Come then into my bosom, & in thy shadow arms bring with
>   thee
> My lovely Enitharmon.   [p. 86]

The burden of negativity which afflicts semiological discussions drops away, and Los makes those "shadow arms" seem beautiful (and perhaps gently humorous) just by accepting them for what they are. His words can be taken as a caveat for literary criticism, a humanistic conviction that after all the shadows of literary representation have been deconstructed and revealed as metaphysical or linguistic illusions, they need to be embraced for what they are. Metaphoricity is embraced, metaphorically.

If the danger in perceiving the distance between signs and their significance is that the signs tend to look less appealing (metaphor as a bad mistake—if not as the Fall), Los performs a correction of desire. Knowing the origins of illusion, he does not turn away, but feels a burst of originating power: "Stern desire / I feel to fabricate embodied semblances in which the dead / May live before us in our places and in the gardens of our labour" (ll. 435–37). He knows semblances for semblances. But he knows also that they can be made to "live before us," and if "before" cannot mean "anterior to," restoring priorities, it can mean "present to us," restoring a sense of presentness as art best can.

CHAPTER 7

Wordsworth: How Shall I Seek the Origin?

> In its origin language belongs in the age of the most rudimentary form of psychology. We enter a realm of crude fetishism when we summon before consciousness the basic presuppositions of the metaphysics of language, in plain talk, the presuppositions of reason. Everywhere it sees a doer and doing; it believes in will as *the* cause; it believes in the ego, in the ego as being, in the ego as substance, and it projects this faith in the ego-substance upon all things—only thereby does it first *create* the concept of "thing." Everywhere "being" is projected by thought, pushed underneath, as the cause; the concept of being follows, and is a derivative of, the concept of ego.
>
> Nietzsche, *Twilight of the Gods*

Early in *The Prelude,* Wordsworth defines what he believes to be his immediate task: "Meanwhile, my hope has been that I might fetch / Invigorating thoughts from former years" (I.648–49).[1] This "meanwhile" was to extend over a lifetime of writing and revising *The Prelude,* and could be said to include the composition of a wide range of shorter poems as well. So commonplace a term, "invigorating thoughts" can stand for assurances of continuity in the face of death, disruption, or loss of power—assurances however ordinary or extraordinary. One can call it cure (*restoration* is his usual term) or a naturalized substitute for what, with a more theological aura, is termed renovation or salvation. However the goal is specified, the point of origin is habitually some incident of an actual or fictional past, or perhaps (and this turns out to be a complex equivocation) some thought about such an incident. To call Wordsworth a "memory poet" is to note how he substitutes personal memories for other assurances of continuity, natural or divine. To refer to Wordsworth's "myth of memory"[2] is to understand that the new myth, like old ones, has a special interest in origins, a special force as a myth abstracted from particular memories, and a special status as a substitute for or reformulation of other myths.

I want to suggest all these concerns at once because they have often been suggested, and we need to confront the fact that a myth of romantic origins—something to be gleaned from other poets—is everywhere on the surface in Wordsworth's poems and close to the center of his best critics' analyses. How readily two lines of Wordsworth introduce us to a host of critical questions about origins! When culled from a Wordsworthian garden, the meanest flower breeds thoughts to fill volumes. Perhaps there is something refreshing in the view, periodically rejuvenated, that Wordsworth is a simple poet of "invigorating thoughts." So Robert Langbaum, reviewing Hartman's *Wordsworth's Poetry*, complains: "The answer to the question so labored throughout this book—the question whether Wordsworth's perceptions come from without or within—is, as Mr. Hartman knows, very simple. They come from both directions."[3] But if we face a myth of origins we must see the laboring (which Langbaum attributes to Hartman) as Wordsworth's almost obsessive labor, and the simplicity of Langbaum's view (which Wordsworth sometimes affects) as the cultivated naiveté of a bare, antimythological perspective. Literal answers about origins, if they did exist, would not be easy; but answers that concern rhetorical and romantic fictions about inspiration are necessarily complex. In what sense are invigorating thoughts "fetched" both from without and from within? Is this "fetching" another formulation, or an earlier hope, compared to the discovery of restoration "knocking at the door / Of unacknowledged weariness" (*Prelude*, IV.147–48)? What is lost in neutralizing the spatial metaphor by which thoughts are fetched the way objects might be from a neighboring room? Any man can summon up invigorating thoughts from the vasty deep—but will they come when he calls them? And were they there or here all along? How errant is the romance journey undertaken to fetch them?

Deceptively easy to read, Wordsworth may be in fact the most difficult of the English Romantics because each incident, each accounting, partly transmits and partly reformulates a myth of origins. The quotation with which I began is but one statement of intention—actually just part of one statement of intention, and part of a passage the poet revised and (redoubling the myth of inspired place back upon itself) revisited with the hope of fetching from this place, from such a passage, "invigorating thoughts." Here is the 1805 text:

> I began
> My story early, feeling as I fear,
> The weakness of a human love, for days
> Disown'd by memory, ere the birth of spring
> Planting my snowdrops among winter snows.
> Nor will it seem to thee, my Friend! so prompt
> In sympathy, that I have lengthen'd out,
> With fond and feeble tongue, a tedious tale.
> Meanwhile, my hope has been that I might fetch
> Invigorating thoughts from former years,
> Might fix the wavering balance of my mind,
> And haply meet reproaches, too, whose power
> May spur me on, in manhood now mature,
> To honorable toil.   [I.640–53]

Like the incidents of childhood to which it refers, the passage itself has "the charm / Of visionary things" (ll. 659–60) partly in the magical sense of *charm* (it is a passage of relaxed but assured power) and partly in the commonplace sense of *charming* (the pleasant replaces the prophetic as a source of "invigoration"). We must add also that the passage is part of a direct address to Coleridge, for one idea of the romance of the origin shared by the two poets is that moments of revelatory conversation can be themselves seminal spots of time from which invigorating thoughts can be said to date. Each point in the poem when Wordsworth looks back on what he has written marks an original place to be revisited, like a tourist spot in part sanctified, in part secularized by public homage.

The story of the composition of *The Prelude* is so complex that it requires a special suspension of anxiety about the actual origins of the poem to take on faith "I began / My story early" and pass on to the more complex temporal problems of the phrases that follow.[4] The present participle "feeling" ("feeling as I fear, / The weakness of a human love, for days / Disown'd by memory") refers to the time of composition. But when was that weakness of human love, or more important, when were days disowned by memory? Most probably he means days earlier than those normally preserved by memory. But the strong verb "disown'd" in so bland a context seems to transcend its metaphor; there emerges something of a power struggle between the "weakness of a human love" that would hold on to past attachments and the stronger ego of an independent Memory that rejects the past as too far gone. In one sense (developed later) the incidents of which he speaks may be said to be disowned by memory because they are mere fictions of what never was— recognized by Memory as being none of hers. This Freudian insight (that our memories are screened reworkings, not natural offspring whom Memory should own as her own) is masked by the conflict between the poet-child holding on to his mystified past and the sterner, parental Memory forcing her fledging from the nest.

We appear very close to a point of origins when Wordsworth approaches the Blakean position that the daughters of memory are not the daughters of inspiration. For Wordsworth, unlike Blake, we may ultimately wish to stop short of the radical independence of the imagination from personal history, and recognize the highly charged area of shady dependencies in which poetic origins seem, like sexual origins, to be a center surrounded by conflict of power and weakness. It is interesting that Wordsworth revised the phrase "weakness of a human love" to "an infirmity of love for days / Disowned by memory." One overtone retained by both variants is that the poet would be misled if his love for days gone by were too weak. While not the primary meaning (indeed, antithetical to it), this idea retains a certain force: he says he is worried about having been too attached to the past, and we hear also the perhaps deeper anxiety about not being attached enough. In an alternate reading he speculates that the desire to find renovation in composing autobiographical narrative may be "but an impotent desire"; in both the 1805 and 1850 texts he couples with the desire for "invigorating thoughts" the wish for reproaches "whose power / May spur me on." The past is asked to act in loco parentis, and we can say that it is fundamental to Wordsworth's myth of romantic origins that the relation of past incident or past self to the present self is that of a powerful, parental predecessor to the weak singer of the present time who, "centering all in love" (XIII.384), finds his emotional investment amply repaid.

This is a *romantic* myth of origins because it is a myth of autogenesis; it is a *myth* of origins because ordinary ideas of the power of the past over the present give way to humanized or superhuman abstractions. Child and parent are not equally participants, not equally "into" the myth; the poet is a natural child of the past, feeling the weakness of a human, all-too-human, love for it, while the past acts with the personified might of a potentially alienated god.

One more revision in this passage serves to exemplify the revisionary mode so essentially Wordsworth's. In place of the metaphor taken from nature, "ere the birth of spring / Planting my snowdrops among winter snows," he substitutes in his last "review" of the poem,

> fancying flowers where none
> Not even the sweetest do or can survive
> For him at least whose dawning day they cheered.[5]

It is a revision like that the Miltonizing bard makes to the desires of the ragged boy of "Nutting." It also seems to take into account what Freud called "secondary revision"—the later operation of fancy on materials not to be preserved by memory of or from dreams. The difference between the two versions of the passage helps define two different ideas of romantic origins. The simple romanticism (a naiveté or literalism not to be despised but returned to, as to a font) holds that the present is fostered by the flowers of the past; the more complex romanticism (sometimes sentimental) finds the labor of fancying flowers a fit substitute for the flowers that have gone, and a fit emblem of a continuity of spirit that survives. The earlier text bursts with enthusiastic trust that though the snowdrops fell, frost-bitten, an imaginative spring ensues; the later reading defines a faith in the power of rhetorical and narrative substitution. Reworking the past, he finds that the present is in turn reinvigorated and reoriginated.

Wordsworth's myth of memory is a myth of revision in several senses: it finds the presentation of the past revisable; it finds the present revisable (capable of renovation) by direct recourse to the powers of the past, or by recourse to a strength guaranteed by analogy: just as I overcame past crises, so will I be sustained in the face of present debility or the abyss of the future.[6] Needless to say, Wordsworth's presentations of this myth are as various as his texts: his mystifications of the myth and demystified skepticisms about it are as various as the turns or "crossings" of the poems. With all its changes, the myth of the revisability of the self, which has its greatest emblem in the repeatedly revised *Prelude,* is a faith for moderns. It is here that Wordsworth seems most to have anticipated the theory and something of the practice of psychoanalysis; here that he formulated the tenets of romanticism by which the literature after him lives.

Since the myth of romantic origins based on revision is itself subject to revision and re-presentation in each text, generalizations falsify as they present. Still, I would like to try to outline what may be called Wordsworth's "revisionary ratios," borrowing the term from Harold Bloom, who uses it to describe six ways in which a poet revises his stance in relation to his precursor. From the perspective of romantic origins, the poet takes none but himself as precursor, and our ratios define various relationships between an earlier myth of romantic origins and a revised one. My six revisionary myths or recollections in tranquillity may seem to bear a shadowy resemblance to Mr. Bloom's interpoetic ones; but my terms—and I hope the revisions themselves—are Wordsworth's own: First, the idea of presences, whether they take their origin in nature or the self. Second, the affections, whose source is a topic of theoretical exploration as well as specific mythmaking in Wordsworth. Third, the idea of freedom or liberty in the politics of the selfhood and nation. Fourth, the idea of Voice—like the others, Wordsworth's term, but the one that most seems to be a poet's response to a critic's notion about interpoetic revisionism. It is as though the concept of daemonization—of a more authentic voice seizing the poet and speaking through him—preceded Wordsworth, who moderates and internalizes the notion. Fifth, the idea of ego, identity, self, or, as he prefers to call it, the soul. Sixth, the idea of power, meaning in general imaginative power, but sometimes abstracted in a way that seems to transcend particular manifestations in sexual, verse-making, or political potency. These six are necessarily overlapping terms, and I cannot imagine a text that does not in some way involve all or most of them. Selecting examples, I hope to outline in this chapter something of the revisionary nature of the myths surrounding the first four. I will omit a separate section on the fifth because the need first to hypothesize a whole (or preexistent) self, and the greater need to come to a sense of the soul as a principle and product of growth, should emerge from the discussion of the first four. I reserve the sixth for a separate chapter in place of a conclusion.

i   Presences

In Book VI of *The Prelude,* Wordsworth recounts the story of a shipwrecked solitary who derived comfort from tracing geometrical figures on the sand: "Mighty is the charm / Of those abstractions to a mind beset / With images, and haunted by itself" (ll. 178–80). Though the analogy between the poet's abstractions and those of geometry is not pursued, the little story is enough to suggest that the self-hauntings of the poet's mind may be more a burden than a comfort. A shipwreck—here Wordsworth's deliberate addition to his source[7]—offers too strong, too romantic an image of man standing as though he were author of himself; to counter it ordinary socialization seems insufficient (the solitary would part from available company to be alone with his geometry) and the age-old science provides a better retreat from too intense a subjectivity.

Wordsworth's poetry has been described by Geoffrey Hartman as "in many ways the most ghostly poetry ever written."[8] If the poet cultivates ghostliness, he desires, like the victim of the shipwreck, some means of self-forgetfulness by which the mind will reappear haunted by others, not by its own invented images and re-presentations of past experience. If to be shipwrecked is to be cut off from past and future and to confront bald, unmediated presence, one seeks in abstractions like those of geometry, or like "the Present," what Hegel calls "mediated simplicity."[9] One turns from the present to ghosts or presences of the past, searching for reassurances, in Derrida's terms, "that the present in general is not primal but reconstituted, that it is not the absolute, wholly living form which constitutes experience, that there is no purity of the living present."[10]

In the search for evidences of continuity, Wordsworth is in a strong position. This is true partly because he desires them more than other men do. (Harold Bloom says the poet begins "by rebelling more strongly against the consciousness of death's necessity.")[11] More important, he knows how to conjure—how to make the past vividly present in imagery and narrative, and how to use inherited literary forms and techniques in such a way that the continuity of method adds force to the particular continuities or presences evoked from the past. Thus Geoffrey Hartman notes, "the archaic or literary forms subsumed by Wordsworth are the literal spooks of Gothic ballad or tale, and the etiolated personifications endemic to poetic diction." [12] As Wordsworth says in another context, "all shall survive," [13] and though the old forms have been naturalized—redecorated, as it were, to suit contemporary taste—their perdurability argues the durability of the self.

In calling the idea of presences a myth, we focus attention on the mechanisms for repressing consciousness of the mind's autonomy. In the magnificent opening of *The Prelude* the poet can assert his independence ("I breathe again!") by representing individual freedom under the shadow of the Exodus from Egypt and the guiding cloud of Jehovah. Though he claims to be free from those types, they remain the spiritual or ghostly presences haunting the air in which he breathes freely. When we first encounter it, we may hardly be sensible of the ghostliness of things in "the calm / That Nature breathes among the hills and groves" (I.284–85). But the characteristic early spot of time in *The Prelude* figures a ghostly presence in nature, haunting the mind like a bad conscience—or, more precisely, haunting the mind like a reproving figure of authority not yet internalized, not yet made the self-hauntings of conscience. Stealing a bird from another's trap, the young poet "heard among the solitary hills / Low breathings coming after me" (I. 329–30).

If the beginning of wisdom is the fear of the Lord, this myth of presences would have it that the romantic origin of poetic wisdom is in the child's fear of some ghostly Lord figure thought to preside in nature. Writing of a later spot of time, Thomas Weiskel identifies the origins of poetic power in the remembered haunting Presence: "Things are invested with a 'visionary' aspect as if in recompense for the prior fear." [14] If all children (and most adults) have these shadowy experiences, children are protopoets, and poets can trace their visionary sense of things to its origin in the presences of childhood. In the process of literary composition, "the thought ghosts of the poet become ghost thoughts." [15]

The first and simplest incident of a haunting presence in *The*

Prelude reveals not only the "breathings" of the ghostly figure that mark its animation but the motion with which it stalks the earth. The child imagines sounds "of undistinguishable motion, steps / Almost as silent as the turf they trod" (I.331–32). Since motion is the most readily perceived sign of life, a shadow moving by itself betokens a mind more than *self*-haunted. So the huge cliff in the boat scene "With measur'd motion, like a living thing, / Strode after me (I.411–12). Originally something like a representation of the superego, warning the child that his actions are not independent of antecedent authority, these ghostly motions come to guarantee that the present self will also not be cut off from futurity. Motion guarantees not only the life of the ghost, but life in general against the stasis and discontinuity of death. Thus in *Tintern Abbey* the sense of a presence in nature is identified with "a motion and a spirit," and in the skating episode, awareness of the earth rolling "with visible motion her diurnal round" replaces the more primitively figured ghosts.

While reserving for later books of *The Prelude* and such poems as *Resolution and Independence* his more sophisticated, more demystified representations of a haunting presence, Wordsworth establishes in the first book a myth of presence that can be recognized as itself haunting other occurrences, be they so natural as old men encountered on the road. Nature early peopled the mind with forms sublime or fair, and the poet continues the work of nature in depicting other encounters, as it were, under the shadow of those early hauntings. The supreme fiction behind this myth is that verse writing continues the writing of nature and constitutes no movement definitively antithetical to it. Perhaps one could say that this is not just a myth about romantic origins but a myth of the origin—a myth needed at a moment of origination to help bridge the discontinuity between nature and the self or between the nonwriting self that was and the new self emerging in the creative process. Enlarged from the sphere of personal creation, the myth of presences can be found at the origin of poetry. Here is Vico:

The first people, simple and rough, invented the gods "from terror of present power." Thus it was fear which created gods in the world; not fear awakened in men by other men, but fear awakened in men by themselves. . . . That such was the origin of poetry is finally confirmed by this eternal property of it: that its proper material is the credible impossibility. It is impossible that bodies should be minds, yet it was believed that the thundering sky was Jove.[16]

In cultural history the gods serve the same function that personal ghosts serve for the poet: men forget that fear was awakened by themselves, and are able to originate poetry.

Though the spans of time Wordsworth explores are usually those of personal memory, he occasionally speculates about mythic prehistory in ways that suggest analogues or archetypes for individual origins.[17] In the extraordinary visions on Sarum's Plain personal history and national history converge, blending together all the more strongly myths of origin and pledges of continuity. The presences of nature assure the poet "that he hath stood / By Nature's side among the men of old, / And so shall stand for ever" (XII.296–98). Insofar as the episode, or group of episodes, is the poet's personal reverie of the British past, we can regard the wolfskin-clad Britons as ghosts like those presences that haunt the boy of Book I. But as vision replaces vision, the poet seems to be attending a panorama of the origins of poetry, and even his own voice ("I called on darkness") is empowered by the change in scene. Fear makes him cry out:

> I called upon the darkness; and it took,
> A midnight darkness seem'd to come and take
> All objects from my sight.   [XII.327–29]

Revising the passage, Wordsworth diminishes the representation of his own agency, and Darkness itself becomes a giant Presence that anticipates his wish:

> I called on Darkness—but before the word
> Was uttered, midnight darkness seemed to take
> All objects from my sight.   [1850, XIII.327–29]

In 1805 his words *took* (took effect); in the revision, the agency of taking seems not to belong to him. The vision that ensues seems to enact Vico's speculation about the origins of religion and poetry. From fearful imaginings of synecdochic "single Britons," "the voice of spears," and other terrible relics, imagination conjures up gods or the worship of them.

The third vision will reveal the Druids as benevolent figures, poet-teachers; the second is mysteriously intermediary, and while depicting human sacrifice, seems to present also a demonic origin of poetry from fear:

> The voice
> Of those that crowd the giant wicker thrills
> The monumental hillocks, and the pomp
> Is for both worlds, the living and the dead.
> [1850, XIII.332–35]

Our ancestors propitiated the gods with human sacrifices under the harsh conviction that nothing is got for nothing. Something in the poet, or in his daemonic half, holds on to that law and presupposes, behind the speaking face of nature, a once-human sacrifice that envoiced the hills. In the 1805 text Wordsworth heard how the collective voice of sacrificial victims "thrill / Throughout the region far and near." In revision, he made the verb transitive, so that the voices of the victims give to the hills what the hills still can be imagined to give back to the poet now. I do not know how to determine the primary meaning of that great, expansive line that has the pomp "for both worlds, the living and the dead." Perhaps the intention of the sacrificers is to appease the gods or ghosts of the dead, while their ceremonies in fact impress the living onlookers, or those shortly to be living no more. At the same time, we recognize that Wordsworth is the living poet contemplating the dead, and so the pomp of ancestral sacrifice both was for the dead (the Druids then living) and is for the world of those presently surviving and reimagining them. The ghastly business of the past has become a ghostly

imagining for the present—and it is *for* the present in the sense
of bequeathing to the living some intimation of one great community, the noble living and noble dead—however shocking or
sublime the origins of this great continuity of spirit.

If each confrontation with a ghostly presence is a return to a
myth of poetic origins, it remains true for Wordsworth that one
myth is privileged above others. Though the authority of the
Christian myth is not usually manifested overtly, its assumed
priority makes other representations seem naturalized redactions
of it. Thus, whether individually apprehended in a particular
place and time or vaguely recast into forms like the One Life or
the Presence in *Tintern Abbey,* one of whose dwelling places is
"the light of setting suns," the presences that Wordsworth discovers can be seen as revisions of the original Presence of God
known to Adam in Eden. In *The Excursion,* the Christian myth
is given priority over all other accounts of man's original,
unmediated relationship to nature and supernature:

> Upon the breast of new-created earth
> Man walked; and wheresoe'er he moved,
> Alone or mated, solitude was not.
> He heard, borne on the wind, the articulate voice
> Of God; and Angels to his sight appeared
> Crowning the glorious hills of paradise;
> Or through the groves gliding like morning mist
> Enkindled by the sun. He sate—and talked
> With winged Messengers; who daily brought
> To his small island in the ethereal deep
> Tidings of joy and love.   [IV.631–41]

Several Miltonic echoes here suggest one way a poet, through his
own involvement with language, recaptures a time when "solitude was not." Much stronger, however, is the impression of how
wholly other is such a time of easy commerce between spirits.
The Wanderer is brought to envision this original plenitude of
spiritual presence by considering how much he would prefer

even rude superstition over dryly reasoned faith, with its "repetitions wearisome of sense." Contra repetition (verbal and experiential) is the imagination of an original Presence, which survives feebly in ordinary superstition, more splendidly in imagined paradises.

"The articulate voice / Of God" speaks no more, or speaks far more indirectly. If the Solitary and Wordsworth's readers are to feel not only that "solitude was not" but that it is not, the poet must provide simulacra or intimations of a Presence that yet survives in nature. At the same time, he must so acknowledge the lapsarian condition as not to violate the distinction between an original and a far more derivative sense of presence.

The poet replaces the articulate voice of God, and often re-places it or finds in the absence of paradise another inspired locus. We can thus call the idea of presences a revisionary myth of romantic origins because the particular genius of the place re-presents an original Presence and an original place now lost. Geoffrey Hartman, tracing the genius loci from its most primitive form to the "secret spirit of humanity," finds it "Wordsworth's fate to return to spirit of place as if that alone were the well-spring of poetry." [18] Perhaps Wordsworth's myth of memory might better be called a myth of forgetfulness insofar as it sanctions taking each particular place and time as the wellspring of poetry, and overlooking the original absence on which all representations, and perhaps speech itself, is founded. If Wordsworth's power of forgetfulness were greater in this matter he might have been, like Blake or Shelley, what we loosely call an apocalyptic poet. But half remembering in some way that the presences he discovers in nature are not the original Presence, he avoids representing apocalyptic or absolute confrontations. When nature is represented as speaking to the poet, it is often to voice the imperative "Be mild!"—less a revelation itself than a directive not to seek revelatory breaks with nature or take any particular envoicing as more than a faint reworking of a lost Presence. In the strange "Invocation to the Earth" (1816), which may appear to have been dictated to the slumbering poet by Blake, a spirit brings earth what seems to be an apocalyptic message:

> "Rest, rest, perturbèd Earth!
> O rest, thou doleful Mother of Mankind!"
> A Spirit sang in tones more plaintive than the wind:
> "From regions where no evil thing has birth
> I come—thy stains to wash away,
> Thy cherished fetters to unbind,
> And open thy sad eyes upon a milder day."

Coming "From regions where no evil thing has birth," the spirit is itself of purer origin and reminds earth of that origin with which it has lost contact. The cry is (since the poem is Wordsworth's, not Blake's) to rest, not to rise, and under a restored blanket of peacefulness subdue the disruptive, destructive impulses of man. Like the cry in Blake's Introduction to *Songs of Experience,* "O Earth, o earth return," this spirit speaks from the hope that a renewed sense of the *whence* will redeem the *whither.*

One could represent the difference between a Wordsworthian search for origins and a more apocalyptic one by juxtaposing the appeal to earth, "open thy sad eyes upon a milder day" to the journey Shelley's Asia takes backward "Through Death and Birth, to a diviner day." Shelley's journey cannot be conceived outside the province of song; Wordsworth's can be said to be actualized with every little nameless act of personal or political kindness and love. Shelley's "diviner day" is transcendent; Wordsworth's "milder day" is immanent, as the second stanza of the Invocation makes clear:

> Upon the act a blessing I implore,
> Of which the rivers in their secret springs,
> The rivers stained so oft with human gore,
> Are conscious.

Consciousness *of blessing* can be imputed to rivers at their sources because such blessing is the state of the source, while sullying occurs in the geographical or temporal distance from original purity. *Consciousness* of blessing can be imputed to inspirited sources just as the poem as a whole figures a vocal spirit addressing a silent, unconscious, blood-stained earth. A poetic fiction of address by a spirit to a place, far from violating the sanctity of an original, "really" inspirited place, raises consciousness of how far we have fallen away, and thus participates in a return to primordial blessedness.

At this point we can isolate the major turn or revision in the myth of presences. The difference between the two versions is elided by the Christian myth, for God is both present to the Christian now—someone he can address as "Father"—and a lost presence ever since the expulsion from Eden. Despite its awkwardness, the simplest way to label the two versions may be paternal and maternal, the first referring to something ghostly that yet survives, the second to an original ideal of presence now largely lost. If we follow Vico in presupposing fear as the origin of the gods, or if we follow the poet's early spots of time in which presences emerge as admonitory shadows, we confront the paternal presence as a representation of what Freud called the superego. In the absence of external figures of authority, the mind remains haunted by father-like ghosts or father-like ideas of God.

There is in Freud, however, a second, more mysterious derivation of the superego, more romantic in its autogenetic origination from a source regarded as "in" or present to the mind: "In the id, which is capable of being inherited, are harboured residues of the existences of countless egos; and, when the ego forms its super-ego out of the id, it may perhaps only be reviving shapes of former egos and bringing them to resurrection."[19] From the idea that the id is inherited one passes beyond romantic origins to the theory of poetic influence and the Bloomian hypothesis that precursors are absorbed into the id, the body of desire, rather than remaining admonitory covering cherubs, superego figures never having assumed the form of desire. Outside the special provenience of literary history, we commonly think of the forms of desire preserved in the id as cathected around the mother.

One may regard Book I of *The Prelude* as the locus of the most primitive representations of the superego or paternal presence, and turn to Book II for the central formulation of the revised, maternal myth of presence. Biographical fact gives us the maternal presence before the ghostly presences of superego figures; but poetically the sense of one great presence, unmoving and unreproving, is a revision of the earlier notion. Since the maternal presence is the one great loss while paternal ghosts continue to haunt us, it may be that the myth of maternal presence is, in any text, properly reserved for a later stage of poetic maturity. (The great exception to this, the paired spots of time in 1805 *Prelude* XI, must be discussed separately.) We can say of the myth of maternal presence either that the representation of it is consciously delayed or that it is cherished in a way that permits the defensive guards around it to be lowered only after the poet has worked up to a certain rhetorical height. In the Intimations Ode the revised myth is saved for the rhetorical climax in the eighth stanza. Recalled now from the soul's home, this sense of eternal presence is represented as the Eternal; the child's early awareness of continuity with the mother and all nature is raised to an intimation of immortality like the Immortal Himself:

> Thou, over whom thy Immortality
> Broods like the Day, a Master o'er a slave,
> A Presence which is not to be put by.

Before turning to Book II of *The Prelude*, I would like to qualify and perhaps justify my designation of the maternal presence as revisionary. In using the shorthand "maternal presence" (rather than an insufficiently specific though more authorized term like "sense sublime") I do not mean that an idea of original communion with the face of nature is denied to the poet of Book I or any of the later episodes in which the element of fear looms as large as the benevolence of the haunting presence. If the myth of presences is truly revisionary, any episode that first presents a paternal presence will reveal a maternal one; or (to remove this for a moment from a shorthand that threatens to mix its signs with its significances) an episode that first presents an admonitory presence as a threat or agent of discontinuity becomes, in retrospective revision, an agent of continuity and assurance. Let me choose one example from a literal revision of the text. In the 1805 version Wordsworth concludes the boat-stealing episode with a description of a general darkness in which the forms of nature give way to "huge and mighty Forms that do not live / Like living men" (I.425–26). Manuscript V continues: "Ah! not in vain, ye Beings of the hills, / And ye that walk the woods and open heaths. . . ." This is revised to the less admonitory, more absolute presence in all subsequent texts: "Widsom and Spirit of the universe! / Thou Soul that art the Eternity of Thought!"

In Book II a symbolic maternal Presence replaces the theological "Spirit of the universe," and the infant babe is seen blessed as one might be by the guaranteed presence of God:

> For him, in one dear Presence, there exists
> A virtue which irradiates and exalts
> Objects through widest intercourse of sense.
>
> [1805, II.238–40]

Insofar as the maternal Presence is the principle of continuity itself, it may be called for Wordsworth, as it was by Stevens, the "purpose of the poem."[20] Maternal Presence gives significance to all the forms of nature, and the meanest flower that blows is beautified by such love. It is no accident that Mary is described later in the poem in similar terms: her presence "such a sweetness breathed" (there is all the difference between these breathings and those of the ghostly fathers pursuing the boy) that flowers and trees seem once more humanized and sensible of her love for them. In the 1805 text the verse paragraph describing her ends with just the theological term used for the infant babe: "her life is *blessedness*" (XI.223).

Revision in the Blessed Babe passage highlights the revisionary nature of the myth of maternal presence. Under the watchful mother's eye, the child is first described as

> eager to combine
> In one appearance, all the elements
> And parts of the same object, else detach'd
> And loth to coalesce.   [II.247–50]

I take it that this early poetic instinct of the child is employed not simply in putting together the mother from her synecdochic parts—assembling a Presence from eye, voice, breast—but in putting together the Presence of nature from its various forms, of which the literal mother figure is chief synecdoche. In revising the passage Wordsworth subdues the poetic activity of the child so that he perceives more than he creates. Instead of originating the Presence in the child's active assimilation (composing one's own mother is a romantic origin indeed), the passage conjures up a picture of origins romantic in the "soft" sense—a prevenient Presence that is there, from the beginning, not just fulfilling but anticipating each want:

> Is there a flower, to which he points with hand
> Too weak to gather it, already love
> Drawn from love's purest earthly fount for him
> Hath beautified that flower; already shades
> Of pity cast from inward tenderness
> Do fall around him upon aught that bears
> Unsightly marks of violence or harm.   [1850, II.245–51]

"Always already!" Derrida exclaims, lamenting the inevitable belatedness of an "originary moment." Wordsworth is creating here a myth of precisely what Derrida denies: real presence, or "original plenitude."[21] The prevenience of the mother's affections makes of the origin of the child's desire no new break in nature, however mild, but a little receptivity toward prevenient

desire, prevenient love. Wordsworth identifies this as "the first /
Poetic spirit of our human life" (II.275–76), but any anxiety
about the solitariness or danger of being first is relieved by the
providential spirit antecedent to and hovering over the child's life.

As the child loses his mother (either traumatically, as Wordsworth did his literal mother, or gradually, as Wordsworth defines
the process of maturation) that original maternal Presence fades
into Nature, and Nature fades into nature. In place of the
earliest fixation the child learns an excursive power—the ability
to move from one to another sign or manifestation of a presence
like the mother's. Geoffrey Hartman singles out as "the one myth
he allows himself" the idea that nature (as Nature) into which
the mother has faded, but not wholly faded out, "could turn
the 'self-haunting-spirit' outward and make it excursive once
more." [22] The original maternal Presence acts like the biblical
God—once fully present, but not wholly absent to man in
lapsarian exile. We can call the maternal Presence, in its godlike
function, the "transcendental signified," borrowing Derrida's
term, and note how it "places a reassuring end to the reference
from sign to sign" [23]—or acts as a reassuring guarantee that all
signs will be valorized, and that the excursive spirit traveling
between them need not be overly anxious about the loss of the
individual sign any more than the poet writing *The Prelude* is
stalled between episodes of his poem. The journeying spirit is
reassured by the memory of that primal Presence whose single
conversion to an absence—but not a total absence—subsumes all
lesser signs of diminishment and death. Derrida sums up his
critique of religious vocabulary, and perhaps Western metaphysics more generally, in noting that he has "identified logocentrism and the metaphysics of presence as the exigent, powerful,
systematic, and irrepressible desire for such a [transcendental]
signified." It is interesting that Wordsworth looks back on his
great presentation of the transcendental signified by recalling,
"I held mute dialogues with my Mother's heart" (II.283). After
infancy the child falls from this central logocentrism (physical

and metaphysical presence) into articulated dialogues and the differences and deferrals of language. Vico held that the gods engaged in mute intercourse, while men fall into speech; in Wordsworth's myth of maternal Presence the (mythic) child holds mute dialogues, and poetic speech reconstitutes that transcendental signified by belatedly (*nachträglich*) representing it.

Writing of the Presence in *Tintern Abbey*, Richard Onorato summarizes the way a myth of an original transcendental signified becomes a guarantor of continuity as the poet moves from sign to sign: "The Presence, a personification that has no one image, is Nature herself and has all of Nature's imagery. It is also the mother projected into Nature; she who was the 'one beloved presence' that once made the imagery of Nature coalesce is now evoked as a Presence by the coalescence of the imagery of Nature." [24] The connector Onorato employs between these two ideas ("it is also") may blur the mythologization of maternal Presence by seeming to present as simultaneous alternatives that which myth orders temporally; but "she who was the 'one beloved presence'" restores the valorization of a romantic *origin*. The Presence thus has two incarnations: it is recalled from (assumed to have presided over) the child's earliest perceptions of the imagery of nature; and it is re-called, reinvoked in philosophic maturity and the awareness of "something far more deeply interfused."

In *Tintern Abbey* the earlier stage of paternal or ghostly presence makes a brief appearance in the description of the youth, "more like a man / Flying from something that he dreads, than one / Who sought the thing he loved." Though already subdued, the presence discerned in the "sounding cataract" haunts the younger man in a sense slightly harsher than that in which we speak of music being borne in the heart long after it is heard no more. Afterward, the "presence that disturbs me with a joy / Of elevated thoughts" comes as a revision of the younger man's sense of haunting presence. Granted that the business of this verse paragraph is to discover a principle of continuity that will override change and time, we can see how the revision in the myth of presences furthers this end by mollifying the change. The intimation of paternal presence is so soft we cannot even tell whether what he dreaded was something in nature or something in social or political life from which he fled, turning to nature. Conversely, the maternal Presence "disturbs" with its joy, coming thus closer to the more worrisome presence than a radical philosophical maturation would otherwise indicate.

While the poet suggests, through carefully tempered diction, the connection between his sentiments in 1793 and those of 1798, the myth of presences also works counter to the ostensible rhetorical aim and reminds us that the state of mind in 1793, like that of "boyish days," was but an interruption in the more important continuity—that between an original Presence and a mature approximation or reapprehension of it. If the new "sense sublime" appears a sophisticated reincarnation of the maternal Presence biographically known—or mythically hypothesized as having been known—much earlier, it must be recognized as both a rediscovery (something perceived) and a screening revision (something half created). Freud speculated of screen memories generally that "in these periods of revival, the childhood memories did not, as people are accustomed to say, emerge; they were formed at that time." [25] But we do well to distinguish in Wordsworth (as in Freud) three kinds of screen memories. Most simply, an adolescent experience screens a childhood one, or an awareness of loss in youth (the poet of 1798 is not that of 1793) screens the more absolute loss of the original Presence. Second, a childhood memory screens or overshadows an adolescent one. While the "glad animal movements" of boyish days mark an earlier period than the poet's 1793 visit to the Wye, he imports from childhood the dizzying raptures that may in fact not have been so dizzying to the twenty-three-year-old. The memory of bounding like a roe, coming from childhood, masks and re-presents the experience of five years past. Then, finding himself empowered (however consciously or unconsciously) to re-present the past, he is moved to create the third and most extravagant screen memory: this visit to the Wye, this moment of togetherness with Dorothy, will screen out past losses and act as a romantic origin—a moment of full, maternal Presence, to nourish future years.

Perhaps the greatest triumph of *Tintern Abbey* is that its revisionism is so gentle, so benevolent, that the repeated shocks of disruption in the poem's own grammar and its reworking of the past are wholly subsumed into a "green pastoral landscape"—as though nothing threatened between the poem's opening scene and that, its penultimate line. I turn last to "Nutting," a poem whose thematic interest in the shock of self-consciousness helps highlight the major turn or crossing in the mythology of presences.

Though an early version of the poem has the child led by "guardian spirits," Wordsworth excised all such statements of maternal Presence from the poem's opening.[26] The poem does picture the child attired by his "frugal Dame"—his literal mother figure—but she is no overriding Presence, no inviolate spirit whom he recognizes, all along, to be equally present in the woods. He is on his own in this nutting expedition, and the little rape committed on the hazel nook fulfills, in pastoral form, the romantic wish to stand at the primal scene.[27] If the bower gives up its "quiet being" to his sexual assault—becoming a Presence at the moment that presence is denied—what he begets there is no mere offspring of later feeling but the paternal Presence or superego representation, imaged as "the intruding sky."

These explicitly sexual terms do a delicate text more violence than the child ever did that bower. We must take note, at a minimum, that the poet was a little more guarded than his critic about the nature of the begetting that took place in the bower. He pauses to question whether the sense of an intruding presence was a vision, a "conception" of that time, or the work of later revision:

> And, unless I now
> Confound my present feeling with the past;
> Ere from the mutilated bower I turned
> Exulting, rich beyond the wealth of kings,
> I felt a sense of pain when I beheld
> The silent trees, and saw the intruding sky.

If his presentation of his feeling then is unconfounded by later conscience, the beholding of the silent trees (like the beholding of the opening scene in *Tintern Abbey*) seems innocence itself, or a figuration of remorse so benign it seems to argue for the continued virginity of the scene. With a sense of pain barely awakened from pleasure, the youth virtually begets his superego, nontraumatically, out of a sentiment that seemed all his own. Of the Freudian model which recognizes that the superego is created by the ego from materials in the id, we could say that the very loveliness of the scene—silent trees, and sky felt as a Presence—is the romantic material from which the poet originates the ghost of paternity.

If his presentation of his feeling at that time *is* confounded by a later sense of remorse or a belated awareness of the possibilities latent in the bland childhood event, then the poem itself is the locus of romantic origination: recounting and confounding, he begets a Presence barely conceived by the child. The temporal gap between the event and the retelling of it becomes the local habitation of the paternal Presence, begotten by the poet out of his own awareness of the difference between childhood and later feelings. "To say that *différance* is originary," writes Derrida, "is simultaneously to erase the myth of a present origin"—a myth in which the nutting scene, rather than the poem "Nutting," is the birthplace of the Presence. "Which is why 'originary' must be understood as *crossed out* [confounded], without which *différance* would be derived from an original plenitude." [28]

"Nutting" ends with a very beautiful, very un-Derridan statement of faith in an "original plenitude":

> Then, dearest Maiden, move along these shades
> In gentleness of heart; with gentle hand
> Touch—for there is a spirit in the woods.

The desire to illustrate or make the reader feel a spirit in the woods may have been the prevenient motivation, the "purpose of the poem." But while it comes to be felt as an "original plenitude," there from the beginning, the spirit is equally an originated plenitude, product of this text's blindness and rediscovery. In its magical innocence, the last line fulfills a pastoral version of an oedipal fantasy: leaving behind the paternal for the fully benevolent, maternal Presence. Or rather, the line does not leave the paternal behind; it discovers the paternal Presence to be a latecomer on a scene shared by the poet-child and the maternal Presence. In one sense rebegotten by the poet and in one sense the maternal figure on whom the vision is begotten, this quiet Being in the woods becomes the great guarantor of continuity over all gaps of oedipal conflict. Sublimed into gentleness of heart, she will survive as the poet's romantic originatrix and symbol of his originality.

ii   The Affections

One can only guess whether Wordsworth would have approved of interweaving myths of the origins of various Presences—from haunting memories of specific events to a "sense sublime / Of something far more deeply interfused." He did approve, or rather repeatedly sought to prove, the Presences as themselves the origin of the affections. Yet even after many readings of *The Prelude* it is something of a shock to come across the title of Book VIII, especially in the 1850 version: "Retrospect.—Love of Nature Leading to Love of Man." In the 1805 version the less surprising "love of mankind" in part explains his meaning: fond memories of incidents and individuals belonging to the natural setting of childhood can lead to the love of man in the abstract.[29] But just as we cannot elide the processes by which "love of nature" half creates the presences of nature, we cannot overlook the way "love of man" in part conceals, in part directs us to two deeper topics: how it is we free ourselves to love, and why it is that coming to love should be considered a problem.

The title "Retrospect" indicates the centrality of Wordsworth's interest in the origins of the affections. When he reminds his readers, "my present Theme / Is to retrace the way that led me on / Through Nature to the love of Human Kind" (VIII.586–88)—a reminder subsequently omitted in revision— he obscures the way this theme is "present" in the largest sense: capable of subsuming or subordinating his other concerns; it is an ever present theme. Repetitions and disclaimers attest to anxiety surrounding the theme, and there is at moments a special reprieve in the fancy that love comes "naturally," neither requiring nor rewarding attention to its origins. In 1805 he slides over the distinction between love of nature and love of man in the magical discovery "that we love, not knowing that we love, / And feel, not knowing whence our feeling comes" (VIII.171–72). In the revision of this passage, obliviousness to origins finds an image in the idea that "noticeable kindliness of heart / Sprang out of fountains" (1850, VIII.124–25).

The most passionate disclaimer of interest in the origins of the affections precedes and energizes the greatest evocation of love and "one dear Presence." In Book II, Wordsworth looks back at the "incidental charms which first attach'd / My heart to rural objects," and pauses before turning to Nature—before converting what would have been a turn to Nature into an evocation of maternal Presence. In the pause he rejects the effort to particularize what comes from what fountain—in distinction from the lofty generalizing image of fountains in Book VIII:

> Who knows the individual hour in which
> His habits were first sown, even as a seed,
> Who that shall point, as with a wand, and say,
> 'This portion of the river of my mind
> Came from yon fountain?" [II.211–15]

If this dismissal marks an abyss to be passed over quickly, what he reaches for on the other side is the reality of present affection: "Thou, my Friend!" He turns to Coleridge ostensibly because Coleridge would know better than to confuse romantic origins with source study. Perhaps beyond a reference to Coleridge's theory of the imagination there is a little joke here at Coleridge's expense, for Wordsworth lauds his philosophic friend as "no slave / Of that false secondary power," a needling understatement in light of Coleridge's energetic castigations of source-hunting scholarship and his dread of the charge of plagiarism. With or without the jest the passage marks a desire for intimacy and a wish that the reality of affection would overshadow—or perhaps preveniently valorize—the succeeding myth of the origin of the affections.

The question "who shall parcel out / His intellect?" may mark a gentle deflection from, rather than an alternate formulation of, the real subject, the originatory components of the affections. In an equally graceful swerve, Wordsworth sets out to praise Coleridge for his intellectual clarity, and praises him for emotional strength:

> to thee
> Science appears but, what in truth she is,
> Not as our glory and our absolute boast,
> But as a succedaneum, and a prop
> To our infirmity.   [II.216–20]

"Science" may mean knowledge in general, but the passage makes more sense if it refers to the science of source hunting, or science understood as the field of inquiry into natural as opposed to romantic origins. "Our infirmity" may refer to our temporal or sciential limitations, but since he turns to Coleridge from considering the problem of autobiographical origins, we may be justified in recalling the problem of "an infirmity of love for days / Disowned by memory" (1850, I.614–15). In part ignorance, the infirmity carries a (superficially antithetical) meaning of "insufficiency of love." Thus science, in the narrow sense, is a sublimation of or a substitute for properly affective attachments to the past. In its spirit we "create distinctions, then / Deem that our puny boundaries are things / Which we perceive, and not which we have made." Self-made distinctions substitute for self-made or romantic origins. "Puny" boundaries are *puis né*, belated distinctions replacing more anxiety-laden problems of belatedness and originality. These are the substitutions others make; dismissing them, Wordsworth rises to a rhetorical climax that transcends its origin or referent:

> Hard task to analyse a soul, in which,
> Not only general habits and desires,
> But each most obvious and particular thought,
> Not in a mystical and idle sense,
> But in the words of reason deeply weigh'd,
> Hath no beginning.   [II.232–37]

Those last words are raised to special importance by their position: they conclude the strongest dismissal of hunting for nonmythic origins, and they introduce the great myth of romantic origins, "Bless'd the infant Babe. . . ." One can emphasize either that *particular* thoughts have no beginning (it is impossible to specify at what point a thought becomes one's own) or that particular *thoughts* (as opposed to affections, which, when we have them, are more truly our own) have no beginning. What resounds most as one turns to the blessed babe are the words "no beginning," cut off to some extent from their grammatical antecedent. Like Milton's injunction to the slumbering Adam and Eve, "know to know no more!" (*PL*, IV.775), this dismissal marks the dividing line between innocence and the romantic denial of beginnings. There are no beginnings in nature, as Coleridge pointed out; but in art and in the mind's artistic re-creation of itself there are mistakings of beginnings, or myths of origin.[30]

At this point one can pursue along two different routes the concept of anxiety about the origins of the affections. If "those first affections, / Those shadowy recollections" (as he calls them in the Intimations Ode) go back to the literal maternal presence, then the personal loss described in *Prelude* II is *the* center of anxiety.[31] Regarded as a preliminary to the great blessed babe passage, Wordsworth's turn to Coleridge would mark a reach for present assurance before leaping over the great abyss of mother-loss. On the other hand, one can focus on the nature of this assurance and its dismissal of literal beginnings. To wish to be presustained by affection for Coleridge is to wish to reverse the priorities in two senses: in terms of importance, mother-loss would be approached as one of many mythic representations, one more obstinate questioning of sense and outward things; and in terms of temporal priority, mother-loss would be not an event of an irrecoverable past but a re-presented event, a story one comes to from one's present psychic composition and composure. Wordsworth praises Coleridge for understanding science to be a "prop / To our infirmity." He then describes the death of his mother in terms that make rhetorical figures seem more primary than the literal figure of maternal presence: "The props of my affections were remov'd, / And yet the building stood, as if sustain'd / By its own spirit!" (II.294–96). If affection for Coleridge is an important part of his own spirit now, then the spirit is excursive, rather than centrally and irretrievably cathected around the mother or the event of mother-loss.

These two theories of the origin of affections correspond to two different ways of understanding psychoanalytic myth and the application of it to literary analysis. In tribute to the poet who so valued "gentleness of heart," as he calls it at the end of "Nutting," and who sought the principles by which we may "gently pass" from one affect to another, I will label the second the gentle, as opposed to the traumatic, theory. Though both theories are present in Freud almost from the start, the distinction is sometimes viewed by his more idealizing followers (like Paul Ricoeur) as a distinction between Freudian theory and their own. The more orthodox theory holds that personality is essentially molded around memories of certain traumatic events (real or re-created); the work of analysis is to expose and decenter these trauma. The gentle theory holds that a far more prominent role is played by memories of nontraumatic difficulties successfully overcome; the work of analysis is to convince a patient that since he has done so much up to now (and played such a large role in reworking his memories of the past), he can continue to remake his past and shape his future.

The difficulty with this distinction is in applying the label "traumatic." Since the analyst's interest is in the event as remembered, rather than the actual event, any incident, however trivial, can function like a trauma; on the other hand, since memories are always creations that our unconscious artistic hands have passed over (remolded) many times, the most dire memory is a proving ground for the power of the mind to pass over (pass beyond). The difficulty is compounded for the analysis of poems. Should incidents like the death of Wordsworth's mother, the death of Lucy, the numerous encounters like that with the leech gatherer in *Resolution and Independence,* be considered trauma? Or should one regard the poet's success in representation as an indication of a crisis so "gentled" that it seems wrong to speak of a crisis? Wordsworth critics often respond to one another by conceiving of their predecessors as being in the traumatic camp. More important to our concerns, Wordsworth's narratives often involve approaching an incident as though someone else—a nervous auditor, or a previous version of the self—considered it traumatic. The poet himself, as gentler revisionist, conceives the preliminaries to the blessed babe passage in Book II, or the turning to "ideal grace" of traumatic incidents in Book V—the one place where he makes explicit reference to his mother, surrounding it by perhaps the richest gathering of gentled crises in the poem.[32]

From the retrospective viewpoint of Book VIII, the gentle theory emerges not as an alternative but as a repeatedly enacted revision of the traumatic theory. This book proposes that real traumas are not early or "original" and therefore not originary of the personality. Wordsworth takes the French Revolution as chief instance and emblem of actual trauma, and presupposes a salvific "sanctity of Nature given to Man" (l. 430), whether evidenced in actual or imagined events of childhood:

> Starting from this point
> I had my face turned toward the truth, began
> With an advantage furnished by that kind
> Of prepossession, without which the soul
> Receives no knowledge that can bring forth good,
> No genuine insight ever comes to her.   [1850, VIII.322–27]

Is "the truth" the world of actuality, of real trauma, or the realm of higher truths not to be forgotten when one encounters the disappointments of politics and social intercourse? Applied to the blessed babe passage, for example, this concept of "prepossession" argues for a continuity of the affections from what the child knew before the loss of his mother to what the adult knows, knowing Coleridge. The address to Coleridge "pre-vents" (comes before) the passage about loss, and it prevents a loss from being The Loss. The gentle theory ultimately holds that all representation of trauma is prevented because the revisionary spirit reworks all events of the past, and it is all the more manifest in poetry than in the psyche generally.

The major incidents of Book VIII involve shepherds. In preparation for the new revisionary myth of the origin of the affections Wordsworth blithely dismisses a more traditional problem in revisionism—the relationship of a given poet's shepherds to pastoral tradition. The priority that concerns him is biographical— "Shepherds were the men who pleas'd me first" (l. 182)—not a matter of literary history. He borrows the richness of association, without the burden of the past, from Arcadian shepherds who "handed down among themselves, / So ancient Poets sing, the golden Age" (ll. 184–85). But he is as indifferent to the historicity of Arcadia as he will be to the question of whether noble visions of rural life are fantasies or memories. In revision he softens the acknowledgment "so ancient Poets sing" to "in

Grecian song renowned" (1850, l. 135)—a statement more reserved about whether those figures had extraliterary life. Even in the sigh of regret, "This, alas! / Was but a dream" (ll. 203–04), the dream is ambiguously something past or something that never was. Like the Wife of Bath bemoaning the vanished reign of incubi, Wordsworth avoids a traumatic demythologization of the past and has the old fiction just fade away: "The times had scatter'd all / These lighter graces." These lines, and the even more triumphant exclamation "love survives" (1850, l. 156), are signs of gentleness, assurances in the poet's voice that the idea of continuity prevents trauma.

It is interesting to consider these pastoral assurances of continuity beside those in the Intimations Ode. There Wordsworth first invokes, then rejects as inadequate, the pastoral vision of present joy: "Shout round me, let me hear thy shouts, thou happy Shepherd boy." While the return of lambs and pipes in stanza ten is a sign that an abyss has been crossed, the intervening stanzas explore a deeper disruption than any acknowledged in *Prelude* VIII. The Ode discovers a transcendent Presence which is not to be discontinued or "put by"; it "Broods like the Day, a Master o'er a Slave." In *The Prelude* the gently giantized shepherd personifies this spirit of immortality, and "his presence in his own domain" is experienced as that of a "Lord and Master" (ll. 392–93). If the more abstract Presence in the ode "Broods like the Day," a half-naturalized version of the Holy Spirit brooding over the waters, then the poet of *The Prelude* could be said to discover in his shepherd figure a presiding Power sufficient to banish from thought any anxiety about the relationship of personified sign to its significance. In the presence of this shepherd, solitude is felt to brood over the solitary like a master—in the most benignant sense—over a servant in his care.

Like the choice of a shepherd rather than an abstraction like Immortality, the choice of narrative over abstract discussion is a mark of gentleness. This is a general principle much explored in *The Excursion,* especially in the revision of the tale of

Margaret into Book I with the invention of a narrator—one who passes over traumatic events, thus embodying as well as teaching principles of continuity. In the 1805 *Prelude* VIII the most extended narrative is the story of a shepherd and his son. As the two search for a lost sheep, the verse becomes unusually thick with place-names. These stand for sources, and we seem to pass beyond sources to a myth of origins when the son first speaks: "Father, with your leave I will go back, / And range the ground which we have search'd before" (ll. 248–49).

Wordsworth presents this story "as recorded by my Household Dame," and we are reminded at this point of the existence of the narrator ranging the ground of her story:

> 'For take note,
> Said here my grey-hair'd Dame, that tho' the storm
> Drive one of those poor Creatures miles and miles,
> If he can crawl he will return again
> To his own hills, the spots where, when a Lamb,
> He learn'd to pasture at his Mother's side.'   [VIII. 252–57]

The lad, "bethinking him of this," seems to hear the old dame's reminder. What he remembers is connected with the idea of the old dame being the teller of this tale, and telling as an aside to her story the principle of return home to a mother's side. She is a literal maternal presence, and she reminds the poet to whom she is actually speaking of an instinct that survives from days when the maternal Presence was all in all. The visitor to the Wye in 1793 had long since renounced "the coarser pleasures of my boyish days / And all their glad animal movements all gone by" (*Tintern Abbey*), but the sheep in this story retains those animal movements and their centripetal pull toward the maternal Presence.

What follows has the narrative simplicity and mimetic complexity of true myth. The boy spots the sheep on a little island of grass in the middle of a stream of growing turbulence. When, "with a prophet's joy," the boy leaps to the island, prophecy turns out to involve prevenience in a lethal sense. On that little island the sheep had gone as far as he could in his homeward journey; the path back to origins is blocked, and the separating stream, differentiating present from past, spells death. Sheep follow their leader; when the boy "prophetically" leaps to the island the sheep leaps from it—to his destruction. Now the idea of prophecy changes its meaning, and the prevenience of the boy's leap over the sheep's becomes the prevenience of the sheep's death that seems to spell the boy's. The sheep's literal spot syndrome (fixation on the place of natural origin) is replaced—re-placed—by the more awesome spot of figurative birth trauma (romantic origin). The boy is stuck on the island, cut off by the rising flood from both the father's and the farther shore.

Can one say which shore represents the past? For the sheep the near shore represented the immediate past and the opposite shore the unreachable territory of the maternal Presence. For the child, contact with the shore from which he has leaped represents both the more immediate paternal presence and the hope for continuity with the future. Postponing recognition, Wordsworth describes the father hearing a whistling sound, and

> not knowing why, as oftentimes
> Long afterwards he has been heard to say,
> Down to the Brook he went. [VIII.299–301]

That "long afterwards" is the poet's prevenient assurance of continuity—the rescue to come which will make of the whole episode a story to repeat in all its details. The unknowingness of the shepherd (the poet could as easily have had him hear a cry recognized immediately as his son's) acts as a new innocence, a new substitute for the dangerous search for origins.

In the rescue, the shepherd succeeds in bringing his son safely back to his shore. In one sense the father here represents a superego figure or paternal presence in distinction to the maternal Presence. The function of the superego (leaving aside for a moment its derivation in the id) is protective; it rescues the ego when the inclinations of the id would prove destructive. But we must distinguish this father from the haunting Presence I have labeled paternal, and restore the superego to its origins: the father re-presents life to his son, whereas the search for the territory of maternal Presence spelled death. We could borrow at this point Geoffrey Hartman's distinction between *apocalypse* (break) and *akedah* (binding) and discover the binding or covenanting between father and son to be the replacement, like that at a puberty rite, for the necessarily rejected first affections and animal movements toward the mother as source.[33] Certainly the biblical diction supports this concept of covenanting:

> The Shepherd heard
> The outcry of his Son, he stretch'd his Staff
> Towards him, bade him leap, which word scarce said
> The Boy was safe within his Father's arms.   [VIII.308–11]

The shepherd newly hearing the cry of his son is like God hearing (newly heeding) the voice of the bound Isaac. But the diction itself seems biblical because of the desire for certainty in the transitions that produces a phrase like "which word scarce said." This is the rhetorical equivalent of evidences for election to the covenant of gentle continuity.

Hartman's terms deal with mediate middles and with ends. If we substitute for *apocalypse* and *akedah* the traumatic and the gentle theories of the affections, we return the tale to its status as a myth of origins. It is a story of gentleness, one in which God's hand is seen, no less than at the binding of Isaac, to avert the wrath of a more primitively conceived paternal presence. The ram substitutes for the boy bound by the original decree: to the ram is assigned the traumatic disjunction from maternal Presence, while the relation of the boy to his father marks the "gentled" or redeemed one. In "The Solitary Reaper" Wordsworth offers his reader a choice typical of tombstone injunctions to the passerby: "Stop here or gently pass." One can say of this story in *Prelude* VIII that it figures that "or" as a revisionary myth. The sheep is stopped here, the boy can gently pass.

Returning to the question of whether one should consider such an incident a traumatic one in a poem, we can now answer yes and no—or rather yes and then no, or rather yes and then a no that restores a pretraumatic no, a gentleness which Book VIII insists is authentic and original. Thus if one said of the shepherd boy that he is a type of Christ—that the story is an Isaac story not just gentled but "Gentiled"—one would have to say also that the old dame's tale detraumatizes or "dechurches" the Christian myth, restoring a spirit of primitive, pretheological Christianity. But even wholly divorced from prevenient myths the myth of the origin of the affections is in and of itself revisionary. The last line of this story, "The Boy was safe within his Father's arms"—so simple one wonders at that point why one ever thought the affections should have to be mythologized as reoriginating—marks the achieved gentleness as an overcoming not simply of trauma but of the idea of representing trauma as trauma. From the new perspective we understand not that something had been presented traumatically but rather that it is impossible to represent without a saving difference. The turn from sheep to boy resembles in miniature the turn from the flood dream of Book V to this flood story in Book VIII: when the earlier story (or the earlier part of a story), which at some point seemed to be traumatic, turns out to mean something nontraumatic, then meaning itself emerges as a function of delay and retrospective re-presentation. In deferment, as Derrida points out, "the perception of the primal scene—whether it be reality or fantasy is unimportant—is lived in its meaning, and sexual maturation is not the accidental form of this delay." [34]

Sexual maturation is not the overt topic of Book VIII, and perhaps that sense of the "love of man" could be said to be deferred, as a topic, to Book XI (1850 Book XII). It is something of an achievement—perhaps something we should call a pastoral achievement—that in Book VIII Wordsworth can regard as inherently gentling the possibility of interpreting a crisis in terms of romantic love. He lets the romantic interest stand for the prevenient work of fancy covering the real trauma of poverty, disease, and death. Strong in imaginative power to pre-vent trauma, the young poet could face a dying woodsman, for example, by inventing for the cause of his languishment a romantic origin:

> I called the pangs of disappointed love,
> And all the sad etcetera of the wrong,
> To help him to his grave.   [1850, VIII.441–43]

Perhaps, in this little episode he tosses off as an aside, Wordsworth is preventing the trauma of the Vaudracour and Julia episode. More generally, and with a little more assurance, we can compare the acts by which the gentle psyche prevents trauma to the acts of revision in which the poet stands before his earlier material and rebegins.

   The most striking example is the one that seems to mark the literal beginning or first conception of *The Prelude* in Manuscript JJ:

> Was it for this
> That one, the fairest of all rivers loved
> To blend his murmurs with my nurse's song
> And from his alder shades and rocky falls
> And from his fords and shallows sent a voice
> To intertwine my dreams? [35]

A myth of romantic origins seems given to the poet from the start in the pathetic fallacy by which the river is said to have "loved / To blend his murmurs" before the poet develops his own affections, love of nature or love of man. If it is a platitude of psychology that we can learn to love because we were loved, it is a platitude invented by Wordsworth that he can come to represent man's love of man by having represented nature's love of man and then man's love of nature. In the last line quoted does "intertwine" mean interweave a voice with "my dreams" or spin these dream-elements into One Dream, the way the maternal Presence is assembled? Later he smooths out the line to read "That flowed along my dreams," thereby exhibiting a certain reverence for romantic origins in further distancing himself from the issue of priority between dreams and river. Later the "this" of the first beginning ("Was it for this?") will be given narrative antecedent, literally pre-venting the crisis just as nature, figuratively, is said to have done.

In other revisions episodes are replaced or re-placed (placed later), and their meaning likewise seems to be as much involved with these external deferrals as with the acts of deferral they internally portray. Reworking his poem from its earliest drafts, Wordsworth reserved the story of the shepherd and his son for the retrospective Book VIII. Similarly, the Snowdon episode comes to be reserved for the concluding book of the poem. One of the most important deferrals for the story of the growth of the affections and sexual maturation is the joint postponement of the two so-labeled spots of time and the internal *espacement* he comes to make between the first and the second. The two spots of time are already present in the first part of the 1799 *Prelude*—before the blessed babe passage.

There are three questions about deferral, the first two of which may be finally subsumed by the third. Why is it Wordsworth comes to reserve these spots of time for a point so late in his poem? Why does the second, involving a paternal Presence, follow the first, already the belated reworking of a maternal Presence? Why do these spots of time, now following his best portrait of (presumably) Mary, frame between them an account of sexual maturation?

Michel Foucault defines man in general, "as opposed to the things whose glittering birth time allows to show in all its density, [as] the being without origin, who has 'neither country nor date,' whose birth is never accessible because it never took 'place.' "[36] As a poem of many places, a poem in which second birth into maturity is constantly taking place, *The Prelude* may be, like *The Excursion,* an argument for the ultimate expatriation of the soul whose country and date are always representations, re-presentations, of a lost singleness of time and place. On the other hand, the spots of time in 1805 Book XI have a privileged status, and mythically grant the soul a country and a date.

If any event in the poet's actual past could serve to represent a clear point of origins, it would be the death of his father, and I want to consider first the spot of time broaching this event. We should note from the start that the passage defers the actual death and concerns rather a moment some days before, when the blow of actuality was not yet felt and the soul supplied its own anxieties original to itself—independent of the poet's father or his death. The scene on which guilt is cathected is one where the poet stood at a crossroads and waited with excessive "anxiety of hope" for a servant from home. An excess of desire? The very triviality of the imputed crime has about it the nagging overtone of first motion or original sin—slight enough to appear nothing itself but the beginning of something else. Retrospectively, the remembered anxiety of hope replaces anxiety about death, allowing for guilt about an event whose causation is otherwise external to the poet's soul. More than replacing, the anxiety of hope precedes, and thus seems to stand as a fictional origin of, that death:

> The event
> With all the sorrow which it brought appear'd
> A chastisement; and when I call'd to mind
> That day so lately pass'd, when from the crag
> I look'd in such anxiety of hope,
> With trite reflections of morality,
> Yet in the deepest passion, I bow'd low
> To God, who thus corrected my desires.   [XI.368–75]

To remember feeling that eagerness actually caused the death— that the father's death, instead of an event unto itself, came about as a chastisement—is to feel guilty of a witchcraft-like arrogation of power, or at least a self-centeredness or solipsism far more guiltworthy than the original anxiety of hope. Looking back now the poet can call such reflections of morality "trite," and perhaps view his childhood piety ("I bow'd low / To God") as primitive. If the God worshiped then seems more a Voodoo than a Christian power, the child's early conjuration of a paternal Presence can still stand as the origin for more sophisticated ideas of presence and self-origination.

The adult, remembering the crossroads scene, retains an interest in causation, though it is now positive affect rather than lethal effect that he is pursuing to its source. In place of the primitive sensation of bringing about the traumatic (calamitous) event, Wordsworth postulates the originating power of the traumatic (in the sense of dream) event, and he details the "aftering" effect of an extraordinary process of secondary revision:

> And afterwards, the wind and sleety rain
> And all the business of the elements,
> The single sheep, and the one blasted tree,
> And the bleak music of that old stone wall,
> The noise of wood and water, and the mist
> Which on the line of each of those two Roads
> Advanced in such indisputable shapes,
> All these were spectacles and sounds to which
> I often would repair and thence would drink,
> As at a fountain.   [XI.376–85]

Baptized in that last line with the traditional image of sources, the spot of time becomes an exemplum for the origins of the affections in—or should one say antecedent to?—the incidents of childhood.

The need for that last qualification may suggest how successful the screening process is in obscuring the distinction between memories of and memories from childhood. The poet remembers the conflation of the crossroads incident and his father's death as The Event, imaginatively making what were two geographic spots—passageways or valleys of the shadow of death—into one poetic passage about a primal scene. Concern for the way geographic passages become poetic ones belongs to the very idea of spots of time, and is so introduced by Wordsworth:

> This efficacious spirit chiefly lurks
> Among those passages of life in which
> We have had deepest feeling that the mind
> Is lord and master.   [XI.269–72] [37]

The actual occurrence of the words "the event" (l. 368), marking a turn from the assembled narrative passage to the passage of interpretation, marks also the point at which we can begin to think of a primal scene. To do so, we must specify something that resembles or replaces a maternal Presence there—wherever we decide "there" is. Looking at the lines about the efficacious spirit, one might be tempted to regard the spirit, insofar as it is retroactively discovered to be "efficacious," as maternal, and insofar as it lurked in the valley of the shadow, as paternal—like the God who sought to slay Moses. But the process of transferring these terms from a misty roadway to clear blank verse is more complex.

Suppose we evoke Freud's distinction between secondary-process thought and primary-process thought (images and affects free of ratiocination) as a ghostly paradigm behind what I have called the paternal and maternal presences. [38] Properly speaking, "primary-process thought" refers not simply to those images of maternal presence that rise from the id unfiltered by any opposi-iton, but to all the imagery, whether its immediate effect is awful or soothing, that lurks in the passages of "deepest feeling." Though it is possible in broad terms to regard the first spot of time as having a greater share not only in the maternal Presence but in primary-process thought generally, we sharpen the distinction between primary and secondary if we understand, within the second spot of time, that the dreamlike reverie at the cross-roads is primary-process thought, and that secondary-process thought enters with the work of rational commentary and interpretation, when the event is said to have appeared "a chastisement." We can then understand the primal scene as the place where the secondary slew the primary—where secondary-process thought took over. For the story in the poem, this spot may be said to be the moment when the poet's father died, for it is from that point that he (fictionally) dates the secondary-process thought in which the crossroads event is moralized. In the poem proper, the passage that begins with the words "The event" thus appears not commentary on an event but itself the magic event— the takeover by secondary-process thought.

A primal scene is a place where the concept of repetition is more a threat than a consolation. One fears that Oedipus has repeated and not deferred and differed from the scene of his father's sexuality, and one recognizes as the sublime or fearful the elements in a subsequent literary scene that suggest repetition of Oedipus's. In Wordsworth's scene the youth stood at a crossroads, emblem and repetition, as in Sophocles' play, of the generational fact that one person comes from two. Recalling the landscape of the crossroads, the poet associates death with his oneness and singles out correlative emblems—"The single sheep, and the one blasted tree."[39] Meanwhile the two roads, either of which leads home, are peopled with "indisputable shapes," what we might call, borrowing from another Wordsworth context, "unfather'd vapours" (VI.527). If we say that the shapes that troubled the boy appeared to be forms assumed by the paternal Presence, they seem all the more awesome for having been thought insistent and "indisputable." Hamlet may have been stronger, more sure of himself than ever again when he called his father's ghost a "questionable shape" and called upon it to stand and answer to him. In Wordsworth's incident, the haunted youth begins rather in weakness, and we might call what he imagined an "unfather'd vapour" in the sense that the Presence appeared unquestionable and wholly paternal, all father and no son, itself unfathered.

Retrospectively, however, what was weakness is seen as strength. The shape can now be recognized as "indisputable" in the sense that it was wholly the boy's creation. The ghost of Hamlet senior was external cause enough to grow weak; that ghost had external being, could be questioned, and could turn the identity of the son into a questionable thing. But what gives the retrospective poet strength is the awareness that the Englishman's ghost, unlike the Dane's, was wholly internal. From this perspective the misty shapes on the road were not father-vapors but fathered vapors— fathered by the boy's imagination. Thus when his father actually dies—is translated from a literal father to a paternal Presence— that death, that translation, appears to be the work of the son completing what he first originated at the crossroads. The child proves father of the man in a double sense: in his anxiety of hope the child conceived of a paternal Presence insubstantially present; and in imaginative transference the child seems to give death to the father and consciousness of independence to himself. He fathers his father image, and he fathers himself as self-conscious man. At the same time, he recognizes this autogenesis as nonviolent and the scene itself as the source or "fountain" whence the growing youth, returning in memory, can be nourished. The scene becomes the locus of primary-process thought— the locus of a sustaining maternal Presence—and guilt surrounding the paternal Presence is transformed into desire for being begotten rather than begetting. Wordsworth seems himself restored "Once more in Nature's presence" (l. 394) and goes on to begin the following book with assurance that the burden of affective autogenesis has been deflected: "From nature doth emotion come."

The first spot of time so denominated complicates the idea of romantic or internal antecedence in a way that can make the second ultimately appear a stark revision of it. Trusting the conscious artist more than his artful disclaimers of artistry, we can find as we read more and more reason for discounting the casualness of the connecting phrase introducing the second spot: "Yet another / Of these, to me, affecting incidents" (XI.343–44). But we do better to defer indefinitely that larger relationship and consider the way the first spot of time, like the second, represents in itself a revisionary ratio in the origin of the affections. The second spot of time, having fixed attention on one physical locus (the crossroads), hurries by and blurs the configuration of the second (the father's deathbed or grave). The first spot of time lingers over the geographic representation of two physical spots: the boy comes to the bottom of a stony moor where a murder was once committed and the murderer's name carved in the turf; but "forthwith I left the spot" (XI.302), and we may distinguish as a second spot the bare common from which the boy sees pool, hills, and a girl with a pitcher on her head forcing her way against the wind. Leaving aside the usually crucial distinction between writing and voice, Jonathan Bishop notes that we "identify the initials on the turf with the voice whose cry climaxes so many 'spots,' but here it appears at the beginning, rather than the end."[40] This composite experience thus has built into it a template for the "pre-posterous" or romantic origin of the affections. Flying from the site of inscription, the boy takes a sense of dreariness with him to the sights he grasps as The Event. He exposes the roots of the affections, as it were, before the growing plant is buffeted by the winds of fortune.

If Derrida is right that "it is by deferment that the perception of the primal scene . . . is lived in its meaning," then the crucial deferment here is the one in which the meaning of the composite incident is made to appear only later, at the time of sexual maturation described between the two great spots of time. But we must defer for a while consideration of that deferment and focus on the prevenient ones. Separated from his father's servant, the boy approaches the scene of the murder eager to have re-presented to himself that surrogate of the paternal Presence. Actually, to spot "honest James" at this point would be a comfort representative of a maternal Presence, for instead the boy finds a sign of a more awesome prevenience or paternity—the fact of death given to us from our birth. "All graphemes are of a testamentary essence," Derrida generalizes, but these more than all the rest.[41] The inscription *represents* death, and as such might be thought to have a meliorating function. Viewing the inscriptions on tombstones (others have died from time to time) can be interpreted as a "gentled" version of seeing the writing on the wall (sensing that one's own death is being announced). But this inscription is different. I take it that the letters are not carved on a stone which is in danger of being obscured by tall grass, but that they are formed, emblematic prophets of negativity that they be, by clearing away the grass, *ciphering* the earth:

> The monumental writing was engraven
> In times long past, and still, from year to year,
> By superstition of the neighbourhood,
> The grass is clear'd away.   [XI.295–98]

The earth is thus reciphered so that the inscription can be deciphered. The neighbors write degree zero—or rather, the zeroing (all flesh is grass; here there shall be no grass) is done "By superstition of the neighbourhood"—as though the ghostly superstition itself, without further human agency, effected inscription. The poet seems to re-present as well as represent that superstition by substituting the abstraction for human agency. One wishes the writing would be done by one for all, and that it would be done once and for all. The past would then stay past (past inscriptions would stand for past deaths) and not appear prophetic of the future. Instead, death is re-presented afresh every time the grass is cleared away, "and to this hour [the hour at which the boy was there? the hour of composition? the hour of reading this passage?—the terrible continuity mounts as one passes from possibility to possibility] / The letters are all fresh and visible" (XI. 298–99).

No Deucalion, who became an originator by stoning the earth, the boy hastens up the stony moor now described as a "bare Common." Whether we consider the literal object of Wordsworth the child (to regain the presence of his father's servant) or the object of Wordsworth the retrospective adult (to bring to the dreary sight that follows a sense of having himself generated the paternal Presence), we find the path too bare, too common, to lead easily from son to father. It is interesting that Wordsworth shifts the statement of limitation, "Faltering, and ignorant where I was" (XI.300), from its placement before the sight of the inscription to the intensified point of confusion after the boy sees it (1850, XII.247). Can the child, lost and terrified after he has seen the murderer's name, father his own reassurance by turning in memory to the incidents of earlier childhood? Or is such a retrospective formula good only later, recollected in tranquillity? How delayed does the turn from trauma to gentle passage have to be?

To pose these as rhetorical questions is to note how far from the child's experience is rhetoric, voice, and the ability creatively to re-present the past. The rhetorical problem is the poet's:

> But I should need
> Colours and words that are unknown to man
> To paint the visionary dreariness
> Which, while I look'd all round for my lost Guide,
> Did at that time invest the naked Pool.   [XI.309–13]

On the other hand the boy on the bare common is overwhelmed by the sensation that nature has already written this scene and decreed that it shall be read as written. The boy continues to see, as Hartman describes them, " 'characters' that subsist against a background of decay: pool, beacon, and woman are, in fact, perceived singly and with the sharpness of individually engraved signs."[42] The signs are new, but their significance is the same. Though the whole episode may date from about the time of the death of Wordsworth's mother, we need not pursue, as Onorato has done, the image patterns that make of the maid a dreamy refiguration of the mother. The maternal Presence is absent here, and that is just the point; mourning has become a melancholia so dominating that all signs seem to refer not to prevenient presences but to the prevenient fact of death.

To make the traumatic gentle, what is required is time—more time than the boy has in turning from gibbet to girl. The boy would find no alternative in the testamentary inscription, "stop

here or gently pass," since he is too stopped, too much arrested
by the writing he has read to pass from incident to incident, or
sign to sign. Hartman calls the necessary delay a "reaching
through time, or temporalizing of this 'spot' ";[43] similarly, Derrida's idea of the deferment of the understanding of a primal
scene brings us to the later point from which the pre-scription
of nature can appear to be for our health. As though he had
heard Derrida's words of comfort—that "sexual maturation is
not the accidental form of this delay"—Wordsworth turns
directly from the boyhood vision of the girl with the pitcher to
the romantic memory of first love. The voice he heeds is no
philosopher's, though the relation of his new awareness to the
old incident (the incident of childhood or the incident as recorded in the 1799 *Prelude* without the turn to a time of
romantic love) marks a growth in awareness like the philosopher's: it is like the relation of the philosophically sophisticated
Presence (that disturbs with elevated thought in *Tintern Abbey*)
to the memory of earliest maternal Presence.

I risk the preposterous in representing Wordsworth founding
his account of sexual maturation on a principle articulated by
Derrida; but the origins of the affections must lie in something
pre-posterous—in the root meaning of that word—if the gentle
theory is to attain priority over the traumatic one. Success in
overcoming difficulties in the prepubescent past casts a moderating influence over difficulties in the socialization of the
adolescent spirit. Only thus does the time of first romance come
to appear "youth's golden gleam" (XI.323) and not a period of
darkness falsely glimmering with a light that never was on sea
or land. Actually, as we look more closely at what Wordsworth
brought from one spot of time to another, we can question the
naiveté of the spirit that supposes all importations are immediate
strengths, all memories a first aid for the struggling affections.
If Wordsworth himself comes to let the thought cross his mind
like a shadow (perhaps in the phrase "I am lost" [XI.330]),

that demystification is deferred while the spirit revels in its evidences of continuity.

The "blessed season," which Wordsworth depicts as having taken place literally "in daily presence of this very scene" (XI.320), is a time of "presence" in its broadest sense; it is a time of what Derrida calls logocentric illusion, founded on the presence of the word—the presence-making power of speech— and the presence of the past.[44] Whether preparing to become a sexual lover or, in the most general sense, a lover of mankind, one feels reassured by the way words flow that the affections can follow suit. The possibility of significant apostrophe is abetted by the evidence of what seems to be the past addressing itself to one now. Speaking memorable things, the past becomes not just a general moderating influence, but a vocal moderator intro- ducing the "speakers" of the present. Here (significantly enough, in an essay on epitaphs) is Wordsworth's dream of communica- tion at the origin of the affections:

It is to me inconceivable, that the sympathies of love towards each other, which grow with our growth, could ever attain any new strength, or even preserve the old, after we had received from the outward senses the impression of death, and were in the habit of having that impression daily renewed and its accompanying feeling brought home to ourselves, and to those we love; if the same were not counteracted by those communications with our internal Being, which are anterior to all these experiences, and with which revela- tion coincides, and has through that coincidence alone (for other- wise it could not possess it) a power to affect us.[45]

The phrase "communications with our internal Being" may have originated as a metaphor for "the faith that Man is an immortal being." If so it is a far-fetched one—one that has been recalled from the altars of religious faith to do service in what he calls the "motions in the life of love."

Caution may be instinctive in the making of libidinal invest- ments once libido has been withdrawn from its primary object in childhood, but the motions toward reinvestment are seconded by voices from our "internal Being" or memories of earlier incidents so internalized that they represent our truest selves speaking. I think it would be wrong to emphasize Wordsworth's egotistical sublime and find him unduly interested in sublimation or unduly cautious about recathecting libido. Whatever was true of Wordsworth the man, Wordsworth the poet is presenting a mythology of the affections, and what emerges at the center— centered between the two spots of time—is a general though extraordinarily personalized account of the revisionary nature of the gentle theory. If time turns trauma into instances of imaginative triumph, then in time the feelings surrounding the gibbet spot come to be seen as evidences of imaginative strength brought to the windy plain where the girl stands. And, at a subsequent time like that of first love, the more recent business of the libido appears the potentially traumatic experience which can be gently passed through under the guidance of memories of earlier passage.

Wordsworth's myth of the origins of the affections thus arises from a conviction that we experience as traumatic not the hauntingly early but that which is too late, too recent, and that temporalizing consciousness will restore memories of gentle passage to their early and important place. A psychoanalytic critic might still judge that to be a defensive origin and propose instead that the gentle theory is invented to disguise the real trauma of the past, just as easy poetic rites of passage (like "The music in my heart I bore / Long after it was heard no more") disguise calamitous incidents (what was happening in the highlands at the time of Wordsworth's tour). But the gentle theory will not let itself be the text and the trauma theory the critic of that text. The gentle theory accords the trauma theory anteriority, and proposes—at least as an offer, if not as a statement about the past—the revisionary possibilities of the mind. Ignoring screen memories, we popularly think of social or sexual maladjustment as traceable to traumatic events; concerned rather with the greater mystery of successful adjustment, Wordsworth offers a myth of the origins of the affections in which restoration forestalls traumatic understanding of events associated with maturation:

> When, in a blessed season
> With those two dear Ones, to my heart so dear,
> When in the blessed time of early love,
> Long afterwards, I roam'd about
> In daily presence of this very scene,
> Upon the naked pool and dreary crags,
> And on the melancholy Beacon, fell
> The spirit of pleasure and youth's golden gleam.

Reading only so much, the trauma theorist might point to the way the pool, crags, and beacon became, at a point in the past, forevermore naked and dreary and melancholy. Focusing on only so much he might believe a later time was shedding on an earlier one a superficial optimistic glow. But if one reads on—literally, or develops techniques for "reading on" past so-called trauma—one discovers that terror remembered is no longer terror but the aesthetically sublime, something that can add a genuine radiance to the romantic youth's (however fictional) golden gleam:

> And think ye not with radiance more divine
> From these remembrances, and from the power
> They left behind? So feeling comes in aid
> Of feeling, and diversity of strength
> Attends us, if but once we have been strong.   [XI.316–26]

According to Freud, "social feelings rest on identification with other people, on the basis of having the same ego ideal,"[46] and we can say of the characteristic turns to a loved one in Wordsworth's work (be it to Dorothy in *Tintern Abbey,* to the maid in "Nutting," or to Coleridge at various averted or overcome crisis points in *The Prelude*) that Wordsworth is founding the affections on the memory—or a representation henceforth to become a memory—of a shared superego. If the myth of the origins of the affections is a myth of *tessera,* whereby sharers of social feelings meet and match up their broken pieces, it is based on the earlier memory of the unbroken vessel (say, "A Girl who bore a Pitcher on her head") so that the piece-holder's primary relation—the one on the basis of which he makes his match—is to the once whole vessel. The passage that begins "When in a blessed season . . ." is not exactly an apostrophe to Mary, to Dorothy, or (quite yet) to Coleridge, but it discovers the social feelings—and perhaps more specifically the romantic sentiments—to rest on the possibility of sharing an ego ideal. Richard Onorato remarks of the simpler pattern in *Tintern Abbey,* "this nurse, guide, guardian of the heart, soul of the moral being, is Nature as the *mother,* before whom brother and sister stand."[47] With or without Dorothy (and Wordsworth changes "with those two dear Ones" to "the loved one at my side" [1850, XII.262]), our passage marks the complexity of the process of reinforcement, because it so clearly depends on a memory when only the poet was present at this place. But sharing the ego-ideal with a former self, he finds he is not wholly alone, not traumatically isolated at just the point when a man must act for himself: the time of early love.

Though "feeling comes in aid of feeling" could be given a general or "weak" reading (one nice sentiment supports another), the strong reading emphasizes that there was nothing nice about the early sentiment in and of itself, and that strength of the self is something newly originated, not wholly continuous with an earlier time when something outside the self made a strong impression. For the traumatic reading of the origin of the affections it matters not whether the event that proved the weakness of the self was real or imaginary; for the gentle theory one might suppose that it matters not whether "if but once we have been strong" refers to a strength actually felt earlier or only retrospectively understood to be the property of a mind that transferred visionary dreariness from the scene of the gibbet to that of the girl. But surely it does matter that Wordsworth has chosen an instance of doubled influence of the past on the more recent past in which the first transference made things dreary, the second brightened the scene. If one inquires when that "once" was when

we were strong, one cannot answer simply "during the first in-
fluencing"; however powerfully the gibbet scene impressed itself
on the boy's mind, that was the power of the scene, not his power,
at the time, in viewing the girl. What makes the power his is the
work of revisionary "after-meditation" (III.648)—the only mental work we can call truly our own, and hence the only source of
a strong self. Something happens to the origins of the affections
in the phrase "radiance more divine / From these remembrances." At first *remembrances* seems to mean "scenes," but it
comes to mean "these acts of transfiguring memory," not the
incidents in their historicity. The triumphant statement, "if but
once we have been strong," though memorializing a past strength
by association with a scene, refers to a time and a strength that
were not—save in the act of strong revision.

More than an instance of such strength, the return to the bare
common during the time of young love represents a myth of the
origin of the affections because Wordsworth is using a geographic
recourse to symbolize what is normally experienced as a vaguer
repetition. In a biblical version of feeling coming in aid of feeling, Isaac takes Rebecca into his mother's tent and finds comfort
for the loss of the maternal Presence that had presided there.
Perhaps one could say that in Wordsworth's myth the *akedah* or
binding of Isaac to the past that prevents apocalyptic or traumatic
destruction in a new situation is the memory of the presence once
in the tent that helps the sexually maturing youth over a potentially difficult present.

The crudeness of my illustration comes from the fact that a
maternal presence might indeed be traumatic for the youth when
the spot is so literally associated with a primal scene (Abraham in
Sarah's tent). In Wordsworth's spot of time, it is not the maternal Presence but a substitute Presence he first encountered, and
so the spot was, from the beginning, a spot of already revised
representation that figured the loss of the maternal Presence in
the very act of figuration. Such, in the end, is the saving difference, which Wordsworth calls the "perception of similitude in

dissimilitude": "This principle is the great spring of the activity of our minds, and their chief feeder. From this principle the direction of the sexual appetite, and all the passions connected with it, take their origin." [48]

iii Freedom

Toward the end of *Prelude* III, Wordsworth formulates an equivalent for the idea of *Nachträglichkeit,* the revisionary aspect of rememoration:

> Of these and other kindred notices
> I cannot say what portion is in truth
> The naked recollection of that time,
> And what may rather have been call'd to life
> By after-meditation.   [III.644–48]

At this point the inability to distinguish the original from the revised, if not yet understood as a source of freedom, is also not felt as a burden. Book III is much concerned with images of circles— figures that know no beginning or end—and power of self-restoration seems guaranteed to the mind that returning back to itself "with prompt rebound seemed fresh as heretofore" (1850, III.97).[49]

In a struggle for freedom, however, "circling back" is the meaning of *revolution* that one wishes to put far off.[50] Turning to France in Book IX the poet optimistically distances himself from "motions retrograde" and the process he sees himself as heretofore having undergone, "Turned and returned with intricate delay" (1850, IX.8). In the opening of Book X the idea of images returning in after-meditation turns into a nightmare. Unable to read the scene of the Carrousel (and thus face the ineluctable anteriority of historical events to which the tourist can be at best a belated receptor of images), Wordsworth retires to his room, where the images of terror he could not conjure come to him of their own accord. If in moments of confidence the soul delights in the liberty it takes with its own—or the country's—

history, in this midnight of the soul the idea of after-meditation takes a darker interpretation in which the new seems but a repetition of the old:

> The horse is taught his manage, and the wind
> Of heaven wheels round and treads in his own steps,
> Year follows year, the tide returns again,
> Day follows day, all things have second birth;
> The earthquake is not satisfied at once.   [X.70–74]

Half recalled from recent history (the September Massacres), half invented in collaboration with literary fantasy (was he reading *Macbeth*?), the terror that haunts him lurks amid these lines in the confusion over just what *recall* means. Things brought back to memory cannot be recalled in the sense of canceled; nor can poetic revocalization constitute revocation. The passage confuses purely temporal cycling (day follows day) with purposeful, human repetition (so horses are taught) and with calamitous repetition ("The earthquake is not satisfied at once"). Mirroring the chaos in nature, the mind finds itself too overwhelmed by the grand triumph of repetition to isolate in it the deliberate from the dire. No salvific prophecy of "second birth" like that promised by St. Paul, Wordsworth's vision threatens that the new testament will be but a return of the old, and that the testamentary quality of signs will forever spell the inability of the spirit to free itself from the burden of the past.

On the other hand, the desire for "second birth" in the best sense motivates the poet personally, much as it seemed to him to have motivated the French Revolution. *The Prelude* opens with a paean to freedom of the spirit, and if it seems in some ways to recall the models of Exodus and *Paradise Lost*, one notes resemblances only to note the differences. The poet sets out "with a heart / Joyous, nor scar'd at its own liberty" (I.15–16), filled with the optimism of the French revolutionary spirit that would, in rejecting an ancient regime, choose its own guides, consecrate its own joys. The desire for freedom brings desire for a romantic reading of the origination of the self. History—be it personal

literary history or national political history—fades, and re-creation
seems pure creation:

>   I pursued
> A higher nature, wish'd that Man should start
> Out of the worm-like state in which he is,
> And spread abroad the wings of Liberty,
> Lord of himself in undisturb'd delight.   [X.835–39]

Like the "redundant energy" of *Prelude* I that "vexes itself *into*
creation, wishing to generate itself by its proper force, disowning
Nature,"[51] the energetic pursuit of higher nature in Book X
would bring its own object into being. In *Prelude* I redundant
energy seems the aftereffect or overrun of the attachment to
liberty; here one glimpses the effect of after-meditation in the best
sense. The passage continues,

> A noble aspiration, *yet* I feel
> (Sustained by worthier as by wiser thoughts)
> The aspiration.   [1850, XI.255–57]

The italicized *yet* and the parenthetical line, both added in
revision, emphasize the relocation of liberty's source in difference
and distance from the high passion of reorigination. Liberty
comes to be rederived, in tranquillity, from the recollected emotion of wishing man to spread his wings, "Lord of himself in
undisturb'd delight."

  The question of what constitutes lordship over the self attains
a perhaps unmatched intensity in *The Borderers*. Against a back-
drop of international dispute concerning sovereignty, Oswald and
Marmaduke play out a drama of lordship and bondage. Dramatic
form itself mingles the themes of personal and political (interpersonal) liberty, as does the plot situation of an outlaw band
dedicated to refounding law by taking questions of property in its
own hands. Oswald hymns the magnanimous freedom of spirit in
terms that may, transcending conscious irony on his part, indicate
a real article of faith:

> Happy are we,
> Who live in these disputed tracts, that own
> No law but what each man makes for himself;
> Here justice has indeed a field of triumph. [II.595–98]

To be sure, the justice he has in mind is closer to "an eye for an eye"—a demonic repetition—but the idealism of freedom is something in which he, if anything, leads the rest.

There are two burdens of the past that could oppress Oswald, one ever present in his consciousness, the other present in our consciousness of him as a dramatic character. Oswald's great prototype is Iago, who, binding himself to Othello, establishes the rites, as it were, for the marriage of minds Oswald would perform with Marmaduke. One way Wordsworth undermines the tyranny of the past is by granting his character more motivation than Iago, so that the specified prevenience in the character's intentionality seems to counter the belatedness of his appearance in literary history. Oswald announces in Act V, "My Master shall become / A shadow of myself—made by myself" (V.2038–39).[52] Reducing highly complex matters of motivation to a politics of power, Oswald would lighten his burden of responsibility—and perhaps Iago's as well.

For all its perversity his statement of intention broaches the revisionary nature of Wordsworth's myth of liberty. Any idea of liberty is revisionary if it substitutes a new order for an old one; but it is something more special so to recast the burden of the past and so to imagine the problem of freedom as an issue in representation. Oswald has made Marmaduke his master, substituting Marmaduke's unwitting, weak lordship over him for the indomitable tyranny of his own past over his present consciousness; and in undoing his new master, Oswald would make of him "A shadow of myself"—a representation reversing the order of priority in mimesis and turning Oswald (for his crime had priority) into the great Original to which Marmaduke, as shadow or copy, would be bound.

The irony at Oswald's expense is that in seeking a ground for freedom, he condemns himself, with Marmaduke, to a repetition compulsion. Though a terrible fate, a repetition compulsion is at some point conceived by the ego as a defense mechanism—not a very good one, as Harold Bloom points out, because the daemonic in oneself blindly overrules the pleasure principle, rather than assay more temporizing accommodation with it.[53] Circumstance makes the new crime even more a repetition of the old than Oswald intended, for Marmaduke does not slay Herbert outright as Oswald urged but abandons the innocent man to his death just as Oswald had done his captain. Marmaduke believes he is trying Herbert by ordeal—higher authority—only to discover that Herbert is condemned by the anterior, rather than superior, authority of Oswald's act. Herbert actually dies because Marmaduke forgets to leave him his scrip of food, and forgetfulness is the rotten core of the repetition compulsion.

Misery loves company, and in expecting as the literal consequence of his perfidy that Marmaduke will be forever bound to him, Oswald substitutes external society for his unbearable association with his former criminal self. He hopes thus for a saving difference amid repetition: one person's immortality broods over him, a master o'er a slave; two people's guilt should constitute a variation of the kind of sharing described by Freud on which the social affections are founded.[54] Oswald wishes to refound, to re-mythologize the social relations first literally between himself and Marmaduke and then (defensively?) in the abstract:

> Ay, we are coupled by a chain of adamant;
> Let us be fellow-labourers, then, to enlarge
> Man's intellectual empire. We subsist
> In slavery; all is slavery; we receive
> Laws, but we ask not whence those laws have come;
> We need an inward sting to goad us on.   [IV.1854–59]

Emphasize *inward* rather than *sting* in the last line and criminality and conscience seem obscured by the idealist's yearning for romantic origins. When a specific crime is romanticized by being reconceived as Original Sin, the new guilt seems an ethereal—

and thus easier to bear—version of the old. Three great causes (statements of motivation) fan the flames in which this sublimation takes place. First, fraternity:

> Know then that I was urged,
> (For other impulse let it pass) was driven,
> To seek for sympathy, because I saw
> In you a mirror of my youthful self.

This is reinterpreted as the short-lived idealism of equality:

> I would have made us equal once again,
> But that was a vain hope. You have struck home,
> With a few drops of blood cut short the business;
> Therein for ever you must yield to me.

And out of such bondage, new liberty:

> But what is done will save you from the blank
> Of living without knowledge that you live:
> Now you are suffering—for the future day,
> 'Tis his who will command it.   [V.1862–73]

Offering Marmaduke this fruit of knowledge, Oswald both represents or dramatizes original sin and re-presents it (makes it appear to be presently occurring, not just faintly echoing an Adamic original). Writing in 1795, Wordsworth was similarly not just representing the fallen ideals of liberty, equality, and fraternity, but re-presenting them in a way that makes the desire for romantic origins seem a new sin against history. If the pastness of the past is denied by every representation, then Oswald's in itself innocent observation, "I saw / In you a mirror of my youthful self," is easily befouled into "my Master shall become / A shadow of myself."

After such knowledge, what forgiveness? If there is any possibility for "second birth" to mean something salvific, some resistance to the idea of representation must constitute the ground for new innocence. Wordsworth struggles with such resistance in *Prelude* X, and more generally, as Thomas Weiskel has shown, he depicts a resistance to reading by which the self finds a saving difference

from the imposed signs of the past.[55] In *The Borderers* this resistance, marking the possibility of a turn from Oswald's concept
of liberty to a genuinely revisionary one, has no space to flourish.
But its roots may be located in Marmaduke's impatience with
Oswald's account of his origins. Marmaduke is not eager to hear
Oswald's story to begin with, and his nervous effort at self-
differentiation redounds upon him with terrible irony:

> The proofs—you ought to have seen
> The guilt—have touched it—felt it at your heart—
> As I have done.

No, the saving difference is not to be found *there*. But as Oswald
continues, Marmaduke's (and our) distance from Oswald's intensity discloses the grounds for our freedom:

> A fresh tide of Crusaders
> Drove by the place of my retreat: three nights
> Did constant meditation dry my blood;
> Three sleepless nights I passed in sounding on,
> Through words and things, a dim and perilous way;
> And, wheresoe'er I turned me, I beheld
> A slavery compared to which the dungeon
> And clanking chains are perfect liberty.
> You understand me—I was comforted.   [V.1769–79][56]

I am tempted, after "You understand me," to interpose, "Who,
me?" Whether Oswald reaches for these words at this point because he believes the thirst for action is something Marmaduke
should understand, or whether he is reassuring himself at a point
he knows Marmaduke could not possibly follow, he leaps with a
"spring of energy" he would have his auditor transfer from rhetoric to the action it describes. If I do understand him he means
that retreat in a convent was for him a form of slavery in comparison with which any life of action—even if it entailed capture
by an enemy and literal dungeon chains—would be "perfect
liberty."

But the important thing is that he is at this point hard to

understand, hard to "follow," because he is leaping in thought
away from referentiality as he leaps from the past:

> I seemed a Being who had passed alone
> Into a region of futurity,
> Whose natural element was freedom—

Oswald's hope is that Wordsworth had in turning to France, the
hope "that future times would surely see / The Man to come
parted as by a gulph, / From him who had been" (*Prelude*
XI.58–60). Wordsworth is definitively arrested in that hope by
the tide of history and made to turn inward to the kinds of gulfs
crossed in the spots of time. Oswald is momentarily arrested by
Marmaduke:

> Stop—
> I may not, cannot, follow thee.   [IV.1817–20]

Marmaduke cannot follow Oswald in the sense that he cannot
understand how anyone could so conceive the intellect to be, in
Hartman's phrase, "basically revolutionary or *contra naturam*." [57]
He also cannot follow in the sense of "go along with" what
Oswald is saying. Oswald rushes "Into a region of futurity,"
while Marmaduke holds on to the image of the dire event Oswald
has recounted to him. Here Marmaduke may seem the traumatist,
Oswald the proponent of a demonic version of the gentle theory.
That the opposite is more true begins to be apparent when one
sees how Marmaduke, in returning to the guilty mariners, attempts to avert a radical break from his earlier idea of Oswald's
innocence.

What Marmaduke cannot follow and what Oswald is presenting is the idea of achieving autonomy of spirit—absolute, free
self-consciousness—at one blow. Oswald's understanding of freedom is radical in the way Hegel's theory of consciousness is, depending as it does on an absolute break:

If [consciousness] has endured not absolute fear, but merely some
slight anxiety, the negative reality has remained external to it, its

substance has not been through and through infected thereby. Since the entire content of its natural consciousness has not tottered and shaken, it is still inherently a determinate mode of being; having a "mind of its own" is simply stubbornness, a type of freedom which does not get beyond the attitude of bondage.[58]

To get beyond the attitude of bondage, Oswald rushes into the futurity where the mind seems all its own, not dependent for its meaning—for its reference—on others' interpretation. In a way, what troubled Oswald about his own original act of abandoning the captain was that the act had some innocence about it; he was ignorant of the betrayal of the mariners—nature's betrayal, as he feels it retrospectively—and could not bear that weak interpretation or "slighting" of his anxiety. He wishes not to be exonerated but to himself *prevent* being judged—to go before, rather than in the wake of, others' opinions. If this is to feel, in a vulgar sense, above society, it seems a little more sophisticated when presented as an abstract theorem in the semiotics of personality studies:

> I now perceived
> That we are praised, only as men in us
> Do recognize some image of themselves,
> An abject counterpart of what they are,
> Or the empty thing that they would wish to be.
>
> [IV.1822–26]

In presenting this account of himself, Oswald would have Marmaduke read *independence;* resisting that reading, Marmaduke understands only *dependence*—that Oswald's perfidy parts by a gulf neither himself nor Marmaduke from the man who was. The inexorable ties of their future to the past they have brought about may find an emblem in the way the revelation of what he has done dawns on Marmaduke. He half-consciously says it, hears Oswald emphasize "Herbert is *innocent,*" and cries, "You do but echo / My own wild words?" (IV.1874–75). Realization comes, by a supreme irony, in that terrible *repetition.*

If we can call Oswald's the more revolutionary theory of free self-consciousness, we can understand it to be such in both senses: at first appearing more radical, rushing into the froward chaos of futurity, it turns out—it turns about, like the French Revolution—to revolve or recoil back upon itself. The revised understanding of freedom gentles the relation of future to past and —renouncing apocalyptic cries of "Liberty!"—discovers independence in the smaller acts of repetition with a difference. So Wordsworth, turning away from the climactic Snowdon episode in *The Prelude,* first apotheosizes Liberty:

> Oh! who is he that hath his whole life long
> Preserved, enlarged, this freedom in himself?
> For this alone is genuine liberty.

And then he *gentles* his relation to that "genuine" abstraction, discovering instead what Ricoeur calls "a freedom which does not posit itself absolutely because it is *not* Transcendence":[59]

> Where is the favoured being who hath held
> That course unchecked, unerring, and untired,
> In one perpetual progress smooth and bright?—
> A humbler destiny have we retraced,
> And told of lapse and hesitating choice,
> And backward wanderings along thorny ways.
>   [1850, XIV.130–38]

We can call this assumption of a "humbler destiny" a *kenosis* or putting off of the godlike "genuine liberty" for an only human freedom. One might call this rejection of the absolute ideal skepticism;[60] but it is an achievement of Wordsworth's myths of revision that the modified notion seems ritualistically rekindled, so that instead of a single lamp of Liberty and some doubt about its light, we may think of two lamps, and the duller one, subject to revision and re-vision, endures.

iv   Voice

The myth of voice is perhaps the area of Wordsworth's fiction-making where the term *myth,* with its connotation of age-old lore, most properly applies. As ancient as poetry itself is the idea that a higher voice—that of a god or muse—speaks through the bard, and Wordsworth sets himself against the background of this myth whenever he depicts Nature or something in nature as having a voice that speaks to him. Perhaps one should, from the start, identify the authoritative voice of a superior power as the first member in a revisionary ratio, on the other side of which stands a modified or internalized voice. But it is hard to identify in Wordsworth's poetry an instance of such higher voice that is not already internalized or in some sense "gentled."

Often the revisionary voice is the only one audible. The sonnet "Composed by the Side of Grasmere Lake" concludes with an address by the god Pan which makes the whole scene, as it were, his mouthpiece:

> Clouds, lingering yet, extend in solid bars
> Through the grey west; and lo! these waters, steeled
> By breezeless air to smoothest polish, yield
> A vivid repetition of the stars;
> Jove, Venus, and the ruddy crest of Mars
> Amid his fellows beauteously revealed
> At happy distance from earth's groaning field,
> Where ruthless mortals wage incessant wars.
> Is it a mirror?—or the nether Sphere
> Opening to view the abyss in which she feeds
> Her own calm fires?—But list! a voice is near;
> Great Pan himself low-whispering through the reeds,
> "Be thankful, thou; for, if unholy deeds
> Ravage the world, tranquillity is here!"

Were Wordsworth a little more like Blake or Shelley, we might have had Pan's voice answer that of Apollo, the warrior sun-god and rival source of inspiration. To borrow Geoffrey Hartman's description of a similar context, there is "a 'pastoral murmur' that replies here to a martial or apocalyptic voice," except that in this sonnet the prevenient apocalyptic voice is to be inferred rather than heard directly.[61] The scene Wordsworth depicts is mysteriously silent—Jove, Venus, and Mars being apprehended visually, without thunder. The only voice anticipating Pan's is that of "earth's groaning field," but like the earth in Genesis

envoiced by Abel's blood crying for vengeance, this earth is not
something we hear but something we hear about. It is neither
the scene up there nor down here by the side of Grasmere Lake
but "at happy distance" from both; it groans rather than cries
out, expecting no auditor, and only indirectly—in a most naturalized sense of inspiration—commands prophetic outcry. The
revelation we do hear (Thus spake Wordsworth in the name of
the reeds in the name of the Great God Pan) is itself a second
dispensation, announcing a reprieve from the energy level and
moral burden of a harsher law.

So characteristic of Wordsworth is the voice of tranquillity
that to find something more like an unmoderated voice we turn
to narratives in which the transmission of voice is given a more
elaborate fictional framework. In *Prelude* V, Wordsworth recounts a dream—itself borrowed, and in the 1805 text presented
as Coleridge's. The dreamer puts a shell to his ear and hears

> A loud prophetic blast of harmony,
> An Ode, in passion utter'd, which foretold
> Destruction to the Children of the Earth,
> By deluge now at hand.   [V.96–99]

"Poetry is allied to apocalyptic destruction," [62] as Thomas Weiskel
points out, and we sense that we are hearing, however distanced
an echo, the voice of a power in whose hands creation and destruction lie. Mysterious and perhaps even more threatening than
the message of apocalyptic destruction is the fact that nature appears to have usurped the human power of poetry-making: the
shell speaks—and speaks something already an ode.

One can emphasize the destructiveness of nature in the dream
(its words and its plans for destruction are already there) or its
benignity (the shell proves nonetheless a joy to hear). Either
way, one can say of the original anxiety about whether poetry
will last that the concern for the future (for the future of poetry
in the natural world) was a displacement of anxiety about the
individuation of the poet's own words from previous writers' and

the individuality of what the poet has himself created and given a life of its own. If all dreams are wish fulfillments, this one could thus be said to transmute anxiety about facing the otherness—the independence and public accessibility—of words already composed, by passing off as Nature's this frightening fact of pre-venience: the shell has an ode to recite before the dreamer can interpret, let alone wake to retell, the story of the shell. J. Hillis Miller notes of poems in general, but of Wordsworth's inscriptions in particular, that texts we read are not records of what was once speech but re-presentations of what was always written, always a trace: "Their 'primary' existence was not as living speech but as marks made with a slate pencil on a stone."[63] We need not take literally Wordsworth's titles to poems that describe inscription on a specific surface at a specific place; but even if the poet did compose in his head while walking, he wrote down and revised phrases "written" in his head. Pre-scription is the very condition of textuality, as well as a fundamental metaphor for intertextuality.

In the dream, as in poetry generally, the problem of ineluctable pre-scription is transmuted into the sanguine possibility of re-inscription—of rewriting or substituting the new form for the old. "This movement of substitution or dislocation," suggests Miller, "may be defined as the fundamental structuring principle of the text as well as its theme."[64] When the shell's ode of destruction is over and the Arab continues, the "structuring principle" becomes a principle of faith, and prophetic foreboding is transformed into the prophet's assurance of consolation just as easily as Isaiah or Jeremiah return to gentle consolation after traumatic threat:

> Th' other that was a God, yea many Gods,
> Had voices more than all the winds, and was
> A joy, a consolation, and a hope.   [V.107–09]

Ignoring the gap between hearing such voices and hearing about them, the dreamer has "perfect faith" not only in what the shell uttered but what "this [Arab] was uttering." Like the abstract phrase "this was uttering" (1850, 1.110), the equivocation "a God, yea many Gods," marks an indefiniteness which Wordsworth associated with poetic efforts to apprehend the sublime. One fades into many at the point where an auditor believes that he is listening—had been listening—to a "prescribed" or pre-scribed superior voice now lost or blurred into "indefinite abstraction."[65]

As the episode of the dream continues, the voice of the Arab replaces the voice of the shell first heard by the dreamer and then described by the Arab. The last words given to the Arab in direct quotation reveal not gentle interpretation but literal reading or re-presentation of the scene. The verbal loses its lead over the visual and failure of difference itself constitutes the threatened deluge: " 'it is,' said he, 'the waters of the deep / Gathering upon us.' " With these words the Arab fades into the landscape while to the dreamer is left the vestige of voice: "I call'd after him aloud." The whole episode becomes, from this perspective, a nightmare version of a scene of instruction in which the professor or muse (the figure of capable voice speaking to the ephebe) departs in a way that leaves the newly awakened poet more aware of his loss than his power. What is left to the dreamer, dreaming or awake, is the nonspeaking sea and the act of reading—standing in a mediated relation to poetic voice.

In one justly celebrated passage Wordsworth represents both the authoritative voice of a superior power and the poet's own power of voice. Perhaps the passage could be described as a bold reversal of the habitual revisionary ratio by which an absolute voice is gentled. It is significant that Wordsworth excerpted the conclusion of the *Recluse* fragment (beginning with the words "On Man, on Nature, and on Human Life"), making this Prospectus, with its unrivaled claim to authoritative voice, drop the progenitor passage like a poor relation. In context, the gentle

voice is Nature's—or rather "that which in stealth [in silence]
by Nature was performed / Hath Reason sanctioned":

> her deliberate Voice
> Hath said; be mild, and cleave to gentle things,
> Thy glory and thy happiness be there.   [*Recluse,* ll. 734–36]

Though it is the poet himself who reasons thus, Reason speaking in the name of Nature assumes the authority of a prophet,
and Wordsworth proceeds as though the mantle were passed on
from Nature to Reason to himself as poet who has, by listening
to a higher voice, attained a special status. Of an analogous context Geoffrey Hartman writes, "An act of listening precedes or
is constitutive of the naturalized oracular voice we hear in
Wordsworth's poem."[66] Does the act of listening to Reason's
deliberate voice here precede or constitute the oracular voice?
As he defines his epic stance—saying farewell to warrior schemes
and accepting the injunction to sing of common things—the
metaphor of heeding a higher voice takes over, and something
called Voice finds its romantic origin:

> Yet in this peaceful Vale we will not spend
> Unheard-of days, though loving peaceful thought,
> A voice shall speak, and what will be the theme?

> On Man, on Nature, and on Human Life,
> Musing in solitude, I oft perceive . . .

The great Prospectus thus introduced could be described as
Wordsworth's most prestigious effort to confront the origin of
his unique poetic voice, or as an ultimate proof against autogenesis because even in self-created myths the poet needs to
hypothesize voice as being given to him. The passage thus stands
like the beginning of Manuscript JJ as it is incorporated into
Prelude I, an origin that is no origin because nature was already
envoiced, and "voiced" the poet. "Was it for this / That one,
the fairest of all Rivers, lov'd / To blend his murmurs with my
Nurse's song?" (*Prelude,* I.271–73). The river murmured before

the poet murmured against his own failure of creativity. It "sent a voice" (1. 275) before the poet had one of his own, and the river's voice, flowing along his dreams, became his own most inward voice, so that in later time, looking back, he remembers as a point of origin a point at which a voice of nature's was already deeply embedded in him.

The voice declaiming "On Man, on Nature, and on Human Life" is backed by a voice already there—in part attributed to nature, in part recognized as Milton's. In his furthest reach the poet sees himself surpassing not just Milton and Milton's Satan, but all chosen people and poets bound to an older notion of prophetic spirit:

> —Beauty—a living Presence of the earth,
> Surpassing the most fair ideal Forms
> Which craft of delicate Spirits hath composed
> From earth's materials—waits upon my steps;
> Pitches her tents before me as I move,
> An hourly neighbor.   [ll. 794–99]

This is not simply to substitute natural beauty for Jehovah the pillar of cloud, but to demystify the idea of a guiding spirit and find a neighbor—one who dwells near the poet—rather than apocalyptically interrupt him in a descent from heaven.[67] The demystification is performed with such flourish, such authority, that the poet seems to usurp the *power* of the voice that commanded, through Reason, "be mild, and cleave to gentle things." Retrospectively it seems that both the heroic bards of the past and the reasonable voice enjoining mildness were modified or mediated voices, while this the poet's truest voice breathes power at its source. Harold Bloom complains of this passage that it "yielded up a Wordsworth who might have been a greater poet than the one he became, a more externalized maker who would have had a subject beyond that of his own subjectivity."[68] That seems to me like bemoaning, when an opera singer makes the major breakthrough of his career, that he will henceforth never be happy at his old trade of cobbling. Yet the Bloomian nostalgia for "a more externalized maker" is rather reinterpreted than rejected outright in the poet's declaration of how exquisitely mind and world are fitted to each other. More an act of creation than perception, the declaration is something that the poet's "voice proclaims" (l. 815) and *it is so*, like God's hexaemeral work.

Wordsworth reserves another such myth of creation by fiat of poetic voice for the climactic episode of *The Prelude*. I want to explore the episode piece by piece, attending both to the overt subject of voice and to the way each portion revises the concept of poetic voice implicit in its predecessor. We may note first generally that the incident concerns an ostensible search for natural origins—the poet sets out to see the sun rise from the top of Mount Snowdon—and that each development in the episode shifts the relation of natural to romantic origins.

The episode begins with an occlusion of visual and aural stimuli, the second diminishment an auxiliary aid in preparing the scene:

> Little could we see
> Hemm'd round on every side with fog and damp,
> And, after ordinary Travellers' chat
> With our Conductor, silently we sank
> Each into commerce with his private thoughts:
> Thus did we breast the ascent.   [XIII.15–20]

Unlike the poet revisiting the scene in memory, the travelers then were intent on seeing the sunrise—a visual revelation, not an apprehension of Voice. They walk right into the mist and expect that at some point it and the night will give way to light. "Travellers' chat" (later revised to the less obtrusively informal "travellers' talk") seems undignified, and they are hushed as an audience might be before a curtain goes up. Sometimes an audience is prematurely hushed, as when the play is expected and instead someone comes onstage to hawk refreshments or programs. Such a little preliminary announcement interrupts the silent climbers:

> and by myself
> Was nothing either seen or heard the while
> Which took me from my musings, save that once
> The Shepherd's Cur did to his own great joy
> Unearth a Hedgehog in the mountain crags
> Round which he made a barking turbulent.
> This small adventure, for even such it seem'd
> In that wild place and at the dead of night,
> Being over and forgotten, on we wound
> In silence as before.   [XIII.20–29]

They return, beyond this small adventure, to their hope of revelation from the sky, not the ground, and something seen, not heard. Silence resumes her reign.

Thomas Weiskel points out generally that "visionary power is associated with the transcendence of the image and in particular with the 'power in sound'; yet it depends upon a resistance within that transcendence of sight for sound."[69] We can regard the little incident of dog and hedgehog as a preliminary testing of that resistance, and what follows as its major manifestation:

> With forehead bent
> Earthward, as if in opposition set
> Against an enemy, I panted up
> With eager pace, and no less eager thoughts.
> Thus might we wear perhaps an hour away,
> Ascending at loose distance each from each,
> And I, as chanced, the foremost of the Band;
> When at my feet the ground appear'd to brighten,
> And with a step or two seem'd brighter still;
> Nor had I time to ask the cause of this,
> For instantly a Light upon the turf
> Fell like a flash.   [XIII.29–40]

If the hedgehog episode may be called abortive revelation, here is abortive revisionism. "Forehead bent / Earthward" signifies

no major turn from external mountains to deep descents into the
the mind, but rather a physical condition that prepares the way
and tests the soundness of the internalization to come. The light
seen first on the turf marks no metaphysical injunction to look
to the common earth rather than the skies searched by predecessors. But obliterating for the while the shadowy thought that
the whole visible scene will be retrospectively recast, the light
on the turf does signal the full-scale visual revelation when the
traveler looks up:

> I looked about, and lo!
> The Moon stood naked in the Heavens, at height
> Immense above my head, and on the shore
> I found myself of a huge sea of mist,
> Which, meek and silent, rested at my feet:
> A hundred hills their dusky backs upheaved
> All over this still Ocean, and beyond,
> Far, far beyond, the vapours shot themselves,
> In headlands, tongues, and promontory shapes,
> Into the Sea, the real Sea, that seem'd
> To dwindle, and give up its majesty,
> Usurp'd upon as far as sight could reach.
> Meanwhile, the Moon look'd down upon this shew
> In single glory, and we stood, the mist
> Touching our very feet.   [XIII.40–54]

We may begin to apprehend how extraordinary a revelation
this is by borrowing from the 1815 Preface Wordsworth's distinction of imagination from "a mode of memory" which binds
the creative powers of the poet to natural experience. Illustrating
how metaphoric language particularizes an impression but remains free from literal representation or bondage to nature,
Wordsworth discovers the "mind in its activity," connecting and
transforming sense impressions: "The processes of imagination are
carried on either by conferring additional properties upon an
object, or abstracting from it some of those which it actually
possesses, and thus enabling it to re-act upon the mind which hath
performed the process, like a new existence."[70] Each occurrence

of a "new existence" marks a place of origins where something is called into being by fiat of poetic voice. When Wordsworth asks of the cuckoo, "Shall I call thee Bird, / Or but a wandering Voice," he passes from the cuckoo as bird, or object of nature, to the new existence, the "wandering Voice" not simply described but, as an entity, brought into being in that line. Capturing the "seeming ubiquity of the voice of the cuckoo," he is true to the particularity of nature; inventing a phrase that "dispossesses the creature almost of a corporeal existence," he confronts a mild form of the shock attendant on the discovery that the limits of nature in however small a way have been transcended and the creative mind, for the moment, stands alone.

It is important to note in the moon passage that we do not yet have an image of voice. There is, however, something like a new existence, or a process of revelation in which a number of phenomena appear like new substances with a life of their own independent of the prevenient consciousness of the traveler or the scene as previously expected. First, the mountain climber with head bent earthward is surprised by a light which seems not of this earth. It may be moonlight, or more probably the light of early dawn before the sun itself emerges. The surprise that makes the brightness seem "a new existence" comes from its being discovered first on the earth—independent of the spectator moon off in the distance looking on this show, and independent of the out-of-sight sun. Moonlight is reflected sunlight and implies the priority of the sun; this brightness is discovered by the traveler before the sun itself comes to view, just as it is discovered by the reader before the moon is brought into the scene by the poet. "Let there be light!" God announced on the first day, before creating sun and moon; this brightness seems such an original thing.

Is this brightness the poet's repetition in finite circumstance of *the* original act of creation, *the* new existence? Milton countered the sublimity of first things in Genesis by supposing a fiat antecedent to the creation of light: "Silence ye troubl'd waves, and thou Deep, Peace" (*PL*, VII.216). Wordsworth defers his act of transumption in which voice regains its priority over visual effect. For the while all is visual, and the revelation a show to which the moon itself seems a spectator. Perhaps we can call this spectator-moon the second "new existence," for the moon seems no longer an inanimate heavenly body but an archetype—not a representation of the poet but an original presence which the poet's re-presents; the moon was presumably there through the night, looking on a scene of more belated creation. Milton solved the Genesis problem of God creating light before he created the sun by supposing "shee in a cloudy Tabernacle / Soujourn'd the while (*PL*, VII.248–49). Wordsworth makes the moon a prevenient onlooker to the show enacted in the mist.

Jonathan Wordsworth describes the sense of new existence in the moon passage by noting how (like the rock in the lines from *Resolution and Independence* Wordsworth singles out in discussing this effect) the inanimate is animated: "The most noticeable feature of this landscape is that it is alive—the moon *stands naked, looks down* on the shew; the mist is *meek and silent, shoots itself* into tongues and headlands, and *touches* the feet of those who are watching—but it is not so easy to define in what sense it is living." [71] Like the moon in Keats's Nightingale Ode, this one seems alive because it lives apart, all involved in a relationship to the rest of the landscape that is self-contained— to the exclusion of the poet. Again as in Keats there is a sense of mysterious life because poetic might seems to be half slumbering on her own right arm. Jonathan Wordsworth: "For the moment all is meek and silent, but the still ocean is composed of a hundred hills, 'their dusky backs *upheaved*,' of vapors that have 'shot themselves / In headlands, tongues, and promontory shapes.' . . . There is a curious sense of potential, of power without motion." [72] The ocean is also *still* in the sense of silent, and the quiet is the scene's greatest sign of potential life. If the real sea— of moving and roaring waves—remains "Usurp'd upon as far as sight could reach," there remains, as in the quietude of Keats's

Saturn, a sense of implicit power and implicit life. Harold Bloom notes of a similar context, "visible traces usurp the hopeful murmur of prophetic voice."[73] Perhaps we can respond to Jonathan Wordsworth's location of the difficulty in specifying in what sense the moon is living by pointing to the murmur of prophetic voice for the moment usurped upon by a power potentially more alive and now more threatening in its silence.

Revising the passage, Wordsworth extended the visual glory of the scene in a way that makes of it a cover for what we feel more surely is a "prophetic murmur" waiting to be free:

> Not so the ethereal vault; encroachment none
> Was there, nor loss; only the inferior stars
> Had disappeared, or shed a fainter light
> In the clear presence of the full-orbed Moon.
>
> [1850, XIV.50–53]

The significance of the terms *encroachment* and *loss* can scarcely be accounted for by the natural fact that the mist seems condensed into a sea of cloud below the traveler's feet, while the sky above is cleared. Surrogates of the power of negativity, the terms stand as earnest of the poet's negative or critical voice in revisionary response to a voice of prophetic revelation. These are not yet images of voice, but they do point to the irresistible power of negation to authenticate itself. When the Psalmist says, "The heavens declare the glory of the Lord," his words engage in an uphill battle with our sense that the heavens do no such declaring; if a poet like Shelley says, "The heavens declare 'There is no god,'" we are impelled, past the fiction that the heavens declare, to the shared negativity of no declaration, no god.[74]

God is not—or not yet—at stake in Wordsworth's lines, but the heavens' negation of mist prophesies a demystification to come. Or rather, the "ethereal vault" would so prophesy if it were envoiced. Now it is but seen, and its silence marks, out there, something like what, deep in the mind of man, constitutes repression. To the question why Wordsworth adds "encroachment none / Was there, nor loss," we may respond with Freud's generalization: "A negative judgment is the intellectual substitute for repression; its 'no' is the hall-mark of repression, a certificate of origin—like, let us say, 'Made in Germany.' " [75] If we ask ourselves what certificate of origin Wordsworth is attaching to this scene—not where he wrote it but in what way he felt that nature wrote it and gave it to him—we come up with nothing as easily tagged as "Made in Germany." Made in the Imaginative States? In the Union of Mountainous Moonlit Republics? A new space opens up, the discovery of which *makes* the scene for the traveler:

> and from the shore
> At distance not the third part of a mile
> Was a blue chasm; a fracture in the vapour,
> A deep and gloomy breathing-place through which
> Mounted the roar of waters, torrents, streams
> Innumerable, roaring with one voice. [XIII.54–59]

With the image of a breathing-place we are almost at the origins of voice—a primal scene in the approach to which a landscape figuration for repression may not have been inappropriate. Pointing to Coleridge's image in "Kubla Khan," "As if this earth in fast thick pants were breathing," Jonathan Wordsworth marvels at the indefiniteness of the breathing-place image: "What is odd is that it should be felt to be so concrete and yet not raise the question answered easily enough on the level of Coleridge's fantasy—as to who is doing the breathing." [76] The uncertainty seems linked to a question about the level on which we are to read this interruption of nature. In Genesis, God breathes into Adam and animates him; if that myth represents a time of origination, this must be the place—the spot where an image of voice stakes its territorial claim. The break in the mist appears to be, or is imaginatively taken to be, the point from which rises the newly noticed sound of the waves. "Excessive loudness alone," wrote Burke, "is sufficient to overpower the soul, to suspend its action, and to fill it with terror." [77] But more than "the roar of waters," he hears—or better, he creates the image of—"streams / Innu-

merable roaring with one voice." In the 1815 Preface Wordsworth proposes that of the many ways in which Imagination
"shapes and *creates*" (italics his), "in none does it more delight
than in that of consolidating numbers into unity, and dissolving
and separating unity into number—alternations proceeding from,
and governed by, a sublime consciousness of the soul in her own
mighty and almost divine powers." In *Resolution and Independence* the shaping, poetic soul finds the voice of the leech
gatherer "like a stream / Scarce heard; nor word from word
could I divide." The *Prelude* image not only displays the soul's
powers in the conceit of waters roaring with one voice; it presents the voice as a type or image of poetic voice, and, like the
voice of God (for it is in speech, not in visual image, that man is
made in God's image), purely creative.

In James Clarke's *Survey of the Lakes* the visitor to Snowdon
is said to be able to tell one water sound from another: "The
voice of extremely distant waterfalls is heard perfectly distinct,
and not one confusing another." [78] Making of Clarke's (or of
Nature's) distinguished voices a sound of streams "roaring with
one voice," Wordsworth found an extraordinary emblem of his
own coming to voice. The poet becomes, like Isaac, the truer
transmitter of the nonapocalyptic covenant of continuity because
he can hear things God's way, rather than seeing them as they
are. Like Isaac's first preference for Esau the natural child,
Wordsworth inclined up to this point to a description of the scene
in wholly visual terms. Like the patriarch pronouncing his blessing, the poet comes to voice deluded by a trick of nature, yet
mysteriously set right: Esau's hands may have stamped the scene,
but the voice is the voice of Jacob. Wordsworth's revisionary
myth of voice is thus like the revision in the story of the patriarchal birthright: a second, aural revelation displaces the be-
nighted visual one. To claim to hear a voice speaking a more
specific revelation ("Do this! . . .") is to lie against nature; but
to hear the waters roaring with one voice is perhaps to hear more

truly than nature—as nature—speaks. *"Hear,* O Israel"—the injunction to the children of Jacob who would inherit the revisionary birthright—"the Lord our God is *One.*"

If the creative soul, imagining the waters to be roaring with one voice, resembles the creative voice of God, it meets a fate like the voice of God: no sooner uttered than displaced by the voices of commentary. Wordsworth begins a new paragraph a few lines later with the words "A meditation rose in me that night"—as though what preceded was incident, what follows, meditation on that incident. Yet even before the "text" paragraph closes, a revisionary voice enters and presents, as though the poet wishes it to be incorporated into the scene itself, a rather strange effort at interpretation:

> The universal spectacle throughout
> Was shaped for admiration and delight,
> Grand in itself alone, but in that breach
> Through which the homeless voice of waters rose,
> That dark deep thoroughfare had Nature lodg'd
> The Soul, the Imagination of the whole.   [XIII.60–65]

Granted that authoritative voice is to be displaced from God to the poet of nature, the burden for such trespass had best be assumed by Nature herself. Nature dislodges the voice of waters from its natural source (the ocean) and makes of the voice's homelessness an emblem of the soul's homelessness—the feeling that man is not wholly from the earth, though destined to return thither. Like the Hebrew language, which means by *nephesh* both soul and throat, Nature places the soul in the place of voice.[79] Throated but not throttled, the soul, the imagination of the whole, rises up as it does in Book VI—"like an unfather'd vapour." If the Snowdon poet's imagination is figured in the voice of the waves, that voice's homelessness is a sign of the exile of poetic discourse from the world of objects. Poetic voice takes its romantic origin at a remove from sources in nature.

Revising the Snowdon episode, Wordsworth omitted the lines that so strongly preempted interpretation, and closed the verse paragraph with two lines extending the absolute dominion of voice: "Heard over earth and sea, and in that hour, / For so it seemed, felt by the starry heavens" (1850, XIV.61–62). To "start with the sun" and strip these lines of nocturnal fantasy, one might distinguish the truth-to-nature in "Heard over earth and sea" (the sound of the waves would have been audible for a distance) from the mind's fiction (the sound was felt by the heavens). The intermediary fiction—that the sound was not just audible but *heard* over earth and sea—glides between natural fact and pathetic fallacy, filling the space between, as it were, and pointing us instead to the space separating this verse paragraph from the paragraph of interpretation which follows.

According to the celebrated definition announced in the Preface to *Lyrical Ballads,* poetry is "the spontaneous overflow of powerful feelings: it takes its origin from emotion recollected in tranquillity." [80] Turning to the paragraph of recollection in tranquillity of the Snowdon vision, we can now place more emphasis than usual on the word "spontaneous," seeing in the theory of spontaneous generation a desire to internalize origins and interpret poetic voice as removed from extrapoetic sources. Tranquillity is the mood in which "successful composition generally begins," and one's tranquillity is one's own, whereas emotions—whether those said to be felt by the starry heavens or those in the traveler's immediate response to the Snowdon scene—seem more definitively fathered. Wordsworth revised his introduction to the paragraph of interpretation by recasting the whole previous paragraph as the *given* and more boldly passing on to his own voice of commentary. Originally,

> A meditation rose in me that night
> Upon the lonely Mountain when the scene
> Had pass'd away, and it appear'd to me
> The perfect image of a mighty Mind. . . .   [XIII.66–69]

Or perhaps one should qualify even "originally," for surely the meditation is the work of secondary revision projected back to that night so as to seem part of the original incident. Interpretation takes shelter, as it were, under the wing of the dove that sat brooding over the vast abyss in that scene and made it pregnant.

The revision is more daring:

> When into air had partially dissolved
> That vision, given to spirits of the night
> And three chance human wanderers, in calm thought
> Reflected, it appeared to me the type
> Of a majestic intellect, its acts
> And its possessions, what it has and craves,
> What in itself it is, and would become.
> There I beheld the emblem of a mind
> That feeds upon infinity. . . .   [1850, XIV.63–71]

"Imagination," wrote Wordsworth in the introduction to *Peter Bell*, "not only does not require for its exercise the intervention of supernatural agency, but . . . though such agency be excluded, the faculty may be called forth as imperiously, and for kindred results of pleasure, by incidents within the compass of poetic probability."[81] Saying of the Snowdon vision that it was "given to spirits of the night" raises the incident beyond the compass of poetic probability and daily life; simultaneously, it looks to find imagination in the new space of interpretation, once the supernatural voice has been rejected.

The 1805 text leaves uncertain just how much of a rejection has taken place:

> one that feeds upon infinity,
> That is exalted by an under-presence,
> The sense of God, or whatsoe'er is dim
> Or vast in its own being.   [XIII.70–73]

Equivocating about the bounds of selfhood, the two great *or*s of this passage point to the indefiniteness of a moment of origins. In revision, this indefiniteness (the abyss between God and one's own being) gives way to a clarity of will—the will to revisit a primal scene and oneself to see one's self created. In place of what is fully realized in 1805, "The perfect image of a mighty Mind," the 1850 text discovers a mind in the making, "what it has and craves, / What in itself it is, and would become." Its "craving" is its intentionality, and "would become" makes the vision less a sign of clear referentiality—pointing to something that *is*, outside the system of signs—than a picture of something evermore about to be:

> There I beheld the emblem of a mind
> That feeds upon infinity, that broods
> Over the dark abyss, intent to hear
> Its voices issuing forth to silent light
> In one continuous stream; a mind sustained
> By recognitions of transcendent power,
> In sense conducting to ideal form,
> In soul of more than mortal privilege.   [1850, XIV.70–77]

The 1805 text contains a slight Miltonism in the image of Mind "that feeds upon infinity." Milton's presence is intensified, however, when Wordsworth borrows from Milton's invocation of the Divine creative spirit the doubled image of the activity of the mind "That feeds upon infinity, that broods / Over the dark abyss." Just as the Holy Spirit broods over the vast abyss and makes it pregnant, the spirit of Milton hovers seminally over this passage in a poetic begetting that must be Wordsworth's own. Harold Bloom complains that Milton's presence in Wordsworth supports "Wordsworth's own Spectre of Urthona, the anxiety-principle that usurps voice in all the great poems, and substitutes for voice various memorial inscriptions, various traces of a Miltonic anteriority." [82] Yet I wonder whether the Snowdon passage does not rather undermine than do obeisance to Milton's anteriority. Beside Wordsworth's image of the mind "intent to hear / Its voices," we can place this line from his sonnet to Milton: "Thou hadst a voice whose sound was like the sea" ("Milton, thou shouldst be living at this hour," 1802). Wordsworth is "intent to hear," from the abyss of his own mind, echoes of voices neither wholly natural nor wholly his but rising through his images "to silent light." What was Miltonic voice returns—not as Milton's voice, which would deny the self-begetting quality of this passage, but as voices of the abyss that beget their begetter, issuing in holy, inspiring light. By themselves, the echoes of Milton are enough to confirm this passage as being about poetic begetting; if in thinking of Milton Wordsworth thinks of his own sonnet to Milton, then his own past composition inspires the great revision of this passage, and the poet stands as begetter of his own voice.

Wordsworth stands in relation to his own Miltonism as the verse paragraph of interpretation stands in relation to the incident-as-text. His is the work of interpretation which Foucault calls commentary rather than criticism, and which sacralizes the incident—or, more precisely, the poetry narrating the incident—giving it a numinous status like that of scripture: "Commentary halts before the precipice of the original text, and assumes the impossible and endless task of repeating its own birth within itself."[83] Foucault means that commentary repeats commentary's birth, but he could as well mean that commentary repeats the begetting (the elevation, in the Christological sense) of the text-as-text. A similar uncertainty attends Wordsworth's pronoun as the mind broods over the abyss "intent to hear / Its voices." Does the moon brood over the breathing-place in the mist the way a mind broods over the abyss in the self, intent to hear the mind's own voices? Or are the terms of nature-as-text and mind-as-commentary more mixed, so that mind broods over nature's abyss, listening to natural voices? A moon can represent a poet, but the craving, the intention, to hear voices is so strongly an aspect of mind—so very much, in Edward Said's sense, a beginning point for the mind—that the tenor seems to usurp the vehicle of the metaphor and carries itself into being.[84] "Voices issuing forth to silent light" issue only in metaphor, for the begetting of light, let alone silent light, from voice can occur only in figurative language removed from correspondence to nature.

More precisely, voices issuing forth to silent light *now* issue only in metaphor. Once, as Wordsworth puts it in *On the Power of Sound,* "A voice to light gave being." The divine fiat, "Let there be light," followed by "and there was light," represented for

Boileau *the* moment of the sublime.[85] Like his relation to Milton, Wordsworth's relation to the language of Genesis leaves the poet far more a rich recipient and remaker than a loser in the comparison. When the "streams / Innumerable" are so removed from literal streams in after-meditation that *stream* becomes a metaphor for rising sound, language leaps beyond referentiality (the sense that scene fathered description) and discovers the power of poetic voice. If God's voice is the original, and the poet's voice the revised myth of voice, then the genesis of rhetorical figures is no defensive or evasive business, carrying man away from his own nature, but man acting most fully in the image of God.

The work of commentary is endless, and after each interpretation more may be said that challenges the authority of what has already been said. This commonplace about literature and literary criticism faintly reflects the relation of scripture to scriptural commentary, and Wordsworth's theological language entails a theologian's commitment to revisionary exegesis as something that gets one closer to, rather than further and further removed from, divine Voice. The poet continues his commentary on the scene:

> above all
> One function of such mind had Nature there
> Exhibited by putting forth, and that
> With circumstance most awful and sublime,
> That domination which she oftentimes
> Exerts upon the outward face of things,
> So moulds them, and endues, abstracts, combines,
> Or by abrupt and unhabitual influence
> Doth make one object so impress itself
> Upon all others, and pervade them so
> That even the grossest minds must see and hear
> And cannot chuse but feel.   [XIII.73–84]

Jonathan Wordsworth complains that Nature is "an ulterior power where none is needed." [86] Though in one sense Wordsworth could only go downhill—especially after the sublimity of the 1850 "voices issuing forth to silent light"—there is a peculiar power to the poet's heavy-handedness in naming Nature as an agent previously not granted its due authority. This exegetical voice is a more prosaic one, yet its power is not to be belittled. After the voice of thunder comes a still small voice, less exciting in its business of philosophic generalization, and cautious in its suggestion of alternate verbs to describe what it has posited as Nature's efforts. The power of this voice lies in its demystification of what was given previously and magically without (or with less) commentary. Jonathan Wordsworth regrets that "the chasm is deprived at a blow of the transcendental power it has come to possess."[87] But I think we can say of the Snowdon episode what Harold Bloom says of *Tintern Abbey*: "Our memory of the poem . . . is finally not a memory of nature's marking nor of Milton's writing, but of hearing again, with Wordsworth, 'these waters. . . .'"[88] That is, if Wordsworth's exegesis seems belated and less grand, it has the effect of allowing us to recollect in tranquillity a voice we heard more truly and more strange, issuing forth to silent light. This is to deny both the pessimism that successive voices (within or between poems) are successive diminishments from original Voice and the idealism that a revisionary voice can, by its sophistication and skepticism, transcend the fiction-making power of its predecessor. What a new voice can do is re-present the relation of one voice to its successor and discover in the representation something like the dawning of "a new existence":

> The Power which these
> Acknowledge when thus moved, which Nature thus
> Thrusts forth upon the senses, is the express
> Resemblance, in the fulness of its strength
> Made visible, a genuine Counterpart
> And Brother of the glorious faculty
> Which higher minds bear with them as their own.
> That is the very spirit in which they deal
> With all the objects of the universe;
> They from their native selves can send abroad
> Like transformation, for themselves create
> A like existence, and, whene'er it is
> Created for them, catch it by an instinct.   [XIII.84–96]

In the 1850 text, the corresponding passage is followed by an extraordinary image that returns, past the question of successive stages of resemblance, to an image of original, authoritative voice: minds at their highest reach are "Like angels stopped upon the wing by sound / Of harmony from Heaven's remotest spheres" (XIV.98–99). In the interim, however, the imagery of voice is dropped in both the 1805 and 1850 versions while the question of "counterpart" (1805) or "resemblance" (1850) is considered abstractly. The "as" in the line "Which higher minds bear with them as their own" reflects the central ambiguity about origins, for it is impossible to say whether higher minds bear this faculty because it is their own or whether they are permitted to bear it as if it were their own. If the uncertainty of that "as" marks the shadowy ground of origins, that place is approached through the poetic labor of representation. Minds involved in the search for origins

> from their native selves can send abroad
> Kindred mutations; for themselves create
> A like existence. . . . [1850, XIV.93–95]

The desire for self-begetting, with the emphasis on *self,* seems compacted, concentrated in the phrase "from their native selves." Then the energy of that desire is released, and the emphasis shifts from the self as source to the act of begetting (again with the accent shifting from modifier to noun) "kindred *mutations*" and "a like *existence.*" In that shift images take their origin and independence, returning to confront the maker of likenesses with their alienated majesty:

> . . . and, whene'er it dawns
> Created for them, catch it, or are caught
> By its inevitable mastery,
> Like angels stopped upon the wing by sound
> Of harmony from Heaven's remotest spheres.
> [1850, XIV.95–99]

It is possible to locate the ambiguity about origins in the space between the pieces of the quotation I have separated in two—

between "create / A like existence" and "it dawns / Created for them." But once "it dawns," the sense of "created for them" takes over. Poetic representations, like the shows of nature, pass their points of origin and are discovered always already created.

Like fathers, poets may wish to retain their hold on what they have created or adopted, but are more likely to be "caught up" by their likenesses than able to "catch up" with those likenesses which, barely originated, have begun to run their own race. Where nature offers the higher mind an adoptable likeness, the mind can "catch it by an instinct" (XIII.96). Revising this passage, Wordsworth acknowledged that even this power cannot be unequivocally claimed as one's own. When a resemblance is *there,* waiting to be perceived, poetic minds can "catch it, or are caught / By its inevitable mastery." Here is a vision of a benign stalemate between image-maker and image, like a resolved generational conflict in which the child alternately masters or is mastered by the imagination of the man. Thomas Weiskel: "What is astonishing is Wordsworth's indifference to priority: creating, catching what is created, or being 'caught / By its inevitable mastery': These are in the end—in perception—equivalent, and one need not worry the difference between what the mind confers and what it receives."[89] Has the imagination conferred on the Snowdon scene whatever significance it has, or has the imagination been caught up by nature's masterful representation—a "something given"?

Less resolved than transcended, the argument about originality closes with the origination of a new figure, wholly refreshing, whose remoteness declares the mind's unvanquished powers of begetting something new—at the same time that, suggesting an infusion from afar, the lines argue for a wholly pre-conceived and received voice: "sound / Of harmony from Heaven's remotest spheres." This sound, like the sound of one voice of waters (half heard, half created) suggests the ultimate triumph of searches for romantic origins over the location of origins. Coming upon what one takes to be a place of origination, one finds one has been mistaken, that a voice has come, and come there before, from a place more remote.

Since poets "need not extraordinary calls / To rouze them" (XIII.101–02), the point taken to be a point of origins does not have to involve a voice from remotest spheres. Whether he conceives of angels "stopped upon the wing" or halted travelers who hear they have mistaken their way, Wordsworth creates images of voice being given to him. For minds that are "powers," the quest for beginnings, for what we might call "consciousness of who they are," opens back at crucial points to what Wordsworth calls "consciousness / Of whom they are":

>   hence religion, faith
> And endless occupation for the soul
> Whether discursive or intuitive.   [XIII.111–13]

This last line is itself an echo of Milton.[90] But acknowledgment of sources is no longer a stumbling block in the quest for origins at this point. Discursive or intuitive, the soul is envoiced, and in communion with voices of the past, present, and future. Far from defeated by the priority of the ocean's, God's, or Milton's voices, the poet discovers a dream of communication—of "communion with the invisible world." Between what he has half created as a beginning and what he half perceives as already given to him, the poet discovers the revisionary nature of his own voice.

From the Seats of Power Divine

> It is the measure of strength to what extent we can admit to
> ourselves, without perishing, the merely *apparent* character, the
> necessity of lies. To this extent, nihilism, as the denial of a truthful
> world of being, might be *a divine way of thinking.*
>
> Nietzsche, *The Will to Power*

Coleridge referred to Wordsworth's *Prelude* as "an unpublished Poem on the Growth and Revolutions of an Individual
Mind."[1] Comparing this to the subtitle posthumously affixed to
the 1850 text, "Growth of a Poet's Mind," we may wonder
whether to consider the mind revealed in the poem anomalous or
poetic in the larger sense of self-conscious and fully human. If
the poet is essentially a man speaking to men—only a little more
articulate than most—then poetic power may be a metaphor for
psychic health and no more a technical problem for writers of
verse than is sexual power a technical matter of the loins.[2] If we
believe that thought has no priority over the way it is articulated—that articulation is all—then the relationship of the poet
to the origins of poetic power could challenge the resolution of the
Oedipus complex as the central symbolism for psychic health—
or even challenge the grounds for considering psychic health more
than an alternate or subsidiary metaphor. The origins of an
individual mind would be essentially romantic in the sense of
being fictive, distanced, related to the written "types and symbols
of eternity," rather than in the sense of being centrally concerned
with the types and symbols of sex and family romance.

How anomalous, how archetypal is the development of the
poet's mind: the concern achieves a special prominence in *Prelude* IV, where it worries the youth who is the subject of the story

as well as the poet-narrator. Composing out loud while saunter-
ing along a public way, the young Wordsworth was grateful to
his dog for warning him of the approach of strangers so that he
could compose himself—in the other sense—and prevent rumors
"such as wait / On men suspected to be craz'd in brain"
(IV.119–20). Earlier in the same book we hear of the London
schoolboy being exhibited to all the neighbors and "willing, nay—
nay—wishing to be led" (l. 57). The poet-as-poet, like the youth-
as-youth, partly desires to make a spectacle of himself, but more
than the youth wishes some assurance that he is not making too
great a spectacle of himself. Compare the role of the dog in
Book IV with that of the shepherd's cur in the concluding episode
on Snowdon: there the question is the dog's relation to the revelation that comes to the poet; here it is a matter of the poet's being
revealed to others, and wishing to appear himself in the proper
light.[3] Book IV ends with an incident suspended between these
two senses of *revelation*: the youth making his appearance known
to a stranger on the road, and the revelation to the youth of that
stranger—an apparition of potentially menacing power. I turn
to that incident because Wordsworth's revision of it seems paradigmatic for the revisionary nature of his concept of poetic power.

Wordsworth composed a version of the episode of the discharged soldier in 1798.[4] Deciding to incorporate the episode
into Book IV, he recognized the relationship of the episode to the
question raised in that book about how social, how self-concerned
a figure the poet is to cut. Earlier in Book IV Wordsworth
distinguishes a new social sense from a more youthful, egotistical sublime:

> Nor less do I remember to have felt
> Distinctly manifested at this time
> A dawning, even as of another sense,
> A human-heartedness about my love
> For objects hitherto the gladsome air
> Of my own private being, and no more;

> Which I had loved, even as a blessed Spirit
> Or Angel, if he were to dwell on earth,
> Might love, in individual happiness.   [IV.222–30]

He becomes less like Milton's Satan and more like Raphael, "the sociable Spirit" (*PL*, V.221), moving from an individual to a human-hearted happiness capable of being shared. This socialization is not altogether easy for the poet, and he first tries to find happiness shared by objects of nature (ll. 233–39) and then to distinguish what he means by human-heartedness from trivial socialization (ll. 315–27). In the passage that ensues he socializes the spirit in bonds that transcend human society—a contradiction in terms, in one sense, and perhaps interpretable as something like a sublimation of the social instinct. Freud used the term *sublimation* when sexuality was the earthiness from which one defended oneself by etherealizing one's desires; but if we regard the social manifestation of personal strength as the base, we can understand the evasive motivation as well as the sophisticated achievement of the great passage in which Wordsworth imagines himself specially empowered by a benevolent Nature:

> I made no vows, but vows
> Were then made for me; bond unknown to me
> Was given, that I should be, else sinning greatly,
> A dedicated Spirit.   [IV.341–44]

He thus approaches the episode of the discharged soldier with an obligation to be true to the bond. The encounter must transcend the kind of socialization the youth rejected in the night of festivity, and it must reject also the wholly "individual happiness" (l. 230) from which he was rescued by the socializing spirit of a power that made vows for him.

The apprehension of that transcendent power was itself an extraordinary display—as well as an account of the origins—of poetic power. If, in a vulgar sense, poetic power means mind over matter, then the youth returning from an all-night dance was empowered to imagine, for example, the sea "laughing at a distance" (l. 333). But that pathetic fallacy is rather subdued, and if anything the poet displays power through his exquisite control of the scene—holding it, with an expertise that seems effortless, at the tensional limit between alien landscape and human-centeredness:

> Magnificent
> The morning was, a memorable pomp,
> More glorious than I ever had beheld.
> The Sea was laughing at a distance; all
> The solid Mountains were as bright as clouds,
> Grain-tinctured, drench'd in empyrean light;
> And, in the meadows and the lower grounds,
> Was all the sweetness of a common dawn,
> Dews, vapours, and the melody of birds,
> And Labourers going forth into the fields.   [IV.330–39]

If a poet is thought to be a man who talks to nature rather than to men, then this scene would represent the pathetic displaced from the social hall to the morning landscape. But if a poet is a man talking to men—one to whom even nature seems to speak as men talk to men—then we can see in this morning landscape a radical humanization of something like the heavenly dawn in *Lycidas*, where the dead poet is entertained by all the saints above "in solemn troops, and sweet Societies." In place of that otherworldly and "unexpressive nupital Song" Wordsworth gives us the melody of birds and the vows nature makes for him. Not solipsistic, the poet is empowered to apprehend, beyond the gaiety and mirth of the meeting hall, an image of nature and man cooperating at the social intercourse of a newborn day: the sea's laughter transcends the dancers', and laborers going forth to the fields seem a higher society than the "promiscuous rout" of the night before.

With this background, the setting of the discharged-soldier episode seems to argue against the solitude of the night-walker and prepare for the socialization to come:

> A favorite pleasure hath it been with me,
> From time of earliest youth, to walk alone

> Along the public Way, when, for the night
> Deserted, in its silence it assumes
> A character of deeper quietness
> Than pathless solitudes. At such an hour
> Once, ere these summer months were pass'd away,
> I slowly mounted up a steep ascent
> Where the road's watry surface, to the ridge
> Of that sharp rising, glitter'd in the moon,
> And seem'd before my eyes another stream
> Creeping with silent lapse to join the brook
> That murmur'd in the valley.   [IV.363–75]

On the level of the mind-over-matter interpretation of poetic power, it is a pretty fancy to imagine the glittering road like a stream. But in the slowed verse line describing the road "Creeping with silent lapse to join the brook" we hear an intimation, in nature, of the human socialization to come: just as the road is asked (by the poet's fancy) to join the stream, so the figure on the road will be asked (by the socializing youth) to join the stream of human life. Objects distinguished in the silent scene appear "dispos'd to sympathy / With an exhausted mind," as though to prompt the youth to the truer socialization, the sympathy he will show with the exhausted mind of the soldier.

In the 1805 text the poet's powers of description are in alliance with the youth's powers of socialization; "poetic power" seems an extension of the power manifest by a man among men, like a physician's power to keep men free from pain, or an electrician's power to connect a remote cabin dweller to the town's source of physical energy. When with exhausted mind the youth proved indifferent to the celestial landscape (IV.381–84), there was a lapse in what Paul Sheats calls "authentic communion"— a lapse corrected by the appearance of the soldier.[5] The poet returns to the episode the way sympathetic nature returns the youth to his awareness of community. We can thus say of the poet, from the viewpoint of this first myth of poetic power, that he has a practical function like that of the physician or electrician or that which he imagines nature to possess. And just as he resocializes his characters by re-presenting reality to their isolate selves, so he represents and re-presents to the company of his readers the individual aged, forlorn, and (momentarily or habitually) "border" figures who had become detached from society.

It seems an act of charity—of poetic power manifest as magnanimity—that Wordsworth omits from the 1805 text the lines that most bluntly isolated the soldier in the earlier version:

> His face was turn'd
> Towards the road, yet not as if he sought
> For any living thing. He appeared
> Forlorn and desolate, a man cut off
> From all his kind, and more than half detached
> From his own nature.

C. F. Stone III notes that these lines add less to our knowledge of the old soldier as such than to our awareness of the youth's determination to remain in control through his power of surmise.[6] Superficially, the act of revision may be thought generous because in omitting the blunt description of the man "more than half detached / From his own nature," the poet helps reattach the soldier to his own nature. More precisely, the poet abets the resocialization of the *youth* by discounting his power to stand aside and sum up the character of another whom he has scarcely seen and not yet met. Omitting this description, Wordsworth hastens a little the movement from the pictorial phase in which the two figures are observer and observed to the dramatic phase and the conversation between the men.

The soldier's words are never presented by direct quotation in *The Prelude*; the poet-youth is the soldier's mediator and humanizer, quoting only himself—and that to show the uniqueness of his role:

> 'No one there,'
> Said I, 'is waking, we must measure back
> The way which we have come: behind yon wood
> A Labourer dwells; and, take it on my word
> He will not murmur should we break his rest. [IV.453–57]

Wordsworth omitted from the 1805 text one line from his quoted speech to the laborer: "The service if need be I will requite." Perhaps that represented too awkward or too vulgar an interference on the part of the youth. But even in the passage just quoted we can see him asking to be accepted as the mediator whose power of word is a power to repair the breach that isolates one man from other men. "Take it on my word" is spoken by the youth to the soldier; it is spoken also by the poet to his readers in a request that we accept his poetic power as the power to turn from words as *signs* of relationship to words as express actualizations of human kindness. This laborer is called upon to fulfill the vision of socialization the poet earlier described on that morning after the dance where dews, birds, and laborers going forth to the fields form one great harmony of things. The laborer's sociability is represented in the last line quoted by the thought that he will not murmur about being awakened. "Murmur" is an important word in this episode, representing in the stream the possibility of all things joining together (l. 375), and in the soldier's lament the failure of that possibility.[7]

The one speech Wordsworth did give the soldier in 1798 concluded with a related image of murmuring:

> He replied, "In truth
> My weakness made me loth to move, and here
> I felt myself at ease & much relieved,
> But that the village mastiff fretted me,
> And every second moment rang a peal
> Felt at my very heart. There was no noise,
> Nor any foot abroad—I do not know
> What ail'd him, but it seemd as if the dog
> Were howling to the murmur of the stream."

Perhaps the poet found he had given the soldier too much life in allowing him to speak, to speak this long, or to entertain a semi-imaginative speculation like that of his last line. In any case Wordsworth banished the barking dog, the murmur of the stream, and the whole audible murmur of the soldier, leaving

himself the sole murmurer of the episode and singly empowered
to humanize the silent figure—half human, half symbol—that
he encounters.

The 1805 version of the discharged-soldier episode represents
what we may call the myth of poetic power in its naive or un-
revised form. It holds that poetic power is at best a synecdoche,
and that autobiographical verse narrative represents, at a literary
remove, a manifestation of power in interpersonal relations. Verbal power "stands for" power to relate efficaciously to other men;
a poetic description of communication is a sign of human
community.

Something develops, however, between the 1805 and 1850
texts that we can allow to represent a revision in the concept of
poetic power and the whole notion of representation. The youth
plays a less obtrusive role in the revised text, and the poet seems
more eager to represent to us the power of an apparition like the
old soldier.[8] The revised episode is introduced this way:

> When from our better selves we have too long
> Been parted by the hurrying world, and droop,
> Sick of its business, of its pleasures tired,
> How gracious, how benign, is Solitude;
> How potent a mere image of her sway;
> Most potent when impressed upon the mind
> With an appropriate human centre—hermit,
> Deep in the bosom of the wilderness;
> Votary (in vast cathedral, where no foot
> Is treading, where no other face is seen)
> Kneeling at prayers; or watchman on the top
> Of lighthouse, beaten by Atlantic waves;
> Or as the soul of that great Power is met
> Sometimes embodied on a public road,
> When, for the night deserted, it assumes
> A character of quiet more profound
> Than pathless wastes.   [1850, IV.354–70]

One could compare this passage with Shelley's "Hymn to
Intellectual Beauty," where the idea of Beauty as an "unseen

Power" plays a role not unlike Wordsworth's Solitude. Shelley's poem ends with a dedication of the poet "To fear himself, and love all human kind." Wordsworth's verse paragraph heads an episode that leads to a similar discovery, though the paragraph itself seems to have originated, at some point in Wordsworth's review of the episode as he first wrote it, from sentiments like those with which Shelley's poem ends. The story seems to have grown from an early representation of the youth's efficacious love for humankind, to an awareness of the awesome powers of the self, to an abstraction of the power of the poet in the form of Solitude. Shelley distinguishes the Power itself from the shadow of the Power; Wordsworth first specifies in the abstract, "How gracious, how benign, is Solitude," and then introduces the shadow of the Power: "How potent a mere image of her sway." The next lines, repeating the word "potent," distinguish a further level in the representation of power: an image of solitude is "Most potent when impressed upon the mind / With an appropriate human centre"—a welcome, but possibly not a required, condition. As the paragraph concludes, Wordsworth seems to capitalize on that uncertainty by introducing as his last example of an image of Solitude an abstraction without human center: "Or as the soul of that great Power is met / Sometimes embodied on a public road." Reading back from the episode that follows (reading forward from the episode whose composition antedates this paragraph) we know that an image of Solitude will be "embodied" in the discharged soldier; but here the poet refers to the soldierless road which itself "assumes / A character of quiet."

The suspension in the significance of the word "embodied" can stand for a suspension in the significance of the soldier figure till the text was revised. Actually, the power of that ghostly shape was there from 1798, only slightly shadowed by the narrator's interest in depicting himself as humanizer. Like the process of revision, the episode itself represents the soldier as there preveniently, and come upon by the youth walking up the road. The youth is the latecomer in the scene, a little like Keats in *The Fall*

of Hyperion, himself made to bear the weight of eternal quietud\
while beholding the arrested figure of his dream vision. In the\
Prelude versions the youth still acts as humanizer, bound by the\
social obligation of bringing the weary soldier to the comforts of\
a home; but the soldier himself is more clearly a figure of the\
unheimlich, an "uncouth shape, / Shown by a sudden turning of\
the road." [9] It is as if that abstract *turning* were the agent, em-\
powered to reveal, in this conversion from self to other, the\
mysterious otherness of an individual as isolate self—not to be\
overpowered by conversation or acts of benevolence.

In revising the 1805 version, Wordsworth restores power to its\
origin. Perhaps one can say of the process of composition that the\
poet abstracted "Solitude" from an originally human encounter.\
But that literal or literary source for this power has nothing to do\
with the awesome appearance of this power in the 1850 version as\
the romantic origin of what follows. If, in revision, Wordsworth\
had simply emphasized the priority of the solitary soldier over the\
youth we could say that the concern with origins was being shifted\
from a psychological perspective (the youth's state of mind is the\
preeminent, the prevenient, fact, and the meeting functions like a\
projection) to a historical perspective (the soldier—the historicity\
of his being, his being there—is the ineluctable fact, and the\
youth's solitariness is a secondary revision designed to make mean-\
ing out of an actual occurrence). These are two perspectives on\
natural origins. What turns Wordsworth into a poet of romantic\
origins is his extraordinary success in representing an abstract\
power that has priority over both soldier and youth, and that\
makes of the soldier not just a "ghastly figure" (1805, l. 468) in\
the sense of "gruesome," but a "ghostly figure" (1850, l. 434)\
from another, prevenient realm of being. The new perspective\
can be called that of romantic myth because, as in the Christian\
story of the Fall, a natural event (an eating or a meeting) brings\
knowledge of remoter origins (the story of Satan, or "the God of\
Heaven" [l. 494]). Perhaps a better analogue would be the story\
of the Fall given by Blake's Ahania, according to which "above"

man "rose a shadow from his wearied intellect" (*Four Zoas*, p. 40). What seems at first a psychological perspective opens out to reveal "that shadowy spirit of the fallen one, / Luvah, descended from the cloud."

Wordsworth's discharged soldier becomes such a shadowy spirit, re-presented to us, as he seemed re-presented to the youth, from a world elsewhere. Originally,

> in all he said
> There was a strange half-absence, and a tone
> Of weakness and indifference, as of one
> Remembering the importance of his theme
> But feeling it no longer.   [IV.474–78]

Deleting the emphasis on the soldier's weakness, Wordsworth made of his "half-absence" not a distance from military strength and an actual past but a romantic distance from a sense of self and a sense of Presence like that Satan knew before his fall:

> in all he said
> There was a strange half-absence, as of one
> Knowing too well the importance of his theme,
> But feeling it no longer.   [1850, IV.442–45]

The earlier concept of poetic power is mimetic; it assumes that the poet, like the soldier, remembers or re-members what once was from fragments shored against the ruins of weakness and indifference. The revised concept finds that in the process of representation, poetic power glimpses an origin and home antedating the incidents and images that represent power. Like paper currency, whose value no longer corresponds to what is or was buried in Fort Knox, poetry discovers that its images transcend their referents, or rather that its real referentiality is to antecedents always mythic in the sense that their reality is only imaged or attested to in any specific embodiment at any spot of time. Before the solitary youth, before the solitary soldier, was, from eternity, Solitude herself. And the poet, in the image of God, rebegets this day—and each common day—something like her Son: "How potent a mere image of her sway!"

Wordsworth's revision of the discharged-soldier episode may be taken as emblematic of the revisionary ratio in the myth of poetic power ordinarily implicit in a single narrative. The boy of Winander episode commences with a shaky image of the power of communion (the boy hoots and the owls hoot back) and revises itself into an awareness of the poet as representer, gaining from the gap between himself as observer and the grave he stands over "Knowledge not purchas'd with the loss of power" (V.449). The visitor to Sarum's plain hopes that by mining the "depth of untaught things" he might become "A power like one of Nature's" (XII.312). He discovers, from his own dreamy reverie, a Druid-like power of representation that transcends the terror-filled images of Druidic community. And on Snowdon, the "power which these / Acknowledge when thus moved" by the shows of nature is the resemblance of a higher power—the power *of* resemblance, ultimately, of remaking oneself in the image of God. "Among the more awful scenes of the Alps," Wordsworth wrote Dorothy, "I had not a thought of man, or a single created being; my whole soul was turned to him who produced the terrible majesty before me." [10] Those who are impressed by nature's representations *as* representations are "By sensible impressions not enthrall'd"; they transcend the limits of a purely mimetic theory and discover themselves in relation to the ultimate Originator:

> Such minds are truly from the Deity,
> For they are Powers; and hence the highest bliss
> That can be known is theirs, the consciousness
> Of whom they are habitually infused
> Through every image.   [XIII.106–10]

At such a height of consciousness, in such relation to the source, one can overleap the distinction between the abstraction and the images or shadows of the abstraction and say, "they are Powers!"

Harold Bloom accounts for the revisionary nature of Wordsworth's concept of poetic power by supposing a process of repression that delays and insists on re-presentation of what could not be fully manifest in its own right and have the poet continue

...ding. What is repressed is "a power so antithetical that it could tear the poet loose from nature and take him into a world of his own, restituting him for the defense of self-isolation by isolating him yet more sublimely."[11] Wordsworth himself singles out "intellectual love" as the sphere where self-isolation is most a danger. I take it that he means by the term not just love of things intellectual but the kind of socializing spirit (love in every inter-personal sense but literal sexuality) which I have identified with what, in a preliminary sense of poetic power, poetry *represents*. "Here," as he writes before turning outward, turning to Coleridge and Dorothy in his peroration, "Here must thou be, O Man! / Power to thyself" (1850, XIV.209–10). Yet if this inner strength, this Imagination necessary to approach outward fellowship, is rooted "far / From any reach of outward fellowship," its origin is not far from the reach of a fellowship with a prevenient self. "So feeling comes in aid / Of feeling, and diversity of strength / Attends us, if but once we have been strong" (XI.326–28). What makes one's strength one's own is the effort to derive present power of self-possession from the revisited scenes of the past. The search for the origins of power may be a romantic search, in the sense that its goal is always in some sense beyond one's grasp, but it is not beyond the searcher's reach:

> The days gone by
> Return upon me almost from the dawn
> Of life: the hiding-places of man's power
> Open; I would approach them, but they close.
>
> [1850, XII.277–80]

I have quoted these famous lines from the 1850 text. In the 1805 version Wordsworth specifies "the hiding-places of my power" (is this the story of the growth of an individual mind? a poetic mind? *this* poetic mind?) and he distinguishes more clearly the temporal dislocation of the search for power from the always distanced sources of it: "I approach, and then they close." Imagination, which is "but another name for absolute power" (1850, XIV.190), requires the temporalization or remythologization of power: first something understood as actualizable in social relations, in "actuality," it then comes to be understood as the soul's essential distance from the reality that poetry re-presents.

Wordsworth called the failure of imagination "despondency," and explored it at greatest length in *The Excursion,* where the Solitary is the figure who denies poetic power in its first sense (as a solitary he dismisses the efficacy of social intercourse) and in its revisionary sense (he understands not the power of representation). The whole enterprise of re-presenting to the self the efficacious power of certain spots of time he dismisses in a parenthesis. He finds,

> Reviewing my past way, much to condemn,
> Little to praise, and nothing to regret,
> (Save some remembrances of dream-like joys
> That scarcely seem to have belonged to me).   [III.271–74]

The Solitary represses the power of such moments, the power that could be his if he pursued it to its romantic origins in such spots of time. A crucial mechanism of this repression is the deflection of concern about origins from personal history to anthropology:

> I, without reluctance, could decline
> All act of inquisition whence we rise,
> And what, when breath hath ceased, we may become.
> Here are we, in a bright and breathing world.
> Our origin, what matters it?   [III.234–38]

The question is followed by speculations about origins that further belittle such concerns. If some can cope with the big *Whence?* by a myth that holds that "men / Leapt out together from a rocky cave," or one that sees men, like grasshoppers, to have sprung "from the soil / Whereon their endless generations dwelt," then what advance, except perhaps in decorum, is there in deducing "the stream of human life / From seats of power divine"?

We can better identify the Solitary's swerve away from concern with romantic origins by juxtaposing two passages of related imagery. For a myth more in keeping with "serious minds," he proposes that,

> as the Hindoos draw
> Their holy Ganges from a skiey fount,
> Even so deduce the stream of human life
> From seats of power divine; and hope, or trust,
> That our existence winds her stately course
> Beneath the sun, like Ganges, to make part
> Of a living ocean.   [III.254–60]

In the Intimations Ode the poet concludes his excursion back to the fount of childhood with grand affirmation:

> Hence in a season of calm weather
> Though inland far we be,
> Our Souls have sight of that immortal sea
> Which brought us hither,
> Can in a moment travel thither,
> And see the Children sport upon the shore,
> And hear the mighty waters rolling evermore.

The first of these passages belittles the act of "deducing" life from an ultimate source of divine power. The second passage attains to something like prophetic strain by tracing the soul (and the *trace,* the *différance,* is crucial) not all the way back to an abstracted Power, but to the image of that power, the "immortal sea" which itself is a representation or vehicle for the first, most metaphoric journey. Denying the distinction between a Power and "a mere image of her sway," the Solitary is cut off from the potency of such images. "Living ocean" in the first passage is an extraordinary extension of a figure of speech which, if the Solitary only paused there, could suffice to cure his despondency. The children sporting on the shore in the second passage have made of a metaphor, more than a vehicle, a dwelling place where meaning appears to have found a proper home. That becomes the spot whence poet and reader can derive the power of renovation. The Solitary easily assimilates "skiey fount" as a figure for a pre-existence and an ultimate power outside metaphor; the concept of preexistence in the Ode becomes transmuted into a feeling we have about the *figure* of the sea—that it could only have been mysteriously "come upon" and not invented. However figurative the seat of power divine may be, or may have been, Wordsworth is in touch with it, and derives hence his poetic power.

After that great stanza of the Intimations Ode it may seem a letdown to approach the consolation Wordsworth voices in language of purest simplicity: "We will grieve not, rather find / Strength in what remains behind." But in accepting the task of deducing the stream of human life from seats of power divine, the poet has come to recognize that strength is always behind him, always a re-presentation of what was never present, what could never be present except in metaphor. Perhaps the Intimations Ode arrives at a more satisfactory resolution than *The Excursion* because even at its low point the Ode is all involved in the problem of representation. Man's whole vocation *is* endless imitation—though of more romantic paradigms than those specters of repetition that haunt stanza seven of the Ode. "From *nuo*, to make a sign," wrote Vico, "came *numen*, the divine will, by an idea more than sublime and worthy to express the divine majesty." [12] Divine majesty is expressed only in signs, in what Wordsworth calls express resemblances—always distanced, always re-presented, because only the shadow of a Power visits us from the seat of romantic origins. But grant the power of metaphor in a moment to travel thither, and one can forever return to hear the mighty waters rolling evermore.

There is an old Hebrew legend that two thousand years before God created heaven and earth he created a Voice that cries, *Return!* [13] Wordsworth's tales of psychic regeneration, like *The Excursion* and the Intimations Ode, are manifestations of extraordinary poetic power that would, by representing prevenient voices yet to be heard, offer a romantic origin for the process of regeneration. Coleridge's ancestral voices prophesying war—insofar as they prophesy a war between the mind and the sky—antedate the creative efforts of Kubla Khan the way the Voice that cries *Return!* antedates God's voice calling all creation into being. For

Byron, poetic power derived its source from fictive worlds else-where. Reaching beyond nostalgia or envy for Shelley's world of high romance, Byron mythologizes the distant place and preserves something that resembles a memory of it despite the enormous success of his satiric spirit in naturalizing man to this earth. Keats came to image himself as auditor of cries from the earth: the voice of the nightingale is the voice of a literal bird heard by the poet on a passing night, but it is also the voice "heard in ancient days." Listening to Saturn in *The Fall of Hyperion*, Keats had his ear to the ground—to the ground of our being in a world far, but not hopelessly far, from its romantic origins: "Methought I heard some old man of the earth / Bewailing earthly loss."[14] Darley found a romantic origin for the voice of regeneration in the yearning of Memnon for his mother, Aurora, and represented his own poetic power in a tale that involved his following a pre-scription from of old. For Blake the question "Whence had thou this song?" was always as seminal as it was terrible. He found it best to "Begin with Tharmas, parent power," taking *as parent of his theme* a power yet to be fully reborn in the integrated self but manifest nonetheless in every prophetic voice that cries "Lost!" and gets him started. As he proceeds Blake finds greater and greater difficulty in giving credence to any hypothesized point of origin, and perhaps Blake is the Romantic poet most haunted by the shadowy thought that the "presence of the word" was always a fiction—that there never was a moment of pure presence. The labor of Los is to forge—I borrow Derrida's formulation once again—

a text nowhere present, consisting of archives which are always already transcriptions. Originary prints. Everything begins with reproduction. Always already: repositories of a meaning which was never present, whose signified presence is always reconstituted by deferment, nachträglich, belatedly, supplementarily.[15]

I want to reserve a special place here for Shelley, because like Wordsworth (perhaps in part from Wordsworth, but that is out-side the domain of romantic origins) he privileged the word *power* and made of a revisionary myth of power a crucial issue in poetic mimesis. Shelley celebrated the revisionary power of representation in the extraordinary *Triumph of Life,* where life turns out to mean, or to be based on, the "track" or *trace* separating a shape from an intention to signify. But the term *power* has a special place in another poem so concerned with the idea of having the last word on matters of romantic origins that we might best accord it something near the honor of that place. In *Mont Blanc* Shelley mythologizes the place "Where Power in the likeness of the Arve comes down," and discovers in the relationship of the likeness of power to The Power an archetype of the relationship of all empowered poetic symbols to their abstract objects.

Of all Shelley's poems, none holds so much promise of revelation about romantic origins as does *Mont Blanc.* Its opening lines cast the whole phenomenal world as a rapid stream and make us wonder (with all the force of going against the current, as it were) what and "where" are its "secret springs." In the second paragraph the stream—or a power behind it—descends from its "secret throne," but the focus is rather on the ravine, addressed in the opening line and still *there,* still the object of direct address as the paragraph, with all its mysterious wanderings, draws to a close.

Moses had a vision of the glory of God not in its presence but as it passed by and became displaced into metaphor (Exod. 33:19). The prophet Ezekiel had a vision of the Power *birom kivod YHVH mimkomo*—"as the glory of the Lord was ascending from its place" (3:12). Like Moses, he thus perceived the power as it was being borne away, and such conveyance is the root meaning of metaphor. In a seminal misreading, Ezekiel is said to have heard a thunderous sound itself voicing (or in response to which *he* voiced the exclamation) *baruch kivod YHVH mimkomo*—"Praised be the Glory of the Lord from His Place!" The Hebrew requires the mistranscription of only one letter for this difference, and in the scribal misplacing of a pen stroke—on the very words that could have been translated "from the seat of power divine"—the origin of poetic voice takes place.[16] Whether the exclamation "Praised be the Glory of the Lord from His Place!" is imagined to be what Ezekiel heard the angels exclaim, or whether it is imagined to be what Ezekiel himself was moved to exclaim in beholding the displacement of the glory of God, tradition holds that this "original" exclamation is repeated by the angels whenever they give voice to their devotional stance. To the ritualistically repeated query "Where is the place of His Glory?" they respond with the reaffirmation borrowed from (or transmitted by) Ezekiel, "Praised be the Glory of the Lord from His Place [wherever that is]." No mere evasion, their speed in replacing the literalistic query with the metaphoric assertion marks their closeness to The Place (itself a trope for God) and the origin of devotional—and all poetic—discourse.

Shelley is not quite of the angels' party, but he inherits from Moses and Ezekiel the prophetic power of voice and the prophetic caution in metaphorizing or transposing away from its place something he is willing, in a poem, to call "the Power." Subtle skeptic that he is, he delays for a while in addressing the Power or the mountain said to be its place, and reserves the second person for the ravine—the figure for *our* place, for all we can know of the phenomenal world. The second paragraph of *Mont Blanc* concludes with the poet searching not the heavens but the displaced place, "the still cave of the witch Poesy," for "some phantom, some faint image," not of the Power or its place, but of the ravine. Overwhelmed by the rhetoric, as men are by religious dread, readers may mistake this "thou" for the Power, but its proper antecedent is the ravine; like the world for which it stands, the ravine is without further antecedent. And so it is only to the ravine that the poet can say, after he emerges from the mystification of metaphor, "Thou art there!" Yet if that "there" is here, the world as we know it, there remains the other "there," the source of the river Arve and the summit or consummate image of the original place. The landscape imagery seems a little ahead of the grammar (or rather, in touch with something psychologically a little further back) and seems to generate from itself, in despite of our good rational sense about grammatical antecedents, the quest for the source. We approach the third section of the poem fully prepared for a revelation of the mountain itself or the Power we have been led to believe resident there.

We are not disappointed: "Mont Blanc appears,—still, snowy, and serene." But the section does not quite begin that way, the way the concluding section of the poem does begin: "Mont Blanc yet gleams on high:—the power is there." Instead, with a delay that marks a crucial difference (a delay itself truer to the romantic origin of power than any specific attempt to image the place of that power), he considers first another aspect of the search for origins. He pauses to dismiss dream vision (which I have assumed to be *the* center or source for him) as a matter of fancy, or at least what others, in their "unseeing of the eye," speculate about: "Some say that gleams of a remoter world / Visit the soul in sleep." Perhaps a joke at Byron's expense (so much for his "remoter world" myth of romantic origins!), the dismissal moves Shelley beyond all poetic or theosophic speculators about a world elsewhere. In distinction to thoughts about a world elsewhere, and to Hamlet-like thoughts about the prospect of thoughts surviving in a world elsewhere, is this poet's plain sight of what looms up before him when he looks on high: not the Infinite in the sky but the real, wholly natural mountain "piercing the infinite sky." Overshadowing the question of whether this be some waking revelation or a special operation of the dreamwork is the sheer presence of the mountain.

But is there a Presence behind the mountain? Is this a thing-in-itself or a sign, even if a sign of the ultimate in-itself quality of all things? The world is no sooner beheld bare of fictions than questions arise, making the power *of* that mountain seem the romantic origin of romantic quest. So "ghastly, and scarred, and riven" is the scene that the poet is driven to ask whether he might not be confronting a place of chaotic origins, "where the old Earthquake-daemon taught her young / Ruin." Or, alternately, "did a sea / Of fire envelop once this silent snow?" While the questions pose as alternatives two theories about the earth's creation, the turn from one to the other is also a turn from mythic to more acceptable scientific inquiry. If this is the place where Earthquake-daemon taught her young, then the place is an aboriginal place, a scene of instruction and destruction like the crossroads where Oedipus slew Laius, only more sublime because older and more deeply engraved in the very surface of the earth. Nature seems to have taught her young from a text with only one word, "ruin," and this is the indelible message which the book of nature offers to readers of the scene.

The second speculation demystifies the first, for if a sea of fire *once* enveloped this silent snow it does so no longer. Origins and ends are different things, and speculation about origins is seen more properly, more scientifically, to concern how the present place, insofar as it is a synecdoche for the earth as a whole, came into being. But there is no end, no purpose or continued message to be read from the scene; by whatever prescription the world was called into being, the writing has faded and no signs survive.

Both mystified and demystified speculations about origins are silenced: "None can reply—all seems eternal now." Then, magically, out of this silence itself emerges a new voice—or rather, the silence itself is figured as a revelatory voice. Mark said that believers in the reborn god "will cast out demons; they will speak in a new tongue" (16:17). Dismissing the Earthquake-daemon and the whole daemonic lure of speculation about origins, Shelley finds that "the wilderness has a mysterious tongue" capable of casting more doubt on previous dogmas about origins than ever Jesus did on the daemonic aspects of the Jaweh of the Old Testament. Is this a tongue of flame as mysterious as those with which the apostles spoke? If this silence can be said to betoken a new faith, it is one *so* mild, *so* serene, that it seems the last vestige of mystification standing in the way of our ability to confront nature in all its barrenness. What the poet imagines is thus nothing like the thunderous voice on Sinai proclaiming God as the creator of the world and recreator of a people liberated from Egypt; neither does it resemble the "sound of a great earthquake" heard by Ezekiel when beholding the cherubim (3:12). It must not be compared to John the Baptist's voice crying in the wilderness and heralding a new dispensation to come. This is a negative voice, crying "NO!" to false revelations about origins and positing its own nonexistence, outside metaphor, as the most original truth available to sensible and sensitive souls. So the prophet Elijah, burdened by the nasty obligation of making God a visible show, has his faith reaffirmed by the "still small voice"—the voice of stillness itself, when all fictions of a thundering god have passed away (I Kings 19:12). And so Wordsworth, beholding the Convent of Chartreuse "In silence visible and perpetual calm" (1850 *Prelude,* VI.429), hears a voice of Nature. Like Elijah's and Wordsworth's, Shelley's speaking silence comes to discredit all more vocal, more specific revelations, and to valorize the idea of prophetic voice as that which denounces them. The silence that speaks to Shelley silences all fictions of romantic origin (from Genesis to Wordsworth) and all codes of woe (from Leviticus to the contemporaneous laws about marital or military alliance against which Shelley inveighed):

> Thou hast a voice, great Mountain, to repeal
> Large codes of fraud and woe; not understood
> By all, but which the wise, and great, and good
> Interpret, or make felt, or deeply feel.

If this be atheism, it is no late arrival in the history of ideas but what Stevens calls the first idea, the idea of the phenomenal world unspoiled, unshadowed by speculation about anterior powers. One may call it the romantic original of all poetic thoughts—or better, the romantic re-originator, perpetually crying like a prophetic voice with two thousand years' priority over the voice calling Creation into being, *Return!* Return to the earth without further fictions of origins!

For Stevens, as for Shelley, the voice that cries "NO!" to previous dispensations must also be recognized as a fiction, but one truer to the "chaos of the sun," the original or unfictionalized world as we know it. So the concluding section of "Sunday Morning" opens:

> She hears, upon that water without sound,
> A voice that cries, "The tomb in Palestine
> Is not the porch of spirits lingering.
> It is the grave of Jesus, where he lay." [17]

This voice never was on sea or land, but it speaks a truth of the present and a truth that had priority over the voices that made Palestine into Zion—the place from which Voice goes forth. Earlier in the same poem Stevens describes this contemplative Sunday as a day "like wide water, without sound, / Stilled for the passing of her dreaming feet." There may have been no resurrected Christ or miraculous walker on the waves; but "dreaming feet" remains a surprising new birth—an extraordinary figure for thoughts that wander back to the Christian myth. Metaphor takes over a "power of the wave or deepened speech." Though the god who appears only in silent shadows and in dreams is dismissed, dreams restore the memory of the grave of Jesus—the vision of unrisen man. Death, not the Virgin Mary, is the mother of this Jesus, and dreaming a little about him returns one to the romance and original beauty of this "our perishing earth."

To reimagine the perishing earth at its origin! The opening of Genesis has been alternatively translated, "In the beginning God created the heaven and the earth. And the earth was without form, and void" or "When God set about creating heaven and earth, the earth was void and without form." We can let the two translations stand for the alternate priorities of formless earth and God. As readers of scripture and literature, but perhaps more especially as readers of the book of nature, we tend to lose the romance of either origin—the excitement of imagining a creator and source at a temporal remove from the phenomenal world, and the excitement of demystifying such myths and discovering, with Wallace Stevens, that what has priority over "And God saw it was good" is the critical realization "Bare earth is best!" Poets restore the romance of both theories of origin. Secular heralds of a second coming, they challenge our complacency about what is first in importance or first in time. When the prophetic cry *Return!* is said to have two thousand years' priority over the voice crying *Let there be light!* we are asked to recognize anew that far more "original" than the story of Adam is the earthiness, the waywardness, of men that requires eternal error, eternal myths of return. But that is to opt for the priority of earth over transcendence; on the other side, the legend can be said to collapse all the work of the Creator into creation and to grant prophetic voice a new priority over the phenomenal world.

Christian myth is similarly romantic in countering original sin with a pre-Genesis account of Satan and Son. But *every* significant act of mythopoesis refreshes the earth, restoring both the limiting awareness that man is dust and the re-presented transcendent origin of man as the image of a prevenient Creator. Thus the lady in "Sunday Morning" hears a new voice that announces a demystifying prophecy for our time, but it takes the exciting form of a fiction of voice, a prophetic cry, nonetheless. Surely the formalists, and more recently the structuralists, were right to ignore cultural traditions, to close their eyes to the specific entanglements of literary history and biography, and to dream of poetry arising by itself out of poetic language—they were right, like the lady in "Sunday Morning," so to *dream*.

"The poem refreshes life so that we share, / For a moment, the first idea." [18] So Stevens, in *Notes toward a Supreme Fiction,* revives a belief in the "immaculate beginning" of poetry—headed toward, but retaining a priority over, a Supreme Fiction. The Christian and the Structuralist hold antipathetic dreams of the first idea, but they share the high romance of such quests, and discover at their best that the path back to origins is double all the way, with one voice crying "Let there be . . . !" echoed antiphonally by a deconstructive murmur, "Let the illusion in 'Let there be . . . !' cease to be!" Keats's Saturn rises to his full magnificence declaiming, "and there shall be / Beautiful things made new,"—despite the fact that Saturn is an old fiction, since replaced by the god of this sun-drenched, demystified world. In his rage for order Saturn gives us, like Wallace Stevens, "of ourselves and of our origins, / In ghostlier demarcations, keener sounds."

Stevens had a better term than *sentimentalism* or *naiveté* to describe speech like Saturn's and mythopoeic labors like Keats's in *Hyperion*. He called it *candor,* and found, in the high romance of all quests for origins,

> An elixir, an excitation, a pure power.
> The poem, through candor, brings back a power again
> That gives a candid kind to everything.[19]

Notes

By searching out origins, one becomes a crab. The historian looks backward; eventually he also *believes* backward.

Nietzsche, *Twilight of the Gods*

Chapter 1. Coleridge and the Ancestral Voices

1. An earlier draft of this chapter was published under the same title in *The Georgia Review* 29(Summer 1975), 469–98, and is used with permission.

2. *The Statesman's Manual,* in *The Complete Works of Samuel Taylor Coleridge,* ed. W. G. T. Shedd (New York: Harper & Brothers, 1884), I, 436.

3. *Aids to Reflection and The Confessions of an Inquiring Spirit* (London: George Bell, 1901), p. 178.

4. *Aids,* p. 44.

5. Notebook 20, fol. 4 verso. Cited by Joseph Anthony Wittreich, Jr., *The Romantics on Milton* (Cleveland: Case Western Reserve University Press, 1970), p. 280.

6. *Collected Letters of Samuel Taylor Coleridge,* ed. Earl Leslie Griggs (Oxford: Clarendon Press, 1956–71), II, 866.

7. From Coleridge's annotations to *Warton's Poems upon Several Occasions,* cited by Wittreich, p. 260.

8. *The Philosophical Lectures of Samuel Taylor Coleridge,* ed. Kathleen Coburn (London: The Pilot Press, 1949), p. 297. Compare pp. 121–22.

9. *The Literary Remains of Samuel Taylor Coleridge,* ed. Henry Nelson Coleridge (London: W. Pickering, 1836), I, 305.

10. *Letters,* III, 355.

11. John Beer, *Coleridge the Visionary* (London: Chatto & Windus, 1959), p. 256. John Livingston Lowes (*The Road to Xanadu* [Boston:

Houghton Mifflin, 1927]) and Norman Fruman (*Coleridge, the Damaged Archangel* [New York: George Braziller, 1971]) are less helpful on this point, but supply invaluable information where indebtedness is a matter of demonstrable fact.

12. *Treatise on Logic*, II, 403–04, cited by Owen Barfield, *What Coleridge Thought* (Middletown, Conn.: Wesleyan University Press, 1971), p. 20.

13. *Aids*, p. 176.

14. Cf. Beer, pp. 207–10.

15. *Literary Remains*, II, 45.

16. Notebook (Sept. 18, 1820), cited by Wittreich, p. 250.

17. *Specimens of the Table Talk of the Late Samuel Taylor Coleridge,* ed. Henry Nelson Coleridge (London: J. Murray, 1835), I, 127.

18. *Biographia Literaria*, ed. J. Shawcross (Oxford: Clarendon Press, 1907), I, 21.

19. *Aids*, p. 172.

20. Sigmund Freud, *The Interpretation of Dreams*, in *The Standard Edition of the Complete Psychological Works of Sigmund Freud*, ed. James Strachey (London: Hogarth, 1953–74), V, 556.

21. Freud, St. Ed. V, 554.

22. *Letters*, IV, 728.

23. *Aids*, p. 171.

24. Michel Foucault, *The Order of Things: An Archaeology of the Human Sciences* (New York: Pantheon Books, 1971), p. xxi.

25. *Aids*, p. 175.

26. *Literary Remains*, I, 175.

27. Appendix B to *The Statesman's Manual*, in *Works*, I, 458.

28. Lecture VII (to the London Philosophical Society). Cited by Wittreich, pp. 200–01.

29. *Aids*, p. 176.

30. *Aids*, p. 40.

31. Reeve Parker, *Coleridge's Meditative Art* (Ithaca: Cornell University Press, 1975), p. 241.

32. Parker, p. 242.

33. Notebooks, cited by Wittreich, p. 250.

34. *Table Talk*, II, 240–41.

35. *Letters*, I, 320–21.

36. Foucault, p. 332.

Chapter 2. Keats and a New Birth

1. An earlier version of the first section of this chapter, "Keats, Milton, and What One May 'Very Naturally Suppose,'" appeared in *Milton and the Romantics* 1 (1975), 4–7, and is used with permission.

2. See Bacon's essay, "Cupid; or the Atom," in *The Wisdom of the Ancients*. I am indebted to Susan H. Brisman for this reference. On the duality of love as both oldest and youngest of the gods see Marsilio Ficino's *Commentary on Plato's Symposium*, trans. Sears R. Jayne (University of Missouri Studies 19, 1944), esp. ch. X, p. 178. In *Beyond the Pleasure Principle* Freud makes a curious effort to combine the significances of the two cupids (St. Ed. XVIII, 50).

3. *A Map of Misreading* (New York: Oxford University Press, 1975), p. 153.

4. On voyeurism free from anxiety see Christopher Ricks, *Keats and Embarrassment* (Oxford: Clarendon Press, 1974), p. 89.

5. Keats to the George Keatses, 14 February–3 May 1819, in *The Letters of John Keats*, ed. Hyder Edward Rollins (Cambridge: Harvard University Press, 1958), II, 106.

6. Keats to James Rice, 24 March 1818, in *Letters*, I, 254–55. I am indebted to Harold McGee for this invaluable reference and for other suggestions about Apollonius and Milton.

7. Cf. Ricks p. 61 on these lines, and pp. 21–23 on the relationship of the embarrassingly "natural" to Milton.

8. For both text and variants I cite *The Poetical Works of John Keats*, ed. H. W. Garrod (Oxford: Oxford University Press, 1958).

9. Keats to John Taylor, 30 January 1818, in *Letters*, I, 218–19.

10. Earl R. Wasserman, *The Finer Tone: Keats' Major Poems* (Baltimore: Johns Hopkins University Press, 1953); Stuart M. Sperry, *Keats the Poet* (Princeton: Princeton University Press, 1973).

11. B. R. Haydon to Edward Moxon (?), 29 November 1845, in *The Keats Circle: Letters and Papers, 1816–1817*, ed. Hyder Edward Rollins (Cambridge: Harvard University Press, 1948), II, 143–44.

12. Knight's essay is in *The Starlit Dome: Studies in the Poetry of Vision* (New York: Barnes & Noble, 1960); Morris Dickstein, *Keats and His Poetry: A Study in Development* (Chicago: University of Chicago Press, 1971), p. 74.

13. In reviewing the 1817 volume, Hunt praised Keats's fancy for being "founded, as all beautiful fancies are, on a strong sense of what really exists or occurs." And he concluded by describing the book with lines from

"L'Allegro": "It is a little luxuriant heap of 'Such sights as youthful poets dream / On summer eves by haunted stream,'" *The Examiner,* July 6 and 13, 1817, pp. 429, 444; reproduced in *The Romantics Reviewed: Contemporary Reviews of British Romantic Writers,* ed. Donald H. Reiman (New York: Garland, 1972), pt. C, I, 429, 431.

14. *Letters,* II, 56. See Walter Jackson Bate, *John Keats* (Cambridge: Harvard University Press, 1963), pp. 501–02.

15. The exclamation point ("Already with thee!") corresponds to modern italics: "Already with *thee* tender is the night." (See Wasserman, *The Finer Tone,* pp. 198–99.) The misunderstanding that has Keats momentarily with the bird ("[I am] already with thee, [and how] tender is the night!") delays what I call the second revision till the line "But here [I mistook my place!] there is no light." The revision is, however, proleptic rather than retrospective, for Keats separates himself from the fancy before articulating it. David V. Erdman clarified this point for me.

16. Eamon Grennan, "Keats's *Contemptus Mundi:* A Shakespearean Influence on the 'Ode to a Nightingale,'" *MLQ* 36 (1975), 276.

17. Martin Heidegger, "The Origin of the Work of Art," in *Poetry, Language, Thought,* trans. Albert Hofstadter (New York: Harper & Row, 1971), p. 42. The following two Heidegger quotations are from pp. 46 and 77–78.

18. Richard Onorato cites Claudio's speech in *Measure for Measure* as a source Wordsworth is "preconsciously recalling" when associating death and darkness "with the '*ghostly* language of the ancient earth' and with the 'viewless winds' of poetry." *The Character of the Poet: Wordsworth in "The Prelude"* (Princeton: Princeton University Press, 1971), p. 114.

19. For a discussion of assumptions about such "consistencies" or developments see the Afterword to Wasserman's *Finer Tone.*

20. *John Keats: His Life and Writings* (New York: Macmillan, 1966), p. 147.

21. *Theocritus,* ed. and trans. A. S. F. Gow (Cambridge: Cambridge University Press, 1952).

22. "Spectral Symbolism and Authorial Self in Keats's 'Hyperion,'" *The Fate of Reading* (Chicago: University of Chicago Press, 1975), 70–73.

23. Compare the Memnon story as revised by George Darley (Chapter 5 of this volume).

24. Foucault, p. 313.

25. *The Vision; or Hell, Purgatory, and Paradise,* trans. Henry Francis Cary (1814; rpt. New York: Appleton, 1865).

26. Paul de Man, "Impersonality in the Criticism of Maurice Blanchot,"

in *Blindness and Insight: Essays in the Rhetoric of Contemporary Criticism* (New York: Oxford University Press, 1971), p. 66.

27. Introduction to *John Keats: Selected Poetry* (New York: New American Library, 1966), p. xii.

28. "Spectral Symbolism," p. 69.

29. For a "suspicious or demystifying" critique of this prospective stance see Harold Bloom, "Keats: Romance Revised," in *Poetry and Repression* (New Haven: Yale University Press, 1976), esp. pp. 112–15, 139–42.

Chapter 3. Byron: Troubled Stream from a Pure Source

1. A version of this chapter appeared as "Byron: Troubled Stream from a Pure Source," *ELH* 42, no. 4 (Winter 1975), 623–50. Copyright © 1975 by The Johns Hopkins University Press; Arnold Stein, Senior Editor.

2. *The Works of Lord Byron: Poetry*, ed. E. H. Coleridge; *Letters and Journals*, ed. Rowland E. Prothero (London: John Murray, 1899–1901), *Letters*, V, 459. This edition will be cited for Byron's prose and manuscript variants in *Lara* and *Manfred*. Poetry quotations are from *The Complete Poetical Works of Byron*, ed. Paul E. More (Cambridge, Mass.: Riverside, 1933). Manuscript information about Don Juan is available in *Byron's Don Juan, a Variorum Edition*, ed. Truman Guy Steffan and Willis W. Pratt (Austin: University of Texas Press, 1957).

3. Michael Cooke, *The Blind Man Traces the Circle: On the Patterns and Philosophy of Byron's Poetry* (Princeton: Princeton University Press, 1969), p. 77.

4. "Le langage est bien le médium de ce jeu de la présence et de l'absence. N'y a-t-il pas dans le langage, le langage n'est-il pas d'abord cela même en quoi pourraient sembler s'unir la *vie* et l'*idéalité*?" (Jacques Derrida, *La Voix et le phénomène* [Paris: Presses Universitaires de France, 1967], p. 9; trans. David B. Allison in *Speech and Phenomena and Other Essays on Husserl's Theory of Signs* [Evanston: Northwestern University Press, 1973], p. 10).

5. Wallace Stevens, *The Auroras of Autumn*, in *The Palm at the End of the Mind* (New York: Alfred A. Knopf, 1971). Copyright 1967, 1969, 1971 by Holly Stevens.

6. *Letters*, V, 470.

7. Gilles Deleuze, *Proust and Signs*, trans. Richard Howard (New York: George Braziller, 1972), p. 72.

8. Wallace Stevens, *The Comedian as the Letter C*, in *The Palm at the End of the Mind* (New York: Alfred A. Knopf, 1971). Copyright 1967, 1969, 1971 by Holly Stevens.

9. *Journal of Conversations with Lord Byron by the Countess of Blessington* (Boston: Veazie, 1859), p. 94.

10. Blessington, *Journal,* pp. 95–96.

11. *Letters,* III, 201.

12. Robert Gleckner, *Byron and the Ruins of Paradise* (Baltimore: Johns Hopkins University Press, 1967), pp. 160–61.

13. Gleckner, p. 161.

14. See *Poetry,* ed. Coleridge, pp. 367–69.

15. Foucault, pp. 333–34.

16. George A. Ellis in *Quarterly Review* 11 (July 1814), 453.

17. Blessington, *Journal,* p. 311.

Chapter 4. Shelley: From the Caverns of Dreamy Youth

1. W. B. Yeats, *Essays and Introductions* (New York: Macmillan, 1951), p. 65.

2. Bryan Cooper, "Shelley's *Alastor:* The Quest for a Vision," *Keats-Shelley Journal* 19 (1970), 71.

3. Norman Thurston, "Author, Narrator, and Hero in Shelley's *Alastor,*" *Studies in Romanticism* 14 (1975), 121.

4. Thurston, pp. 121–22.

5. Earl Wasserman, *Shelley: A Critical Reading* (Baltimore: Johns Hopkins University Press, 1971), p. 40. See also pp. 12, 44, 56.

6. Thurston, p. 122.

7. Thomas Weiskel, *The Romantic Sublime: Studies in the Structure and Psychology of Transcendence* (Baltimore: Johns Hopkins University Press, 1976), p. 145.

8. *Shelley: A Critical Reading,* p. 38.

9. Earl Wasserman, "Shelley: *Mont Blanc,*" in *The Subtler Language* (Baltimore: Johns Hopkins University Press, 1959), p. 231.

10. Stuart Curran, *Shelley's Annus Mirabilis: The Maturing of an Epic Vision* (San Marino, Calif.: Huntington Library, 1975), pp. 105–06.

11. Wasserman, *Prometheus Unbound: A Critical Reading* (Baltimore: Johns Hopkins University Press, 1965), p. 116; reprinted in *Shelley: A Critical Reading,* pp. 309–10.

12. The finest analysis of the problem of voice is by Susan Hawk Brisman, "'Unsaying His High Language': The Problem of Voice in *Prometheus Unbound,*" *Studies in Romanticism* 16 (1977), 51–86.

13. Wasserman, *Shelley: A Critical Reading,* p. 437.

14. Harold Bloom, *Shelley's Mythmaking* (New Haven: Yale Univer-

sity Press, 1959; rpt. Ithaca: Cornell University Press, 1969), pp. 220–26, 236–37.

15. Harold Bloom, *Poetry and Repression: Revisionism from Blake to Stevens* (New Haven: Yale University Press, 1976), p. 100.

16. This is the suggestion of John A. Hodgson, "The World's Mysterious Doom: Shelley's *The Triumph of Life,*" *ELH* 42 (1975), 595–622. See especially pp. 606–07 concerning the idea of stages of an afterlife as a reinterpretation of Wordsworth's Intimations Ode.

Chapter 5. George Darley: Buoyant as Young Time

1. A portion of this chapter appeared as "George Darley: The Poet as Pigmy" in *Studies in Romanticism* 15 (1976), 119–41, and is used here with the permission of the Trustees of Boston University.

2. Claude Colleer Abbott, *The Life and Letters of George Darley, Poet and Critic* (London: Oxford University Press, 1928), p. 224.

3. *Thomas à Becket: A Dramatic Chronicle* (London: Edward Moxon, 1840).

4. Ramsay Colles, ed., *The Complete Poetical Works of George Darley* (London: George Routledge, 1908). Verse quotations, except those from *Becket,* are from this edition.

5. *The Works of Beaumont and Fletcher,* with an Introduction by George Darley (London: Edward Moxon, 1839), p. xxxvii.

6. "How few have read 'Comus,' who have 'The Corsair' by heart! Why? Because the former, which is almost 'dark with the excessive bright' of its own glory, is deficient in human passions & emotions; while the latter possesses these, altho little else" (Abbott, p. 78). For more of Darley's reservations about Byron, see Abbott, pp. 23, 28, 41, 43–46, 123.

7. Int. to *Beaumont and Fletcher,* p. x. See also p. xvii, and Abbott, pp. 116, 219.

8. *Becket,* p. v.

9. "The Enchanted Lyre," in Guy Penseval [pseud. of Darley], *The Labours of Idleness; or, Seven Nights' Entertainments* (London: John Taylor, 1826), p. 42.

10. "Remains and Remarks," in *Labours of Idleness,* p. 90.

11. *On the Origin of Language,* trans. John H. Moran and Alexander Gode (New York: Frederick Ungar, 1966), p. 13.

12. *The Double Dream of Spring* (New York: E. P. Dutton, 1970), p. 17, © 1970 by John Ashbery. Quoted by permission.

13. Allardyce Nicoll, ed., *Chapman's Homer* (New York: Bollingen Foundation, 1956), II, 156, 158.

14. Foucault, p. 155.

15. "Intentional Structure of the Romantic Image," in *Romanticism and Consciousness,* ed. Harold Bloom (New York: Norton, 1970), p. 69.

16. Stevens' myth of Major Man, from which these lines are taken, is in section viii of "It Must Be Abstract," in *Notes toward a Supreme Fiction,* quoted from *The Palm at the End of the Mind* (New York: Alfred A. Knopf, 1971). Copyright 1967, 1969, 1971 by Holly Stevens.

17. Int. to *Beaumont and Fletcher,* p. xlvi.

18. Abbott, p. 124.

19. "Stanzas" by H. [Hood?] in an article, "Memnon's Head," *The London Magazine* 3 (February 1821), 125–28.

20. G. W. F. Hegel, *The Philosophy of Fine Art,* trans. F. P. B. Osmaston (London: G. Bell, 1920), III, 42. T. M. Knox renders this particular sentence a little less well in *Aesthetics: Lectures on Fine Art by G. W. F. Hegel* (Oxford: Clarendon Press, 1975), II, 643.

21. "Memnon's Head," p. 125.

Chapter 6. Re: Generation in Blake

1. See "Remembering, Repeating, and Working-Through," St. Ed. XII, 147. The change in Freud's focus from single, "real" origins to composite, fictional ones is discussed by David Carroll, "Freud and the Myth of the Origin," *New Literary History* 6 (1975), esp. p. 515.

2. Not to add to the difficulty in reading Blake, I quote from the punctuated edition with normalized spelling, *The Poems of William Blake,* ed. W. H. Stevenson, text by David V. Erdman (London: Longman, 1971). Reference is made to, and prose quotations are taken from, *The Poetry and Prose of William Blake,* ed. David V. Erdman, commentary by Harold Bloom (New York: Doubleday, 1965). Reference to the manuscript is made by way of the facsimile edition of *Vala or The Four Zoas,* ed. G. E. Bentley, Jr. (Oxford: Clarendon Press, 1963). Again to avoid distracting scrupulosity I refer to the central man as Albion always, whether or not Blake uses the name in a particular context.

3. Foucault, p. 330.

4. Carroll, p. 517.

5. See *Beyond the Pleasure Principle,* St. Ed. XVIII, esp. p. 62.

6. *Beyond the Pleasure Principle,* p. 28.

7. "Screen Memories," St. Ed. III, 322.

8. "Screen Memories," p. 316.

9. "Le texte n'est pas pensable dans la forme, originaire ou modifiée, de la présence. Le texte insconcient est déjà tissé de traces pures, de différences où s'unissent le sens et la force, texte nulle part présent, constitué d'archives qui sont *toujours déjà* des transcriptions. Des estampes originaires. Tout commence par la reproduction. Toujours déjà, c'est-à-dire dépôts d'un sens qui n'a jamais été présent, dont le présent signifié est toujours reconstitué à retardement, *nachträglich,* après coup, *supplémentairement:* nachträglich veut dire aussi supplémentaire" ("Freud et la scène de l'écriture," in *L'Ecriture et la différence* [Paris: Editions du Seuil, 1967], p. 314; trans. Jeffrey Mehlman in *French Freud* [Yale French Studies no. 48, 1972], p. 92).

10. *Blake's Apocalypse: A Study in Poetic Argument* (New York: Doubleday, 1963; rpt. Ithaca: Cornell University Press, 1970), p. 222.

11. Mary Lynn Johnson and Brian Wilkie, "On Reading *The Four Zoas:* Inscape and Analogy," in *Blake's Sublime Allegory: Essays on "The Four Zoas," "Milton," "Jerusalem,"* ed. Stuart Curran and Joseph Anthony Wittreich, Jr. (Madison: University of Wisconsin Press, 1973), p. 210.

12. *Beyond Good and Evil,* sect. 138.

13. *Blake's Apocalypse,* p. 241.

14. *Fearful Symmetry: A Study of William Blake* (Princeton: Princeton University Press, 1947), p. 285.

15. Johnson and Wilkie, p. 215.

16. *Blake's Apocalypse,* pp. 242–43. Cf. Johnson and Wilkie, p. 216.

17. "Avec l'altérité de l'inconscient', nous avons affaire non pas à des horizons de présents modifiés—passés ou à venir—mais à un 'passé' qui n'a jamais été présent et qui ne le sera jamais, dont l'a-venir' ne sera jamais la *production* ou la reproduction dans la forme de la présence" ("La Différance," in *Marges de la philosophie* [Paris: Editions de Minuit, 1972], p. 22; trans. in *Speech and Phenomena,* p. 152).

18. Thomas Weiskel, "Darkening Man: Blake's Critique of Transcendence," in *The Romantic Sublime,* pp. 73–74.

19. "Remembering, Repeating, and Working-Through," in St. Ed. XII, 153.

20. "Remembering, Repeating," p. 151.

21. "A vrai dire, Husserl n'est pas *conduit* à reconnaître cette hétérogénéité: celle-ci constitue toute la possibilité de la phénoménologie qui n'a de sens que si une présentation pure et originaire est possible et originale" (*La Voix et le phénomène,* p. 50n; trans. in *Speech and Phenomena,* p. 45n).

22. "La *perception n'existe pas* . . . ce qu'on appelle perception n'est

pas originaire . . . d'une certaine manière tout 'commence' par la 're-présentation' (proposition qui ne peut évidemment se soutenir que dans la
rature de ces deux derniers concepts: elle signifie qu'il n'y a pas de 'com-
mencement' et la 're-présentation' dont nous parlons n'est pas la modification d'un 're' *survenue* à une présentation originaire)" (*La Voix,*
p. 50n; trans. in *Speech and Phenomena,* p. 45n).

  23. "Le 'corps' phénoménologique du significant semble s'effacer dans
le moment même où il est produit. Il semble appartenir d'ores et déjà à
l'élément de l'idéalité" (*La Voix,* p. 86; trans. in *Speech and Phenomena,*
p. 77).

  24. "Elle peut *montrer* l'objet idéal ou la *Bedeutung* idéale qui s'y
rapporte sans s'aventurer hors de l'idéalité, hors de l'intériorité de la vie
présente à soi" (*La Voix,* p. 87; *Speech and Phenomena,* p. 78). Derrida
claims that "dans le colloque, la propagation des signifiants *semble* ne
rencontrer aucun obstacle parce qu'elle met en rapport deux origines *phé-
noménologiques* de l'auto-affection pure" (p. 89). ("In colloquy, the
propagation of signs does not seem to meet any obstacles because it brings
together two phenomenological origins of pure auto-affection" [p. 80].)
Blake's colloquy between Shadow and Spirit is *all* obstacle, and the limitation of these voices challenges the "phenomenological origins" of each by
making the auto-affection or self-presence of one voice dependent on the
other.

  25. *Blake's Night: William Blake and the Idea of Pastoral* (Cambridge:
Harvard University Press, 1973), p. 222.

  26. "Si le langage n'échappe jamais à l'analogie, si même il est analogie
de part en part, il doit, parvenu à ce point, à cette pointe, assumer libre-
ment sa propre destruction et lancer les métaphores contre les métaphores;
ce qui est obéir au plus traditionnel des impératifs, qui a reçu sa forme
la plus expresse, mais non la plus originelle dans les *Ennéades* et n'a
jamais cessé d'être fidèlement transmis jusqu'à l'*Introduction à la Métaphysique* (surtout de Bergson). C'est au prix de cette guerre du langage
contre lui-même que seront pensés le sens et la question de son origine"
(*La Voix,* p. 13; *Speech and Phenomena,* pp. 13–14).

  27. "Ce qui fait l'originalité de la parole, ce par quoi elle se distingue
de tout autre milieu de signification, c'est que son étoffe semble être
purement temporelle. Et cette temporalité ne déroule pas un sens qui
lui-même serait intemporel. Le sens, avant même d'être exprimé, est
temporel de part en part" (*La Voix,* p. 93; *Speech and Phenomena,* p. 83).

  28. *The Phenomenology of Internal Time-Consciousness,* trans. James
Churchill (Bloomington: Indiana University Press, 1964), p. 131. The
passage is cited by Derrida.

29. If Blake's vision of masculine sexual desire is as caustic as the one the Spectre assumes concerning feminine desire, then it may be that Los experiences a regeneration of desire precisely by confronting his shadowy rival lover in the Spectre. Where the Shadow found a father figure Los discovers a brother and "another self."

30. *The True Christian Religion* (New York: American Swedenborg Printing and Publishing Society, 1973), sect. 658.

Chapter 7. Wordsworth: How Shall I Seek the Origin?

1. *The Prelude: or Growth of a Poet's Mind,* ed. E. de Selincourt, 2d ed. rev. Helen Darbishire (Oxford: Clarendon Press, 1959). Because my argument concerns the revisionary nature of Wordsworth's quests for origins, I quote in this chapter and the following one (except as otherwise noted) from the 1805 text, overlooking the greater familiarity of the 1850 text and Wordsworth's own belief that in textual matters the last specifications of an author should be followed.

2. See Harold Bloom, *The Visionary Company: A Reading of English Romantic Poetry,* rev. ed. (Ithaca: Cornell University Press, 1971), pp. 131–40; and Thomas Weiskel, *The Romantic Sublime,* pp. 143, 152–53, 158.

3. Robert Langbaum, "Magnifying Wordsworth," *ELH* 33 (1966), 275.

4. Compare the opening of MS JJ ("Was it for this?") with the paragraphs Wordsworth came to place before that point in *The Prelude.*

5. MS E, as cited by de Selincourt, app. crit.

6. Cf. Weiskel's formula in *The Romantic Sublime,* pp. 142–43.

7. See Raymond Dexter Havens, *The Mind of a Poet: A Study of Wordsworth's Thought with Particular Reference to "The Prelude"* (Baltimore: Johns Hopkins University Press, 1941), p. 412.

8. "The Use and Abuse of Structural Analysis: Riffaterre's Interpretation of Wordsworth's 'Yew Trees,'" *New Literary History* 7 (1975), 186.

9. G. W. F. Hegel, *The Phenomenology of Mind,* trans. J. B. Baillie, 2d ed. (London: George Allen, 1931), p. 153.

10. "Que le présent en général ne soit pas originaire mais reconstitué, qu'il ne soit pas la forme absolue, pleinement vivante et constituante de l'expérience, qu'il n'y ait pas de pureté du présent vivant, tel est le thème, formidable pour l'histoire de la métaphysique, que Freud nous appelle à penser à travers une conceptualité inégale à la chose même" (*L'Écriture,* p. 314; *French Freud,* p. 93).

11. *The Anxiety of Influence: A Theory of Poetry* (New York: Oxford University Press, 1973), p. 10.

12. "The Use and Abuse of Structural Analysis," p. 169.

13. *Home at Grasmere,* l. 743, in *"The Poetical Works of William Wordsworth,* ed. E. de Selincourt and Helen Darbishire (Oxford: Clarendon Press, 1940–49; rev. eds. 1952–54), V. 337. (This edition is used *passim* and referred to henceforth as *Poetical Works.*)

14. Weiskel, p. 179.

15. Hartman, "The Use and Abuse of Structural Analysis," p. 170.

16. *The New Science of Giambattista Vico,* rev. trans. of 3d ed. (1774) by Thomas Goddard Bergin and Max Harold Fish (Ithaca: Cornell University Press, 1968), p. 120.

17. *Descriptive Sketches,* for example, compares Rousseauistic—at least Swiss—man to his primeval ancestors, recalling an age of freedom when man was "Nature's Child" (1849 text, ll. 433–60). Several of the sonnets envision a primitive responsiveness to nature now lost. See in particular "Hail Twilight, sovereign of one peaceful hour!" and "The World is too much with us; late and soon."

18. *Wordsworth's Poetry 1787–1814* (New Haven: Yale University Press, 1971), p. 140.

19. *The Ego and the Id,* St. Ed. XIX, 38.

20. *The Auroras of Autumn,* III.

21. *L'Ecriture,* pp. 314, 303; *French Freud,* pp. 92, 81.

22. "The Use and Abuse of Structural Analysis," p. 177.

23. This and the closely following quotation are from *De la grammatologie* (Paris: Editions de Minuit, 1967), p. 71: "Peirce va très loin dans la direction de ce que nous avons appelé plus haut la dé-construction du signifié transcendantal, lequel, à un moment ou à un autre, mettrait un terme rassurant au renvoi de signe à signe. Nous avons identifié le logocentrisme et la métaphysique de la présence comme le désir exigeant, puissant, systématique et irrépressible, d'un tel signifié." (Trans. by Gayatri Chakravorty Spivak in *Sub-Stance* 10 [1974], 149.)

24. Onorato, p. 76.

25. "Screen Memoirs," St. Ed. III, 322. The discussion that follows reflects Susan H. Brisman's view of the ways in which the idea of screen memories applies to *Tintern Abbey.*

26. See the draft of the poem in *The Letters of William and Dorothy Wordsworth: The Early Years, 1787–1805,* ed. Ernest de Selincourt, rev. ed. Chester L. Shaver (Oxford: Clarendon Press, 1967), p. 241.

27. In an unpublished 1973 Cornell University dissertation ("Authorial Awarness in Wordsworth's Early 'Spots of Time.'") C. F. Stone III suggests that we need not regard the version of the poem in which the boy is led by guardian spirits as spoiled by prevenient consciousness of maternal Presence. "Encouragement from frugal dames or guardian spirits in fact

could be simply adjuncts to the boy's vision of himself as harboring a great but hidden power" (p. 37). "Nutting" would thus concern a process of education by which the poet learns to respect his own terms more: first used as a dead metaphor—an easy representation of what is believed to be internal—the idea of a Presence comes to dawn on the poet with something of the power of an epiphany.

28. "Dire qu'elle est originaire, c'est du même coup effacer le mythe d'une origine présente. C'est pourquoi il faut entendre 'originaire' *sous rature*, faut de quoi on dériverait la différance d'une origine pleine. C'est la non-origine qui est originaire" (*L'Ecriture,* pp. 302–03; *French Freud,* p. 81).

29. Havens argues that Book VIII treats "the lofty conception of man, not the love of him" (p. 452).

30. For Coleridge's understanding of the fictionality of beginnings, see Chapter 1 of this book; for a general discussion of the difficulties in locating a point one can call a beginning, see the opening chapter of Edward Said's *Beginnings: Intention and Method* (New York: Basic Books, 1975).

31. See Onorato, *passim.*

32. See especially the episode of the drowned man, but also the dream of the Arab and the boy of Winander.

33. Cf. Hartman, *Wordsworth's Poetry,* pp. 225–31.

34. "C'est à retardement que la perception de la scène primitive—réalité ou fantasme, peu importe—est vécue dans sa signification et la maturation sexuelle n'est pas la forme accidentelle de ce retard" (*L'Ecriture,* p. 317; *French Freud,* p. 96).

35. See the Appendix to the De Selincourt–Darbishire *Prelude,* p. 633.

36. Foucault, pp. 331–32.

37. For discussion of the literary and experimental meaning of "those *passages* of life," see Weiskel, p. 169.

38. For discussion of primary- and secondary-process thought, see *Project for a Scientific Psychology* (St. Ed. I, 326–27) and *The Interpretation of Dreams, VII* (St. Ed. V, 558–609).

39. "I and my two brothers" in the 1805 version becomes, perhaps to obfuscate the theme, perhaps to direct attention to the more central one—two distinctions, "I and my three brothers" at the funeral.

40. "Wordsworth and the 'Spots of Time,'" *ELH* 26 (1959), 56.

41. "Tout graphème est d'essence testamentaire" (*Grammatologie,* p. 100; *Sub-Stance,* p. 168). Cf. Harold Bloom, in *Poetry and Repression:* "To see the writing or marking of nature is to see prophetically one's own absence or imaginative death. . . . And Nature will not stop writing" (pp. 81, 76).

42. *Wordsworth's Poetry,* p. 216.

43. *Wordsworth's Poetry,* p. 217.

44. See Walter J. Ong, *The Presence of the Word: Some Prolegomena for Cultural and Religious History* (New Haven: Yale University Press, 1967).

45. "Essay upon Epitaphs," [I] in *The Prose Works of William Wordsworth,* ed. W. J. B. Owen and Jane Worthington Smyser, II (Oxford: Clarendon Press, 1974), 51–52.

46. *The Ego and the Id,* St. Ed. XIX, 37.

47. Onorato, p. 34.

48. Preface to *Lyrical Ballads,* in *Poetical Works,* II, 400.

49. I am indebted to Roger Morrow for an unpublished essay discussing the circles of Book III. Morrow suggests that even the notorious line "And at the Hoop alighted, famous Inn" has a significant place in this book because the line is itself a signpost of the circle motif.

50. See the discussion of Wordsworth's concept of freedom in M. H. Abrams, *Natural Supernaturalism: Tradition and Revolution in Romantic Literature* (New York: Norton, 1971), pp. 366–72.

51. Geoffrey Hartman, *The Unmediated Vision: An Interpretation of Wordsworth, Hopkins, Rilke, and Valéry* (New York: Harcourt, Brace, and World, 1966), p. 12.

52. See Hartman's interpretation of Oswald and Iago in *Wordsworth's Poetry,* pp. 125–26.

53. *The Anxiety of Influence,* p. 97.

54. *The Ego and the Id,* St. Ed. XIX, 37.

55. Weiskel, pp. 175, 185, 197.

56. D. G. James discusses the coincidence of Oswald's words with those of the Solitary in *Scepticism and Poetry: An Essay on the Poetic Imagination* (London: G. Allen & Unwin, 1937), p. 152.

57. *Wordsworth's Poetry,* p. 126.

58. *Phenomenology,* p. 240.

59. Paul Ricoeur, *Freedom and Nature: The Voluntary and the Involunatary,* trans. Erazim V. Kohak (Evanston: Northwestern University Press, 1966), p. 486.

60. See James, esp. pp. 146–55 on loss of faith in Wordsworth.

61. "The Use and Abuse of Structural Analysis," p. 184.

62. Weiskel, p. 187.

63. J. Hillis Miller, "The Stone and the Shell: The Problem of Poetic Form in Wordsworth's Dream of the Arab," *Mouvements Premiers: Etudes critiques offertes à Georges Poulet* (Paris: Corti, 1972), p. 128.

64. Miller, p. 135.

65. Preface to the 1815 edition, in *Poetical Works,* II, 439.

66. "The Use and Abuse of Structural Analysis," p. 169.

67. Wordsworth wrote "my hourly neighbour" before revising the phrase to the slightly more grand, less homey "an hourly neighbour." Similarly, "Beauty—a living Presence" was originally "Beauty, whose living home is the green earth." See the transcription of three manuscripts of the Prospectus in the Appendix to M. H. Abrams, *Natural Supernaturalism,* pp. 470–79.

68. *The Anxiety of Influence,* p. 125.

69. Weiskel, p. 175.

70. Preface to the 1815 edition, in *Poetical Works* II, 438.

71. "The Climbing of Snowdon," in *Bicentenary Wordsworth Studies in Memory of John Alban Finch,* ed. Jonathan Wordsworth (Ithaca: Cornell University Press, 1970), p. 458.

72. "The Climbing of Snowdon," p. 459. What makes these lines seem instinct with life may be the fact that the spirit of Milton is hovering behind them. For a discussion of their Miltonism see James Rieger, "Wordsworth Unalarmed," in *Milton and the Line of Vision,* ed. Joseph Anthony Wittreich, Jr. (Madison: University of Wisconsin Press, 1975), p. 199.

73. *Poetry and Repression,* p. 56.

74. Compare *Queen Mab,* VII. 13–26.

75. "Negation," St. Ed. XIX, 236.

76. Jonathan Wordsworth, p. 462.

77. Edmund Burke, *A Philosophical Enquiry into the Origin of Our Ideas of the Sublime and Beautiful,* ed. J. T. Boulton (Notre Dame, Ind.: University of Notre Dame Press, 1958), p. 82. See the closely following section entitled "Intermitting": "Now some low, confused, uncertain sounds, leave us in the same fearful anxiety concerning their causes, that no light, or an uncertain light does concerning the objects that surround us" (pp. 83–84). Wordsworth's description of "voices issuing forth to silent light" thus presents a sublime source for the glorious in the uncanny.

78. James Clarke, *A Survey of the Lakes* (London, 1787), p. 73. Cited by Jonathan Wordsworth, p. 453.

79. Compare Isa. 5:14 and Hab. 2:5. The nether world, lengthening its throat, is a source of voice not unlike Wordsworth's "dark deep thoroughfare" where Nature lodges the soul.

80. Preface to the second edition of *Lyrical Ballads,* in *Poetical Works,* II, 400.

81. Dedicatory Epistle to *Peter Bell,* in *Poetical Works,* II, 331.

82. *Poetry and Repression,* p. 58.

83. Foucault, p. 81.

84. Said comments about the Snowdon scene, "The 'glorious faculty' is the power to begin poetry, which is itself not mere effusion but a meaning that is embedded in human circumstances" (p. 45).

85. Longinus begins Section IX of his treatise *On the Sublime* by turning to the source of the sublime that transcends rhetoric: "But tho' the first and most important of these Divisions, I mean Elevation of Thought, be rather a natural than an acquired Qualification, yet we ought to spare no Pains to educate our Souls to Grandeur, and impregnate them with generous and enlarged Ideas." The example from Genesis follows in this chapter: "So likewise the Jewish Legislator, no ordinary Person, having conceiv'd a just Idea of the Power of God, has nobly express'd it, in the beginning of his Law. '*And God said*—What?—*Let there be Light, and there was Light. Let the Earth be, and the Earth was.*' "

Boileau closes his Preface to the translation of the treatise by turning to Genesis I:

Le Souverain Arbitre de la Nature d'une seule parole forma la lumiere. *Voila qui est dans le Stile Sublime: cela n'est pas neanmoins Sublime: parce qu'il n'y a rien là de fort merveilleux, et qu'un autre ne pust aisément trouver. Mais.* Dicu dit: Que la lumiere se fasse, et la lumiere se fit. *Ce tour extraordinaire d'expression qui marque si bien l'obeissance de la Creature aux ordres du Createur est veritablement Sublime et a quelque chose de divin. Il faut donc entendre par Sublime dans Longin, l'Extraordinaire, le Surprenant et comme je l'ay traduit, le Merveilleux dans le Discours.*

The William Smith translation and the Boileau Preface are quoted from *Longinus on the Sublime: The "Peri Hupsous" in Translations by Nicolas Boileau–Despréaux (1674) and William Smith (1739)*, ed. William Bruce Johnson (New York: Scholars' Fascimiles & Reprints, 1975).

86. Jonathan Wordsworth, p. 463.
87. Jonathan Wordsworth, p. 464.
88. *Poetry and Repression,* p. 81.
89. Weiskel, pp. 50–51.
90. See *PL,* V.486–88.

Reintroduction: From the Seats of Power Divine

1. See De Selincourt's discussion of the title in *Prelude,* p. xxxvii.
2. I am indebted to M. A. Roberts and the late Thomas Weiskel for calling attention to the centrality of *power* as a critical term in Wordsworth's vocabulary and symbol-making.
3. A dog played a large role in the discharged-soldier episode itself:

> I wished to see him move, but he remained
> Fixed to his place, & still from time to time
> Sent forth a murmuring voice of dead complaint,
> A groan scarce audible. Yet all the while
> The chained mastiff in his wooden house
> Was vexed, & from among the village trees
> Howled never ceasing.

And the soldier diagnoses his own dis-ease:

> "In truth
> My weakness made me loth to move, and here
> I felt myself at ease & much relieved,
> But that the village mastiff fretted me,
> And every second moment rang a peal
> Felt at my very heart. There was no noise,
> Nor any foot abroad—I do not know
> What ail'd him, but it seemd as if the dog
> Were howling to the murmur of the stream."

These and other manuscript quotations are from the transcription by Beth Darlington in *Bicentenary Wordsworth Studies,* ed. Jonathan Wordsworth, pp. 425–48.

4. See Darlington, in *Bicentenary Wordsworth Studies,* p. 427.

5. Paul D. Sheats, *The Making of Wordsworth's Poetry, 1785–1798* (Cambridge: Harvard University Press, 1973), p. 169.

6. "Narrative Variation in Wordsworth's Versions of 'The Discharged Soldier,' " *Journal of Narrative Technique* 4 (1974), 36.

7. Stone discusses the soldier's murmur and its relation to the entry in Dorothy Wordsworth's journal describing the dog howling "at the murmur of the village stream" ("Narrative Variation," pp. 37–38).

8. I am indebted to Anne L. Aronson for pointing out, in an unpublished essay, how much the concern with the power of the solitary figure was a product of Wordsworth's revision of the text. De Selincourt finds the change "regrettable" (*Prelude,* p. lxi), and Miss Aronson has similar reservations about my enthusiasm for the later text.

9. In 1798:

> While thus I wandered step by step led on,
> It chanced a sudden turning of the road
> Presented to my view an uncouth shape.

In 1850:

> Sound there was none—but, lo! an uncouth shape,
> Shown by a sudden turning of the road.

10. *Letters,* ed. De Selincourt–Shaver, p. 34.

11. *Poetry and Repression,* p. 76.

12. *The New Science,* p. 119.

13. The whole passage from Midrash Tihillim is of interest in connection with the origins of metaphor: "In the beginning, two thousand years before the heaven and the earth, seven things were created: the Torah written with black fire on white fire, and lying in the lap of God; the Divine Throne, erected in the heaven which later was over the heads of the Hayyot; Paradise on the right side of God, Hell on the left side; the Celestial Sanctuary directly in front of God, having a jewel on its altar graven with the Name of the Messiah, and a Voice that cries aloud, 'Return, ye children of men'" (Louis Ginzberg, *The Legends of the Jews,* trans. Henrietta Szold [Philadelphia: The Jewish Publication Society of America, 1913], I,3).

The Torah written (in fire) before it is written (engraved in stone) is a central trope for the always-already quality of speech; in Jewish tradition the oral law forever struggles for priority with the written, but the Torah (which can only symbolically, or in shorthand, be said to have ever been engraved in stone) is the arche-trace teaching that all commentary, and all existence, is belatedness, "after-meditation." The Divine Throne is the central figure for metaphor as displaced place, the "seat" of power referred to in the title of this chapter. The name of the messiah (with priority over the messiah?) may point to the redemptive ideal when all peoples shall be one, and the priority of the sign over its referent will be universally acknowledged.

14. *The Fall of Hyperion,* I.436–38. For a more somber reading of these lines and their relation to poetic power, see Weiskel, pp. 189–90.

15. See note 9 to Chapter 6 of this book.

16. The word *baruch,* translated as "praised be" or "blessed be," literally refers to homage done in bowing by bending the knee. The break in the knee, like the break in the modern Hebrew letter forming *baruch* from *birom* (BRK from BRM) or the break in linear scribal transcription of the ancient Phonecian letter (where the K and M are mirror images) may be associated with the "blessed rage" to order words from the sea (in Stevens's "The Idea of Order at Key West"), where *blessed* retains a similar sense of break (Fr. *blessé,* wounded). This break or wound in the perfect fabric of representation opens the space for the origination of poetic voice.

Samuele Davide Luzzatto, commenting on Ezekiel 3:13, observed that the letters *mem* and *kaf* "are very close in Phonecian writing which is the early Hebrew script in which the prophets wrote their books." Luzzatto believes that the prophet must have written "in the ascent of the Glory of the Lord" rather than "Praised be the Glory of the Lord" because loud noise and audible speech (even though Hebrew uses the same word for sound and voice) are incompatible. He cites a host of examples in which *mem* and *kaf* were mistaken for one another. *Perushe Shmuel David Luzzatto Zichrono Livracha al Yirmiyahu, Yichezkel, Mishleh viEyov* (Lemberg: A. Isaak Menkes, 1876; reprinted Jerusalem: Makor, 1968). I am indebted to Professor Michael Fishbane of Brandeis University for this reference.

17. Wallace Stevens, "Sunday Morning," in *The Palm at the End of the Mind* (New York: Alfred A. Knopf, 1971). Copyright 1967, 1969, 1971 by Holly Stevens.

18. Wallace Stevens, *Notes toward a Supreme Fiction,* in *The Palm at the End of the Mind.*

19. Wallace Stevens, *Notes toward a Supreme Fiction.*

Index

index

ROMANTIC ORIGINS

Designed by R. E. Rosenbaum.
Composed by York Composition Company, Inc.,
in 11 point Intertype Baskerville, 2 points leaded,
with display lines in Monotype Baskerville.
Printed letterpress from type by York Composition Company
on Warren's 1854 Text, 50 pound basis.
Bound by John H. Dekker & Sons, Inc.
in Joanna book cloth
and stamped in All Purpose foil.

Library of Congress Cataloging in Publication Data
(For library cataloging purposes only)

Brisman, Leslie
  Romantic origins.

  Includes bibliographical references and index.
    1. English poetry—19th century—History and
criticism. 2. Romanticism—England. 3. Creation
(Literary, artistic, etc.) I. Title.
PR590.B84   821'.7'09   77-90898
ISBN 0-8014-1024-X